SOMETHING ABOUT THE AUTHOR

SOMETHING ABOUT THE AUTHOR

Facts and Pictures about Contemporary Authors
and Illustrators of Books for Young People

Anne Commire

VOLUME 4

GALE RESEARCH
BOOK TOWER
DETROIT, MICHIGAN
48226

Also Published by Gale

CONTEMPORARY AUTHORS:
A Bio-Bibliographical Guide to
Current Authors and Their Works

(Now Covers More Than 30,000 Authors)

Special acknowledgment is due to the members of the *Contemporary Authors* staff who assisted in the preparation of this volume, and to Gale's art director, Chester Gawronski.

Library of Congress Catalog Card Number: 70-127412
© 1973 by Gale Research Company. All rights reserved.

GRATEFUL ACKNOWLEDGMENT

is made to the following publishers, authors, and artists, for their kind permission to reproduce copyrighted material. ■ **ABELARD-SCHUMAN LTD.** Illustration by Elizabeth Donald from *Pet Parade* by James Sterling Ayars. © 1960 by James Sterling Ayars. Reprinted by permission of Abelard-Schuman Ltd. ■ **ABINGDON PRESS.** Illustration by Fritz Kredel from *The Silent Storm* by Marion Marsh Brown and Ruth Crone. © 1963 by Abingdon Press. Reprinted by permission of Abingdon Press. ■ **ADDISON-WESLEY PUBLISHING CO., INC.** Illustration by Willi Baum from *Birds of a Feather* by Willi Baum. © 1969 by Willi Baum, an Addisonian Press Book. Reprinted by permission of Addison-Wesley Publishing Co. ■ **ATHENEUM PUBLISHERS.** Illustration by Gail Garraty from *The Tombs of Atuan* by Ursula K. Le Guin. © 1971 by Ursula K. Le Guin. /Illustration by Joseph Schindelman from *The Great Picture Robbery* by Leon A. Harris. Illustrations © 1963 by Joseph Schindelman. /Photograph by Arline Strong from *The World of the Living* by Earl Ubell. Photographs © 1965 by Arline Strong. /Illustration by E. L. Konigsburg from *From the Mixed-Up Files of Mrs. Basil E. Frankweiler* by E. L. Konigsburg. © 1967 by E. L. Konigsburg. /Illustration by Tom O'Sullivan from *The Muskie Hook* by Peter Zachary Cohen. © 1966 by Peter Zachary Cohen. /Illustration by Leonard Shortall from *Rita the Weekend Rat* by Sonia Levitin. © 1971 by Sonia Levitin. /Illustration by Richard Cuffari from *The Far Side of Evil* by Sylvia Louise Engdahl. © 1971 by Sylvia Louise Engdahl. /All reprinted by permission of Atheneum Publishers. ■ **THE BOBBS-MERRILL CO.** Illustration from *Pebbles from a Broken Jar* by Frances Alexander. © 1963, 1967 by Frances Alexander. /Illustration by Frank Bozzo from *The Beasts of Never* by Georgess McHargue. © 1968 by Georgess McHargue. Both reprinted by permission of The Bobbs-Merrill Co., Inc. ■ **CONSTABLE YOUNG BOOKS LTD.** Photograph by Marcus Crouch from *Britain in Trust* by Marcus Crouch. Photograph © 1963 by Marcus Crouch. Reprinted by permission of Constable Young Books Ltd. ■ **COWARD, McCANN & GEOGHEGAN, INC.** Illustration by Elton C. Fax from *Tales from the Story Hat* by Verna Aardema. © 1960 by Coward-McCann & Geoghegan, Inc. /Illustration from *Taro and the Sea Turtle* by Arnold Dobrin. © 1966 by Coward-McCann & Geoghegan, Inc. /Illustration by Susan Perl from *Sir Howard the Coward* by William Wise. /Illustrations © 1967 by Susan Perl. All reprinted by permission of Coward, McCann & Geoghegan, Inc. ■ **THOMAS Y. CROWELL CO.** Illustration by Louise E. Jefferson from *Understanding Africa* by E. Jefferson Murphy. Illustrations © 1969 by Louise E. Jefferson. /Illustration by Charles W. Walker from *This Snake is Good* by Helen Copeland. © 1968 by Helen Copeland. /Illustration by Don Madden from *Why Frogs are Wet* by Judy Hawes. Illustrations © 1968 by Don Madden. /Illustration from *Do You Want to be My Friend?* by Eric Carle. Illustrations © 1971 by Eric Carle. /Illustration by John Gretzer from *Grettir the Strong* by Robert Newman. © 1968 by Robert Newman. /Illustration by Don Madden from *Gravity is a Mystery* by Franklyn M. Branley. Illustrations © 1970 by Don Madden. /Illustration by Nils Hogner from *Birds of Prey* by Dorothy Childs Hogner. Illustrations © 1969 by Nils Hogner. /Illustration by David Palladini from *The Sword and the Grail* by Constance Hieatt. Illustrations © 1972 by David Palladini. /Illustration by Enrico Arno from *How Our World Came to Be* by Stanley W. Angrist. Illustrations © 1969 by Enrico Arno. /Illustration by Arnold Roth from *Isabel's Noël* by Jane Yolen. Illustrations © 1967 by Arnold Roth. Reprinted by permission of Funk & Wagnall, Inc. All reprinted by permission of Thomas Y. Crowell Co. ■ **CURTIS BROWN LTD.** Illustration by Ernest Shepard from *The Pooh Cook Book* by Virginia H. Ellison. © 1969 by Daphne Dorothy Milne and Spencer Curtis Brown. Reprinted by permission of Curtis Brown Ltd. ■ **DELACORTE PRESS.** Illustration by Mary Frank from *Buddha* by Joan Lebold Cohen. © 1969 by Mary Frank. /Illustration by J. C. Kocsis from *Edge of Two Worlds* by Weyman Jones. © 1968 by J. C. Kocsis. Reprinted by permission of The

Dial Press. Both reprinted by permission of Delacorte Press. ■ **T. S. DENISON & CO., INC.** Illustration by June Talarczyk from *A Mouse in the House* by Betty Jane Reed. © MCMLXXI by T. S. Denison & Co., Inc. Reprinted by permission of T. S. Denison & Co., Inc. ■ **DODD, MEAD & CO., INC.** Illustration by Laszlo Kubinyi from *And Tomorrow the Stars* by Kay Hill. © 1968 by Kay Hill. Reprinted by permission of Dodd, Mead & Co., Inc. ■ **DOUBLEDAY & CO., INC.** Illustration by Edward Sorel from *The Duck in the Gun* by Joy Cowley. © 1969 by Doubleday & Co., Inc. /Illustration by Ib Ohlsson from *Room 10* by Agnes McCarthy. © 1966 by Agnes McCarthy. /Illustration from *The Best Thing to Be* by Julia Noonan. © 1971 by Julia Noonan. /Illustration by Paul Galdone from *The Shy Stegosaurus of Indian Springs* by Evelyn Sibley Lampman. © 1962 by Evelyn Sibley Lampman. /Illustration from *The Fox Went Out on a Chilly Night* by Peter Spier. © 1961 by Peter Spier. All reprinted by permission of Doubleday & Co., Inc. ■ **E. P. DUTTON & CO., INC.** Illustration by Ernest Shepard from *The Pooh Cook Book* by Virginia H. Ellison. © 1969 by Daphne Dorothy Milne and Spencer Curtis Brown. Copyright for text: *Winnie-the-Pooh* by A. A. Milne. © 1926 by E. P. Dutton & Co., Inc. Renewed 1954 by A. A. Milne; *The House at Pooh Corner*, © 1928 by E. P. Dutton & Co., Inc. Renewal, 1956 by A. A. Milne. /Illustration by William Wiesner from *Ghosts and Goblins* by Wilhelmina Harper. © 1965 by E. P. Dutton & Co., Inc. /Photograph by Ulli Steltzer from *The Night Workers* by Alvin Schwartz. Photograph © 1966 by E. P. Dutton & Co., Inc. /Illustration by Nora S. Unwin from *Amos Fortune, Free Man*. © 1950 by Elizabeth Yates McGreal. All reprinted by permission of E. P. Dutton & Co., Inc. ■ **FARRAR, STRAUS & GIROUX, INC.** Illustration by Harriet Pincus from *Tell Me a Mitzi* by Lore Segal. Illustrations © 1970 by Harriet Pincus. /Illustration by Garth Williams from *The Cricket in Times Square* by George Selden. © 1960 by George Selden Thompson and Garth Williams. Both reprinted by permission of Farrar, Straus & Giroux, Inc. ■ **FEARON PUBLISHERS.** Illustration by Robert Haydock from *Teaching Without Tears* by Jenny Gray. © 1968 by Fearon Publishers /Lear Siegler, Inc. Reprinted by permission of Fearon Publishers. ■ **FOLLETT PUBLISHING CO.** Illustration by Don Madden from *The Zoo That Moved* by Gloria D. Miklowitz. Illustrations © 1968 by Don Madden. /Illustration by Charles Liese from *Claudia* by Barbara Wallace. © 1969 by Barbara Wallace. /Book jacket by Ted Lewin from *More Than Halfway There* by Janet Halliday Ervin. Illustrations © 1970 by Follett Publishing Co. All reprinted by permission of Follett Publishing Co., division of Follett Corporation. ■ **GARRARD PUBLISHING CO.** Illustration by Dom Lupo from *Knute Rockne* by George Sullivan. © 1970 by George Sullivan. /Illustration by Gerald McCann from *Benjamin Franklin* by Charles P. Graves. © 1960 by Charles P. Graves. /Illustration by Cary from *Thomas Alva Edison* by Mervyn D. Kaufman. © 1962 by Mervyn D. Kaufman. All reprinted by permission of Garrard Publishing Co., Champaign, Illinois. ■ **GOLDEN GATE JUNIOR BOOKS.** Illustration by F. Leslie Matthews from *Higher Than the Arrow* by Judy Van der Veer. © 1969 by Judy Van der Veer. /Reprinted by permission of Golden Gate Junior Books. ■ **GRANADA PUBLISHING LTD.** From *Martin Luther* by Leonard W. Cowie. Reprinted by permission of Rupert Hart-Davis Educational Publications Ltd. © 1969 by Rupert Hart-Davis. ■ **GROSSET & DUNLAP.** Illustration by Darryl Sweet from *The Wonders of the Human Body* by Martin L. Keen. © 1966 by Grosset & Dunlap, Inc. Reprinted by permission of Grosset & Dunlap, Inc. ■ **HAMISH HAMILTON LTD.** Illustration by Eileen Armitage from *The High House* by Honor Arundel. /Illustrations © 1967 by Eileen Armitage. Reprinted by permission of Hamish Hamilton Ltd. ■ **HARCOURT BRACE JOVANOVICH, INC.** Illustration by Mary Shepard and Agnes Sims from *Mary Poppins Opens the Door* by P. L. Travers. © 1943, 1971 by P. L. Travers. /Illustration by Robert Parker from *Touch of Light: The Story of Louis Braille* by Anne E. Neimark. © 1970 by Harcourt Brace Jovanovich, Inc. /Illustration by Katharina Barry from *Spaghetti for Breakfast* by Sesyle Joslin. Illustration © 1965 by Katharina Barry. /Illustration from *Emmy Keeps a Promise* by Madye Lee Chastain. © 1966 by Harcourt Brace Jovanovich, Inc. /Illustration by Edward Ardizzone from *The Witch Family* by Eleanor Estes. © 1960 by Eleanor Estes. /Illustration by Margery Gill from *Over Sea, Under Stone* by Susan Cooper. © 1965 by Jonathan Cape Ltd. /Illustration from *The Ballooning Adventures of Paddy Pork* by John S. Goodall. Illustrations © 1969 by John S. Goodall. /Illustration by Erika Weihs from *The Mountain and the Summer Stars* by Michael Baker. © 1968 by Michael Baker. Reprinted by permission of Victor Gollancz Ltd. All reprinted by permission of Harcourt Brace Jovanovich, Inc. ■ **HARPER & ROW, PUBLISHERS.** Illustration by Marc Simont from *A Tree is Nice* by Janice May Udry. Picture © 1956 by Marc Simont. /Illustration by Emily McCully from

Steffie and Me by Phyllis Hoffman. Picture © 1970 by Emily Arnold McCully. /Illustration from *Morris Goes to School* by B. Wiseman. © 1970 by Bernard Wiseman. /Illustration by Mary Chalmers from *Goodnight Andrew, Goodnight Craig* by Marjorie Sharmat. Picture © 1969 by Mary Chalmers. /Illustration by Joan Sandin from *A Year in the Life of Rosie Bernard* by Barbara Brenner. © 1971 by Barbara Brenner. /Illustration by James Barkley from *Sounder* by William H. Armstrong. © 1969 by William H. Armstrong. /Illustration by Tom Eaton from *Steven and the Green Turtle* by William J. Cromie. © 1970 by Tom Eaton. /Illustration by Charles Geer from *Polliwog* by Arthur D. Stapp. © 1962 by Arthur D. Stapp. /Illustration by Wallace Tripp from *No Flying in the House* by Betty Brock. © 1967 by Wallace Tripp. /Illustration by Emily McCully from *Twin Spell* by Janet Lunn. © 1969 by Harper & Row, Publishers. /Illustration by Ronni Solbert from *Bronzeville Boys and Girls* by Gwendolyn Brooks. © 1956 by Gwendolyn Brooks Blakely. /Title page from *The Sea-Dragon* by George Sanderlin. © 1969 by George Sanderlin. All reprinted by permission of Harper & Row, Publishers. ■ **HARVEY HOUSE, INC.** Illustration by Ursula Koering from *Man Against Winter* by Oren Arnold. Illustrations © 1966 by Harvey House, Inc. Reprinted by permission of Harvey House, Inc. ■ **WILLIAM HEINEMANN LTD.** Illustration by Bernadette from *One's None* by James Reeves. Illustrations © William Heinemann Limited 1968. Reprinted by permission of William Heinemann Ltd. ■ **HOLT, RINEHART & WINSTON, INC.** Illustration by Leo Carty from *50,000 Names for Jeff* by Anne Snyder. Illustrations © 1969 by Leo Carty. /Illustration by Leo and Diane Dillon from *Shamrock and Spear* by F. M. Pilkington. Illustrations © 1968 by Holt, Rinehart & Winston, Inc. /Illustration by Jane Castle from *The Story of Irving Berlin* by David Ewen. © 1950, by Holt, Rinehart & Winston, Inc. All reprinted by permission of Holt, Rinehart & Winston, Inc. ■ **HOUGHTON MIFFLIN CO.** Illustration from *A Mouse Named Mus* by Irene Brady. © 1972 by Irene Brady Kistler. /Illustration by Walter Lorraine from *David McCheever's 29 Dogs* by Margaret Holt. © 1963 by Walter H. Lorraine. /Illustration by Joe and Beth Krush from *Mrs. Wappinger's Secret* by Florence Hightower. © 1956 by Florence C. Hightower and Mary Elizabeth and Joseph Krush. /Illustration by Leo and Diane Dillon from *The Untold Tale* by Erik Christian Haugaard. © 1971 by Erik Christian Haugaard. /Illustration by Peggy Fortnum from *A Bear Called Paddington* by Michael Bond. © 1958 by Michael Bond. All reprinted by permission of Houghton Mifflin Co. ■ **J. B. LIPPINCOTT CO.** Illustration by Burmah Burris from *Gretchen's Hill* by Jeannette Eyerly. © 1965 by Jeannette Eyerly. /Photograph by Marcia Kay Keegan from *Only the Moon and Me* by Richard J. Margolis. Illustrations © 1969 by Marcia Kay Keegan. /Illustration by Wendy Worth from *The House of Secrets* by Nina Bawden. Illustrations © 1964 by Wendy Worth. /Illustration by Edward A. DeVille from *Fundamental Physical Forces* by Raymond A. Wohlrabe. © 1969 by Raymond A. Wohlrabe. /Illustration by W. T. Mars from *Trouble in the Jungle* by John Rowe Townsend. Illustrations © 1969 by J. B. Lippincott Co. All reprinted by permission of J. B. Lippincott Co. ■ **LONGMAN YOUNG BOOKS LTD.** Illustration from *Hey Riddle Diddle!* by Rodney Peppe. © 1971 by Rodney Peppe. Reprinted by permission of Longman Young Books Ltd. ■ **THE MACMILLAN CO.** Illustration by Doreen Roberts from *Young Louis XIV* by Burke Wilkinson. © 1970 by Burke Wilkinson. © 1970 by The Macmillan Co. /Illustration by Nonny Hogrogian from *In School* by Esther Hautzig. Illustration © 1969 by Nonny Hogrogian. Illustration by Jose Aruego from *Whose Mouse Are You?* by Robert Kraus. Illustrations © 1970 by Jose Aruego. /Illustration by Helga Aichinger from *Bear Weather* by Lillie D. Chaffin. Illustrations © 1969 by Helga Aichinger. /Illustration by Eros Keith from *The House of Dies Drear* by Virginia Hamilton. Illustrations © 1968 by the Macmillan Co. /Illustration by Peter Bramley from *The Bonus of Redonda* by Robert D. Abrahams. © 1969 by The Macmillan Co. /Jacket cover by Emanuel Schongut from *The Seal Singing* by Rosemary Harris. All reprinted by permission of The Macmillan Co. ■ **McCLELLAND AND STEWART LTD.** Illustration by Ernest Shepard from *The Pooh Cook Book* by Virginia H. Ellison. Reprinted by permission of The Canadian Publishers, McClelland and Stewart Limited, Toronto. ■ **McGRAW-HILL BOOK CO.** Illustration by Jean Zallinger from *Discovering What Frogs Do* by Seymour Simon. © 1969 by Seymour Simon and Jean Zallinger. Reprinted by permission of McGraw-Hill Book Co. ■ **DAVID McKAY CO., INC.** Book jacket by Genia from *A Break in the Circle* by Jean Fiedler. © 1971 by Jean Fiedler. Reprinted by permission of David McKay Co., Inc. ■ **METHUEN & CO. LTD.** Illustration by Richard Kennedy from *Cut Off from Crumpets* by Margaret J. Baker. © 1964 by Margaret J. Baker. Reprinted by permission of Methuen & Co. Ltd. ■ **MILWAUKEE ART CENTER.** Painting by Colleen Browning from *Who Look at Me* by June

Jordan. Reprinted by permission of the Milwaukee Art Center. ■ **WILLIAM MORROW & CO.** Illustration by Robert Quackenbush from *Mrs. Herring* by Margaretha Shemin. Illustrations © 1967 by Lothrop, Lee & Shepard Co., Inc. Reprinted by permission of William Morrow & Co. ■ **PARENTS' MAGAZINE PRESS.** Illustration by Harold Berson from *Watermelons, Walnuts and the Wisdom of Allah* by Barbara Walker. Illustrations © 1967 by Harold Berson. Reprinted by permission of Parents' Magazine Press. ■ **PUBLISHERS-HALL SYNDICATE.** Illustration of "Mark Trail" episode by Ed Dodd. Reprinted by permission of Publishers-Hall Syndicate. ■ **FREDERICK A. PRAEGER, INC.** Illustration from *Martin Luther: Leader of the Reformation* by Leonard W. Cowie. © 1969 by Frederick A. Praeger, Inc. ■ **RAND McNALLY & CO.** Illustration by Jerome P. Connolly from *Adelbert the Penguin* by Ross E. Hutchins. © 1969 by Rand McNally & Co. Reprinted by permission of Rand McNally & Co. ■ **RANDOM HOUSE.** Illustration by John Kaufmann from *Unusual Careers* by Martha E. Munzer. © 1962 by The Conservation Foundation. /Illustration from *Two If By Sea* by Leonard Everett Fisher. © 1970 by Leonard Everett Fisher. /Illustration by Don Bolognese from *Headed for Trouble* by Barbara Rinkoff. Illustrations © 1970 by Donald Bolognese. All reprinted by permission of Alfred A. Knopf and Random House. ■ **REILLY & LEE.** Photograph from *How A Family Grows* by Arthur Shay. © 1968 by Arthur Shay. Reprinted by permission of Reilly & Lee. ■ **SCHOLASTIC BOOK SERVICES.** Illustration from *Clifford's Tricks* by Norman Bridwell. © 1969 by Norman Bridwell. Reprinted by permission of Scholastic Book Services, a division of Scholastic Magazines, Inc. ■ **CHARLES SCRIBNER'S SONS.** Illustration by Richard Floethe from *If I Were Captain* by Louise Lee Floethe. © 1956 by Louise Lee Floethe and Richard Floethe. Reprinted by permission of Charles Scribner's Sons. ■ **THE SEABURY PRESS.** Illustration from *Why the Jackal Won't Speak to the Hedgehog* by Harold Berson. © 1969 by Harold Berson. Reprinted by permission of The Seabury Press. ■ **STECK-VAUGHN CO.** Illustration by J. M. Roever from *The Coyote* by Iona Seibert Hiser. © 1968 by Steck-Vaughn Co. Reprinted by permission of Steck-Vaughn Co. ■ **UNITED STATES SIGNAL CORP.** Photograph from *The Battle of the Bulge* by Stephen W. Sears. Reprinted by permission of the United States Signal Corp. ■ **THE VIKING PRESS, INC.** Illustration by Margaret Gordon from *Noah's Journey* by George MacBeth. © 1966 by George MacBeth and Margaret Eastoe. /Illustration by Leo Politi from *Looking-for-Something* by Ann Nolan Clark. © 1952 by Ann Nolan Clark and Leo Politi. /Illustration from *The Twenty-One Balloons* by William Pene du Bois. © 1947 by William Pene du Bois. /Illustration by Ted Coconis from *The Summer of the Swans* by Betsy Byars. © 1970 by Betsy Byars. /Illustration by Emily A. McCully from *Friday Night is Papa Night* by Ruth A. Sonneborn. Illustrations © 1970 by Emily A. McCully. /Illustration by Arabelle Wheatley from *The Beachcomber's Book* by Bernice Kohn. © 1970 by Bernice Kohn. /Illustration by Kurt Wiese from *Silver from the Sea* by Ruth Tooze and Kurt Wiese. © 1962 by Ruth Tooze and Kurt Wiese. /Illustration from *The Man with the Bushy Beard* by Susanne Suba. © 1969 by Susanne Suba. All reprinted by permission of The Viking Press, Inc. All rights reserved. ■ **HENRY Z. WALCK, INC.** Illustration by Frederick T. Chapman from *Castles* by Fon W. Boardman, Jr. © 1957 by Henry Z. Walck, Inc. Reprinted by permission of Henry Z. Walck, Inc. ■ **FREDERICK WARNE & CO., INC.** Illustration by W. T. Mars from *The Crab from Yesterday* by John F. Waters. Illustrations © 1970 by W. T. Mars. Reprinted by permission of Frederick Warne & Co., Inc. ■ **FRANKLIN WATTS, INC.** Illustration by Bernadette Watts from *One's None* by James Reeves. Illustrations © 1968 by William Heinemann Ltd. /Illustration by Bruce Bacon from *The First Book of Local Government* by James A. Eichner. © 1964 by Franklin Watts, Inc. /Illustration by Mimi Korach from *Let's Find Out about Bread* by Olive Burt. © 1966 by Franklin Watts, Inc. /Illustration by Joseph Escourido from *Mystery in the Ravine* by Carol Farley. © 1967 by Carol J. Farley. /Illustration by Polly Bolian from *Safety* by Polly Bolian and Shirley Hinds. © 1970 by Franklin Watts, Inc. /Illustration from *The Rain Man* by Helga Aichinger. Illustrations © 1970 by Neugebauer Press (Badgoisern, Austria). /Illustration by Cliff Roberts from *The First Book of Jazz* by Langston Hughes. © 1955 by Franklin Watts, Inc. All reprinted by permission of Franklin Watts, Inc. ■ **THE WESTMINSTER PRESS.** Illustration by Edward J. Smith from *The Threatening Fog* by Leon Ware. © MCMLXII by Leon Ware. Reprinted by permission of The Westminster Press. ■ **ALBERT WHITMAN & CO.** Illustration from *Who Lives There?* by John Hawkinson. © 1970 by Albert Whitman & Co. /Illustration from *When the Moon is New* by Laura Bannon. © 1953 by Laura Bannon. Both reprinted by permission of Albert Whitman & Co. ■ **THE WORLD PUBLISHING CO.** Illustration by David K. Stone from *Where Condors*

Fly by Robert F. Burgess. /Illustrations © 1969 by David K. Stone. Reprinted by permission of The World Publishing Co./Illustration from *Arm in Arm* by Reme Charlip. Reprinted by permission of the author. Jacket cover from *The Stainless Steel Rat's Revenge* by Henry Harrison. Reprinted by permission of the author. Illustration of "The Last Tribe" by Henry C. Pitz. Reprinted by permission of the artist.

PHOTOGRAPH CREDITS

Helga Aichinger: Foto Studio Roemer; Stanley Angrist: Robert W. Hornbeck; Honor Arundel: Anne Christie; Fon W. Boardman, Jr.: Congrat-Butlar; Franklyn M. Branley: Compliments T. Y. Crowell; Edith Brecht: Peel's Studio; Barbara J. Brenner: George Ancona; Curtis Casewit: Courtesy of J. B. Lippincott Co.; Ann Nolan Clark: Jack Sheaffer Photographers; Susan Cooper: Babette Whipple; Helen Copeland: Howard C. Copeland; Burke Davis: Colonial Williamsburg Photograph; Sylvia Louise Engdahl: Edmund Keene, Portland, Oregon; Eleanor Estes: Jim Theologos; D. X. Fenton: Studio of The New York Times; Louise and Richard Floethe: St. Petersburg Times; Virginia Hamilton: Audree Distad; Rosemary Harris: Jerry Bauer; Hal Hellman: Hy Rosen; Langston Hughes: Courtesy of Dodd, Mead; Weyman B. Jones: Greene-DeVito; Bil Keane: Markow Photography; Bernice Kohn: Edward Lavitt; Ursula K. LeGuin: Wes Guderian, *The Oregonian;* Janet Lunn: Lloyd E. Thompson; Charles Paul May: Paul F. May; Georgess McHargue: Polushkin/Robbins; Grace Mintonye: Harry Barth; Anne E. Neimark: Philip Banks; Susan Beth Pfeffer: Chris Emanuel; Laurence Pringle: Judith Pringle; Russell P. Reeder: *Pacific Stars and Stripes;* Barbara Rinkoff: Herbert Rinkoff; Alvin Schwartz: Ulli Steltzer; Stephen W. Sears: Emma Landau; Marjorie Sharmat: Jay Te Winburn, Jr.; Peter Spier: Peter Beckett; Fred J. Steinberg: Vernon L. Smith; George Sullivan: Conrad Brown; John Rowe Townsend: R. Smith, *The Guardian*, courtesy of J. B. Lippincott Co.; P. L. Travers: Helen Piers; Kurt Unkelbach: Paul Norman Kammet; Judy Van der Veer: Gordon Nicholason; Richard J. Walton: Henrik Krogius; Don Whitehead: Wilson Woolley; Raymond A. Wohlrabe: Kennell-Ellis, Inc.; Jane H. Yolen: David Stemple.

VERNA AARDEMA

AARDEMA, Verna (Norberg) 1911-

PERSONAL: Surname is pronounced *ar*-da-ma; born June 6, 1911, in New Era, Mich.; daughter of Alfred Eric (a businessman) and Dorothy (VanderVen) Norberg; married Albert Aardema, May 29, 1936; children: Austin, Paula. *Education:* Michigan State University, B.A., 1934. *Politics:* Republican. *Religion:* Baptist. *Home:* 3313 McCracken St., Muskegon, Mich. 49441.

CAREER: Grade school teacher in Pentwater, Mich., 1934-35, Muskegon, Mich., 1935-36, 1945-46, 1951—, currently at Lincoln School, Mona Shores. *Muskegon Chronicle,* Muskegon, Mich., staff correspondent, 1951—. Sunday school teacher for twelve years. *Member:* National Education Association, Woman's National Book Association, Juvenile Writers' Workshop (publicity chairman, 1955-69), Michigan Education Association, Mona Shores Education Association (corresponding secretary, 1965-67).

WRITINGS: Tales from the Story Hat, Coward, 1960; *Otwe,* Coward, 1960; *The Sky-God Stories,* Coward, 1960; *The Na of Wa,* Coward, 1960; *More Tales from the Story Hat,* Coward, 1966; *Tales for the Third Ear,* Dutton, 1969; *Behind the Back of the Mountain,* Dial, 1973. Columnist, "Lincoln Lingo," *Muskegon Heights Record,* 1949-51; articles in *Instructor* and *Christian Life.*

WORK IN PROGRESS: A collection of African folk tales rewritten for children; a collection of Chicano heritage tales translated from Spanish and retold.

SIDELIGHTS: "I was eleven years old when the desire to write hit me. Because I took after my older brother, I was born loving to read. But for a girl in our household, reading was a form of laziness. Our folks had nine children. So, to Mama, help with the housework was a matter of survival. As a helper, I was a great disappointment even to myself. My younger sister could beat me either washing or drying the dishes.

"Then came the day when I got an 'A' on a poem at school. Mama read it and said, 'Why, Verna, you're going to be a writer like my grandpa!' That was the first time I had been noticed for any good reason. I decided to make a career of being like my ancestor who had published frequently in religious magazines.

"Mama set me up in business. She found a big gray ledger for me left from the days when my father had owned a store. She tore out the used pages saying, 'Those people will never pay anyway.' About half of the book was left. The paper was lined and smooth, far superior to a 'Big Chief' tablet.

"I soon learned that imitating Great-Grandfather worked as well as practicing the piano for getting out of dishes. It seems he had done his thinking while walking in the country. I discovered that I could get away with taking a few dishes from the dining table out to the kitchen, then flying out the back door. I'd hear Mama say, 'Let her go. She's going to the swamp.'

"Our town, New Era, Michigan, in those days was one large square. Everyone lived on some edge of it. Our side overlooked a cedar swamp. That's where I did my 'thinking.' I'd sit on a log, dig my heels into the spongy black earth and think and think—until I'd think my sisters must be finished with the dishes. So my mother nurtured that faltering desire to write. And the gray ledger began to fill with little stories born in the swamp. A person can't sit in perfect solitude without thinking of something!

"When I was fourteen, an uncle gave me a part-time job in his lumber company office. The pay was twenty-five cents an hour, some of which I saved for college. Later, the experience helped me get a job in the publications department of my college.

"After college I taught school for two years then got married. I entered marriage with the idea that at last I'd have lots of time to write. But it didn't work out that way. My husband was jealous of the men in the stories I had done in college. I tore up the most offensive manuscripts, and with them tore up my desire to write.

"Years later it was my little daughter who got me started writing children's stories. She wouldn't eat without a story. And she could make a scrambled egg last all the way through 'Little Red Riding Hood.' After a time, I began to

Leopard was very much embarrassed by his failures. ■ (From *Tales from the Story Hat* by Verna Aardema. Illustrated by Elton C. Fax.)

make up little feeding stories. That way she didn't know how far off the end would be. Because I was usually reading about Africa, the feeding stories were apt to be set in Ashantiland or the Kalahari Desert.

"I sold one of those feeding stories to the *Instructor Magazine*. And it was that little story that got me into the Coward-McCann stable of authors. The editor, Alice Torrey, asked me to use it as chapter one of a juvenile novel. I countered with the suggestion of a collection of African folk tales which had not been done for children. She told me to go ahead.

"Then I set to work. I was like the Ekoi mouse who listens to the tales people tell. When she hears one she likes, she takes it home with her, makes a new garment for it, and it becomes her story child.

"I burrow into old library books, many obtained through inter-library loan, to find my stories. Then I have to make new garments for them. For although the African storyteller embellishes his tales with plenty of songs, descriptions, and explanations when he is performing for an audience, he's apt to clam up for an anthropologist with a pencil. So the versions available to me are likely to be incomplete.

"In order to place a story in its proper setting, I have to read other books about the area from which it comes. Often a song is mentioned, but not given. And I have to make one up out of whole cloth. Sometimes I have to change episodes because the original action is taboo in our culture.

"I tighten the tales by emphasizing cause and effect relationships. I always strive for brevity, sometimes eliminating unimportant episodes to achieve it. Like the African storyteller, I retell a tale to make it more satisfying and more understandable to my audience, my readers."

FOR MORE INFORMATION SEE: Muskegon Chronicle, April 12, 1960; *Grand Rapids Press,* April 17, 1960; *Junior Libraries,* November, 1960; *Cleveland Press,* November 8, 1960; *Michigan State University Magazine,* October, 1961.

ABRAHAMS, Robert D(avid) 1905-

PERSONAL: Born September 24, 1905, in Philadelphia, Pa.; son of William and Anne (David) Abrahams; married Florence Kohn, November 21, 1929; children: Richard Irving, Roger David, Marjorie (Mrs. Clifford Slavin). *Education:* Dickinson School of Law, LL.B., 1925. *Religion:* Jewish. *Home:* 8204 Cedar Rd., Elkins Park, Philadelphia, Pa. 19117; and Morning Star, Fig Tree, Nevis, West Indies. *Office:* Land Title Building, Philadelphia, Pa. 19110.

CAREER: Admitted to Pennsylvania Bar, 1925; secretary to commissioner general to Europe for Sesquicentennial Exposition, Philadelphia, Pa., 1925; assistant city solicitor, Philadelphia, Pa., 1927-32; consul for Dominican Republic, Philadelphia, Pa., 1931-62; Legal Aid Society, Philadelphia, Pa., assistant chief counsel, 1933-50, chief counsel, 1950—; Abrahams & Loewenstein (law firm), Philadelphia, Pa., partner, 1953—. Temple University, lecturer

When I first came to live in gran'pa's shack I was a little fellow, scared of everything and especially of the sea, which I knew had taken my father from me. ■ (From *The Bonus of Redonda* by Robert D. Abrahams. Illustrated by Peter Bramley.)

in law, 1959—. Philadelphia Neighborhood Law Office Plan (first successful legal service plan for middle income group), founder, 1939; president of Community Health Center, 1945-52, Jewish Family Service, 1951-54, and Pennsylvania Prison Society, 1968-72; executive director, Community Legal Service, 1966-67. Trustee, Dickinson School of law.

MEMBER: National Legal Aid Association (vice-president, 1957), International Bar Association, American Bar Association, Pennsylvania Bar Association, Philadelphia Bar Association (chairman of committee on public service, 1961-62), Tau Epsilon Rho, Philmont Country Club, Locust Club, Consular Association of Philadelphia. *Awards, honors:* Order of Duarte, 1945, and Order of Christopher Columbus, 1957 (both from Dominican Republic); Reginald Heber Smith Award of National Legal Aid Association, 1962.

WRITINGS—Adult: *Come Forward* (poems), Humphries, 1928; *New Tavern Tales* (fiction), Neale, 1930; (with M.J. Meyer) *Handbook of Collection Practice for Attorneys, Collection Agencies, Credit Houses, Managers and Business Men,* Soney & Sage, 1931; *The Pot-Bellied Gods* (poems), Dorrance, 1932; *Death After Lunch* (novel), Phoenix Press, 1941; *Death in 1-2-3* (novel), Phoenix Press, 1942; *Three Dozen* (poems), Dorrance, 1945.

Juvenile: *Mr. Benjamin's Sword,* Jewish Publication Society, 1948; *Room for a Son,* Jewish Publication Society, 1954; *The Commodore: Uriah P. Levy,* Jewish Publication Society, 1954; *The Uncommon Soldier: Major Alfred Mordecai,* Farrar, Straus, 1959; *Sound of Bow Bells,* Farrar, Straus, 1962; *Humphrey's Ride,* Crowell, 1965;

The Bonus of Redonda, Routledge & Kegan Paul, 1968, Macmillan (New York,) 1969.

Contributor to legal journals; contributor of articles and poems to *Esquire, Story, Saturday Evening Post,* and other magazines. Editor, *Independent* (weekly), 1932.

AICHINGER, Helga 1937-

PERSONAL: Born November 29, 1937, in Linz, Austria; daughter of Franz (an artist) and Anna (Bernhard) Aichinger. *Education:* Attended Linz Art School, 1955-61. *Home:* Luefteneggerstrasse 10, A 94020, Linz/Danube, Austria, and Reichenstein, Austria.

CAREER: Artist, author, and illustrator of children's books; also maker of handmade puppets and appliques. *Awards, honors:* Prize for *Der Rattenfaenger* at Brussels World's Fair, 1958; culture prize of Upper Austria for illustrative art, 1964; award from Austrian Ministries of Commerce and Reconstruction for *Die Bunte Maerchentruhe,* 1965; award from International Biennale in Bratislava, 1969, and 1971.

And the next time the Rain Bird sings, the whole game will start over: Rain Man will come back—and it will rain!

WRITINGS—All self-illustrated: *Der Rattenfaenger*, Neugebauer Verlag, 1958; *Der Elefant, die Maus und der Floh*, Middlehauve Verlag, 1966, translation published as *The Elephant, the Mouse and the Flea*, Atheneum, 1967; *Der Hirte*, Neugebauer Verlag, 1966, translation published as *The Shepherd*, Crowell, 1967; *Die Regenmaus*, Neugebauer Verlag, 1968, translation published as *The Rainmouse*, Watts, 1968; *Der Regenmann und die Regenfrau*, Neugebauer Verlag, 1968, translation published as *The Rainmouse and His Wife*, Watts, 1968.

Illustrator: *Die Wichtelreise*, Benziger Verlag, 1963; *Die Bunte Maerchentruhe*, Trauner Verlag, 1965; *Die Schoepfung*, Ernst Kaufmann Verlag, 1965; *Der verlorene Sohn*, Ernst Kaufmann Verlag, 1965; *Mein Lesebuch fuer das 2, Schuljahr*, Bayerischer Schulbuch Verlag, 1969; *Bear Weather*, Macmillan, 1969; *Ein Koernchen fuer den Pfau*, Ernst Kaufmann Verlag, 1970; *Jonah and the Great Fish*, Crowell, 1970; *Der Regenbogen*, Artemis Verlag, 1972, translation published as *The Rainbow*, Watts, 1972.

Leporellos: *Von den Bienen*, Ernst Kaufmann Verlag, 1963; *Die Verwandlung des Raeupleins*, Ernst Kaufmann Verlag, 1963; *Die Katze Mimi*, Ernst Kaufmann Verlag,

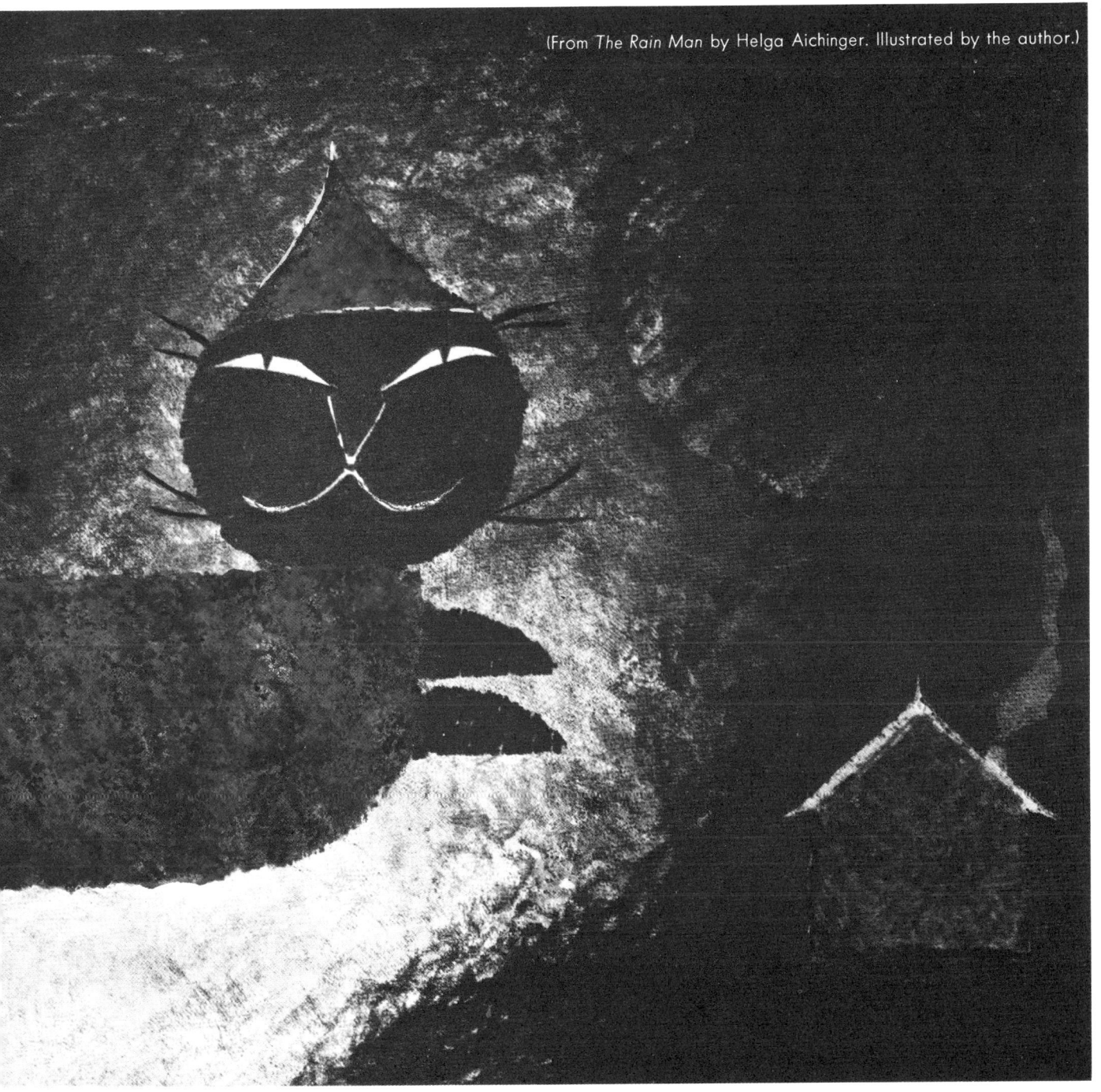

(From *The Rain Man* by Helga Aichinger. Illustrated by the author.)

1964; *Die Waldameisenburg,* Ernst Kaufmann Verlag, 1965; *Leuchtkaeferchen,* Ernst Kaufmann Verlag, 1965.

SIDELIGHTS: "I think that my illustrations tell more about me and the goals of my work than a statement. By my work I want to inform children again and again about my world, to show them something of this world condensed in pictures and simple sentences, and to have them experience those things that daily give me joy, sometimes grief and sorrow, that always give, however, the treasures of a more profound life, a touch with all living things. To that end it is probably more important to have remained a child at heart, i.e., to have remained open and flexible, rather than to have children; to experience even in the smallest detail the enormity of the world; to view everything with a fresh outlook (as on the First Day).

"I paint out of a joy for painting, I paint like the bird sings, I listen for the inaudible tone of tones, and I attempt to say what no word can express, to paint what no picture can convey. Very young children always understand me. I believe that the actual, the essential life is not to be found in the turmoil of city life, although one can also perceive it there when one knows where the sources are, and when one has an ear for it. Whoever has experienced it can never lose it again. Again and again I seek the stillness to find myself there. I live as often and as long as I can in my house in the woods. Here one lives not only the pastoral life—there is also hard work, a severe winter, and problems with harvest.

"From time to time exhibits, transactions with publishers or ceremonies in large cities are unavoidable. I like to travel, but I shy away from the official tumult and speeches. I have therefore decided in the future in such circumstances to allow myself to be represented by my besom [broom]. I am not very adept at interpreting myself. Thus my brush could really represent me quite well. A short time ago I read about a Japanese painter who had the same thought. My books and illustrations should speak for themselves; why should I say something more? Perhaps it happens sometimes that someone looks deeply into my works and sees something that is not at all perceptible. Perhaps my books help someone to develop in a way suitable to his own life. That is reward enough for me."

HOBBIES AND OTHER INTERESTS: Collecting rocks and natural formations of wood; studying insects and flowers.

FOR MORE INFORMATION SEE: Oberoesterreich Kulturbericht, November 15, 1963; *Oberoesterreich Nachrichten,* December, 1963; *Zeitschrift alte und moderne Kunst,* November/December, 1965; *Presse* (Vienna), March 26, 1967; *Jugend und Buch* (Vienna), 1970 *Bookbird* (Vienna), 1970; *Graphis 155,* Volume 27, Graphis Press, 1971-72; *Welt der Frau,* 1972.

ALEXANDER, Frances (Laura) 1888-

PERSONAL: Born February 12, 1888, in Blanco, Tex.; daughter of Thomas Jefferson (a druggist) and Ella Joe (Carson) Alexander. *Education:* Baylor University, B.A., 1911; Columbia University, M.A., 1918; University of Texas, graduate study, 1946-47. *Politics:* Democrat. *Religion:* Baptist. *Home and office:* 2708 Enfield Rd., Austin, Tex. 78703.

CAREER: High school mathematics and English teacher in San Marcos, Port Arthur, and Houston, Tex.; Texas College of Arts and Industries, Kingsville, professor of English, 1925-46; University of Texas, Austin, instructor in English, 1946-48. *Member:* Poetry Society of America, Texas Institute of Letters, Texas Poetry Society, American History Club of Austin. *Awards, honors:* Texas Institute of Letters award ($100), 1938, for *Time at the Window;* Cokesbury Award of the Texas Institute of Letters, 1969, for *Pebbles from a Broken Jar.*

WRITINGS: Seven White Birds (verse), Kaleidograph Press, 1938; (editor and translator with others) *Mother Goose on the Rio Grande* (Mexican nursery folklore with rhymed English translations), Banks Upshaw, 1944; *Time at the Window* (verse), Kaleidograph Press, 1948; *Conversation with a Lamb,* privately printed, 1955; (with Mary C. Alexander) *Handbook on Chinese Art Symbols,* Von Boeckman-Jones, 1958; *Shanghai Internment* (biographical), privately printed, 1962; *Pebbles from a Broken Jar* (Chinese folk tales), Von Boeckman-Jones, 1963,

HELGA AICHINGER

Yi was so pleased with his new wife that he sat on the porch talking to her instead of planting his rice. ■ (From *Pebbles from a Broken Jar* by Frances Alexander. Illustrated with scissor cuts.)

Bobbs, 1969; *Mary Charlotte Alexander* (biography), privately printed, 1968; *Choc, the Chaschalaca*, privately printed, 1969; *The Diamond Tree* (children's verse), Von Boeckman-Jones, 1970; *Orphans on the Guadalupe*, Nor-Tex Publishers, 1971. Occasional contributor to magazines.

WORK IN PROGRESS: Two novels; a collection of her "choicest poems."

SIDELIGHTS: "I remember back in 1938 when I wrote my first book of poetry. I felt like a fish in a bowl because I was the only one writing for publication on the campus at Kingsville. I was embarrassed. I wouldn't admit it to anyone except my mother. She asked how much I was asking for the book. I told her the publisher was asking $1.50. 'Oh, Frances,' she said, '50 cents would have been plenty.' But then a friend sent me a *Houston Post* review of the book, and after I read it I thought maybe the book was pretty good."

ANDREWS, J(ames) S(ydney) 1934-

PERSONAL: Born December 14, 1934, in Belfast, Northern Ireland; son of David (a company director) and Helene L. (Baud) Andrews; married Judith Ann McCartan, June 1, 1962; children: Rona Mary, Susan Helene, Eileen Pamela. *Education:* Attended Rossall School, Fleetwood, Lancashire, England, 1946-50. *Home:* Dunyvaig, Pier Road, Tarbert (L. Fyne), Argyll, Scotland. *Agent:* Marilyn Marlow, Curtis Brown Ltd., 60 East 56th St., New York, N.Y. 10022.

CAREER: Isaac Andrews & Sons Ltd. (millers) and associated companies, Belfast, Northern Ireland, director. *Member:* Society of Authors, Royal Ulster Agricultural Society, National Geographical Society, Ulster Archaeological Society, Royal North of Ireland Yacht Club, Royal Yachting Association, Amateur Yacht Research Society, Clyde Cruising Club.

WRITINGS: *The Bell of Nendrum,* Bodley Head, 1969, published in America as *The Green Hill of Nendrum,* Hawthorn, 1970; *The Man from the Sea,* Bodley Head, 1970, Dutton (Junior Literary Guild selection), 1971. Contributor to yachting journals.

WORK IN PROGRESS: *Cargo for a King,* a novel based in the early thirteenth century; an instruction handbook, *Simple Sailing;* a book of stories for younger children; a novel set in the Bronze Age; technical articles for the yachting press.

SIDELIGHTS: "My main interests lie in sailing, navigation, archaeology, photography, driving, wildlife, open countryside, strumming assorted musical instruments and singing, quite apart from seeing my family enjoying much the same things. I have been handling a wide range of sail boats since early childhood and have mostly lived by or near the sea. I have traveled over most of Britain, some of France (speak French rustily), Switzerland, Holland, South Norway, and Malta.

J. S. ANDREWS

STANLEY W. ANGRIST

"My particular interests in sailing and archaeology provide ample material for all my writing of books and technical or descriptive articles. I believe modern life in cities lacks natural excitement needed by growing children and young adults, so my novels tend to try to picture exciting events in the distant past, etc. I also try to show that men living three, four, or five thousand years ago reacted and behaved very much as we do today, despite different environments. People don't change, really. That's why we all need a little excitement, now and then. If we can't find it naturally, we tend simply to *make* it—hence student riots, etc."

FOR MORE INFORMATION SEE: *Times Literary Supplement,* June 26, 1969; *Horn Book,* December, 1970, December, 1971.

The Coyote-man took that mud and scattered it about him and it became earth. ■ (From *How Our World Came To Be* by Stanley W. Angrist. Illustrated by Enrico Arno. Reprinted by permission of Thomas Y. Crowell Co.)

ANGRIST, Stanley W(olff) 1933-

PERSONAL: Born June 3, 1933, in Dallas, Tex.; son of Isadore (an accountant) and Freda (Beck) Angrist; married Shirley Bloomstone (a college professor), February 6, 1955; children: Joshua, Misha, Ezra. *Education:* Texas A&M University, B.S., 1955; Ohio State University, M.S., 1958, Ph.D., 1961. *Home:* 152 Maple Heights Rd., Pittsburgh, Pa. 15232. *Office:* Carnegie-Mellon University, Schenley Park, Pittsburgh, Pa. 15213.

CAREER: Canadair Ltd., Montreal, Quebec, design engineer, 1955; Ohio State University, Columbus, instructor in mechanical engineering, 1957-61; Carnegie-Mellon University, Pittsburgh, Pa., assistant professor, 1962-67, associate professor mechanical engineering, 1967-71, professor of mechanical engineering, 1971—. *Military service:* U.S. Air Force, 1955-57; became captain. U.S. Air Force Reserve, 1957-67. *Member:* American Society of Mechanical Engineers, American Society for Engineering Education, American Association of University Professors, Sigma Xi, Tau Beta Pi. *Awards, honors:* U.S. Air Force research grant, 1962; National Science Foundation laboratory grant, 1963; Western Electric Fund award for excellence in engineering instruction, 1967.

WRITINGS: Direct Energy Conversion, Allyn & Bacon, 1965, 2nd edition, 1971; (with Loren G. Hepler) *Order and Chaos,* Basic Books, 1967; *How Our World Came to Be* (juvenile), Crowell, 1969; (with Alvin S. Weinstein) *An Introduction to the Art of Engineering,* Allyn & Bacon, 1970; *Other Worlds, Other Beings* (juvenile), Crowell, 1972; *Sensible Speculating in Commodities,* Simon & Schuster, 1972; *Feedback: Closing the Loop* (juvenile), Crowell, 1973. Contributor to *Scientific American.*

FOR MORE INFORMATION SEE: Christian Science Monitor, November 6, 1969; *Horn Book,* April, 1970.

ANTHONY, C. L.
See SMITH, Dodie

ARCHER, Jules 1915-

PERSONAL: Born January 27, 1915, in New York, N.Y.; married Eleanor McMahon, May 2, 1942; children: Michael, Dane, Kerry. *Education:* College of the City of New York, diploma in advertising. *Politics:* Independent. *Home:* Pine Plains, N.Y. 12567. *Agent:* Edith Margolis, Lenniger Literary Agency, 437 Fifth Ave., New York, N.Y. 10016.

CAREER: Publicity and advertising copywriter for Universal Pictures and other companies, prior to World War II; free-lance writer, 1940—. *Military service:* U.S. Air Force, World War II; served in Pacific with 5th Air Force, and as war correspondent.

WRITINGS: I Sell What I Write, Fell, 1950; *Sexual Conduct of the Teen-Ager,* Greenberg, 1951; (with Abel Green and Joe Laurie) *Show Biz,* Henry Holt, 1951;

JULES ARCHER

Front-Line General: Douglas MacArthur, Messner, 1963; *Twentieth Century Caesar,* Messner, 1964; *Man of Steel: Joseph Stalin,* Messner, 1965; *Fighting Journalist: Horace Greeley,* Messner, 1966; *Battlefield President: Dwight D. Eisenhower,* Messner, 1967; *The Dictators,* Hawthorn, 1967; *Laws That Changed America,* Criterion, 1967; *World Citizen: Woodrow Wilson,* Messner, 1967; *Red Rebel: Tito of Yugoslavia,* Messner, 1968; *Science Explorer: Roy Chapman Andrews,* Messner, 1968; *The Unpopular Ones,* Crowell Collier, 1968; *African Firebrand: Kenyatta of Kenya,* Messner, 1969; *Angry Abolitionist: William Lloyd Garrison,* Messner, 1969; *The Executive "Success,"* Grosset, 1969; *The Extremists: Gadflies of American Society,* Hawthorn, 1969.

Colossus of Europe: Metternich, Messner, 1970; *Congo: The Birth of a New Nation,* Messner, 1970; *Hawks, Doves and the Eagle,* Hawthorn, 1970; *Indian Foe, Indian Friend,* Crowell Collier, 1970; *Philippines' Fight for Freedom,* Crowell Collier, 1970; *Thorn in Our Flesh: Castro's Cuba,* Cowles, 1970; *Ho Chi Minh: Legend of Hanoi,* Crowell Collier, 1971; *1968: Year of Crisis,* Messner, 1971; *Revolution in Our Time,* Messner, 1971; *Treason in America: Disloyalty Versus Dissent,* Hawthorn, 1971; *Mao Tse-tung: Red Emperor,* Hawthorn, 1972; *Our Exasperating Friends, the French,* Four Winds, 1972. Contributor of short stories and articles to *Good Housekeeping, Cosmopolitan, Look, Esquire, Playboy, This Week, Pageant, Family Circle,* and other magazines.

SIDELIGHTS: "I originally became interested in writing books for young people because I have three sons, and I was dismayed at the clap-trap they were given to read in school during their junior high and high school years. The textbooks did not tell the full truth about how our government operates, nor about our history at home and abroad. Facts were distorted; only one side of controversial issues was presented. Books for supplementary reading often presented only portraits with halos of famous American figures, instead of showing them as the very human people they were with failings as well as virtues. Most American youngsters, in short, were being fed pap and Pollyanna tales instead of the honest truth; the good and the bad alike.

"I began writing my books with the premise that I respected the intelligence of youth who would read them, and that if they were given the whole truth about our society, our disgraceful failures as well as our glowing successes, they would be able to make intelligent decisions and value judgments, and as citizens seek to correct our nation's weaknesses, improve our democracy, bring about greater social justice for all. Young people must first recognize when the Emperor is naked, for all his pretense of wearing finery, if they are to clothe him.

"I cannot tell how much good my books have done in developing a new awareness of the whole truth about America—and the rest of the world—in the younger generation, although they are fortunately in tune with the thinking of many young people about what is wrong in our society and how to correct it.

"The unusual, intriguing and little-known facts that go into most of my biographies and books on history come from intensive research in many different sources. Sometimes I go back to original records never before published anywhere, as in my biographies of William Lloyd Garrison and science explorer Roy Chapman Andrews. Sometimes I have worked with my subjects or those close to them, as in my biographies of Douglas MacArthur and Dwight Eisenhower. Sometimes I obtain material from other countries, through my own travel and foreign sources, as in *The Philippines' Fight for Freedom* and my biographies of Tito and Mussolini.

"My wife is Australian; she assists me in my research and does the indexes for my books. In my quest for material I've shot rapids in a foldboat, had dinner with Elvis Presley as well as the High Talking Chiefs of Samoa, snorkeled among the barracuda of the West Indies reefs of Tobago, had tea with two Prime Ministers of Australia, sailed the fjords of Norway, climbed a live volcano by camel in the Canary Islands, flown with skip bombers in New Guinea, swam the Seine in Paris at midnight, driven through total cloud in Moroccan mountain passes, biked around Europe's youth hostels, invaded eyries of the gannets on the cliffs of Bonaventure Island in the Gaspe, been 'rescued' from the Aran Islands off the coast of Ireland by a British coast guard cutter and watched grain ground in an ancient wooden windmill in Portugal. A one-time ardent skier, I've hung up my skis for different thrills in chess."

Archer's stories, books, and articles have been adapted for television, translated into twelve languages, and reprinted by U.S. Department of State for distribution overseas.

ARMSTRONG, William H. 1914-

PERSONAL: Born September 14, 1914, in Lexington, Va.; son of Howard Gratton and Ida (Morris) Armstrong; married Martha Stonestreet Williams, August 24, 1942 (died, 1953); children: Christopher, David, Mary. *Education:* Augusta Military Academy, student, 1928-32; Hampden-Sydney College, A.B. (cum laude), 1936. *Home:* Kimadee Hill, Kent, Conn. 06757.

CAREER: Kent School, Kent, Conn., history master, 1945—. *Awards, honors:* National School Bell Award of National Association of School Administrators, 1963, for distinguished service in the interpretation of education; Newbery Medal, 1970, for *Sounder*.

WRITINGS: *Study is Hard Work*, Harper, 1956, 2nd edition, 1967; *Through Troubled Waters*, Harper, 1957; (with Joseph W. Swain) *The Peoples of the Ancient World*, Harper, 1959; *87 Ways to Help Your Child in School*, Barron's, 1961; *Tools of Thinking*, Barron's, 1968; *Sounder* (*Horn Book* Honor List), Harper, 1969; *Barefoot in the Grass: The Story of Grandma Moses*, Doubleday, 1970; *Sour Land*, Harper, 1971; *Animal Tales*, translated from Czechoslovakian, Doubleday, 1971; *My Animals*, Doubleday, 1972; *Hadassah: Esther, the Orphan Queen*, Doubleday, 1972.

WORK IN PROGRESS: *The MacLeod Place*.

SIDELIGHTS: Armstrong's children wrote in *Horn Book*, that their father's "lifelong love of history took root at a very early age. He rode the same hills in the Shenandoah Valley over which Robert E. Lee had ridden his famous horse Traveller after the Civil War, when Lee came to Lexington to be the president of Washington College. The self-discipline of the mighty Stonewall Jackson also left its impression on the boy, who was reminded often by this or that Sunday School teacher that Stonewall had once taught Sunday School 'in this very same church.'

"In Augusta Military Academy [Armstrong's] interest in history found further stimulation. The school had been founded by Colonel Charles Roller after his return from the Civil War. The Old Stone Church at the edge of the campus had been built with stones carried on horseback from Middle River six miles away by the women of the community.

"In his English composition class [Armstrong] presented his first literary effort. The assignment was to write an original story. Cadet Armstrong wrote a story of what went on inside the mind of a crippled boy who sat helplessly at his window, looking out at the apple orchard where he would never be able to run and jump. At the climax of the story the boy's pet cat climbed one of the trees and destroyed a nest of baby birds. Helplessly the boy watched the parent birds flutter in anguish and finally fly away.

"Then other members of the class read their stories. There was the usual collection of compositions about winning football games, trips in summer, and visits to grandmothers. When the class ended, Cadet Armstrong was asked to stay behind. The instructor wanted to know from what source he had copied his story. An ordeal that took the young man first to the head of the English department, and next to the headmaster of the school—both of whom also doubted that the work was original—prompted the decision on the part of young Armstrong to write English themes from that day forth exactly like those that everybody else wrote. He ended his creative writing career at that school as he left the headmaster's office. But as a freshman in college he submitted the same story to the literary magazine and it was published."

Many years later *Sounder* came to be. Armstrong pondered its evolution: "Was it the hoot of an owl that had gorged itself on field mice and was sending a chill vibrating across October fields, polished to a golden sheen by a Hunter's moon, that brought me up sharp? Did the oot-whoo-whoo of the owl strike a chord of memory on a quiet road along the Housatonic River in Connecticut? Did the wind in the hemlocks add a second chord of legend, and another and another, until there was a night song far removed—back and back, loud enough to cross time until it was long ago, and far away, in the flatlands and the pine uplands of the South? Was the October night's song lasting enough to let a lone walker's ears pick up the faint, distant voice of Sounder, the great coon dog, a voice the stroller in the night had never heard, but had only heard about, so many year's ago from a black man? The answer to all the questions is yes.

"But what good is a sprig of memory except to twirl between the fingers of the mind as one walks? Who looks a second time at the dead twig that has been snapped from a branch while walking, peeled of its dead bark,

WILLIAM H. ARMSTRONG

"There's plenty of wood, and I must go back to school," the boy told his mother. [He had] read in his book: "Only the unwise think that what has changed is dead." He had asked the teacher what it meant, and the teacher had said that if a flower blooms once, it goes on blooming somewhere forever. It blooms on for whoever has seen it blooming. ■ From the movie, "Sounder," © 1972 by 20th Century-Fox Film Corp. Ltd.

glanced briefly at its velvety smooth nakedness, then cast away in a bed of fallen leaves? Ah! But Prometheus was punished for a thousand years because he gave man memory, that man might distill and purify his thoughts. Fire too he gave. And both can warm man or destroy him.

"How then should I use this sprig of memory? For Zeus, who punished Prometheus, had decreed as a law of life that 'Man must learn through suffering. So, drop by drop, in sleep upon the heart fall the heavy memory of pain. Against one's will comes wisdom.

"So the sprig of memory is rolled between the fingers of the mind, first smooth, then sharpened until its point becomes a splinter. And on the night walk along the Housatonic it pricks and pricks; agonizing, destroying the rhythm of leaves dancing, wrinkling the golden carpet that a Hunter's Moon has laid upon October fields.

"I must use this memory. I must write *Sounder*. But not yet. Autumn is too beautiful. It must wait for winter. Be compressed like a winter's day with darkness ever hurrying to shut off the light. And when in winter? Not in the quiet peace of evening, but the cold dark of early morning, with anxious glances toward the mountain beyond the river to see if dawn will ever break, but knowing that it will.

"And for whom shall *Sounder* be written? For boys because it was a boy who loved a dog named Sounder. For men because Sounder loved a man a little more than he loved a boy.

"Why not use the freedom that the vast aloneness of pre-dawn affords? Why not be arrogant, with no one watching? For more than two thousand years Herodotus has been enjoyed by two classes of readers—children and philosophers. I'll write *Sounder* for both the boy and man.

"So easy the thought on the night walk. So hard to write. To name the man and boy. Impossible, they have a thousand names. Children speak. Why don't the children speak? Three sharpened pencils; and the children remain silent. Props on a stark stage. Why doesn't the mother say more. What more is there for her to say?

"The winter was still long when *Sounder* was finished. Then it lay on the shelf till winter shortened. In the back pasture in March, looking for the bluebirds that nest year after year in a hollow maple, so old that only half a tree is left, I saw my neighbor sawing wood across the fence. I climbed the fence, crossed his brook, and asked him to read my story. So this is how *Sounder* came to be."

Armstrong raises purebred Corriedale sheep on a rocky hillside in Connecticut. He lives in a house built entirely by his own hands and says he "prefers stone masonry and carpentry to writing."

Sounder has been translated into eight languages and was filmed by Radnitz-Mattel, and distributed by 20th-Century Fox, 1972.

FOR MORE INFORMATION SEE: Horn Book, Octo-

A lone figure came on the landscape as a speck and slowly grew into a ripply form through the heat waves. ■ (From *Sounder* by William H. Armstrong. Illustrated by James Barkley.)

ber, 1969, August, 1970, June, 1971; *Christian Science Monitor,* November 6, 1969; *New York Times Book Review,* May 9, 1971; *Time,* December 27, 1971; *Third Book of Junior Authors,* edited by de Montreville and Hill, Wilson, 1972.

ARNOLD, Oren   1900-

PERSONAL: Born July 20, 1900, in Minden, Tex.; son of William Daniel and Laetitia (Barry) Arnold; married Adele Roensch, July 11, 1926; children: Judy (Mrs. P.W. O'Reilly), Rosemary (Mrs. J.F. Detwiler), Gail (Mrs. R.L. Turek). *Education:* Attended Rice University. *Politics:* Republican. *Religion:* Presbyterian (United). *Home and office:* 2353 2-G Via Mariposa West, Laguna Hills, Calif. 92653.

CAREER: Houston Post, Houston, Tex., Sunday editor, 1925; *Houston Chronicle,* Houston, Tex., reporter, 1925; *Harlingen Star,* Harlingen, Tex., editor, 1925-26; *Arizona Republic,* Phoenix, Ariz., Sunday editor, 1927; *Arizona Farmer,* advertising manager, 1928-31; free-lance writer, 1931—. *Member:* Arizona Writers (president), Phoenix Executives Club (director, program chairman, president),

Hail comes as a surprise to people. ■ (From *Man Against Winter* by Oren Arnold. Illustrated by Ursula Koering.)

Dons Club (charter member, president, Phoenix), Mariners Club (charter member, president, Phoenix). *Awards, honors:* Arizona Governor's Plaque for Outstanding Service to State; Phoenix Man-of-the-Year Award for distinguished service to city of Phoenix; Literary Award from Elsevier Press, 1956, for *The Golden Chair* (best in contest for seven southwestern states).

WRITINGS: Superstition's Gold, Arizona Printers, 1934; *Wild Life in the Southwest,* Banks Upshaw & Co., 1935; *Wonders of the West,* Banks Upshaw & Co., 1936; *Wild Americans,* Whitman, 1937; *Border Patrol,* Whitman, 1937; (editor) *Roundup of Western Literature* (anthology for juniors), Banks Upshaw & Co., 1937; *Flame Boy,* Whitman, 1938.

Desert Plants and Animals, Arizona Printers, 1940; (with John P. Hale) *Hot Irons,* Macmillan, 1940; *Sun in Your Eyes,* University of New Mexico Press, 1947; *Arizona Brags,* Bargeo, 1947; *California Brags,* Brags, 1947; *The Widening Path,* Kiwanis International, 1949.

Savage Son, University of New Mexico Press, 1951; *Thunder in the Southwest,* University of Oklahoma Press, 1952; *New Mexico Brags,* Bob Petley Studios, 1953; *Colorado Brags,* Bob Petley Studios, 1953; *Ghost Gold,* Naylor, 1954, revised edition, 1971; *The Golden Chair,* Elsevier Press, 1954; *Wild West Joke Books,* Fell, 1956.

OREN ARNOLD

The Chili Pepper Children, Broadman, 1960; (with Robert Howard) *Rodeo, Last Frontier of the West,* Signet Books, 1961; *The Sky Y Train,* Broadman, 1961; *White Danger,* Holiday House, 1962; *Marvels of the Sea and Shore,* Abelard, 1963; *Marvels of the U.S. Mail,* Abelard, 1964; *Are We All Here?,* Grosset, 1964; *Irons in the Fire,* Abelard, 1965; *The Golden Strand: An Informal History of the Rotary Club of Chicago,* Quadrangle, 1965; *The Story of Man Against Winter,* Harvey House, 1966; *Hidden Treasure in the Wild West,* Abelard, 1966; *Hidden in the Hills,* Broadman, 1967; *The Great Sleepy Gun Animal Hunt,* Fell, 1968; *Arizona Under the Sun,* Bond Wheelwright, 1968; *Young People's Arizona,* Naylor, 1968; *Steeple Stories* (church-related humor), Kregel, 1968; *More Steeple Stories,* Kregel, 1969.

Snappy Steeple Stories, Kregel, 1970; *Your Career in Cattle Ranching,* Rosen Press, 1971; *Arnold's Sourcebook of Family Humor,* Kregel, 1972; *The Mystery of Superstition Mountain,* Harvey House, 1972; *Marvels of the U.S. Mint,* Abelard, 1972. Contributor of more than 2,000 articles to periodicals. Regular columns in *Better Homes and Gardens, Household, Your Life, Home Life, Presbyterian Life, Kiwanis Magazine, Desert, Point West Magazine* and *Sunday Digest.*

WORK IN PROGRESS: Adult fact book on service clubs; a historical novel for teen-agers; a modern novel for junior readers; an adult biography.

SIDELIGHTS: Speaks Spanish, German, and French.

HOBBIES AND OTHER INTERESTS: Sea lore, desert flora and fauna, golf, and raising flowers.

FOR MORE INFORMATION SEE: Collier's, April 29, 1950; *American Home,* October, 1945; *Sunset,* August, 1943.

ARUNDEL, Honor (Morfydd) 1919-

PERSONAL: Born August 15, 1919, in North Wales; daughter of Hubert (an engineer) and Constance (Sawyer) Arundel; married Alex McCrindle (an actor), 1952; children: Suzanna, Catherine, Jessica; one stepdaughter. *Education:* Attended Somerville College, Oxford, 1938-39. *Religion:* None. *Home:* 3 Castle Wynd North, Edinburgh 1, Scotland. *Agent:* Scottish Casting Office, Television, Theatre, Screen Ltd. (S.C.O.T.T.S.), 2 Clifton St., Glasgow C.3, Scotland.

CAREER: Writer. *Member:* Society of Authors.

WRITINGS: (Co-editor) *New Lyrical Ballads,* Poetry London, 1945; *Green Street,* Hamish Hamilton, 1965, Hawthorn, 1970; *The Freedom of Art,* Lawrence & Wishart, 1965; *The High House* (juvenile; illustrated by Eileen Armitage), Hamish Hamilton, 1966, Meridith, 1968; *The Amazing Mr. Prothero,* Hamish Hamilton, 1968; *The Two Sisters* (Junior Literary Guild selection), Heinemann, 1968, Meridith, 1969; *Emma's Island* (Junior Literary Guild selection), Hamish Hamilton, 1968, Hawthorn, 1970; *The Longest Weekend,* Hamish Hamilton, 1969, Nelson, 1970; *The Girl in the Opposite Bed,* Hamish Hamilton, 1970, Nelson, 1971; *Emma in Love,* Hamish

HONOR ARUNDEL

Hamilton, 1970; *The Terrible Temptation,* Hamish Hamilton, 1971; (contributor) *Young Winter's Tales,* Macmillan, 1971; *A Family Failing,* Hamish Hamilton, 1972.

Plays: "The Home Game," produced by B.B.C. Sound, 1960. Contributor of poetry, critical articles, and reviews to British journals.

SIDELIGHTS: "I started writing children's books when I was about forty. Until then I'd written poetry, articles, criticism, reviews and plays. Writing plays is a heartbreaking business, you have to please so many people and just as it looks as though one is going to be produced, the director emigrates, fashion changes or the company goes bankrupt. I wrote thirteen plays and sold only two and was always in a state of anguish—hope or despair.

"At this time my twin daughters, then aged about ten, were short of reading matter and I suddenly thought why don't I write a children's book. Of a different sort. Not about jewel thieves and smugglers and secret passages and incognito royalty at boarding schools but about a real family. With real problems. And bringing in social questions like what-is-wrong-with-our-schools and the way city planners rip down old-fashioned pleasant streets. That book became *Green Street* and though I thought of it only in terms of entertaining my own children and children in Edinburgh, it was immediately accepted by Hamish Hamilton in London. Very surprising. And rather nice.

"I feel very strongly that social and political questions should not be kept out of children's books—after all they suffer from wars and economic slumps and are often the victims of racial or religious prejudice and a writer who suggests that everything in the garden is lovely is not being truthful.

"What interests me is people growing up, overcoming difficulties, learning about relationships and situations and how to cope with them.

"I was a rebellious teenager myself and utterly despised

She was working in her studio, wearing very grubby slacks and a huge black sweater, with an old shirt which she used instead of a proper painter's smock flapping round her shoulders. ■ (From *The High House* by Honor Arundel. Illustrated by Eileen Armitage.)

my plushy middleclass background so I feel particular sympathy with anyone trying to make a life of his own regardless of what Mummy or the neighbors think. I think, in general, that far more parents are domineering, unjust and (psychologically) cruel than children are selfish, rude and irresponsible.

"When people ask how I get my ideas I always answer that if I knew I'd get them more often. It's impossible to say when an idea, a character, a situation will fire one's imagination and turn into a book. I rely a lot on my daughters who tell me about themselves and their friends and generally keep me in touch.

"I live with my husband, who is an actor, in one of the highest flats in Edinburgh—it is featured on the cover of my book, *The High House*—but we also have a small cottage in the Borders where we spend most weekends and a lot of the summer. Our daughters, now both at university, have left home with our encouragement to live in a flat of their own. But it is quite near and we still meet most days."

ATKINSON, M. E.
See FRANKAU, Mary Evelyn

AYARS, James S(terling) 1898-

PERSONAL: Born November 17, 1898, in Wilmette, Ill.; son of Henry Magill and Jeannie Wickes (Lord) Ayars; married Rebecca Caudill (writer); children James Sterling, Jr. (deceased), Rebecca Jean (Mrs. Carl J. Baker, Jr.). *Education:* Northwestern University, B.S., 1922; graduate study at University of Chicago and University of Illinois. *Religion:* Quaker. *Home:* 510 West Iowa St., Urbana, Ill. 61801.

CAREER: Paw Paw (Mich.) public schools, teacher, 1922-28 (as employee of Western Michigan University, 1924-28); *Athletic Journal*, Chicago, Ill., staff of editorial and advertising departments, 1928-37; Illinois Natural History Survey, Urbana, Ill., technical editor and head of section of publications and public relations, 1937-65. *Military service:* U.S. Army, 1918-19. *Member:* Illinois State Academy of Science (publicity adviser, 1953-60), American Civil Liberties Union (chairman, Champaign County chapter, 1961-63), American Institute of Biological Sciences, Council of Biology Editors (chairman of Committee on Form and Style, 1964-71, during production of third edition of *CBE Style Manual*), Society of Midland Authors, Children's Reading Round Table, Sigma Delta Chi. *Awards, honors:* (With Rebecca Caudill) Children's Reading Round Table award, 1969, "for distinguished service in the field of children's reading"; Society of Midland Authors Clara Ingram Judson Award, 1969, for *The Illinois River*.

WRITINGS: Basketball Comes to Lonesome Point, Viking, 1952; *Caboose on the Roof*, Abelard, 1956; *Pet Parade*, Abelard, 1960; *Happy Birthday, Mom!*, Abelard, 1963; (with Milton W. Sanderson) *Butterflies, Skippers, and Moths*, Whitman, 1964; *Another Kind of Puppy*, Abelard, 1965; *John James Audubon: Bird Artist*, Garrard, 1966; *The Illinois River*, Holt, 1968; (with Rebecca Caudill) *Contrary Jenkins*, Holt, 1969. Contributor of short stories and articles to youth publications, and of articles to agricultural and outdoor magazines. Editor of contributors pages, *Target*, 1930-41, and *Boys Today*, 1941-47.

JAMES S. AYARS

SIDELIGHTS: "Although I was born in a north shore suburb of Chicago, when I was about five years old my family moved to a farm near Paw Paw, Michigan, where I grew up. There I became well acquainted with birds and mammals, tame and wild. Our home was well supplied with good books, and on many long winter evenings my father or mother read aloud to my three sisters and me.

"Before my first book was published, I had written many short stories, articles, and poems that were published in magazines for young people and many articles (most of them related to farming or wildlife) that were published in magazines for adults.

"Growing up on a farm (in a family that loved reading), teaching school, and doing editorial work have all contributed to my writing. Being married to another writer

The next day, Jonathan put Bashful on the concrete walk near the kitchen door and tried to teach him to crawl through a hoop when he blew a whistle. ■ (From *Pet Parade* by James Sterling Ayars. Illustrated by Elizabeth Donald.)

and ex-editor has also been helpful. We each do our own writing but each receives, carefully weighs, and sometimes accepts editorial suggestions from the other.

"Most of my books of fiction have been based at least partially on experiences of our son or daughter or their friends. My book on the Illinois River was based on long acquaintance with parts of the river, shorter acquaintance with all of it, and much reading from the records of people who made history along the river. I wanted to show the river as seen through the eyes of people who were there.

"At various times I have talked to adult groups about juvenile or scientific writing, but I especially enjoy talking with small groups of boys and girls who have read my books."

HOBBIES AND OTHER INTERESTS: Gardening, photography.

AYLESWORTH, Thomas G(ibbons) 1927-

PERSONAL: First syllable of surname rhymes with "sails"; born November 5, 1927, in Valparaiso, Ind.; son of Carroll Wells (a salesman) and Ruth (Gibbons) Aylesworth; married Virginia L. Boelter (a teacher), August 13, 1949; children: Carol Jean, Thomas Paul. *Education:* Indiana University, A.B., 1950, M.S., 1953; Ohio State University, Ph.D., 1959. *Home:* 48 Van Rensselaer, Stamford, Conn. 06902.

CAREER: High school teacher in Harvard, Ill., 1951-52; junior high school science teacher in New Albany, Ind., 1952-54; head of science department at a high school in Battle Creek, Mich., 1955-57; Michigan State University, East Lansing, assistant professor of education, 1957-61; Wesleyan University, Middletown, Conn., lecturer in science and senior editor of *Current Science*, 1961-64; Doubleday & Co., Inc., and Natural History Press, New York, N.Y., senior editor, 1964—. Visiting faculty member at Ohio State University, 1962, at Wisconsin State University at Whitewater, 1964. *Military service:* U.S. Army, Medical Department, 1946-47. *Member:* National Science Teachers Association, National Association of Biology Teachers, National Association for Research in Science Teaching, Central Association of Science and Mathematics Teachers, New York Academy of Sciences, Phi Delta Kappa.

WRITINGS: Planning for Effective Science Teaching, American Education Publications, 1963; *Our Polluted World* (juvenile,) American Education Publications, 1964; (editor) *It Works Like This* (juvenile,) Natural History Press, 1968; *This Vital Air, This Vital Water* (juvenile), Rand, 1968; (with Gerald Reagan) *Teaching for Thinking,* Doubleday, 1969; *Into the Mammal's World* (juvenile), Natural History Press, 1970; *Traveling into Tomorrow* (juvenile), World Publishing, 1970; *Servants of the Devil* (juvenile), Addisonian, 1970; *Mysteries from the Past* (juvenile), Natural History Press, 1971; *Werewolves and other Monsters* (juvenile), Addisonian, 1971; *Alchemy,* Addisonian, 1971; *Monsters from the Movies* (juvenile), Lippincott, 1972; *Vampires and other Ghosts* (juvenile), Addisonian, 1972. Contributor to science and nature journals. New England editor, *American Biology Teacher,* 1962-64.

WORK IN PROGRESS: A book on microbiology, for Watts; a book on alchemy and a textbook on junior high school biology, for Addison-Wesley.

SIDELIGHTS: "I have been writing for young people for about ten years, starting out as the senior editor of a weekly junior high science newspaper, *Current Science*. About six years ago I got into the book business and really began having a good time. My first books, of course, were science books, but one summer we had a house guest from England who was an astrology buff and claimed to have attended witches' coven meetings at home. This got me started on the occult.

"Now I have the best of both worlds, since one nice thing about writing books on both science and the occult is that it makes for a good change of pace. I can write one book about something that I've been trained in and the next on something that is new to me.

"Since I hold down a full-time job editing other people's books for young readers, I am forced to do most of my writing on weekends. This can be a bore, since I often

THOMAS G. AYLESWORTH

miss skiing trips, tennis matches, and sailing excursions, but it does have an advantage in that I can usually beg off from mowing the lawn and caulking the boat.

"Outside of actually receiving a finished book that I have written, the most fun I get out of writing is when the neighbors drop in and look at my home reference library. The mixture of biology and witchcraft books is rather astounding. Then, too, another joy is confusing friends with foreign editions of one's own work—particularly the Chinese, Bengali, Thai, and Portuguese editions of *This Vital Air, This Vital Water*."

BAKER, Margaret 1890-

PERSONAL: Born April 8, 1890, in Langley Green, Oldbury, Birmingham, England; daughter of Harry (a works chemist) and Mary (Eccles) Baker. *Education:* Privately educated. *Politics:* Liberal. *Religion:* Society of Friends. *Home:* Tarver's Orchard, Sutton-under-Brailes, near Banbury, Oxfordshire, England.

CAREER: Writer of books for children, most of them illustrated (largely in silhouette) by her sister, Mary Baker. National British Women's Total Abstinence Union, honorary superintendent of local and county work, 1910-28; lecturer throughout England on total abstinence, prior to 1939. *Member:* Society of Authors.

WRITINGS: The Black Cat and the Tinker's Wife, Duffield & Co., 1923; *The Dog, the Brownie and the Bramble-Patch*, Duffield & Co., 1924; *The Little Girl Who Curtsied to the Owl*, Duffield & Co., 1925; *Pedlar's Ware*, Duffield & Co., 1925; *Four Times Once Upon a Time*, Duffield & Co., 1926; *Here's Health to You?*, Grange Court (Leominster), 1927, 6th edition, 1935; *The Lost Merbaby*, Duffield & Co., 1927; *The Pixies and the Silver Crown*, Duffield & Co., 1927; *The Water Elf and the Miller's Child*, Duffield & Co., 1928; *Tomson's Hallowe'en*, Duffield & Co., 1929.

Noddy Goes A-Plowing, Duffield & Co., 1930; *Peacock Eggs,* Duffield & Green, 1932; *Cat's Cradles for His Magesty,* Duffield & Green, 1933; *Patsy and the Leprechauns,* Duffield & Green, 1933; *Pollie Who Did as She Was Told,* Dodd, 1934; *Tell Them Again Tales,* Dodd, 1934; *The Button Who Had a Sense of Humour,* Basil Blackwell, 1934; *Nick and the Diccon,* Oxford University Press, 1935; *Three for an Acorn,* Dodd, 1935; *Wife for the Mayor of Buncastle,* Basil Blackwell, 1935; *Diccon, the Pedlar,* Basil Blackwell, 1936; *Victoria Josephine,* Dodd, 1936 (published in England under title *The Roaming Doll,* Basil Blackwell, 1936); *Matter of Time,* Basil Blackwell, 1937; *Mrs. Bobbity's Crust,* Dodd, 1937; *Tales of All the World,* Oxford University Press, 1937; *Dunderpate,* Dodd, 1938; *Fifteen Tales for Lively Children,* Dodd, 1938; *Margaret and Mary Baker Story Book,* Laurie, 1939; *The Puppy Called Spinach,* Dodd, 1939; *Very Little Dragon,* Oxford University Press, 1939; *Witch's Broom,* Oxford University Press, 1939.

Lady Arabella's Birthday Party, Dodd, 1940; *The Baker's Big Book,* Dodd, 1941; *The Wishing-Nut Tree,* Basil Blackwell, 1941; *Tinker Tailor and Other Nonsense Tales,* Dodd, 1942; *Weathercock and Other Stories,* University of London Press, 1943; *Nightingale,* Basil Blackwell, 1944; *The Wind's Adopted Daughter,* University of London Press, 1944; *Trotters,* Basil Blackwell, 1947; *Seven Times Once Upon a Time,* Carwal, 1948; *Book of Happy Tales,* University of London Press, 1948.

The Wishing Well, University of London Press, 1954. *The Key of Rose Cottage,* Collins, 1964; *Juby,* Hutchinson, 1969.

Writer of books and booklets for World Woman's Christian Temperance Union, including *Temperance Tales to Tell With a Blackboard,* 1959. Editor and illustrator of children's page in *White Ribbon* (periodical of British Women's Total Abstinence Union), 1923-62, and of a monthly leaflet for The Band of Hope Union, 1940-61. Contributor of stories to British Broadcasting Corp. "Children's Hour."

SIDELIGHTS: "My work is almost all for children.... My only visit to the U.S.A. was at the age of five! I used to be very fond of mountain climbing—not rock climbing. Holidays are always spent in wild, picturesque country—English lakes, west coasts of Ireland and Scotland, the Hebrides, etc. I am a keen gardener and enjoy being a great-aunt ten times over."

FOR MORE INFORMATION SEE: More Junior Authors, edited by Kunitz and Haycraft, Wilson, 1951.

BAKER, (Robert) Michael (Graham) 1938-

PERSONAL: Born February 12, 1938, in Northwood, Middlesex, England; son of Ernest Robert (a civil servant) and Kathleen Muriel (Balls) Baker; married Beryl Johnson, April 8, 1967; children: Alison, Katharine, Rachel. *Education:* Attended Merchant Taylors' School, 1951-56; King's College, University of London, L.L.B., 1959. *Politics:* Liberal ("in European sense"). *Religion:* Anglican. *Home:* 24 Sherfield Ave., Rickmansworth, Hertfordshire, WD3 1NL, England. *Office:* Post Office Solicitor, Euston Tower, 286 Euston Rd., London NW1 3DE, England.

CAREER: Potter, Sanford & Cosgrove, Solicitors, London, England, articled clerk, 1959-62; Bird & Lovibond, Solicitors, Uxbridge, England, assistant solicitor, 1962-64; Post Office, London, England, legal assistant to the solicitor, 1964-70, senior legal assistant, 1970—. New Philharmonia Orchestra Trust, member. *Member:* Law Society, Civil Service Legal Society, Civil Service Motoring Association, Youth Hostel Association of England and Wales, Holiday Fellowship, Grand Union Canal Society, Society of Civil Servants, Festiniog Railway Society.

WRITINGS: The Mountain and the Summer Stars: An Old Tale Newly Ended (children's novel), Gollancz, 1968, Harcourt, 1969.

WORK IN PROGRESS: A children's novel set in Scotland.

SIDELIGHTS: "*The Mountain and the Summer Stars* was written as an engagement present for the lady who is now my wife. It is a reworking of the old Welsh tale of the Lady of Llyn y Fan Fach, a lake high on the slopes of the Van or Black Mountain or Carmarthenshire. Throughout the 1939-45 War my parents and I spent our holidays staying with my aunt and uncle in the town of Carmarthen, which seemed then (and still does) a magical place to me. For a start, there was, not far from the shop my uncle kept with his father, a huge old tree-stump, Merlin's Oak, carefully propped up in case of the fulfillment of the wizard's prophecy:

When Priory Oak shall tumble down

Then shall fall Carmarthen Town.

"Then from the window of the room where I slept in my uncle's house I could look up the valley of the winding River Towy. Last thing at night in the summer, and first thing in the morning, I could see in the distance a dark slanting hump like a giant's elbow looming beyond the nearer hills; and that was the Black Mountain. We never went there; it was too far to walk and there was no petrol for cars, it being wartime. Closer at hand was an odd conical hummock, like a wizard's hat—Merlin's Hill. I remember creating a terrible scene when my parents suggested walking up there and picnicking; the wizard might have caught us. I forget whether the plan went through on that occasion but when they eventually got me up there I was very disappointed because there is nothing there except the view.

"All this lay dormant until the autumn of 1967. I was courting in a tentative way, I was in a job I found uncongenial, and I was upset at the number of broken homes I was dealing with as a lawyer and, as I thought, making bad worse. I set off for a holiday at my uncle's, which I had not visited for many years. I drove down to Carmarthen by car. It took all day, and when I arrived I had the story mapped out. I started writing it that evening."

It was as if she wore color itself, which shifted and changed as she moved . . . And I just stood there, gaping like a fool. ■ (From *The Mountain and the Summer Stars* by Michael Baker. Illustrated by Erika Weihs.)

MICHAEL BAKER

HOBBIES AND OTHER INTERESTS: Travel, walking, railways, history, mythology, listening to music, and "everything else."

BARRY, Katharina (Watjen) 1936-

PERSONAL: Born March 31, 1936, in Berlin, Germany; daughter of Heinrich Eduard (a lawyer) and Irene (Sarre) Watjen; married Robert E. Barry (a graphic artist), December 28, 1958; children: John Eduard, Christopher Luis. *Education:* Attended school in Zurich, Switzerland. *Religion:* Roman Catholic. *Home:* "Driftwood," Cliff Ave., Newport, R.I.

AWARDS, HONORS: A Is for Anything, which was illustrated by the author, listed among fifty best books of the year 1962, American Institute of Graphic Arts.

WRITINGS: A Is for Anything, Harcourt, 1961; *A Bug to Hug,* Harcourt, 1964.

Illustrator: Sesyle Joslin, *Spaghetti for Breakfast,* Harcourt, 1965; Sesyle Joslin, *There is a Bull on My Balcony,* Harcourt, 1967.

SIDELIGHTS: For a year after their marriage, the Barrys lived in San Juan, Puerto Rico, where they discovered some old wooden type in a small printing shop. From this stemmed Ms. Barry's idea for *A Is for Anything,* in which many of the old wooden letter forms are used.

"L'aragosta fa una buon'insalata"
lah-rah-go'-stah fah oo'-nah b'woh-neen-sah-lah'-tah
is the way to say "The lobster makes a good salad."
And this is when to say it. ■ (From *Spaghetti for Breakfast* by Sesyle Joslin. Illustrated by Katharina Barry.)

BAUM, Willi 1931-

PERSONAL: Born March 10, 1931, in Biel, Bern, Switzerland; son of August and Johanna (Jseli) Baum. *Education:* Studied in Dresden, Germany, 1937-47, and Switzerland, 1947-51. *Home and office:* 550 Marin Ave., Mill Valley, Calif. 94941.

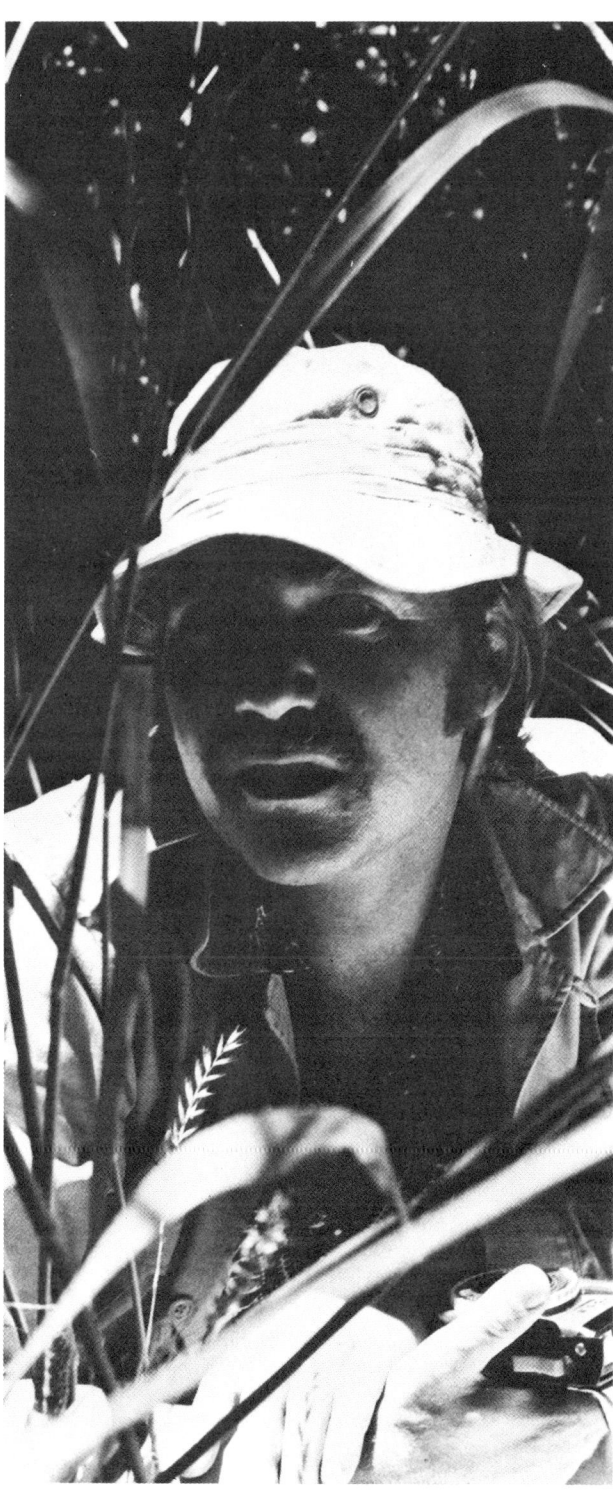

WILLI BAUM, on safari in Kenya

(From *Birds of a Feather* by Willi Baum. Illustrated by the author.)

CAREER: Served apprenticeship as a designer in Bern, Switzerland, 1947-52; designer with South African advertising firm, Capetown, 1952-54; art director of Lintas, Hamburg, Germany, and London, England, 1956-58; free-lance designer and illustrator in the United States, principally in San Francisco, Calif., 1959—. *Awards, honors:* Awards from Art Directors Club of New York, Art Directors Club of Los Angeles, and American Society of Illustrators Art Directors Club of San Francisco.

WRITINGS—Self-illustrated: *Birds of a Feather* (juvenile), Addison-Wesley, 1969.

Illustrator: Caroline Arnett Leach, *The Miracle of the Mountain,* Addison-Wesley, 1969; Doris Orgel, *Baron Munchausen,* Addison-Wesley, 1971.

WORK IN PROGRESS: Books without words.

SIDELIGHTS: "I am an illustrator and designer. Now mainly involved with illustrating children's books and readers for educational purposes. Until four years ago I worked principally in advertising as a free-lance illustrator and designer, but prefer the greater freedom for imagination and style of children's book illustration. It is not the drawing of children but drawing for children, simplicity of the image, a graphic approach if you will, and the abundant possibilities for the fanciful, imagination and storytelling.

"Since I am not a writer, I see a possibility in telling stories with images only, like a short film, as demonstrated in *Birds of a Feather.* In this manner I intend to do more work, preferably with themes relevant to our times. Eventually it might all lead to animated film, but that's after I have studied that medium more thoroughly. As far as illustrating stories goes, I delight in the fantastic and exotic—a chance to use color and shapes that are not of everyday occurrence in this country. Having lived and traveled in Africa, Europe, and Asia, many notes I took during that time are a good background for tales of foreign lands. In fact, travel is still a passion, and to my mind my best work are the watercolors done on the spot. Also the camera comes in handy to record experiences that I would want to put on paper later on."

BAWDEN, Nina
See KARK, Nina Mary

BECHTEL, Louise Seaman 1894-

PERSONAL: Surname is pronounced *Beck*-tel; born June 29, 1894, in Brooklyn, N.Y.; daughter of Charles Francis (a railroad accountant) and Anna (Van Brunt) Seaman; married Edwin De Turck Bechtel, February 28, 1929 (deceased). *Education:* Packer Collegiate Institute, student, 1909-11; Vassar College, A.B., 1915; Yale University, graduate study, 1915-18. *Home:* Bedford 4 Corners, Mount Kisco, N.Y. 10549.

CAREER: Macmillan Co., New York, N.Y., head of juvenile department, 1919-34; *New York Herald Tribune Book Review,* New York, N.Y., editor of reviews of children's books, 1949-56. *Member:* Metropolitan Museum of Art (honorary member), Morgan Library, Bedford Garden Club (former president; honorary member), Cosmopolitan Club.

WRITINGS: Books in Search of Children (R.R. Bowker Memorial lecture), New York Public Library, 1946; *The Brave Bantam* (juvenile), Macmillan, 1946; *Mr. Peck's Pets* (juvenile), Macmillan, 1947; *The Boy with the Star Lantern: Edwin De Turck Bechtel, 1880-1957* (memoir), privately printed, 1960; (Virginia Haviland, compiler and author of introduction) *Books in Search of Children: Speeches and Essays,* Macmillan, 1969. Writings include a pamphlet, *... About Bedford Four Corners and Our Home on One Corner,* 1963. Associate editor and director, *Horn Book,* 1935-69, now honorary director.

SIDELIGHTS: "Having been the first editor of the first college newspaper at Vassar, I looked forward to a career in journalism. Being turned down many times as too young, I took a job teaching at a private school in New Haven. To my surprise, I loved teaching, and would have continued except that Carl Van Doren, who had summoned me to New York when he was head of Brearley, turned me down. So I turned to a publisher who had turned me down in 1915, and he took me on in his advertising department.

"This was Mr. George Brett of Macmillan, who soon made me head of his juvenile department, the first of its kind in any publishing house. At first, besides editing and 'making' their children's books, I did the adult trade department publicity. Considering the size of both lists, this was quite a job, but of course it was very rewarding, to know authors in both fields, and to cover lists of the London publishers with whom Macmillan of New York was connected.

"Soon I had a 'back list' of several hundred books plus forty to sixty new books each year created by myself. Soon I began to make selling trips across America, often lecturing at schools and libraries, the first woman to do this sort of selling and lecturing.

"The records are not complete, but during my active years, I made over 200 speeches on books and reading. At one time, I used lantern slides to brighten my talks on my own books. During one Book Week, I spoke, in one day, eight or ten times, in a store, a library, a bookshop, at club luncheons, etc. At the same time I was contributing pieces on children's books to many periodicals, the *New York Times,* the *Atlantic Monthly, Horn Book,* and writing my own catalogues, some of which were really little books. I was also the first to broadcast children's books regularly on radio—a weekly program.

"After marriage in 1929, my publishing years brought my books three Newbery Medals. I retired in 1934, but continued writing and lecturing, served on a local library board, etc. In 1969 Macmillan celebrated the 50th anniversary of my department. Authors and artists whom I had published honored me at a gala reception, and the book edited by Ms. Haviland was published.

"As the years went by, I was often asked to make speeches, especially those celebrating great dates in library work with children. Then in 1949, Irita van Doren asked me to follow May Lamberton Becker as the reviewer of children's books for the *Herald-Tribune.* Thus at last I did enter the newspaper world, and very exciting it was. I wrote weekly columns, and twice a year did most of the big spring and fall survey issues. I also helped manage the popular Spring Festivals originated by Ms. Becker.

"After 1931, I shared in the gardening and landscaping at our home in the country, especially in work on my husband's rose garden. This led to sharing his talks on roses, showing my slides, or labeled examples of the many kinds of roses he grew, and writing for English and American rose magazines.

"This is more than enough to show what a busy, fascinating life I have had. It includes travels all over America, trips to England, France, Spain, Italy, Morocco, Egypt. I have wonderful memories!"

FOR MORE INFORMATION SEE: Elinor W. Field, *Horn Book Reflections,* Horn Book, 1969; Virginia Haviland, *Books in Search of Children,* Bowker.

BERNADETTE
See WATTS, Bernadette

BERSON, Harold 1926

PERSONAL: Born November 23, 1926, in Los Angeles, Calif.; married Paula (an artist). *Education:* University of California, Los Angeles, B.A., 1953. *Home:* 172 Stanton St., New York, N.Y. 10002.

CAREER: Worked briefly for Bureau of Public Assistance, Los Angeles, Calif., before becoming a full-time illustrator; began illustrating books in the late 1950's, mainly working in brush and ink and in watercolor.

WRITINGS—Self-illustrated adaptations of folktales: *Raminagrobis and the Mice,* Seabury, 1965; *Pop! Goes the Turnip,* Grosset, 1966; *Why the Jackal Won't Speak to the Hedge-Hog: A Tunisian Folk Tale* (Junior Literary Guild selection), Seabury, 1969; *The Devil Gets His Due,* Crown, 1972; *The Thief Who Hugged a Moonbeam,* Seabury, 1972.

Illustrator: Mary Coyle Chase, *Loretta Mason Potts,* Lippincott, 1958; Rutherford G. Montgomery, *In Happy Hollow,* Doubleday, 1958; Helen Diehl Olds, *Silver Button,* Knopf, 1958; William Rose Littlefield, *Seventh Son of a Seventh Son,* Lothrop, 1959; Daniel Walden, *Nutcracker,* Lippincott, 1959.

HAROLD BERSON

Elizabeth Reeve Morrow: *A Pint of Judgement*, Knopf, 1960; Leland B. Jacobs, *Belling the Cat, and Other Stories,* Golden Press, 1960; Ilo Orleans, *The Zoo that Grew,* Walck, 1960; Frances Hodgson Burnett, *Racketty-Packetty House, and Other Stories,* Scribner, 1961; Phyllis McGinley, *Mince Pie and Mistletoe* (poems), Lippincott, 1961; Hans Christian Andersen, *The Nightingale,* Lippincott, 1962; Dana Faralla, *Swanhilda-of-the-Swans,* Lippincott, 1964; Odille Ousley, *Mr. Bear's Bow Ties,* Ginn, 1964; Betsy Cromer Byars, *The Dancing Camel,* Viking, 1965; Dana Faralla, *The Wonderful Flying-Go-Round,* World Publishing, 1965; Beman Lord, *The Perfect Pitch,* Walck, 1965; Hilaire Belloc, *The Bad Child's Book of Beasts, and More Beasts for Worse Children,* Grosset, 1966; Mary McBurney Green, *When Will I Whistle?,* Watts, 1967; Barbara K. Walker, *Watermelons, Walnuts, and the Wisdom of Allah,* Parents' Magazine Press, 1967; *A Treasury of Mother Goose,* Grosset, 1967; Edward Lear, *The Pelican Chorus,* Parents' Magazine Press, 1967; Beman Lord, *The Day the Spaceship Landed,* Walck, 1967; Nikolai Semenovich Leskov, *The Wild Beast,* Funk, 1968; Beman Lord, *Shot-Put Challenge,* Walck, 1969; Barbara Walker, *Pigs and Pirates: A Greek Tale,* David White, 1969; Al Perkins, *King Midas and the Golden Touch,* Beginner Books, 1969; Mabel Watts, *The King and the Whirley-Bird,* Parents' Magazine Press, 1969; Miriam B. Young, *A Bear Named George,* Crown, 1969.

Edmund W. Hildick, *The Dragon that Lived Under Manhattan,* Crown, 1970; Harry Behn, *What a Beautiful Noise,* World Publishing, 1970; Beman Lord, *Shrimp's Soccer Goal,* Walck, 1970; Beman Lord, *The Spaceship Returns,* Walck, 1970; Miriam Chaikin, *Ittki Pittki,* Parents' Magazine Press, 1971; Ivana Brlic-Mazuranic, *The Brave Adventures of Zapitch,* Walck, 1972.

Also contributes illustrations almost monthly to *Humpty Dumpty's Magazine,* where his work first appeared, 1958.

SIDELIGHTS: "I've been illustrating books for about fifteen years and figure I must have done about seventy or eighty. They range from picture books for small children in color, to teenage books in black and white. I love illustrating. I usually work in pen or brush and ink, mainly the latter. I use watercolor for color, usually preseparated.

"I'm originally from Los Angeles, but New York is my home now. I live in Manhattan with my wife. We travel

Together they pulled up all of the weeds, and planted the wheat. ■ (From *Why the Jackal won't Speak to the Hedgehog* by Harold Berson. Illustrated by the author.)

when we can. Most recently to France, Sicily and Tunisia. We're interested in picking up stories on our travels. For example, the 'Hedgehog and Jackal' story was told to us in Tunis. The photo was also taken in Tunis. The hat is a Tunisian chechia and the caftan is Tunisian too. The rest is 100% American."

HOBBIES AND OTHER INTERESTS: Music, ballet.

FOR MORE INFORMATION SEE: *Horn Book*, February, 1970.

BOLIAN, Polly 1925-

PERSONAL: Surname is pronounced *Bol*-yun; born September 20, 1925, in Mississippi. *Education:* Studied at Corcoran Gallery of Art and George Washington University, 1943-45; Rhode Island School of Design, B..A., 1947. *Residence:* Easthampton, N.Y.

CAREER: Free-lance artist and writer, New York, N.Y., and vicinity, 1948—. As artist, works in variety of mediums—painting, drawing, lithographs, silk screens, photography, plastics, wood, clay, and papier-mache. Consultant to Head Start, Job Corps, private organizations, and New York State agencies.

WRITINGS—All self-illustrated youth books: (With Marilyn Schima) *I Know a House Builder*, Putnam, 1968; (with Schima) *I Know a Nurse*, Putnam, 1969; (with Schima) *Something Grows*, Prentice-Hall, 1969; (with Schima) *Magic of Life*, Prentice-Hall, 1970; (with Shirley Hinds) *First Book of Safety*, Watts, 1970; *Growing Up Slim*, American Heritage Press, 1971. Contributor of health and education materials to periodicals.

WORK IN PROGRESS: Three books: two non-fiction, one novel; audio-visual aids.

SIDELIGHTS: "I am a multi-media person and work in whatever medium best suits the job (or whatever mixed media)—from planar (flat) images of all types (photography, silk screens, litho, paintings, drawings, etc.) to three-dimensional (plastics, wood, mache, clay, etc.). Most of my writing pertains to health area education materials."

You should stand absolutely still until the snake losses interest. Snakes strike at moving objects. ■ (From *Safety* by Polly Bolian and Shirley Hinds. Illustrated by Polly Bolian.)

BRADY, Irene 1943-

PERSONAL: Born December 29, 1943, in Ontario, Oregon; daughter of Dave (a farmer) and Gwynne Brady; married Larry Kistler (a phlebotomist), March 4, 1969. *Education:* Attended high school in Caldwell, Idaho. *Home:* Ashland, Ore.

CAREER: Botanical and paleontological illustrator at Harvard University, Cambridge, Mass., 1968-70.

WRITINGS—Self-illustrated juveniles: *America's Horses and Ponies,* Houghton, 1969; *A Mouse Named Mus,* Houghton, 1972.

WORK IN PROGRESS: A bestiary; books about animals for younger children; collaborating with her husband, Larry Kistler, on a children's book of African adventures; a science fiction novel.

SIDELIGHTS: "I'm chiefly an arts-and-crafter, and al-

IRENE BRADY

Nothing stirred that she could see, but just to make sure she waited for quite a while longer before she ventured down. ■ (From *A Mouse Named Mus* by Irene Brady. Illustrated by the author.)

though I love illustrating I do the writing mostly as a chore that must be done. My husband and I are the same age, usually have a cat around the house, like to travel in our VW camper, and have moved around quite a bit. At present we're beginning to settle comfortably into a permanent home in a small town, and loving every minute of it!"

HOBBIES AND OTHER INTERESTS: Weaving, macrame, making animal toys, collecting seashells, camping trips around the United States.

BRANLEY, Franlyn M(ansfield) 1915-

PERSONAL: Born June 5, 1915, in New Rochelle, N.Y.; son of George Percy and Louise (Lockwood) Branley; married Margaret Genevieve Lemon (an elementary school teacher), June 26, 1938; children: Sandra Kay (Mrs. Edward C. Bridges), Mary Jane (Mrs. Robert Day). *Education:* New Paltz Normal School (now State University College of New Paltz), lifetime license, 1936; New York University, B.S., 1942; Columbia University, M.A., 1948, Ed.D., 1957. *Religion:* Unitarian. *Home:* 4 London Ct., Woodcliff Lake, N.J. 07680. *Office:* American Museum-Hayden Planetarium, 81st St. and Central Park W., New York, N.Y. 10024.

CAREER: Elementary, junior, and senior high school teacher in Spring Valley, N.Y. 1936-42, Nyack, N.Y., 1942-44, New York City, 1944-54; Jersey State Teachers College, Jersey City, N.J., associate professor of science, 1954-56; American Museum of Natural History, Hayden Planetarium, New York, N.Y., director of educational services, 1956—, associate astronomer, 1956-63, astronomer, 1963—, chairman, 1968—. Part-time instructor at Columbia University, 1945, Alabama State Teachers College, 1947, Southwest Louisiana College, 1949, New York University, 1962. National Science Foundation, referee, 1960—, advisor to Teacher Education Project, 1961; advisor to U.S. Science Exhibit of Century 21 Exposition, World's Fair, Seattle, Wash., 1962; advisor or director of various conferences and institutes sponsored by National Science Foundation and other scientific organizations.

MEMBER: American Astronomical Society (director, Program of Visiting Professors in Astronomy, 1958—; Committee on Education in Astronomy, 1958—), National Science Teachers Association, American Association for the Advancement of Science (fellow), Royal Astronomical Society (fellow), Authors Guild. *Awards, honors:* Edison Award for outstanding children's science book of 1961, for *Experiments in Sky Watching;* named Outstanding Citizen, Newburgh, N.Y., 1965.

WRITINGS—All juveniles: *Lodestar, Rocket Ship to Mars: The Record of the First Operation Sponsored by the Federal Commission for Interplanetary Exploration, June 1, 1971* (science fiction), Crowell, 1951; *Experiments in the Principles of Space Travel,* Crowell, 1955; *Mars,* Crowell, 1955; *Exploring by Satellite: The Story of Project Vanguard,* Crowell, 1957; *Solar Energy,* Crowell, 1957; *A Book of Satellites for You,* Crowell, 1958, 2nd edition, 1971; *Man Moves Toward Outer Space,* Saga Press, 1958; (contributor) Lawrence M. Levin, editor, *The Book of Popular Science, 1958 Edition,* Grolier Society, 1958; (contributor) Clarence W. Sorenson, *A World View* (social studies text), Silver Burdett, 1958; *A Book of Moon Rockets for You,* Crowell, 1959, 3rd edition, 1970; *Experiments in Sky Watching,* Crowell, 1959, revised edition, 1967.

A Guide to Outer Space, Home Library Press, 1960; *The Planets and Their Satellites,* Science Materials Center, 1960; *A Book of Planets for You,* Crowell, 1961, revised edition, 1966; *Exploring by Astronaut: The Story of Project Mercury,* Crowell, 1961; (editor) *Reader's Digest Science Reader* (stories and articles), three books, Reader's Digest Services, red book, 1962, green book, 1963, orange book, 1964; (author of preface) *The Natural History Library,* American Museum of Natural History and Doubleday, 1962; *A Book of Astronauts for You,* Crowell, 1963; *Exploration of the Moon,* published for American Museum of Natural History by Natural History Press, 1963, revised edition, 1966; *Apollo and the Moon,* published for American Museum-Hayden Planetarium by Natural History Press, 1964; (with Milton O. Pella and John Urban) *Science Horizons,* two volumes, Ginn, Grade 7, *The World of Life,* 1965, Grade 8, *The Physical World,*

FRANKLYN M. BRANLEY

Earth's Natural Satellite, 1960, revised edition, 1971; *Mars, Planet Number Four,* 1962, revised edition, 1966; *The Sun, Star Number One,* 1964; *The Earth, Planet Number Three,* 1966; *The Milky Way: Galaxy Number One,* 1969.

"Let's Read and Find Out" series (for young children), all published by Crowell: *The Moon Seems to Change,* 1960, *Big Tracks, Little Tracks,* 1960, *What Makes Day and Night,* 1961, *Rockets and Satellites,* 1961, revised edition, 1970, *The Sun, Our Nearest Star,* 1961, *The Air is All Around You,* 1962, *The Big Dipper,* 1962, *What the Moon is Like,* 1963, *Rain and Hail,* 1966, *Snow is Falling,* 1963, *Flash, Crash, Rumble, and Roll,* 1964, reissued as *Flash, Crash, Rumble, and Roll Alphabet Teaching Book,* 1966, *North, South, East and West,* 1966, *High Sounds, Low Sounds,* 1967, *Floating and Sinking,* 1967.

Adult books: *Science, Seven and Eight* (textbook), Saga Press, 1945; (editor) *Scientist's Choice: A Portfolio of Photographs in Science,* Basic Books, 1958; (editor) *Earth, Air and Space* (symposium on International Geophysical Year, September 12, 1957), American Museum-Hayden Planetarium, 1958. Also author of introduction to *Astro-Murals,* Astro Murals, 1960. Contributor of weekly article to *Young America* (now defunct); contributor to *Grade Teacher Magazine, Curator, New York Times Magazine, Natural History, Elementary School Science Bulletin, Nature and Science,* and other periodicals. First chairman of editorial board, Natural History Press, 1962—; advisor, *Science and Children,* 1963, *Nature and Science,* 1963-69.

1965; *A Book of the Milky Way Galaxy for You,* Crowell, 1965; *The Christmas Sky,* Crowell, 1966; *A Book of Stars for You,* Crowell, 1967; *A Book of Mars for You,* Crowell, 1968; *The Mystery of Stonehenge* (*Horn Book* Honor List), Crowell, 1969; *A Book of Venus for You,* Crowell, 1969.

A Book of Outer Space for You, Crowell, 1970; *Man in Space to the Moon,* Crowell, 1970; *Gravity is a Mystery,* edited by Roma Gans, Crowell, 1970; *Oxygen Keeps You Alive,* Crowell, 1971; (editor with Roma Gans) Philip Balestrino, *The Skeleton Inside You,* Crowell, 1971; *Weight and Weightlessness,* Crowell, 1972.

Juvenile books with Nelson Frederick Beeler, all published by Crowell: *Experiments in Science,* 1947, revised and enlarged edition, 1955, *Experiments with Electricity,* 1949, *More Experiments in Science,* 1950, *Experiments in Optical Illusion,* 1951, *Experiments in Chemistry,* 1952, *Experiments with Airplane Instruments,* 1953, *Experiments with Atomics,* 1954, *Experiments wih Light,* 1957, *Experiments with a Microscope,* 1957.

Juvenile books with Eleanor K. Vaughan, all published by Crowell: *Mickey's Magnet,* 1956, *Rusty Rings a Bell,* 1957, *Timmy and the Tin Can Telephone,* 1959.

"Exploring Our Universe" series, all published by Crowell: *The Nine Planets,* 1958, revised edition, 1971; *The Moon,*

Lift your little brother . . .
. . . then try to lift your father. ■ (From *Gravity Is a Mystery* by Franklyn M. Branley. Illustrated by Don Madden. Reprinted by permission of Thomas Y. Crowell Co.)

WORK IN PROGRESS Several books on astronomy and general science.

SIDELIGHTS: "There is a need for accurate, readable material for young people. They are the nation's most important resource, and any investment in them will be repaid many fold." Branley first noticed the tremendous dearth of science education books for children while teaching grade school in New York, and has been helping to fill the gap ever since. S.V. Keenan writes that Branley's own education began after his mother's death in 1918, when he was boarded with his brothers and sister at Plattekill, N.Y., "listening to the recitations of the other classes in a country school which had a 'woodshed, outhouse, water pail and dipper, double desks, pot-belly stove.'" Keenan also notes that Branley believes "'children's ability to understand, study, and persevere is terribly underrated by adults.... We throw away a tremendous potential when we delay the exposure of young people to the excitement of science until they have become cynical sophisticates—say twelve years old.'"

In *Books Are By People* Lee Bennett Hopkins calls Branley a man with "tremendous foresight," mentioning that *Exploring by Satellite* was published the day after Russia launched Sputnik (October 4, 1957). He quotes the scientist as saying: "'To write is to accept a challenge. You have to find out what children really want to know, assess yourself, and determine what skills you have to give them. Each book should be important, interesting, contain an element of surprise for *every* reader, whether it is about the sonic boom or honeybees or how a baby is conceived. Actually, a good book for children is also a good book for adults.'"

HOBBIES AND OTHER INTERESTS: Oil paintings, scuba diving, fishing, gardening, boating.

FOR MORE INFORMATION SEE: Wilson Library Bulletin, September, 1961; *More Junior Authors,* edited by Muriel Fuller, Wilson, 1963; *Young Reader's Review,* December, 1966; Lee Bennett Hopkins, *Books Are By People,* Citation, 1969; *New York Times Book Review,* September 7, 1969; *Horn Book,* October, 1969, April, 1970; *Natural History,* December, 1970.

BRATTON, Helen 1899-

PERSONAL: Born July 17, 1899, in Albany, N.Y.; daughter of Hiram and Josephine (Ashton) Stott; married George S. Bratton, September 27, 1923; children: Joyce (Mrs. W.R. Derlacki), Betty (Mrs. E.S. Smith), Carol (Mrs. J.H. Lienhard). *Education:* Studied at Washington University, St. Louis, Mo., 1925-26, St. Louis Institute of Art, four years, and St. Louis Institute of Music, six years. *Home address:* Box 2325, Carmel, Calif. *Agent:* Edith Margolis, August Lenniger Literary Agency, 11 West 42nd St., New York, N.Y. 10036.

CAREER: Civil Service employee in Washington, D.C., 1918-20; assistant court reporter and public stenographer in Aberdeen, Miss., 1920-23. *Member:* Authors Guild of the Authors League of America.

WRITINGS—Young adult fiction: *It's Morning Again,* McKay, 1964; *The Amber Flask,* McKay, 1964; *Only in Time,* McKay, 1967.

WORK IN PROGRESS: Beyond the Sun.

HOBBIES AND OTHER INTERESTS: Literature, art, music, gardening, and adult education.

BRENNER, Barbara (Johnes) 1925-

PERSONAL: Born June 26, 1925, in Brooklyn, N.Y.; daughter of Robert Lawrence (in real estate) and Marguerite (Furboter) Johnes; married Fred Brenner (an illustrator), March 16, 1947; children: Mark, Carl. *Education:* Seton Hall College, student, 1942-43; extension courses at Rutgers, The State University, 1944-46. *Politics:* Independent. *Home:* 11 Richard Dr., West Nyack, N.Y. 10994.

CAREER: Prudential Insurance Co., copywriter, 1942-46; free-lance artist's agent, 1946-52; free-lance writer, mainly of juveniles, 1957—. Committee for a Sane Nuclear Policy, county chairman, 1960-61. *Member:* Authors Guild. *Awards, honors: N.Y. Herald Tribune* Children's Spring Book Festival honor book award for *Barto Takes the Subway; Book World* Children's Spring Book Festival Honor Book Award for *A Snake-Lover's Diary.*

WRITINGS: Somebody's Slippers, Somebody's Shoes, W.R. Scott, 1957; *Barto Takes the Subway,* Knopf, 1960; *A Bird in the Family* (Junior Literary Guild selection), W.R. Scott, 1961; *Amy's Doll,* Knopf, 1963; *Careers and Opportunities in Fashion* (young adult book) Dutton, 1964; *The Five Pennies,* Knopf, 1964; *The Flying Patchwork Quilt,* W.R. Scott, 1965; *Beef Stew,* Knopf, 1965; *Mr. Tall and Mr. Small,* W.R. Scott, 1966; *Nicky's Sister,* Knopf, 1966; *Summer of the Houseboat,* Knopf, 1968; *A Snake-Lover's Diary* (ALA Notable Book), Addison-Wesley, 1970; *Faces,* Dutton, 1970; *A Year in the Life of Rosie Bernard,* Harper, 1971; *Is it Bigger than a Sparrow?,* Knopf, 1972; *Bodies,* Dutton, 1972. Also wrote a children's rock musical, "Ostrich Feathers," 1965.

WORK IN PROGRESS: Six story books for language development program to be published by Center for Media Development.

SIDELIGHTS: "I have been interested in writing since I was nine years old, although I took almost every detour one could imagine before I got to doing what I wanted to do. But I guess you finally write because you can't help it, and I started working at it seriously when I was about twenty-five. I write for young people because I feel a special sense of communication with them and because I honestly feel that part of my function as a writer is an educational one and I would like to educate the young because there is more chance for openness of mind there. What I try to say in all my books, beneath the obvious theme or plot is that the world is a vastly interesting and exciting place, that it is good to be curious, that biologically we are part of a vast and remarkable chain of life.

"All this may seem vague, but I think that if you read my work it speaks to these ideas rather consistently. I am particularly interested in nature and so several of my books have themes related to nature and natural science.

BARBARA J. BRENNER

Their mood toward each other was generous and warm. It was turning out to be a perfect day. ■ (From *A Year in the Life of Rosie Bernard* by Barbara Brenner. Illustrated by Joan Sandin.)

"I am also interested in social questions, and several of my books are directed to contemporary social problems. In particular, my work for Bank Street College of Education has been mainly in the area of reading books for urban children with special focus on literature for minority groups.

"I get my ideas from many sources—my own reading and my hobbies and interests. My children's interests very often spark an idea, and I also have a group of young friends who can usually be depended upon to contribute ideas.

"I consider writing books for children a very difficult and challenging art form."

HOBBIES AND OTHER INTERESTS: Bird-watching, gardening, keeping reptiles, Yoga, sports, traveling, and fossil hunting.

FOR MORE INFORMATION SEE: Horn Book, August, 1970.

BRIDWELL, Norman 1928-

PERSONAL: Born February 15, 1928, in Kokomo, Ind.; son of Vern Ray (a factory foreman) and Leona (Koontz) Bridwell; married Norma Howard (an artist), June 13, 1958; children: Emily Elizabeth, Timothy Howard. *Education:* Attended John Herron Art Institute, Indianapolis, Ind., 1945-49, and Cooper Union Art School, New York, N.Y. 1952-53. *Politics:* Independent. *Religion:* Unitarian. *Home address:* Box 869, High St., Edgartown, Mass. 02539.

CAREER: Started as messenger for a lettering company, New York, N.Y.; Raxon Fabrics Co., New York, N.Y., artist-designer, 1951-53; H.D. Rose Co. (filmstrips), New York N.Y., artist, 1953-56; free-lance artist, New York, N.Y., 1956—.

WRITINGS—All self-illustrated: *Clifford the Big Red Dog*, 1962, *Zany Zoo*, 1963, *Bird in the Hat*, 1964, *Clifford Gets a Job*, 1965, *The Witch Next Door*, 1965, *Clifford Takes a Trip*, 1966, *Clifford's Halloween*, 1966, *A Tiny Family*, 1968, *The Country Cat*, 1969, *What Do They Do When It Rains?*, 1969, *Clifford's Tricks*, 1969, *How to Care for Your Monster*, 1970, *The Witch's Christmas*, 1970, *Monster Jokes and Riddles*, 1972, *Clifford the Small Red Puppy*, 1972 (all published by Scholastic Book Services).

Illustrator: Jean Bethell, *How to Care for Your Dog*, Scholastic Press, 1964; Mae Freeman, *The Real Magnet Book*, Scholastic Press, 1967.

SIDELIGHTS: "I started writing books about nine years

I said, "Clifford, play dead." ■ (From *Clifford's Tricks* by Norman Bridwell. Illustrated by the author.)

NORMAN BRIDWELL

ago. I was a free-lance artist at that time. It was a bad year for artists. I made some samples of art for children's books. Nobody wanted my art so I made up a little story and illustrated it. I was shocked but very happy when it was accepted by the first publisher that saw it.

"I enjoy making up stories that I hope are funny enough to amuse children. It isn't easy all the time. I have about thirty rejected books for the fourteen I have sold. I try to spend five hours a day at my desk. If the weather is good that isn't easy. I try to get all my ideas by myself. I do accept editorial suggestions because my editors are pretty nice people and have been extremely helpful."

BROCK, Betty 1923-

PERSONAL: Born August 31, 1923, in Biltmore, N.C.; daughter of Aleck R. and Kathleen (Lipe) Carter; married Clarence C. Brock (a captain in the U.S. Navy), June 9, 1943; children: Leslie Elizabeth, Alison Carter. *Education:* University of North Carolina at Greensboro, student, 1941-42; George Washington University, Junior College Diploma, 1943, *Religion:* Episcopalian. *Home:* Potomac Ct., Alexandria, Va. 22314.

MEMBER: Children's Book Guild of Washington, D.C., Pi Beta Phi.

WRITINGS: *No Flying in the House* (juvenile), Harper, 1970; *The Shades,* Harper, 1971.

WORK IN PROGRESS: A fantasy.

SIDELIGHTS: "When my own children were almost grown, I realized that we shared a fondness for children's literature, especially fantasy. Writing had been a hobby since childhood, and though my first attempt to write a fantasy for children was unsuccessful, I enjoyed the experience so much I started *No Flying in the House*.

"The setting for *No Flying in the House* is an old villa on the water which we rented one year in Rhode Island. The setting for *The Shades* is imaginary, inspired by homes, circa 1850, which I visited in Newport, Rhode Island on a house tour. My own happy childhood in western North Carolina, growing up in a home where love of flowers and nature and belief in fairies were taken for granted, my fondness for New England where much of my adult life was spent, and my interest in art, antiques, gardens, and travel have influenced my writing."

FOR MORE INFORMATION SEE: *New York Times Book Review,* August 16, 1970, November 7, 1971; *Horn Book,* February, 1972.

BRONSON, Lynn
See LAMPMAN, Evelyn Sibley

BURGESS, Robert F(orrest) 1927-

PERSONAL: Born November 30, 1927, in Grand Rapids,

ROBERT F. BURGESS

There stood the jaguar, head lowered in a half crouch near the edge of the swale. ■ (From *Where Condors Fly* by Robert F. Burgess. Illustrated by David K. Stone.)

Mich.; son of Forrest L. (a watchmaker) and D. LaVerne (Brown) Burgess; married Julia A. Scarborough, June 22, 1956. *Education:* Student at Grand Rapids Junior College, 1945-46, and University of Neuchatel, Neuchatel, Switzerland, 1948-49; Michigan State University, A.B., 1951. *Home:* Chattahoochee, Fla. *Agent:* Paul R. Reynolds, Inc., 599 Fifth Ave., New York, N.Y. 10017.

CAREER: Former railroad section hand, truck driver, seaman on the Great Lakes, lineman, laboratory technician, maintenance man painting high tension wire towers, Y.M.C.A. instructor, member of surveying crew, and magazine editor; free-lance writer and photographer for national outdoor magazines here and abroad, 1953—. *Military service:* U.S. Army, 1946-48; served with Ski Troops in Italy. *Member:* International Oceanographic Foundation, Mote Marine Laboratory, Florida Shark Club (Jacksonville).

WRITINGS: *International Diner's Phrase Book,* Museum Press, 1965; *The Mystery of Mound Key* (juvenile), World Publishing, 1966; *A Time for Tigers* (juvenile), World Publishing, 1968; *Where Condors Fly* (teen book), World Publishing, 1969; *The Sharks,* Doubleday, 1970; *Sinkings, Salvages and Shipwrecks,* American Heritage

Press, 1970; *Exploring a Coral Reef,* Macmillan, 1972; *Gold, Galleons and Archaeologists,* Random House, in press.

WORK IN PROGRESS: A book with working title of *Those Magnificent Men in Their Diving Machines,* for American Heritage Press.

SIDELIGHTS: Burgess lived in France, Italy, Switzerland, and Spain for a total of seven years and has toured Europe, with his wife, on a motor scooter. His major fields of interest are ichthyology, oceanography, archaeology, paleontology, all subjects for his camera.

HOBBIES AND OTHER INTERESTS: Sailing, scuba diving and shark fishing.

BURT, Olive Woolley 1894-

PERSONAL: Born May 26, 1894, in Ann Arbor, Mich.; daughter of Jed F. (a teacher) and Agnes (Forsyth)

Our lunch may be a sandwich or a hamburger or hot dog on a bun.
■ (From *Let's Find Out about Bread* by Olive Burt. Illustrated by Mimi Korach.)

OLIVE W. BURT

Woolley; married Clinton Ray Burt, June 7, 1922 (deceased); children: Eda Forsyth (Mrs. Winton R. Boyd), Beverly Anne (Mrs. Burt E. Nichols), Clinton Robin. *Education:* University of Utah, B.A.; Columbia University, graduate study. *Politics:* Republican. *Home and office:* 777 East South Temple 12D, Salt Lake City, Utah 84102.

CAREER: Elementary teacher in rural districts of Utah, 1913, 1916-17, 1923-27; high school teacher, in Afton, Wyo., 1918-20, American Fork, Utah, 1920-22; *Salt Lake Tribune,* Salt Lake City, Utah, children's feature editor-librarian, 1927-45; *Deseret News,* Salt Lake City, Utah, magazine editor-librarian, 1947-57. Teacher of creative writing at University of Utah, 1947, adult education classes, Brigham Young University, 1958-59. *Member:* Mystery Writers of America, Western Writers of America, National Federation of American Press Women, National League of American Pen Women, League of Utah Writers, Utah Historical Society (fellow), Utah Folklore Society, Chi Delta Phi. *Award, honors:* Maude Adams Playwriting Prize, 1918, for "Sara"; Boys' Clubs of America Award, 1955, for *Camel Express;* Edgar Allan Poe Award of Mystery Writers of America, 1959, for *American Murder Ballads and Their Stories:* Woman of Achievement Award of National Federation of Press Women, 1964; service to journalism award of Sigma Delta Chi, 1965; Delta Kappa Gamma "service to education" award, 1967; Merit Honor Award, Emeritus Club, University of Utah, 1972.

WRITINGS—Adult: *American Murder Ballads and Their Stories,* Oxford University Press, 1958.

Juvenile: *Choice Recitations for the Grammar Grades,* Bugbee, 1928; *Our Magic Growth,* Caxton, 1937; *God Gave Me Eyes,* Gabriel, 1942; *Peter's Story Goes to Press,* Henry Holt, 1943; *Peter's Silver Dollar,* Henry Holt, 1945; *Luther Burbank,* Bobbs, 1948; *Prince of the Ranch,* Bobbs, 1949.

Canyon Treasure, Bobbs, 1950; *Cloud Girl,* Bobbs, 1951; *Jedediah Smith,* Messner, 1951; *God Gave Me Friends,* Gabriel, 1952; *Peter Turns Sheepman,* Henry Holt, 1952; *John Wanamaker, Merchant Boy,* Bobbs, 1952; *The Oak's Long Shadow,* Winston, 1952; *Ouray, The Arrow,* Messner, 1953; *Peter's Sugar Farm,* Henry Holt, 1954; *Young Jed Smith, Westering Boy,* Bobbs, 1954; *Camel Express,* Winston, 1954; *John Charles Fremont, Pathmarker,* Messner, 1955; *When I Pray,* Gospel Trumpet, 1956; *Brigham Young,* Messner, 1956; *Jim Beckwourth, Crow Chief,* Messner, 1957; *Ringling Brothers, Circus Boys,* Bobbs, 1958; *They Knew Jesus,* Gospel Trumpet, 1959.

First Woman Editor, Sarah J. Hale, Messner, 1960; *Cave of Shouting Silence,* John Day, 1960; *Space Monkey: The True Story of Miss Baker,* John Day, 1960; *I Challenge the Dark Sea,* John Day, 1962; *Petticoats West,* Messner, 1963; *First Book of Utah,* Watts, 1963; *First Book of salt,* Watts, 1964; *Wind Before the Dawn,* John Day, 1964; *John Alden, Puritan Boy,* Bobbs, 1964; *I Am an American,* John Day, 1965; *Old America Comes Alive,* John Day, 1966; *Jayhawker Johnny,* John Day, 1966; *Let's Find Out About Bread,* Watts, 1966; *Chief Joseph, Boy of the Nez Perce,* Bobbs, 1966; *Mountain Men of the Early West,* Hawthorn, 1967; *Born to Teach,* Messner, 1967; *First Book of Copper,* Watts, 1968; *Story of the National Road,* John Day, 1968; *Young Wayfarers of the Early West,* Hawthorn, 1968; *Negroes in the Early West,* Messner, 1969; *The Story of American Railroads,* John Day, 1969; *Bulgaria,* Messner, 1970; *Mary McCleod Bethune: Girl Devoted to Her People,* Bobbs, 1970; *How the Horse Helped Build America,* John Day, in press; *The Danube,* Messner, in press; *Physician to Millions,* Messner, in press; *Black Women of Valor,* Messner, in praess. Author of adult and juvenile short stories, articles, poems, and plays. Editor, *Utah Woman,* at intervals, 1945-47, 1950-57.

SIDELIGHTS: "As a child I began to write for a very good reason: It was the only way I had to earn spending money. My brothers—I had eight, no sisters—could sell papers, collect and sell junk, carry a paper route, run errands for the neighbors, work in the corner grocery store. None of these jobs were open to little girls, and, as it was before the day of allowances for children, I had to use my wits. Several newspapers, such as the *San Francisco Examiner,* paid a dollar—sometimes two dollars—for verses. I discovered I could write verses that they would buy—and my career was settled.

"As I grew older, I seemed to find so many ways to use what talent I had: As a teacher, I wrote the recitations and the plays for my classes to present. As a newspaper woman, I received extra recognition, a by-line, and sometimes extra pay for special articles. As a mother, I could entertain my children and my grandchildren. There were always opportunities to use verses, short stories, and plays. And there was nothing else I knew how to do.

"At times I tried other activities: I managed clerking in a store for one whole week. I picked fruit for a part of one summer. As a waitress I lasted only one order, which I got so mixed up and was so clumsy in serving that I gave up.

"When I discovered that I could write books, publishers would pay me for them, people would read them—Well, I thought that was just fine. And I have never held a new book in my hand that I have not felt that thrill of pride and happiness that I felt with the first one. My books have been translated into nine different languages. To see children in Thailand, or India, or Japan reading the stories I've written gives me a special satisfaction. That is one of the extra joys I've found in my travels all over the globe.

"Now folks say, 'Why don't you stop writing? Just relax and rest.' But for me, writing is relaxation; it is rest. I think I shall never quit as long as children will read the new books I write. The old ones are safe enough, but as long as I can still entertain and teach through my books, I'll be putting them out."

With the sole exception of 1904, Ms. Burt has sold something for publication every year since she was eight. Her travels include United States, Central and South America, Europe, and the Orient.

FOR MORE INFORMATION SEE: *Literateur of Chi Delta Phi,* April, 1955; *Utah Library Association Newsletter,* spring, 1956; *Deseret Evening News,* May 4, 1963; *Writer,* February, 1972.

BYARS, Betsy 1928-

PERSONAL: Born August 7, 1928, in Charlotte, N.C.; daughter of George Guy and Nan (Rugheimer) Cromer; married Edward Ford Byars (a professor of engineering at West Virginia University), June 24, 1950; children: Laurie, Betsy Ann, Nan, Guy. *Education:* Furman University, student, 1946-48; Queens College, Charlotte, N.C., B.A., 1950. *Home:* 641 Vista Pl., Morgantown, W.Va. 26505.

CAREER: Writer of books for children. *Awards, honors:* John Newbery Medal of American Library Association, 1971, for *The Summer of the Swans.*

WRITINGS: *Clementine,* Houghton, 1962; *The Dancing Camel,* Viking, 1965; *Rama the Gypsy Cat,* Viking, 1966; *The Groober,* Harper, 1967; *The Midnight Fox,* Viking, 1968; *Trouble River,* Viking, 1969; *The Summer of the Swans* (Junior Literary Guild selection, ALA Notable Book, *Horn Book* Honor List), Viking, 1970; *Go and Hush the Baby,* Viking, 1971; *The House of Wings,* Viking, 1972. Contributor of articles to *Saturday Evening Post, TV Guide, Look,* and other magazines.

SIDELIGHTS: "Most of the ideas for my books come from real-life incidents. The idea for *Summer of the Swans,* for example, came from an article in my college alumni magazine about the swans at the university who persisted in leaving their beautiful lake for less desirable ponds. I moved the swans to West Virginia and the story began. I particularly enjoy writing books about boys and girls in the world today because it seems to me we are living in an exciting and lively period and that the young people are very bright and individualistic.

"My writing is done during the winter months because my husband's hobby is gliding, and my summers are filled with putting a sailplane together, taking it apart, taping and polishing it and driving a thirty-five-foot trailer around the country."

FOR MORE INFORMATION SEE: *New York Times Book Review*, September 14, 1969; *New York Times*, January 23, 1971; *Horn Book*, February, 1971; *Saturday Review*, May 20, 1972; *Third Book of Junior Authors*, edited by de Montreville and Hill, Wilson, 1972.

BETSY BYARS

Slowly she slipped off her tennis shoes and looked down at her feet, which were dyed blue. Then she got up quickly and went to get ready for the party. ■ (From *The Summer of the Swans* by Betsy Byars. Illustrated by Ted CoConis.)

CARLE, Eric 1929-

PERSONAL: Born June 25, 1929, in Syracuse, N.Y.; son of Erich W. (a civil servant) and Johanna (Oelschlaeger) Carle; married Dorothea Wohlenberg, June, 1954 (divorced); children: Cirsten, Rolf. *Education:* Attended Akademie der bildenden Kuenste, Stuttgart, Germany, 1946-50. *Home:* 50 West 12th St., New York, N.Y. 10011.

CAREER: Lived in Germany, 1935-52. U.S. Information Center, Stuttgart, Germany, poster designer, 1950-52; *New York Times*, New York, N.Y., graphic designer, 1952-56; L.W. Frohlich & Co., New York, N.Y., art director, 1956-63; free-lance illustrator and designer, 1963—, working almost exclusively on children's books, 1967—. Pratt Institute, guest instructor, 1964. *Military service:* U.S. Army, 1952-54. *Member:* American Institute of Graphic Arts. *Awards, honors:* Awards from New York Art Directors Show, New York Type Directors Show, Society of Illustrators Show, Best Book Jacket of the Year Show, and American Institute of Graphic Arts Show; International Children's Book Fair [Bologna, Italy], First Prize for Picture Books, 1970, for *1, 2, 3 to the Zoo*; Deutscher Jugendpreis, 1970, for *1, 2, 3 to the Zoo*.

WRITINGS—Self-illustrated juveniles: *1, 2, 3 to the Zoo*, World Publishing, 1968; *The Very Hungry Caterpillar*

■ (From *Do You Want to Be My Friend?* by Eric Carle. Illustrated by the author. Reprinted by permission of Thomas Y. Crowell Co.)

(*New York Times* 10 Best List), World Publishing, 1969; *The Tiny Seed,* Crowell, 1970; *Pancakes, Pancakes* (Child Study Association book list), Knopf, 1970; *Do you Want to Be My Friend?* (ALA Notable Book), Crowell, 1971; *The Secret Birthday Message,* Crowell, 1972; *Walter the Baker,* Knopf, 1972; *The Rooster Who Set Out to See the World,* Watts, in press.

Illustrator: Bill Martin, *The Sun is a Star,* Holt, 1963; Bill Martin, *Gravity at Work and Play,* Holt, 1963; Bill Martin, *If You Can Count to Ten,* Holt, 1964; Lila Perl, *Red-Flannel Hash and Shoo-Fly Pie,* World Publishing, 1965; Samm S. Baker, *Indoor and Outdoor Grow-it-Book,* Random House, 1966; Bill Martin, *Brown Bear, Brown Bear,* Holt, 1967; Eleanor B. Heady, *Tales of the Nimipoo,* World Publishing, 1970; William Knowlton, *The Boastful Fishermen,* Knopf, 1970; George Mendoza, *The Scarecrow Clock,* Holt, 1971; Aileen Fisher, *Feathered Ones and Furry,* Crowell, 1971.

SIDELIGHTS: "In the course of my freelance career since 1963, I occasionally had the opportunity to illustrate books for Bill Martin. I found Bill's approach to the world of the preschool and first grade child very stimulating; it reawakened in me struggles of my own childhood.

"Until I was six years old I lived in Syracuse, N.Y., where I went to kindergarten. I remember happy days with large sheets of paper, bright colors and wide brushes. Then my parents returned to their native Germany. I had to learn German and go to grammar school. School was strict, corporal punishment not excluded. I also remember receiving a small piece of paper, a hard pencil and an eraser with the warning not to make mistakes. However, later I had the good fortune to have a wonderful art teacher, as well as a kind and gentle librarian.

"From 1946-50 I studied under Professor Ernst Schneidler

at the Akademie der bildenden Kuenste, a great teacher, to whose ideas and attitudes I am still deeply committed.

"I strongly believe that the period before and after my transplant from the U.S. to Germany had caused conflicts in the preschool and first grade area in me which remained hidden until the opportunity and insight presented themselves. Through my work with Bill Martin an unfinished area of my own growing up had been touched. It was then that I met Ann Beneduce (then editor with World), and with her kind help and understanding I created my first two books: *1, 2, 3 to the Zoo* and *The Very Hungry Caterpillar*. A mixture of negative and positive influences had led to a fruitful expression.

"As a child in Germany I kept asking, 'When are we going home?' (meaning America). I also wanted to build a bridge from Germany to America, but was told that the ocean is much too deep for such a thing. Today I know that such a bridge is possible. A bridge to one's own childhood—the key to everything creative."

FOR MORE INFORMATION SEE: Graphis, Number 86; *Horn Book,* August, 1971; *Christian Science Monitor,* November 11, 1971.

ERIC CARLE

CASEWIT, Curtis 1922- (D. Green, D. Vernor, K. Werner)

PERSONAL: Born March 21, 1922, in Mannheim, Germany; came to United States in 1948; married Charlotte Fischer-Lamberg, February, 1954. *Education:* Florence Language School, Florence, Italy, student, 1933-38; other courses in journalism and writing at University of Denver and University of Colorado. *Home:* 355 Lowell, Denver, Colo. 80219.

CAREER: Book buyer in department store in Denver, Colo., 1959-64; free-lance writer. Denver Opportunity School, teacher of creative writing, 1961-62. Translator in German, French, and Italian. Consultant, *Writer's Digest*. *Military service:* British Army, interpreter, 1945-47; became sergeant. *Member:* Society of Magazine Writers, Colorado Authors League, Colorado Mountain Club, Mile Hi Writers (president, 1954—). *Awards, honors:* Mystery Writers of America Edgar Allan Poe Award ("Edgar") for best book reviewing, 1956; *Writer's Digest,* short short story contest award, 1955; Dutton Award for article published in *Best Articles of 1964* and *1966*.

WRITINGS: Accent on Treason, Popular Library, 1954; *The Peacemakers,* Avalon, 1960, MacFadden, 1966; *Ski Racing: Advice by Experts,* Arco, 1964; *Adventure in the Cave,* Doubleday, 1965; *Ski Racer,* Four Winds, 1968; *United Airlines Guide to the West,* Doubleday, 1968; *Mountaineering Handbook,* Lippincott, 1968; *Hiking-Climbing Handbook,* Hawthorn, 1969; *How to Get a Job Overseas,* Arco, 1970; *Skier's Handbook,* Winchester Press, 1972; *Mountain Troupers,* Crowell, 1972. Short stories and articles published in more than fifty newspapers and magazines (in seven countries), including *Saga, Argosy, Catholic Digest, Readers' Digest, Coronet, Overseas Weekly,* and *Science and Mechanics*.

SIDELIGHTS: "I tailor my writing to public needs, but I only select subjects that truly interest me. Research is thorough and realistic: for a climbing book, I climb. My great love is fiction, but I cannot indulge in writing it, for financial reasons."

CURTIS CASEWIT

CHAFFIN, Lillie D(orton) 1925-

PERSONAL: Surname is pronounced *Cha*-fin; born February 1, 1925, in Varney, Ky.; daughter of Kenis Roscoe and Fairy Belle (Kelly) Dorton; married Thomas Chaffin (self-employed in a trucking business), August 6, 1942; children: Thomas Randall. *Education:* University of Akron, part-time student, 1952-53; Pikeville College, B.S., 1958; Eastern Kentucky University, M.A., 1971, further study, 1971—. *Address:* Box 42, Meta Station, Pikeville, Ky. 41501.

CAREER: Elementary teacher in Barberton, Ohio, 1951-52, and Pikeville, Ky., 1954-68; Kimper School, Kimper, Ky., librarian, 1968—. *Member:* National Federation of State Poetry Societies, Kentucky State Poetry Society (honorary member), Kentucky State Pen Women (vice-president). *Awards, honors:* First prize for poem, United Press Women; first prize for picture book, National League of American Pen Women, for *A Garden Is Good;* International Poetry Prize, for *A Stone for Sisyphus;* named poet of the year, Alice Lloyd College, 1968; named outstanding alumna of the year, Pikeville College, 1971; Child Study Association Children's Book Award, 1972, for *John Henry McCoy.*

WRITINGS—Juvenile: *A Garden Is Good,* Rand, 1964; *Tommy's Big Problem,* Lantern Press, 1965; (with Miriam Butwin) *America's First Ladies,* two volumes, Lerner, 1969; *I Have a Tree,* David White, 1969; *Bear Weather* (poem), Macmillan, 1969; *In My Backyard,* Goldenhorseshoe, 1969; (with R.E. Simon, Jr.) *A World of Books,* Childrens Press, 1970; *John Henry McCoy,* Macmillan, 1971; *Freeman* (fiction), Macmillan, in press.

Adult poetry: *Lines and Points,* Pikeville College Press, 1967; *A Stone for Sisyphus,* South & West, 1967; *First Notes,* Goldenhorseshoe, 1969.

Several hundred poems and stories have been published in anthologies, magazines, education journals, and newspapers, including *Child Life, Jack and Jill, Humpty Dumpty, Prairie Schooner,* and *Lyric.* Assistant editor, *Twigs* (magazine), 1970; fiction editor, *Pen Woman,* 1970—.

WORK IN PROGRESS: Two books for young people, *Lonesome Valley* and *Tomorrow's Children.*

SIDELIGHTS: "I am vitally concerned about stripmining and pollution of the air and water, about so many people's lack of concern for their fellowmen, about the involvement of children who are physically and mentally deprived by the inequities in our society, and by the failure among all of us in communicating our real needs and our emotions. I have tried to probe these feelings in my stories and poems.

"My concern with a situation has so little to do with physical features that I find describing characters or surroundings the most difficult part of writing. I am interested in how a character feels about things in his life, how he reacts to them, how he relates to his family and friends. Because I must be alone and become one with my characters, I do most of my creative writing at 'odd' hours, mostly from two a.m. to six a.m. As a homemaker and librarian, my writing time is limited, but I love working with boys and girls and introducing them to good books and guiding their reading interests.

"Reading is my chief means of relaxation and my leisure activity. I like drama and attend dramatic programs as often as possible. I enjoy art and music, fancy myself a potential artist, but simply cannot find time—or make time—for proving myself. Perhaps my own love of music has somewhat found expression in my son, who plays practically everything, majored in music in college, and has his own rock dance band. My husband plays guitar and banjo for his own relaxation."

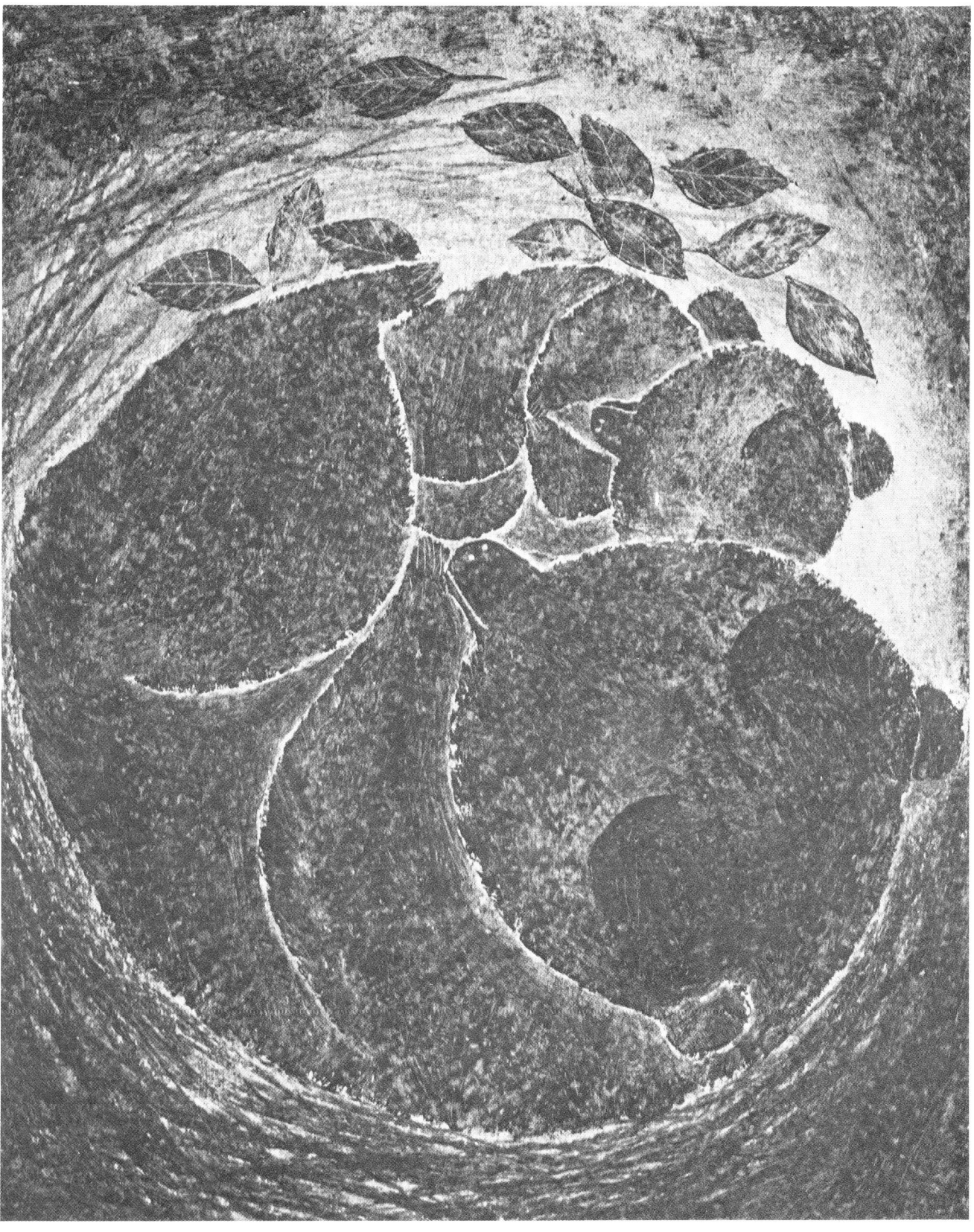

Snug and warm in their deep, dark den,
Cuddled up close with cheek to chin,
Sleeping through dark, sleeping through light.
They never knew the day from night. ■ (From *Bear Weather* by Lillie D. Chaffin. Illustrated by Helga Aichinger.)

LILLIE D. CHAFFIN

CHARLIP, Remy 1929-

PERSONAL: Surname is pronounced Shar-lip; born January 10, 1929, in Brooklyn, N.Y.; son of Max (a house painter) and Sarah (Fogel) Charlip. *Education:* Studied at various times at Cooper Union, Black Mountain College, Reed College, Juilliard School of Music, Merce Cunningham Studio, Connecticut College, and Art Students' League of New York. *Home:* 47 Rue Vaneav, Paris VIIe, France.

CAREER: Actor, dancer, stage director and designer, and author and illustrator of children's books; also involved in experimental theater, conductor of drama workshops, stager of "happenings," and film maker. Choreographer and actor with original Living Theatre company; member of Merce Cunningham Dance Company for eleven years; director, designer, actor, and dancer at American Place Theatre, Cafe La Mama, Open Theatre, Pocket Theatre, and other playhouses; founding member of The Paper Bag Players and actor in first four original productions; director with Shirley Kaplan of children's theater at Sarah Lawrence College, 1967-71, and co-conductor of classes called "Workshop in Making Things Up" and "Inlets and Outlets"; toured with his own company in the series "Intermedia 68," sponsored by National Endowment for the Arts; director of "Biography," opening piece presented by National Theatre of the Deaf on tour, 1971-72; lecturer, workshop director, or consultant at School of Visual Arts, Penland School of Crafts, Radcliffe College, Washington State University, New School for Social Research, "The Place" [London], and other schools. Staged the opening of the Pepsi-Cola/EAT Pavilion at Expo '70 in Japan, using five hundred yards of China silk in a spectacle called "Hommage a Loie Fuller"; staged the "Book Event: The Book is Dead! Long Live the Book!" for a cultural festival in Caen, Normandy, 1972. Designer and developer with four other artists of a Black and Puerto Rican heritage museum in the Bronx, under grant from New York State Council of the Arts; member of advisory panel for Connecticut Commission on the Arts "Project Create," the Brooklyn Children's Museum "Muse," and Judson Poets' Theatre and Dance Theatre.

AWARDS, HONORS: Village Voice Obie Award for director of "A Beautiful Day" at Judson Poets' Theatre, 1966; Boys' Clubs of America Gold Medal, jointly with Burton Supree, 1967, for *Mother, Mother, I Feel Sick, Send for the Doctor, Quick, Quick, Quick;* Yale University grant for work on "Writing with the Camera," 1968-69; *Arm in Arm* was selected by the *New York Times* as one of the ten best books of 1969 and received first prize at the Bologna Book Fair, 1971; two Gulbenkian Awards, for the Scottish Theatre Ballet and The London Contemporary Dance Theatre, 1972.

WRITINGS—Author and illustrator: *Dress Up and Let's Have a Party,* W.R. Scott, 1956; *Where Is Everybody?,* W.R. Scott, 1957; *It Looks Like Snow,* W.R. Scott, 1957; *Fortunately* (play), Parents' Magazine Press, 1964; *I Love You,* McGraw, 1967; *Arm in Arm: A Collection of Connections, Endless Tales, Reiterations, and Other Echolalia,* Parents' Magazine Press, 1969.

Author with Judith Martin, and illustrator: *The Tree Angel* (story and play), Knopf, 1961; *Jumping Beans,* Knopf, 1962.

Author with Burton Supree, and illustrator: *Mother, Mother, I Feel Sick, Send for the Doctor, Quick, Quick, Quick,* Parents' Magazine Press, 1966; *Harlequin and the Gift of Many Colors,* Parents' Magazine Press, 1973.

Illustrator: Margaret Wise Brown, *David's Little Indian,* W.R. Scott, 1956; Bernadine Cook, *The Curious Little Kitten,* W.R. Scott, 1956; Margaret Wise Brown, *The Dead Bird,* W.R. Scott, 1958; Betty Miles, *What Is the World,?* Knopf, 1958; Ruth Krauss, *A Moon or a Button,* Harper, 1959; Betty Miles, *A Day of Summer,* Knopf, 1960; Betty Miles, *A Day of Winter,* Knopf, 1961; Margaret Wise Brown, *Four Fur Feet,* W.R. Scott, 1961; Sandol Stoddard Warburg, *My Very Own Special Particular Private and Personal Cat,* Houghton, 1963; Ruth Krauss, *What a Fine Day for...,* Parents' Magazine Press, 1967.

WORK IN PROGRESS: Making Things Up, based on teaching the use of personal material (things unique to the person) for the creation of original work, whether it be a play, book, dance, painting, or film.

REMY CHARLIP

PART MAN PART GOAT PART FISH PART BIRD PART SNAKE PART BUG

(From *Arm in Arm* by Remy Charlip. Illustrated by the author.)

SIDELIGHTS: "I'm living in Paris now doing paintings for *Harlequin* and research in my home town in Italy. The old country is naturally an inspiration for such a work. I have never before tried to draw and paint in such detail: hair, eyelashes, stones, perspective, etc. I'm learning.

"In doing my own work like *Arm in Arm* and *Harlequin*, I use the book to find out where I am at the moment. I do the thing for myself and itself. If it interests others, I'm sure it's because they see how involved I was in it when I did it. A lot of the time too, I do something so I can get rid of it—put it out in the world so I don't have to think about it anymore and can start something else."

FOR MORE INFORMATION SEE: *Third Book of Junior Authors*, edited by de Montreville and Hill, Wilson, 1972.

CHASE, Alice
See McHARGUE, Georgess

CHASTAIN, Madye Lee 1908-

PERSONAL: Born December 15, 1908, in Texarkana, Tex.; daughter of Fred C. and Roxana H. (Bledsoe) Chastain; married Henry Kurt Stoessel (an artist), October 9, 1936; children: Roxana Ellen (Mrs. David Farnham Bartlett). *Education:* Studied at Oglethorpe University, Art School of High Museum, Atlanta, Ga., Grand Central Art School, New York, N.Y., and Columbia University. *Home:* 2100 Linwood Ave., Fort Lee, N.J. 07024.

CAREER: Artist (portraits and etchings), 1932-38; writer and illustrator.

WRITINGS—Author and illustrator: *Roxana Pretends*, Rachman, 1945; *Susan and the Rain*, Whitman, 1947; *Nellie*, Whitman, 1948; *Let's Play Indian*, Grossett, 1950; *The Sailboat that Ran Away*, Whitman, 1950; *Loblolly Farm*, Harcourt, 1950; *Steamboat South*, Harcourt, 1951; *Bright Days*, Harcourt, 1952; *Fripsey Summer*, Harcourt, 1953; *Dark Treasure*, Harcourt, 1954; *Fripsey Fun*, Harcourt, 1955; *Emmy Keeps a Promise*, Harcourt, 1956; *Leave it to the Fripseys*, Harcourt, 1957; *Jerusha's Ghost*, Harcourt, 1958; *Summer at Hasty Cove*, Harcourt, 1959; *Plippen's Palace*, Harcourt, 1961; *Magic Island*, Harcourt, 1964.

HOBBIES AND OTHER INTERESTS: Theatre, art, music (plays in recorder group), boating, and travel.

MADYE LEE CHASTAIN

She had decided to go down Broadway and inquire in all the stores whether or not they needed a willing girl as a helper after school. ■ (From *Emmy Keeps a Promise* by Madye Lee Chastain. Illustrated by the author.)

CLAPP, Patricia 1912-

PERSONAL: Born June 9, 1912, in Boston, Mass.; daughter of Howard (a dentist) and Elizabeth (Blachford) Clapp; married Edward della Torre Cone (a transportation consultant), March 3, 1933; children: Christopher, Patricia (Mrs. John R. Shelter), Pamela (Mrs. William K. Wakefield). *Education:* Columbia University, journalism student, two years; various writing courses later. *Religion:* Protestant. *Home:* 83 Beverley Rd., Upper Montclair, N.J. 07043.

AWARDS, HONORS: National Book Award runner-up and Lewis Carroll Shelf Award, 1969, for *Constance*.

WRITINGS—All plays except as noted: *Peggy's On the Phone* (one-act), Dramatic Publishing, 1956; *Smart Enough to Be Dumb* (one-act), Dramatic Publishing, 1956; *The Incompleted Pass* (three-act), Dramatic Publishing, 1957; *Her Kissin' Cousin* (three-act), Heuer Publishing, 1957; *The Girl Out Front* (three-act), Dramatic Publishing, 1958; *The Ghost of a Chance* (three-act), Heuer Publishing 1958; *The Curley Tale* (three-act), Art Craft, 1958; *Inquire Within* (three-act), Row, 1959; "The Girl Whose Fortune Sought Her" (one-act), in *Children's Plays From Favorite Stories,* edited by S.E. Kamerman, Plays, 1959.

Edie-Across-the-Street (three-act), Baker Co., 1960; *The Honeysuckle Hedge* (three-act), Eldridge Publishing, 1960; *Never Keep Him Waiting* (three-act), Dramatic Publishing, 1961; *Red Heels and Roses* (one-act), McKay, 1961; *If a Body Meet a Body* (three-act), Heuer Publishing, 1963; *Now Hear This* (one-act), Eldridge Publishing, 1963; "The Magic Bookshelf" (one-act), in *Fifty Plays for Junior Actors,* edited by Kamerman, Plays, 1966; *Constance: A Story of Early Plymouth* (juvenile novel), Lothrop, 1968; *Jane-Emily* (juvenile novel), Lothrop, 1969; "The Other Side of the Wall" (one-act), in *Fifty Plays for Holidays,* edited by Kamerman, Plays, 1969; "The Do-Nothing Frog" (one-act), in *100 Plays for Children,* edited by A.S. Burack, Plays, 1970; *The Invisible Dragon* (one-act with music), Dramatic Publishing, 1971; *A Candle on the Table* (one-act), Baker Co., 1972; *The Retirement* (one-act), Eldridge Publishing, 1972; *A Specially Wonderful Day* (one-act), Encyclopedia Britannica, 1972. "A Feather in His Cap," "The Wonderful Door," "A Wish is for Keeping," "Susan and Aladdin's Lamp," "The Signpost," "The Friendship Bracelet," "Christmas in Old New England," "The Straight Line from Somewhere," published in *Instructor Magazine, Plays Magazine,* or *Grade Teacher Magazine,* 1958-68. Also has had poems published. Editor of little theater publications.

SIDELIGHTS: "Whatever writing I do is a very occasional thing. I am not 'professional' in the sense of writing for a living, and therefore there is no financial drive. When I write it is for (a) the pleasure of putting words on paper, (b) the job of escape into a world of my own creating, and (rather importantly) (c) the thrill of seeing my own work in print.

"I never know where ideas come from, they are just suddenly there. I envy any writer who has a plethora of ideas, mine seem rare and scarce, and the harder I strive for one, the less likely it is to appear. I am always happier when I am writing something, and yet I find myself putting it off week after week. I am unable to view my own work objectively, and I am never sure whether it is fair, good, or very good. I have to trust an editor implicitly. Of course, editors don't always agree. I have had a play turned down with a deflating thud by one editor, only to have it greeted with little cries of joy by another.

"I have an abundance of activities aside from writing, all of which are consuming enough to keep me away from the typewriter. With nine fascinating grandchildren to watch, tend and play with; an administrative position with an almost professional non-professional theatre; a large house to keep in order; frequent trips to other countries; fancy handwork; indoor gardening—plus the daily details of life that keep any housewife busy, my time is crammed.

PATRICIA CLAPP

"I write the sort of thing that, as a young girl (which was some time ago), I enjoyed reading. They are romantic, but not (I hope) smarmy; they have humor, that greatest necessity in life; they are affirmative rather than negative. I have no desire to handle the frightening problems of present-day living, nor do I feel I am equipped to do so. There is a great deal of happiness, laughter, kindness and love in the world today, just as there has always been, and it cannot do any harm to spread it as far as possible. This, perhaps, is my aim, if indeed I have one.

"I am a strong believer in the virtues of conservatism, optimism, good manners, thoughtfulness, kindness and those outmoded beautiful words 'ladies' and 'gentlemen'. Deplore untidiness of any sort, moral, spiritual or physical.... Think every younger generation rebels, but some generations do it more gracefully than others. I love London, Cape Cod, Lucerne, part of Connecticut, and Florence. Dislike Rome, California and the middle west. Enjoy traveling but prefer staying home."

FOR MORE INFORMATION SEE: Book World, May 5, 1968; New York Times Book Review, August 18, 1968; Commonweal, May 23, 1969; Horn Book, October, 1969.

CLARK, Ann Nolan 1898-

PERSONAL: Born 1898, in Las Vegas, N.M.; daughter of Patrick Frances and Mary (Dunne) Nolan; married Thomas Patrick Clark, 1919 (deceased); children: Thomas Patrick, Jr. (pilot, killed in World War II). Education: Attended New Mexico Highlands University. Home: P.O. Box 164, Cortaro, Ariz. 85230.

CAREER: Bureau of Indian Affairs, Washington, D.C., education specialist, 1930—; International Cooperation Administration, Washington, D.C., education consultant, Latin-American Bureau, 1946—. Institute of Inter-American Affairs, former materials specialist; U.S. delegate to UNESCO conference, Brazil. Member: P.E.N. (New York), National Council of Women, International Council of Women, Alpha Delta Kappa, Altrusa International. Awards, honors: New York Herald Tribune Spring Festival Award for In My Mother's House, 1941, Looking-for-Something, 1952; Newbery Medal, 1952, for Secret of the Andes; U.S. government's Distinguished Service Award, 1962; Regina medal, 1963.

WRITINGS: Who Wants to Be a Prairie Dog?, U.S. Office of Indian Affairs, 1940; Little Herder in Spring, U.S. Office of Indian Affairs, 1940; Little Herder in Autumn, U.S. Office of Indian Affairs, 1940; Little Boy with Three Names, U.S. Office of Indian Affairs, 1940; The Pine Ridge Porcupine, U.S. Office of Indian Affairs, 1941; In My Mother's House (Junior Literary Guild selection), Viking, 1941; (with Frances Carey) A Child's Story of New Mexico, University Publishing, 1941, 3rd edition, 1960; The Slim Butte Raccoon, U.S. Department of the Interior, Bureau of Indian Affairs, 1942; Little Herder in Winter, U.S. Office of Indian Affairs, 1942; Little Herder in Summer, U.S. Office of Indian Affairs, 1942; Buffalo Caller, Row, Peterson & Co., 1942; About the Slim Butte Raccoon, U.S. Office of Indian Affairs, 1942; Young Hunter of Picuris, U.S. Office of Indian Affairs, 1943; Little Navajo Bluebird (Junior Literary Guild selection), Viking, 1943; Bringer of the Mystery Dog, Department of the Interior, Bureau of Indian Affairs, 1943; Singing Sioux Cowboy Reader, U.S. Indian Service, 1947.

Magic Money (Junior Literary Guild selection), Viking, 1950; Little Herder in Spring, in Summer (incorporating two earlier primers), U.S. Indian Service, 1950; Little Herder in Autumn, in Winter (incorporating two earlier primers), U.S. Indian Service, 1950; Little Navajo Herder (compilation of four earlier books), U.S. Indian Service, 1951; Secret of the Andes (Junior Literary Guild selection), Viking, 1952; Looking-for-Something (Junior Literary Guild selection), Viking, 1952; Blue Canyon Horse, Viking, 1954; Santiago, Viking, 1955; The Little Indian Pottery Maker, Melmont, 1955; Third Monkey, Viking, 1956; The Little Indian Basket Maker, Melmont, 1957; There Still Are Buffalo, Haskell, 1958; A Santo for Pasqualita, Viking, 1959; World Song, Viking, 1960; Paco's Miracle, Farrar, Straus, 1962; The Desert People, Viking, 1962; Tia Maria's Gardens, Viking, 1963; Medicine Man's Daughter, Farrar, Straus, 1963; Father Kino, Farrar, Straus, 1963; Bear Cub, Viking, 1965; This for That, Golden Gate, 1965; Brother Andre, Farrar, Straus, 1965; Summer is for Growing, Farrar, Straus, 1967; Along Sandy Trails, Viking, 1969; Circle of Seasons, Farrar,

ANN NOLAN CLARK

Straus, 1970; *These Are the Valiant,* Horn, 1970; *Journey to the People,* Viking, 1970; *Hoofbeat on the Wind,* Viking, 1972.

Supervised the preparation of materials for adult literacy, Bureau of Indian Affairs, and reading texts for several countries in Latin America, including Guatemala.

SIDELIGHTS: "In college I planned a two-fold career: teaching English and/or history to high school age children and writing historical materials on the 1800's in the Southwest. Both of these interested me and still do, even though I did not continue along the path I had planned.

"My first teaching experience was as assistant to the English instructor in what is now Highlands University at Las Vegas, New Mexico, my birthplace. My first writing experience was Southwestern historical articles for the *New Mexico* Magazine.

"The first World War changed my life. I was asked to teach a one-room school in a pro-German community. I would have rather been an ambulance driver in 'the War' but I had a firm mother so I did my war work teaching. Many things happened—none of which was appreciated by my dear, patient mother—and I finally found myself teaching older Indian children in a U.S. Government school. I became lastingly involved in the educational and other needs of Indian children.

"After several years teaching older Indian children, the Tesugue Pueblo people asked John Collier if I could come to them—a one-room school from pre-school to fourth grade. I was delighted because by this time I wanted to follow the development of an Indian child from pre-school to boarding school age. The superintendent of the Santa Fe Indian School, where I was teaching said I could go but if I went from a large boarding school to a tiny one-room school my career as an Indian educator would be ended.

So, of course, I went. I stayed four years and it was the richest, most satisfying experience I have had. This prepared me for other experiences, which were rich and good.

"From the beginning, at the Tesugue School, I realized that the children must have instructional materials geared to their language needs and reading materials in which they could identify. At that time school appropriations at small schools covered little more than mops and brooms and yellow soap. My salary covered a little more, but not much. So I could not buy books—I had to write them.

"At first these books were about Indians and for Indians, but there soon became a demand for books about Indians for Indian and also non-Indian children. The situation and, perhaps, my choice made me change my goals from teaching history and writing historical materials for adults. My specialty became teaching children to talk and think, to write and read a secondary language.

"The second World War changed my life and my goals again. My teaching now was geared toward helping in the development of understanding, acceptance and respect (giving and receiving). My world became wider—many kinds of people—many kinds of needs.

"All of my books are based upon actual experiences, knowing the people and places I write about, having been there."

FOR MORE INFORMATION SEE: Junior Book of Authors, edited by Kunitz and Haycraft, H.W. Wilson, 2nd edition, 1951; *Publishers' Weekly,* March 14, 1953; *Library Journal,* March 15, 1953; *Horn Book,* August, 1953, December, 1969, February, 1970, August, 1970; *Elementary English,* October, 1953; *Newbery Medal Books: 1922-1955,* edited by Miller and Field, Horn Book, 1955; Nancy Larrick, *A Parent's Guide to Children's Reading,* 3rd edition, 1969.

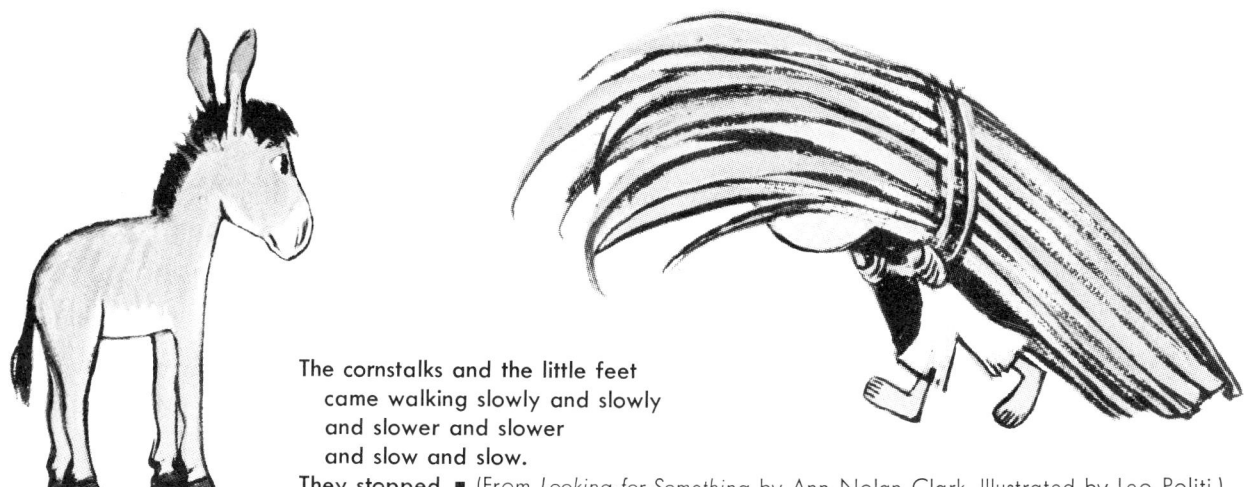

The cornstalks and the little feet came walking slowly and slowly and slower and slower and slow and slow.
They stopped. ■ (From *Looking-for-Something* by Ann Nolan Clark. Illustrated by Leo Politi.)

COFFMAN, Ramon Peyton 1896- (Uncle Ray)

PERSONAL: Born July 24, 1896, in Indianapolis, Ind.; son of Walter McDowell (a mechanical engineer and inventor) and Effie (Stringer) Coffman; married Nelle Ruth Gratton, December 14, 1929; children: Gratton Eugene, Peyton, Roger, Kathleen. *Education:* University of Wisconsin, student, 1914-15, A.B., 1926; studied at Yale University, 1915-16, New School for Social Research, 1918-19. *Religion:* Unitarian Universalist. *Home:* 641 S.E. Poinciana Dr., Fort Lauderdale, Fla. 33301. *Office:* Publishers Newspaper Syndicate, 400 North Michigan Ave., Chicago, Ill. 60611.

CAREER: Founder and editor of *Typical Boy* (magazine), 1912-14; reporter, later children's editor on newspapers in Milwaukee, Wis., 1920-22; began writing newspaper feature for children as Uncle Ray, 1922, and daily column, "Uncle Ray's Corner," has been syndicated in American newspapers, 1925—. Author of juvenile books, 1924—; founding editor and publisher of *Uncle Ray's Magazine*, 1946-57. *Member:* Sigma Delta Chi.

WRITINGS: *The Child's Story of the Human Race*, Dodd, 1924; *The Story of America*, five books, F.A. Owen, 1927-34; *Our America*, Dodd, 1930; (author of brief text) *Picture Story of Robinson Crusoe*, illustrated by Frank C. Pape, Reilly & Lee, 1932; *Uncle Ray's Story of the Stone-Age People*, Rand, 1936; (under pseudonym Uncle Ray) *The Child's Story of Science*, Putnam, 1939.

(With Nathan G. Goodman) *Famous Explorers for Boys and Girls*, A.S. Barnes, 1942 (reissued as *Famous Explorers for Young People*, Dodd, 1956); (with N.G. Goodman) *Famous Authors for Boys and Girls*, A.S. Barnes, 1943 (also issued as *Famous Authors for Young People*, Dodd, 1943); (with N.G. Goodman) *Famous Generals and Admirals for Boys and Girls*, A.S. Barnes, 1944; (with N.G. Goodman) *Famous Pioneers for Young People*, A.S. Barnes, 1945; *Famous Kings and Queens for Young People*, A.S. Barnes, 1947.

WORK IN PROGRESS: A sixteen-volume set of writings.

SIDELIGHTS: Coffman has made seven trips to Europe and traveled around the world, writing about customs in other lands for young readers. Newspaper articles and books have been translated into a total of four languages.

COHEN, Joan Lebold 1932-

PERSONAL: Born August 19, 1932, in Highland Park,

JOAN LEBOLD COHEN

He became ill, but still insisted on beginning the journey. ■ (From *Buddha* by Joan Lebold Cohen. Illustrated by Mary Frank.)

Ill.; daughter of Samuel N. (a businessman) and Patricia (Aloe) Lebold Tucker; married Jerome Alan Cohen (a professor of law at Harvard University), June 30, 1954; children: Peter Lebold, Seth Aloe, Ethan Randolph. *Education:* Attended Girls Latin School, Chicago, 1938-48, and Shipley School, 1948-50; Smith College, B.A., 1954. *Politics:* Democrat. *Home:* 21 Bryant St., Cambridge, Mass. 02138. *Office:* Museum School, Museum of Fine Arts, Boston, Mass. 02115.

CAREER: Corcoran Gallery of Art, Washington, D.C., registrar, 1955-56; professional and volunteer worker for Democratic Party in Virginia, California, and District of Columbia, 1956-60; volunteer teacher of English at youth clubs in Hong Kong, 1963-64; Museum of Fine Arts, Boston, Mass., lecturer and member of department of public education staff, 1964—, lecturer in art history at college level, School of the Museum, 1968—. Tufts University, lecturer in art history, 1969.

WRITINGS: *Buddha* (juvenile), Seymour Lawrence, 1969; (with Bela Kalman) *Angkor, Monuments of the God-Kings,* Abrams, 1972. Television scripts include: "Images" (series); "An American Romance: 19th Century Landscape," 1965; "The Journey of the Buddha," 1965; "A Survey of American Art" (six shows); and three segments for "Highlights of Japanese Art." Contributor of articles and reviews to museum and other publications.

WORK IN PROGRESS: The Avatars of Vishnu.

SIDELIGHTS: "[When] my husband was a law professor at the University of California, . . . he was offered an opportunity to study Chinese Law for four years. I realized I would be living with China for a long time, and it was clear that I too should immerse myself in Chinese studies.

"I have combined the study of Buddhism with the study of tennis and I have also been taught how to wrap chiao-tze and to fry rice by a succession of Chinese language tutors. All this was consummated in Hong Kong during 1963-64, where we went to live for a year when our boys were two, four, and six. It was a good year and we learned every day, often painfully, about values other than our own.

"My interest in writing and teaching about Asian themes is to help Westerners understand those ideas so foreign to them."

COHEN, Peter Zachary 1931-

PERSONAL: Born October 27, 1931; married, wife's name Suzanne; children: Jay, Todd. *Education:* University of Wyoming, B.S., 1953, M.A., 1961. *Home:* Alta Vista, Kan. 66834. *Office:* Department of English, Kansas State University of Agriculture and Applied Science, Manhattan, Kan.

CAREER: Kansas State University of Agriculture and Applied Science, Manhattan, instructor in English, 1961—. Member of Wabaunsee County (Kan.) Planning Commission, 1969—. *Military service:* U.S. Army, 1954-56. *Member:* American Association of University Professors, Authors Guild, and several wildlife organizations.

WRITINGS—All juveniles: *The Muskie Hook,* Atheneum, 1969; *The Bull in the Forest* (Junior Literary Guild selection), Atheneum, 1969; *Morena* (Junior Literary Guild selection), Atheneum, 1970; *The Authorized Autumn Charts of the Upper Red Canoe River Country,* Atheneum, 1972; *Foal Creek,* Atheneum, in press. Author of two movie scripts for Xerox Educational Films.

WORK IN PROGRESS: Children's books.

SIDELIGHTS: "I enjoy almost anything connected with the field-and-stream out-of-doors; live on a small farm raising sheep, horses and chickens under fence, coyotes, rabbits, owls, and the evening stars, too, I guess, by letting them run loose. I return from those contacts with a renewed sense of wonder at the world. And I write to try to discover more about the 'whys' and 'what ifs' of the attitudes and situations I feel and observe. The extra fun is to try to discover them in an interesting way."

FOR MORE INFORMATION SEE: Junior Literary Guild Catalog, fall, 1969, fall, 1970; *Horn Book,* August, 1969, October, 1969, December, 1970.

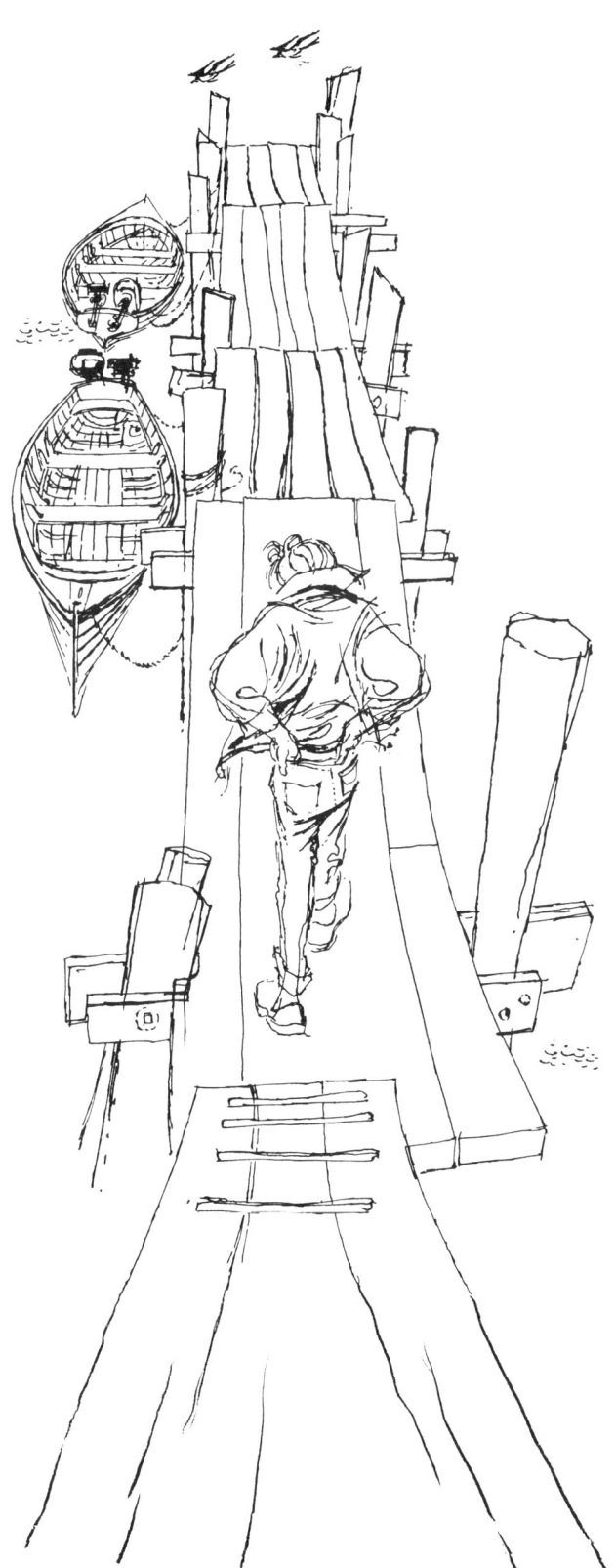

He saw the water blankly reflecting the darkening sky, without a riffle, and he sniffed and felt of the crisp dry air, and he knew he couldn't hope for the weather to turn stormy again. ■ (From *The Muskie Hook* by Peter Zachary Cohen. Illustrated by Tom O'Sullivan.)

PETER ZACHARY COHEN

SUSAN COOPER

COOPER, Susan 1935-

PERSONAL: Born May 23, 1935, in Burnham, Buckinghamshire, England; came to United States in 1963; daughter of John Richard and Ethel May (Field) Cooper; married Nicholas J. Grant (a college professor), August 3, 1963; children: Jonathan, Katharine; stepchildren: Anne, Bill, Peter. *Education:* Somerville College, University of Oxford, M.A., 1956. *Home:* 10 Leslie Rd., Winchester, Mass. 01890.

CAREER: Writer; *Sunday Times,* London, England, reporter and feature writer, 1956-63. *Member:* Society of Authors (United Kingdom), Author's Guild.

WRITINGS: (Contributor) Michael Sissons and Philip French, editors, *The Age of Austerity: 1945-51,* Hodder & Stoughton, 1963, Penguin, 1965; *Mandrake* (novel), J. Cape, 1964, Penguin, 1966; *Behind the Golden Curtain: A View of the U.S.A.,* Hodder & Stoughton, 1965, Scribner, 1966; *Over Sea, Under Stone* (Horn Book Honor List; first in five-part series, *The Dark Is Rising*), J. Cape, 1965, Harcourt, 1966; (editor and author of preface) J.B. Priestley, *Essays of Five Decades,* Little, Brown, 1968; *J.B. Priestley: Portrait of an Author,* Heinemann, 1970, Harper, 1971; *Dawn of Fear* (*Horn Book* Honor List, ALA Notable Book). Harcourt, 1971. Contributor to London *Sunday Times.* Regular weekly column, "Susan Cooper in America," in *Western Mail.*

WORK IN PROGRESS: "*Over Sea, Under Stone,* my book for children published in 1965, has turned out to be the first part of a five-part work *The Dark is Rising.* I am now completing the second volume, also called *The Dark is Rising,* which will be published by Atheneum as a Margaret McElderry Book and by Chatto, Boyd & Oliver in Britain. I shall spend the next three or four years on the remaining volumes in the sequence, which are provisionally entitled *Greenwitch, Fire on the Mountain* and *Silver on the Tree.* This whole project has a certain inevitability about it for me, since it is a kind of distillation of all the things that have taken deepest root in my imagination since I was a child. I draw on the major English and Celtic myths, and many others which have affected the complicated British Isles, for a story of the endless battle between good and evil which moves between various modern English settings and involves both modern children and one or two figures from myth. This has gathered momentum now and I shan't do any adult books until the sequence is finished."

SIDELIGHTS: "I write books simply because I always have, from the age of about eight. My material comes from everything I have ever done, read, or dreamed and my children's books are written, I suspect, for the child I used to be (and perhaps in some measure, like most children's writers, still am).

"I travel a good deal. This includes an annual visit to Britain and two to the British Virgin Islands, where we have a small remote house in which we spend much of the summer, and in which I do a great deal of work."

FOR MORE INFORMATION SEE: New York Times Book Review, October 27, 1968; *Horn Book,* October,

There was not much inside: some old newspapers, a big pair of leather gloves, two or three heavy woollen sweaters and, half hidden, a small black-covered book. A very dull treasure. ■ (From *Over Sea, Under Stone* by Susan Cooper. Illustrated by Margery Gill.)

1970; *Books,* November, 1970; *Chicago Tribune* Children's Book World, November 8, 1970.

COPELAND, Helen 1920-

PERSONAL: Born April 23, 1920, in Rochester, Minn.; daughter of James Carruthers (a physician) and Marion (Knowles) Masson; married H.J. Copeland, June 4, 1945 (divorced, 1958); children: Howard, Marion, Bill, James. *Education:* Wheaton College, Norton, Mass., B.A., 1942. *Home:* 1850 Maryland Ave., Charlotte, N.C. 28209. *Agent:* John Schaffner, 425 East 51st St., New York, N.Y. 10022.

WRITINGS—All children's books: *Meet Miki Takino,* Lothrop, 1963; *Duncan's World,* Crowell, 1967; *This Snake Is Good,* Crowell, 1968; *The Festival in the Park,* Crown, 1970.

WORK IN PROGRESS: An adult novel, *The Light in the Lower Barn.*

HELEN COPELAND

SIDELIGHTS: "The series of three juvenile books for Crowell began with a short story for adults called 'This Snake Is Good.' It was a story that *had* to be written to cool down somewhat my anguish at what had happened to my seven-year-old son, Bill, at summer camp.

"It was a good camp run by good people, and the woods were full of Bill's special enthusiasm—harmless snakes. He hoped to bring a lot home with him for the terrariums he had built in the back yard. But he hadn't reckoned with the world's most persistent prejudice, the fear and hatred of all snakes good and bad. Before his horrified eyes little garter snakes were caught by the boys, stamped into the ground, slapped against trees and cut in pieces with knives. Not a friend, a counsellor or the director understood his yearning, his feeling of outrage at this brutality, and being only seven and shy, he didn't have the words to argue or the courage to take on the bigger boys. There was no one to fight for him. He began to wet the bed; his counsellor thought he was homesick.

"When finally camp was over and he told me of his ordeal I was heartsick. 'What did you do, Bill?' I asked him, and he said he would just kind of turn around so nobody could see there were tears in his eyes. I couldn't get this tearful little boy out of my mind, and I asked myself, How old does a boy have to be to stand up and fight for what's right, for what he believes, for what belongs to him, so that people will listen and be convinced, change their attitudes in the light of new evidence? And suddenly I had a plot powered by great emotion and dramatic possibility.

"I hoped my short story would carry the impact of Katherine Anne Porter's story, 'The Downward Path to Wisdom.' But it was not destined to be published as a short story. My agent showed it to Elizabeth Riley at T.Y. Crowell, and on the telephone she asked if I could expand it and rewrite from the boy's point of view for a juvenile novel. Oh, yes! I said. And when it was finished Ms. Riley said, Now lay it aside and write us another book establishing the background for the main character, Duncan McKenna. I wrote *Duncan's World* then, depicting Duncan as a sturdy twelve-year-old with more than the usual knowledge of nature since his father was the director of the children's nature museum in his hometown of Charlotte, N.C. Since I was a zoology major in college I was bent in this direction myself; my four children, all animal lovers have educated me further. Several of the incidents depicted in *Duncan's World,* including the mysterious midnight vandalism at the Nature Museum came from real life.

"The third book of the series is set in the midst of Charlotte's annual 'Festival in the Park.' In this book an old Charlotte character, a hermit with a pack of Afghan dogs, is brought back to life. A new animal character is Big Neck, a vicious soft-shell turtle, and a new human character is Joey the clown, a television personality who plays a double role in helping Duncan and his friends through a hair-raising situation.

The snake was overhead, coiled around the dead limbs, close enough for Duncan to see in detail the black scales and the pale yellow bands like links in a chain. ■ (From *This Snake Is Good* by Helen Copeland. Illustrated by Charles W. Walker. Reprinted by permission of Thomas Y. Crowell Co.)

"I don't write for the sheer entertainment of children. I like adults to read these books so they will better understand the thinking of children which is rarely verbalized by the children. And I like for my young readers to identify with Duncan, to pick up his positive attitudes toward life. In these books I introduce many subjects which could be carried on by my readers into full-fledged hobbies or vocations. In addition to the animal lore, my plots have become involved with judo, rock collecting, first-aid, meteorites, TV filming, building with cement, parachutes, etc. A boy like Duncan, full of fun, capable of great enthusiasm for work and willing to fight to defend what he values is a good model for younger boys who haven't yet gained a strong sense of their own worth. I have written these stories of Duncan at a fast pace, knowing that elementary school readers lose interest quickly without continuing tension in the story.

"I hope, in addition to increasing an interest in reading, that this series, which began because of a miserable camp experience for a seven year old, will give pleasure and reassurance to a lot of children as they encounter the mixed offering of experiences that awaits them in the real world."

COWIE, Leonard W(allace)   1919-

PERSONAL: Born May 10, 1919, in Brighton, Sussex, England; son of Reginald George (a clerk in holy orders) and Ella Constance (Peerless) Cowie; married Evelyn Elizabeth Trafford (now a lecturer at King's College), August 9, 1949; children: Alan Leonard. *Education:* Pembroke College, Oxford, M.A., 1941; University of London, Ph.D., 1954. *Politics:* Conservative. *Home:* 38 Stratton Rd., Merton Park, London, S.W. 19, England.

CAREER: Clergyman, Church of England. Assistant curate, High Wycombe, Buckinghamshire, England, and history master at Royal Grammar School, High Wycombe, 1943-45; College of St. Mark and St. John, Chelsea, London, England, lecturer in history, 1945-68; Whitelands College, London, lecturer in history, 1969—.

WRITINGS: Henry Newman, An American In London 1708-43, S.P.C.K., 1956; *About the Bible,* Muller, 1958; *Seventeenth-Century Europe,* G. Bell, 1960; *The March of the Cross,* Weidenfeld & Nicolson, 1962; *Eighteenth-Century Europe,* G. Bell, 1963; *The Reformation,* Granada, 1965; *Hanoverian England,* G. Bell, 1966; *Martin Luther,* Granada, 1967; *Industrial Evolution,* Nelson, 1968; *Plague and Fire,* Wayland, 1969; *The Super-Powers,* Nelson, 1970; *The Pilgrim Fathers,* Wayland, 1971; *The Black Death and the Peasants' Revolt,* Wayland, 1972; *The Age of Drake,* Wayland, 1972; *The Trial and Execution of Charles I,* Wayland, 1972.

COWLEY, (Cassia) Joy   1936-

PERSONAL: Born August 7, 1936; daughter of Peter (a builder) and Cassia (Gedge) Summers; married Malcolm John Mason (accountant and author), c.1970; children (by previous marriage): Sharon, Edward, Judith, James. *Education:* Attended girls' high school in Palmerston North, Wellington, New Zealand. *Politics:* None. *Religion:* "Embrace all beliefs; adhere to none." *Home:* 29 Everest St., Khandallah, Wellington, New Zealand.

CAREER: Pharmacists' apprentice in New Zealand, 1953-56, and farmer's wife, 1956-67; full-time writer, 1967—. *Awards, honors:* New Zealand Buckland Literary Award, 1970, for *Man of Straw.*

WRITINGS: Nest in a Falling Tree (novel), Doubleday, 1967; *The Duck in the Gun* (Junior Literary Guild selection; with illustrations by Edward Sorel), Doubleday, 1968; *Man of Straw,* Doubleday, 1970; *Of Men and Angels,* Doubleday, 1972. Stories have appeared in New Zealand literary periodicals and school readers; writer of radio scripts for New Zealand Broadcasting Corp.

WORK IN PROGRESS: The Silent One, a children's novel set in the South Pacific; *The Mandrake Root,* an adult novel.

JOY COWLEY

It did seem silly to blow up freshly painted houses. Besides, he had become rather fond of the Prime Minister's daughter. ■ (From *The Duck in the Gun* by Joy Cowley. Illustrated by Edward Sorel.)

SIDELIGHTS: "Writing for young people requires a memory; more than that—before starting a book it's necessary to peel away years of adult experience like the layers of an onion, and expose a self that's of an age corresponding with character and reader. Only by being once more ten or fourteen or whatever age I'm writing for, can I evaluate the work. I can 'live' with my characters and understand them as equals.

"The actual writing is no different from that of adult novels. The prose must be as good as I can make it. I reread and rewrite until I've said exactly what I wanted to say and in a minimum number of words.

"I like to receive the opinions of my readers. Young people are generally honest. They like or dislike a book and will say so without ulterior motive.

"I strongly dislike the adult view that writing for children is a second-rate occupation."

Nest in a Falling Tree is being adapted by Roald Dahl for filming by Commonwealth Townsend.

HOBBIES AND OTHER INTERESTS: Painting, handicrafts, continental cuisine, photography, gardening, "in other words a domestic cabbage that is also creative."

FOR MORE INFORMATION SEE: New York Times Book Review, August 13, 1967; Best Sellers, August 15, 1967; Observer Review, October 22, 1967; New Statesman, October 27, 1967; Listener, January 4, 1968.

CROMIE, William J(oseph) 1930-

PERSONAL: Born March 12, 1930, in New York, N.Y.;

WILLIAM J. CROMIE

son of Harry Joseph and Margaret (Terrifoy) Cromie; married Alicia M. Connors, December 28, 1958; children: Steven William. *Education:* State University of New York Maritime College, student, 1951-53; Columbia University, B.S., 1956, graduate study in journalism, 1960-61. *Home:* 515 Inwood, Tomball, Tex. 77375. *Office:* Universal Science News, 314 West Commerce, Tomball, Tex. 77375.

CAREER: U.S. Merchant Marine, 1945-50; Anaconda Mining Co., Butte, Mont., geologist, 1956; Arctic Institute of North America, member of International Geophysical Year Expedition to Antarctica, 1956-58; Columbia University, Lamont Geophysical Observatory, research scientist on expeditions, 1958-60; Brown & Root, Inc., Houston, Tex., public information director for Project Mohole, 1962-63; with World Book Encyclopedia Science Service, Houston, Tex., 1963-70; with Universal Science News, Tomball, Tex., 1970—. Archaeological Research Foundation, geologist on 1964 Mount Arat Expedition. Columbia University Oral History Program, interviewer. Operation Green Turtle, biologist, 1966 and 1968. *Military service:* U.S. Naval Reserve, 1948-53. *Member:* American Association for the Advancement of Science, International Oceanographic Foundation, Council for the Advancement of Science Writing, Press Club of Houston. *Awards, honors: Steven and the Green Turtle* was selected as one of the Child Study Association's Books of the Year, 1970.

When Nicky was one year old, Steven needed two hands to pick the turtle up. ■ (From *Steven and the Green Turtle* by William J. Cromie. Illustrated by Tom Eaton.)

WRITINGS: Earthquakes, Science Service and Doubleday, 1961; *Volcanos,* Science Service and Doubleday, 1962; *Exploring the Secrets of the Sea,* Prentice-Hall, 1962; *Why the Mohole,* Little, Brown, 1964; *Living World of the Sea,* Prentice-Hall, 1966; *Steven and the Green Turtle,* Harper, 1970; *Secrets of the Sea,* Reader's Digest Books, 1971. Contributor to *Life's* "Nature Series," *Reader's Digest, Natural History, Science World, Science Digest, U.S. Naval Institute Proceedings.* Writer of by-line articles for International Science News Service.

SIDELIGHTS: Cromie's Geophysical Year activities included nine months at Little America, a four-month Ross Ice Shelf traverse over previously unexplored regions, and an expedition to the Indian Ocean and Red Sea as chief officer and oceanographer aboard the three-masted research schooner, "Vema", in 1958. He also served aboard Drifting Station Charlie, a research outpost on an ice floe in the Arctic Ocean in 1959. Mount Cromie in Antarctica is named in his honor.

CRONE, Ruth 1919-

PERSONAL: Born June 24, 1919, in Lincoln, Neb.; daughter of Burley R. and Willie Ethel (Jones) Crone. *Education:* Nebraska State College, A.B., 1942; George Washington University, M.A., 1945; New York University, PhD., 1960. *Politics:* Independent. *Home:* Apt. 53, 418 South 38th Ave., Omaha, Neb. 68131.

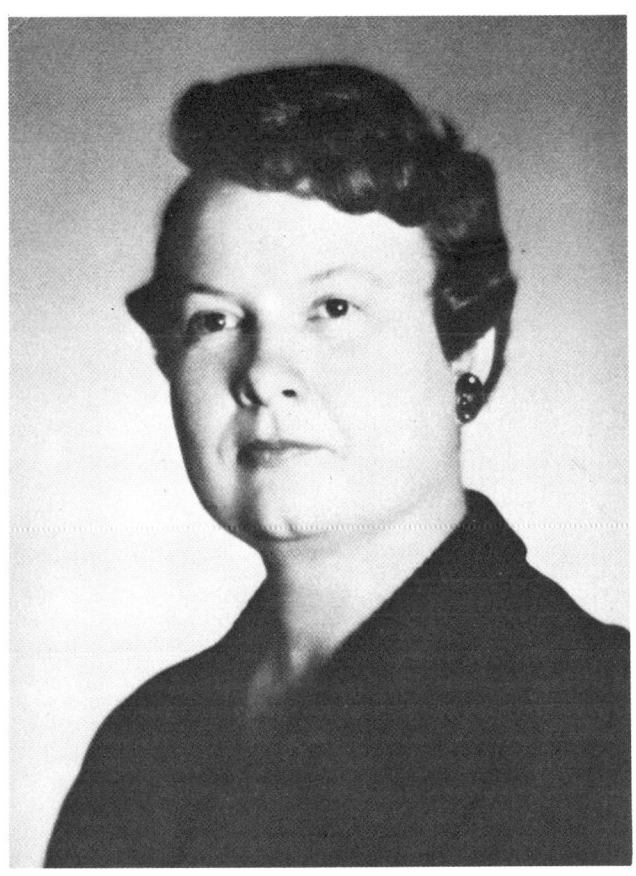

RUTH CRONE

CAREER: U.S. Department of Commerce, Washington, D.C., writer, 1940-44; Port of New York (N.Y.) Authority, reports editor, 1944-49; U.S. Department of State, information specialist, writer-editor, in Shanghai, China, and Seoul, Korea, 1949-52; staffer, *New York Times,* New York, N.Y., 1952-53, *Beatrice Daily Sun,* Beatrice, Neb., 1953-58; Gustavus Adolphus College, St. Peter, Minn., assistant professor of English and journalism, 1958-59; Nebraska State Teachers College, Peru, assistant professor of literature, 1959-60; General Beadle State College, Madison, S.D., assistant professor of English and journalism, 1960-63; Omaha (Neb.) public schools, teacher, 1962-63; Wisconsin State College, Superior, assistant professor of English and journalism, 1963-64; Mankato State College, Mankato, Minn., assistant professor of English and journalism, 1965-70; Bellevue College, Bellevue, Neb., associate professor, chairman of communicative arts, 1970—.

MEMBER: National Council of Teachers of English, American Association of University Women, The Poetry Group of Omaha, Omaha Press Club, Brownville Historical Society, Willa Cather Pioneer Memorial, Joslyn Art Museum, Mari Sandoz Heritage Foundation (charter member), Nebraska Writers Guild, Sigma Tau Delta, Kappa Delta Pi. *Awards, honors:* Adult fiction award, National Federation of Presswomen; twelve first-place awards, Nebraska Presswomen; Best Biography for Youth Award, National Federation of Press Women; Theta Sigma Phi (University of Nebraska), special commendation.

WRITINGS: (With Marion Marsh Brown) *The Silent Storm* (Junior Literary Guild selection), Abingdon, 1963; (with M.M. Brown) *Willa Cather: The Woman and Her Works,* Scribner, 1970. Contributor of articles, features, and reviews to magazines.

WORK IN PROGRESS: Third book in collaboration; articles, short stories.

FOR MORE INFORMATION SEE: Omaha World-Herald, July 8, 1963.

CROUCH, Marcus 1913-

PERSONAL: Born February 12, 1913, in Tottenham, Middlesex, England. *Education:* University of London, B.A., 1934. *Home:* 34 Glebe Lane, Maidstone, Kent, England. *Office:* Springfield, Maidstone, Kent, England.

CAREER: Kent County Library, Maidstone, England, deputy county librarian, 1948—. *Member:* Library Association (fellow), Society of Authors.

WRITINGS: (Editor) *Chosen for Children: An Account of the Books Which Have Been Awarded the Library Association's Carnegie Medal, 1936-1957,* Library Association, 1957, revised, 1966; *Beatrix Potter,* Bodley Head, 1960, 2nd edition, 1969; *Treasure Seekers and Borrowers: Children's Books in Britain, 1900-1960,* Library Association, 1962; *Britain in Trust: England and Wales,* Constable, 1963; (editor) *Books about Children's Literature,* Library Association, 1963, 2nd edition, 1966; *Rivers of England and Wales,* Constable, 1965; *Kent,* Hastings,

This extraordinary [half-timber] building, dating originally from early Tudor times, totters alarmingly above the moat into which it seems always about to fall. ■ (From *Britain in Trust* by Marcus Crouch. Photograph by the author.)

1966, 2nd edition, Batsford, 1967; *Fingerprints of History*, Longmans, 1968; *Heritage of Essex*, Hastings, 1969; The *Heritage of Sussex*, Macdonald & Co., 1969.

FOR MORE INFORMATION SEE: Brian Doyle, *The Who's Who of Children's Literature*, Schocken, 1968.

DAVIS, Burke 1913-

PERSONAL: Born July 24, 1913, in Durham, N.C.; son of Walter Burke and Harriet (Jackson) Davis; married Evangeline McLennan, 1940; children: Angela, Burke III. *Education:* Studied at Duke University, 1931-32, 1933-34, Guilford College, 1935-36; University of North Carolina, A.B. in Journalism, 1937. *Home:* Williamsburg, Va. *Office:* Public Relations Department, Colonial Williamsburg, Williamsburg, Va.

CAREER: Charlotte News, Charlotte, N.C., sports editor, editor, 1937-47; *Baltimore Evening Sun*, Baltimore, Md., reporter, 1947-51; *Greensboro Daily News*, Greensboro, N.C., reporter, 1951-60; Colonial Williamsburg, Va., writer, 1960—. *Member:* Nefarian Society. *Awards, honors:* Fletcher Pratt Award of Civil War Round Table of New York for *Jeb Stuart, The Last Cavalier*, 1958; Mayflower Cup of Society of Mayflower Descendants in North Carolina for *To Appomattox*, 1959.

WRITINGS: Whisper My Name, Rinehart, 1949; *The Ragged Ones*, Rinehart, 1951; *Yorktown*, Rinehart, 1952; *They Called Him Stonewall*, Rinehart, 1954; *Gray Fox: Robert E. Lee and the Civil War*, Rinehart, 1956; *Roberta E. Lee* (juvenile), Blair, 1956; *Jeb Stuart, The Last Cavalier*, Rinehart, 1957; (editor) *I Rode With Jeb Stuart*, Indiana University Press, 1957; *To Appomattox*, Rinehart, 1959; *Our Incredible Civil War*, Holt, 1960; *Marine! The Life of Lt. General Lewis B. (Chesty) Puller*, Little, Brown, 1962; *America's First Army*, Colonial Williamsburg, 1962; *The Cowpens-Guilford Courthouse Campaign*, Lippincott, 1962; *Appomattox* (juvenile), Harper, 1963; *The Summer Land*, Random House, 1965; (with Evangeline Davis) *Rebel Raider*, Lippincott, 1966; *The Billy Mitchell Affair*, Random House, 1967; *A Williamsburg Galaxy*, Colonial Williamsburg, 1968; (with Roy King) *The World of Currier and Ives*, Random House, 1968; *Get Yamamoto*, Random House, 1969; *Yorktown: Closing Struggle of the War of Independence*, Harper, 1969; *The Billy Mitchell Story*, (juvenile) Chilton, 1969; *The Campaign that Won America*, Dial, 1970; *Getting to Know Jamestown*, (juvenile) Coward, 1971; *Getting to Know Thomas Jefferson's Virginia* (juvenile), Coward, 1971; *Heroes of the American Revolution*, (juvenile) Random House, 1971; *Amelia Earhart* (juvenile), Putnam, 1972; *Biography of a Leaf* (juvenile), Putnam, 1972; *Sherman's March*, Holt, 1973.

WORK IN PROGRESS: A narrative of Washington and the Revolution, for Random House; a life of Andrew Jackson, for Dial.

SIDELIGHTS: "I live in a woodland near Williamsburg, Va., overlooking a marsh where herons, raccoons and muskrats make their homes. I raise an organic garden on a terraced hillside above Queens Creek, a stream once well known to George Washington. From spring through fall I take crabs from crab pots. I sleep on an outside sleeping porch the year round, where I can see woods, marsh and stream through a glass and screened enclosure.

"By day, I work in a small office in Williamsburg, accompanied by two German shepherds and warmed by a log-burning fireplace. After writing twenty or more books on historical subjects, I am turning to the writing of nature books for children. In my youth I trained as a botanist and forester and once wished to become a herpetologist—a specialist in the study of snakes. I wear moccasins instead of shoes and refuse to wear shirts with ties and collars."

BURKE DAVIS

MONICA DICKENS

DICKENS, Monica (Enid) 1915-

PERSONAL: Born May 10, 1915, in London, England; daughter of Henry Charles (a lawyer) and Fanny (Runge) Dickens; married Roy O. Stratton (author and retired U.S. Naval officer), December 7, 1951; children: Pamela, Prudence. *Education:* Attended St. Pauls School for Girls, London, England, and studied at Cordon Bleu, Paris, France. *Religion:* Roman Catholic. *Home:* Main St., North Falmouth, Mass.

CAREER: Expelled from dramatic school and bored with social life, the great-granddaughter of Charles Dickens tried her hand as cook and maid in private homes in London for two years (twenty different jobs), studied nursing, worked as mechanic in aircraft engine repair factory, and as reporter on provincial weekly—and each experience turned in time into a book. Life as the British wife of a U.S. Naval Officer in Washington, D.C., also resulted in a book, and others have followed from North Falmouth, Mass., where the author and her American-born husband live.

WRITINGS: One Pair of Hands, Harper, 1939; *The Moon Was Low,* Harper, 1940; *One Pair of Feet,* Harper, 1942; *The Fancy,* M. Joseph, 1943 (published in United States under title *Edward's Fancy,* Harper, 1944); *Thursday Afternoon,* M. Joseph, 1945; *The Happy Prisoner,* M. Joseph, 1946; *Joy and Josephine,* M. Joseph, 1948; *Flowers on the Grass,* McGraw, 1949; *My Turn to Make the Tea,* M. Joseph, 1951; *The Nightingales Are Singing,* Little, Brown, 1953; *The Winds of Heaven,* Coward, 1955; *The Angel in the Corner,* M. Joseph, 1956; *Man Overboard,* M. Joseph, 1958; *The Heart of London,* Coward, 1961; *Cobbler's Dream,* Coward, 1963; *Kate and Emma,* Coward, 1965; *The Room Upstairs,* Doubleday, 1966; *My Fair Lady,* Four Winds, 1967; *The Landlord's Daughter,* Doubleday, 1968; *The End of the Line,* Doubleday, 1970; *The Horse at World's End* (Junior Literary Guild selection), Doubleday, 1971; *Summer at World's*

End, Doubleday, 1972; *Cape Cod,* Viking, 1972; *World's End in Winter,* Doubleday, 1973. Contributor to *Life* and to London newspapers and magazines.

SIDELIGHTS: "After school, my mother wanted me to be a debutante. I was presented at Court, and went to one debutante ball. I was very fat and shy and nobody danced with me. I spent all evening reading in the ladies' room, and the next morning I decided to end this shameful career, even if it meant a job. I went to a domestic agency and said I was a cook. I assumed that cooking was something you could learn as you went along. I was right. In two years I had about twenty jobs: cook, parlormaid, charwoman, waitress, kitchenmaid, nursemaid, and housekeeper.

"I started to write because a publisher asked me to write a book about these experiences. I have been writing since 1938, a book about every two years, now more frequently, as I am doing children's books, which take just as much trouble to write, but are shorter.

"The material comes from my own experiences, or from research in whatever field I am interested in and want to write about. I prefer to have a strong sociological background to my fiction—cruelty to children, cruelty to animals, suicide, the plight of the elderly, race problems in London, etc. This sounds very weighty, but it isn't at all, as humor is the dominant thing in my writing, and I don't believe in propaganda, but in giving people the entertainment they seek when they read a novel. That, and learning something about a side of life they perhaps were not involved with before.

"I keep regular hours when writing a book, working about four hours a day, usually in the morning, composing in longhand and correcting on the typewriter. I have written six children's books, all of which will eventually be published in the U.S., and all about the relationship between people and animals."

Thirteen of Miss Dickens' books have been book club selections. *Cobbler's Dream* inspired the British television series, "Follyfoot," 1971; *The House at World's End* is being filmed by David Paradine Productions, for 1973.

HOBBIES AND OTHER INTERESTS: Riding, gardening, music, theater, ballet.

FOR MORE INFORMATION SEE: Saturday Review, July 2, 1966; *Detroit News,* February 19, 1967; *Horn Book,* February, 1971; *The Stage,* June 24, 1971; *Christian Science Monitor,* November 11, 1971.

DOBRIN, Arnold   1928

PERSONAL: Born June 6, 1928, in Omaha, Neb.; son of Ralph and Ethel (Abrahamson) Dobrin; married Norma Zane Chaplain (a sociologist), June 29, 1956; children: Adam, Brian. *Education:* Studied at Chouinard Art Institute, at Academie de la Grande Chaumiere, Paris, France, and at New York University. *Home:* 8 Cross Hwy., Westport, Conn. 06880. *Agent:* Marie Rodell, 141 East 55th St., New York, N.Y. 10022.

CAREER: Free-lance art director and designer, 1948-52; staff designer for Metro-Goldwyn-Mayer and then for 20th Century-Fox studios, 1952-56; free-lance art director and designer, 1956-62; began to write in 1962 and now devotes more time to writing than art. *Member:* Authors Guild.

WRITINGS—Youth books, most self-illustrated: *Little Monk and the Tiger,* Coward, 1965; *Taro and the Sea Turtles,* Coward, 1966; *Carmello's Cat: The Story of a Roman Christmas,* Coward, 1967; *Aaron Copeland: His Life and Times,* Crowell, 1967; *The Snow Fox,* Coward, 1968; *Italy: Modern Renaissance,* Thomas Nelson, 1968; *Marshes and Marsh Life,* Coward, 1969; *Igor Stravinsky: His Life and Times,* Crowell, 1970; *Gerbils,* Lothrop, 1970; *Ireland: The Edge of Europe,* Nelson, 1970; *Scat!,* Four Winds Press, 1970; *The New Life: The Mexican Americans Today,* Dodd, 1970; *To Katmandu,* Crowell, 1971; *Voices of Joy, Voices of Freedom,* Coward, 1972; *Josephina's 'Magination,* Four Winds Press, 1973; *Vincent Van Gogh,* Frederick Warne, 1973; *Jillions of Gerbils,* Lothrop, 1973. Contributor of travel articles to publications.

ARNOLD DOBRIN

There were three pirates, each one uglier than the other. ■ (From *Taro and the Sea Turtle* by Arnold Dobrin. Illustrated by the author.)

SIDELIGHTS: "I am not sure when I first began to think of myself as an artist. Perhaps it was some time during the third-grade when a memorable teacher began to hold my paintings before the class for them to admire. (I have always been grateful to her for this but I cannot help shuddering when I recall that her way of punishing an unruly class was to scrape her exceptionally long fingernails across the blackboard.) It was about this time that I became fascinated with the wonderful shapes and textures that brushes make on paper. As my skill developed, more praise came and I knew that some day I would become a professional artist.

"Soon after leaving art school I found myself earning a living as a designer and illustrator. Although I loved the work, my need to write gradually became more insistent. I had taken many classes in creative writing at college but I was not able to conceive of myself as a writer. It was not until I was thirty-six that I wrote my first children's story, *Little Monk and the Tiger*. The first publisher who read it accepted it and my career as a writer had begun.

"After doing several picture books the challenge of different, larger forms began to attract me. *Gerbils* came out of a long love affair between my family and several of these beguiling small creatures. Biographies of Aaron Copeland and Igor Stravinsky grew out of my admiration for these men and their music. Books on Italy and Ireland came out of travels in those countries and soon any trip abroad that did not produce a book I considered a failure. I now spend the greater part of my time writing and the rest illustrating.

"To write is to do many things. To write is to reflect on past experience, to give voice to my fears and hopes for the future. Writing is also an act of love—a celebration not only of life but death also, of the fullness and wonder of existence."

Dobrin lived in Japan in 1957 and Rome, 1962-64, and travels abroad annually. He was a fellow at the MacDowell Colony in Peterborough, N.H.

DODD, Ed(ward Benton) 1902-

PERSONAL: Born November 7, 1902, in LaFayette, Ga.; son of Jesse Mercer (a Baptist minister) and Effie (Cooke) Dodd; married Rebecca Bowles, 1930 (divorced, 1932); married Miriam Croft, February 26, 1938 (died, 1943); married Elsa Norris (an artist), July 25, 1958 (divorced, 1968). *Education:* Studied at Georgia Institute of Technology, 1921-22, and Art Students' League of New York, 1923-24; studied animal drawing and illustration under Dan Beard. *Politics:* Republican. *Religion:* Presbyterian. *Home:* 6955 Brandon Mill Rd. N.E., Atlanta, Ga. 30328. *Agent:* Toni Mendez, Inc., 140 East 56th St., New York, N.Y. 10022.

CAREER: Dan Beard Camp for Boys, instructor, later director, 1920-38; New York Military Academy, Cornwall, N.Y., instructor in outdoor activities, 1926-27; commercial artist, New York, N.Y., 1929-30; cartoonist doing "Back Home Again", for United Feature Syndicate, 1930-45, and "Mark Trail" for Hall Syndicate 1946—. National chairman, National Wildlife Week, 1952, 1953. *Member:* National Press Club (Washington, D.C.); Homassassa Atlanta Club (Homassassa, Fla.), Piedmont Driving Club (Atlanta), Campfire Club (New York). *Awards, honors:* Award from Delta Sigma Chi for best cartoon strip, 1948; special award for outdoor writing, Georgia Sportsman Federation, 1960; awards for service to conservation from National Forest Association, 1951, Men's Garden Clubs of America, 1964, National Wildlife Federation (for greatest contribution to conservation in the United States), 1967, and other organizations.

WRITINGS—Self-illustrated: *Mark Trail's Book of North American Mammals,* Hawthorn, 1955; *Chipper the Beaver* (juvenile), Putnam, 1968; *Flapfoot* (juvenile), Random House, 1968; *Mark Trail's Camping Tips,* Essandess, 1969; *Mark Trail's Fishing Tips,* Essandess, 1969; *Mark Trail's Hunting Tips,* Essandess, 1969; *Careers in Conservation,* Macmillan, in press; *Old Chips and Charlie,* Coca Cola Co., in press. Author of NBC documentary "Our Endangered Wildlife," and "Mark Trail's Man in Atlanta," for WAII-TV, Atlanta. Contributor to national magazines.

SIDELIGHTS: Dodd has traveled extensively throughout the United States, Canada, Alaska, and visited in Europe, Central America, and Cuba.

HOBBIES AND OTHER INTERESTS: Fishing, outdoor cooking, horse training, reading, and wing shooting.

A typical Sunday "Mark Trail" episode by Ed Dodd. Courtesy of Publishers-Hall Syndicate.

ED BENTON DODD

du BOIS, William (Sherman) Pene 1916-

PERSONAL: Born May 9, 1916, in Nutley, N.J.; son of Guy (an artist) and Florence (Sherman) Pene du Bois; married Willa Kim (a theatrical designer), March 26, 1955. *Education:* Attended Miss Barstow's School, New York, Lycee Hoche, Versailles, France, 1924-28, Lycee de Nice, Nice, France, 1928-29, Morristown School, N.J., 1930-34. *Politics:* Democrat. *Religion:* Protestant. *Agent:* Ann Watkins, Inc., 77 Park Ave., New York, N.Y. 10016.

CAREER: Author and illustrator of children's books. *Paris Review,* art editor and designer. *Military service:* U.S. Army, more than four years, correspondent for *Yank. Awards, honors: New York Herald Tribune* Spring Book Prize for *The Twenty-One Balloons,* 1946, and *Lion,* 1955; Newbery Medal, 1948, for *The Twenty-One Balloons; New York Times* "Best Illustrated Book" list, 1971, for *Bear Circus; Bear Circus,* was selected a Children's Book Showcase Title, 1972.

WRITINGS—All self-illustrated: *The Three Policemen* Viking, 1938, reissued, 1960; *The Flying Locomotive,* Viking, 1941; *The Great Geppy,* Viking, 1942; *The Twenty-One Balloons,* Viking, 1946; *Peter Graves,* Viking,

The island looked beautiful from the air. Its vegetation was so rich, warm, and soft-looking. ■ (From *The 21 Balloons* by William Pene du Bois. Illustrated by the author.)

1950; *Bear Party,* Viking, 1951; *Squirrel Hotel,* Viking, 1952; *The Giant,* Viking, 1954; *Lion,* Viking, 1956; *Otto at the Sea,* Viking, 1958; *Otto in Texas,* Viking, 1959; *Otto in Africa,* Viking, 1961; *Elizabeth the Cow Ghost,* Viking, 1964; *The Alligator Case,* Harper, 1965; *Lazy Tommy Pumpkinhead,* Harper, 1966; *The Horse in the Camel Suit,* Harper, 1967; *Pretty Pretty Peggy Moffitt,* Harper, 1968; *Porko Von Popbutton,* Harper, 1969; *Otto and the Magic Potatoes,* Viking; 1970; *Call Me Bandicoot,* Harper, 1970; *Bear Circus,* Viking, 1971; *William's Doll,* Harper, 1972.

Illustrator: Rumer Godden, *The Mousewife,* Viking, 1951; Claire H. Bishop, *Twenty and Ten,* Viking, 1952; Marguerite Clement, *In France,* Viking, 1956; George MacDonald, *Light Princess,* Crowell, 1962; Rebecca Caudill, *A Certain Small Shepherd,* Holt, 1965; Roald Dahl, *The Magic Finger,* Harper, 1966; Betty Yurdin, *The Tiger in the Teapot,* Holt, 1968; Edward Fenton, *Fierce John,* Holt, 1969; Richard Wilbur, *Digging for China,* Doubleday, 1970; *Three Little Pigs,* Viking, 1970; Isaac B. Singer, *Topsy-Turvy, Emperor of China,* Harper, 1971; Edward Lear, *The Owl and the Pussy Cat,* Doubleday; and others.

SIDELIGHTS: "I trace my artistic heritage as far back as 1738 when my ancestors came to New Orleans. Since then the Pene du Bois name has been identified with paintings, music, books, cathedrals, and cinema and theater design throughout America and abroad.

"I was born in Nutley, New Jersey, the son of a painter and art critic. I attended school at the Lycee Hoche (Versailles) in France—and made many weekly excursions to the French circus—from the time I was eight until I was fourteen years old."

In his Newbery Award acceptance speech, Pene du Bois recalled that "as a child I hardly read at all, although I loved to look at books. I was the sort of fellow who just looks at the pictures. I try to keep such impatient children in mind in making my books. The only extensive reading I did, other than required reading, was in copies of two ferocious and forbidden magazines while in school in France. These could be concealed neatly in our large geography books and were called *Les Aventures de Nick Carter* (pronounced Neeck Cartaire), and *Les Aventures de Buffalo Bill.* I also did some scattered reading of a peculiar type in other adventure books. If, for instance, I read a caption under a thrilling frontispiece which said, 'Bill Ballantine slipped from his trapeze and fell into the lion cage below (see page 178),' I would quickly turn to page 178 to find out whether or not he was chewed up.

"This lack of interest in reading was probably due to the fact that I was never too familiar with the language of the country in which I was living. I was just barely starting to read English when . . . I left for France; and just fairly proficient in reading French when . . . I returned to America.

"The biggest influence in drawing I've had other than my father's came from a teacher I had at the age of ten, Professor Diremaire. Monsieur Diremaire didn't teach drawing nor was he an artist, but his influence on his class along parallel lines was tremendous.

"Every morning after entering Monsieur Diremaire's class, we would spend ten minutes of complete agony. He would stack our homework papers in a neat pile in the middle of his desk, and then proceed to look at them one by one, not as correct or incorrect papers, but as neat or sloppy examples of orderly procedure. He would hold them up as if he were studying etchings, look at the name of the student, and express his critical opinion of the work. He would either say, 'Ah, c'est beau!' and stack it in a pile to his right, or make a sad dejected grimace, and tear it in four equal parts which he stacked to his left. I remember doing a magnificent page of arithmetic, my favorite subject, in which I neglected to rule one short line under a subtraction of two one-digit figures. This little line must have jumped off the page and struck Monsieur Diremaire between the eyes. 'What have we here,' he said, 'an artist? Monsieur du Bois is drawing free hand.' He neatly tore my work in four pieces. We were able to do these over during recess. . . . But those first ten minutes of inspection never failed to scare us out of our wits.

WILLIAM PENE du BOIS

"To make ten-year-old boys consider their homework as works of art is an extraordinary feat, and I must say that the sense of order and careful planning gained therefrom has been to me of infinite use and influence."

FOR MORE INFORMATION SEE: Young Wings, June, 1947, February, 1951; *Horn Book,* July-August, 1948, December, 1971; *Junior Book of Authors,* edited by Kunitz and Haycraft, H.W. Wilson, 2nd edition, 1951; *Newbery Medal Books: 1922-1955,* edited by Miller and Field, Horn Book, 1955; *Bulletin* of the New York Public Library, April, 1957; *Young Readers' Review,* November, 1966; Diana Klemin, *The Art of Art for Children's Books,* Clarkson Potter, 1966; *Book World,* September 10, 1967; Brian Doyle, *The Who's Who of Children's Literature,* Schocken, 1968; *Library Journal,* May 15, 1969; *New York Times Book Review,* November 7, 1971; *Christian Science Monitor,* November 11, 1971.

DUPUY, T(revor) N(evitt) 1916-

PERSONAL: Born May 3, 1916, in New York, N.Y.; son of R. Ernest (Army officer, writer) and Laura (Nevitt) Dupuy; married Christine Geissbuhler, 1957; children: Trevor, Ernest, George, Laura, Charles, Mirande, Arnold, Fielding. *Education:* St. Peter's College, student, 1933-34; U.S. Military Academy, B.S., 1938; Harvard University, graduate study in public administration, 1953-55. *Home:* 8016 North Park St., Dunn Loring, Va. 22027. *Office address:* P.O. Box 157, Dunn Loring, Va. 22027.

CAREER: U.S. Army, Artillery, from second lieutenant to colonel, 1938-58; during World War II commanded an American artillery battalion, a Chinese artillery group, and the artillery of the British 36th Division in Burma, later serving in Washington, in Operations Division, War Department General Staff; after war attended British Joint Services Staff College, 1948-49, commanded 5th Field Artillery Battalion in Germany, served as operations and planning officer on SHAPE staff in Paris, as professor of military science and tactics at Harvard University, and as director of military history courses at The Ohio State University; retired from Army, 1958. Writing, teaching, research, 1958—; Historical Evaluation and Research Organization, Washington, D.C., president and executive director, 1962—. Rangoon University, Burma, professor of International Relations, 1959-60. Institute for Defense Analyses, International Studies Division, Washington, D.C., member, 1960-62. College of the Potomac, trustee, 1968—.

MEMBER: American Military Institute (president, 1958-59), American Historical Association, Institute for Strategic Studies (London), United States Naval Institute, Army-Navy Club and Cosmos Club (both Washington). *Awards, honors*—Military: Legion of Merit, Bronze Star Medal, Air Medal, British Distinguished Service Order, Chinese Cloud and Banner. Civilian: co-winner of Fletcher Pratt Memorial Award Round Table of New York, for *Compact History of the Civil War* as best Civil War book of 1960.

WRITINGS: (With father, R. Ernest Dupuy) *To the Colors,* Row, Peterson & Co., 1942; *Faithful and True* (privately printed history of Fifth Field Artillery Bat-

talion), Schwabisch-Hall, 1949; (with R.E. Dupuy) *Military Heritage of America*, McGraw, 1956; *Campaigns of the French Revolution and of Napoleon*, Harvard University, Department of Military Science and Tactics, 1956; (with R.E. Dupuy) *Brave Men and Great Captains*, Harper, 1959; (with R.E. Dupuy) *Compact History of the Civil War*, Hawthorn, 1960; *First Book of Civil War Land Battles* (for teen-agers), Watts, 1961; *First Book of Civil War Naval Actions* (for teen-agers), Watts, 1961; *Military History of World War II*, nineteen volumes, Watts, 1962-65; (with R.E. Dupuy) *Compact History of the Revolutionary War*, Hawthorn, 1963; (editor and co-author) *Holidays: Days of Significance for All Americans*, Watts, 1965; *Military History of World War I* (twelve volumes), Watts, 1967; *The Battle of Austerlitz*, Macmillan, 1968; *Modern Libraries for Modern Colleges: Research Strategies for Design and Development*, Communications Service Corp., 1968; *Ferment in College Libraries*, Communications Service Corp., 1968; *The Military History of the Chinese Civil War*, Watts, 1969; (with Richard Ernest Dupuy) *Encyclopedia of Military History*, Harper, 1970; (with Gay M. Hammerstern), *The Military History of Revolutionary War Land Battles*, Watts, 1970; (with Grace P. Hayes) *The Military History of Revolutionary War Naval Battles*, Watts, 1970; (editor and co-author) *Almanac of World Military Power*, T.N. Dupuy Associates, 1970.

"Military Lives" Series: *Alexander the Great of Macedon, Hannibal: Father of Strategy, Julius Caesar: Imperator, Genghis: Khan of Khans, Gustavus Adolphus: Father of Modern War, Frederick the Great of Prussia, George Washington: American Soldier, Napoleon: Emperor of the French, Abraham Lincoln: Commander-in-Chief, Hindenburg and Ludendorff of Imperial Germany, Adolph Hitler: Fuhrer of Germany, Winston Churchill of Britain* (all published by Watts, 1969-70).

Contributor to *Encyclopaedia Britannica, Grolier Encyclopedia,* to periodicals and newspapers, including *US News and World Report, American Heritage, Boston Globe, New York Herald Tribune* (Paris edition), and to military publications.

DWIGGINS, Don 1913-

PERSONAL: Born November 15, 1913, in Plainfield, N.J.; son of Clare Victor (a cartoonist) and Betsey (Lindsay) Dwiggins; married; children: Don Lindsay, Toni Kay. *Education:* Los Angeles Junior College, student, 1932-33. *Home:* 3816 Paseo Hidalgo, Malibu, Calif. 90265. *Agent:* Lenninger Literary Agency, 437 Fifth Ave., New York, N.Y. 10016.

CAREER: Commercial pilot; aviation editor of *Los Angeles Daily News,* Los Angeles, Calif., 1947-54, and *Los Angeles Mirror News,* 1956-62 (both newspapers defunct); space technology consultant, Lockheed Aircraft Co., Burbank, Calif., 1964; news writer, KTTV, Los Angeles, Calif., 1964; editor of "Mickey Mouse Newsreel," Disney Studios, Burbank, Calif., 1965; freelance writer for magazines and television. *Military service:* U.S. Army Air Forces, 1942-43; became master sergeant.

(From *The Military History of Civil War Land Battles* by Trevor Nevitt Dupuy. Illustrated by Leonard Everett Fisher.)

DON DWIGGINS

Member: Aviation Aerospace Writers Association (vice-president), Screen Actors Guild, Writers Guild of America (West), Motion Picture Pilots Association, Sheriff's Aero Squadron (Los Angeles). *Awards, honors:* Award for best California news story of 1960 for coverage of Chessman execution; Aviation Aerospace Writers Association award for best aviation feature in metropolitan newspaper, 1961, and best aviation book, *Hollywood Pilot,* 1968; *Eagle Has Landed* was selected as one of the Child Study Association's Books of the Year, 1970.

WRITINGS: "Frankie" (Frank Sinatra), Paperback Library, 1961; *The S. O. Bees,* New American Library, 1963; *They Flew the Bendix Race,* Lippincott, 1965; *The Air Devils,* Lippincott, 1966; *Hollywood Pilot,* Doubleday, 1967; *Space and the Weather,* Golden Gate, 1968; *The Barnstormers,* Grosset, 1968; *Famous Flyers and the Ships They Flew,* Grosset, 1969; *Bailout,* Crowell Collier, 1969; *Voices in the Sky,* Golden Gate, 1969; *On Silent Wings,* Grosset, 1970; *Eagle Has Landed,* Golden Gate, 1970; *Spaceship Earth,* Golden, 1970; *Into the Unknown,* Golden Gate, 1971; *Robots in the Sky,* Golden Gate, 1972. Writer of more than five hundred articles, appearing in *Saturday Evening Post, Reader's Digest, Collier's, True, Argosy, This Week, Parade,* and other magazines; former writer for television; currently contributing editor, *Plane and Pilot Magazine.*

WORK IN PROGRESS: *Pilots' Bible,* for Doubleday.

SIDELIGHTS: "I think I inherited my love of writing for children from my father, the cartoonist Dwig, whose 'School Days' panels ran in some 200 papers during the first quarter of the Twentieth Century. Now, writing about my love for aviation and space technology, I use my son and his two boys as a 'captive audience' in trying out ideas. We live in a marvelously exciting age, and I find it a challenge to translate the complexities of the new frontiers of space into human terms that will appeal to younger readers."

FOR MORE INFORMATION SEE: *Horn Book,* December, 1969.

EDMUND, Sean
See PRINGLE, Laurence

EDWARDS, Dorothy

PERSONAL: Born in Teddington, Middlesex, England; daughter of Charles and Alice (Saunders) Brown; married Francis P. Edwards (a lecturer on communications, medieval research, and drama); children: Jane Brunt, Francis C.F. *Education:* Attended grammar school in England. *Politics:* Liberal. *Religion:* Christian. *Home:* 17 Effingham Rd. Reigate RH 2 7JN, Surrey, England.

CAREER: Worked as secretary until her marriage. *Member:* P.E.N. International, Society of Authors.

WRITINGS—All for children: *My Naughty Little Sister,* Methuen, 1952, Puffin Picture Books, 1959; *More Naughty Little Sister Stories,* Methuen, 1957; *My Naughty Little Sister's Friends,* Methuen, 1962, Puffin Picture Books, 1968; *When My Naughty Little Sister was Good,* Methuen, 1968, Puffin Picture Books, 1968; *Tales of Joe and Timothy,* Methuen, 1969; *All About My Naughty Little Sister* (omnibus volume), Methuen, 1969; *Listen, Listen,* B.B.C., 1970; *Peter Nick-Nock and the Cuckoo Clock,* Transworld 1971; *Roger's Trains,* Transworld, 1971; *Joe and Timothy Together,* Methuen, 1971; *Listen and Play Rhymes: One,* Methuen, 1972; *Listen and Play Rhymes: Two,* Methuen, 1972; *Look, Look a Cookery Book,* Methuen, 1972; *Look, Look, My Garden Book,* Methuen, 1972; *Sam's Woolly Hat,* Transworld, 1972; *James' Cooking Day,* Transworld, 1973. Writer and producer of scripts for British Broadcasting Corp. series, "Listen with Mother." Also writer of short stories, articles, and verse.

WORK IN PROGRESS: Another collection of "Naughty Little Sister" stories; more 'baby' and 'verse' books; writing and producing material for casettes for younger children; editing collection of tales from B.B.C.'s "Listen with Mother" repertoire.

SIDELIGHTS: "My interests are wide. In my time I ran an antique shop and also wrote for and ran a drama school for the Surrey Community Players. I am very absorbed by my husband's researches in mediaeval drama, art and culture and interested too in music and films. In addition I have written scripts and participated in the production of radio scripts for small children.

"When I was small I lived in Teddington on the River Thames and the places in my stories are all there, including the place where my little sister fell in the river. I write my stories for under-fives mainly for reading aloud or telling and they were first heard on 'Listen with Mother' where they proved very successful and have been ever since.

"I am a grandmother, very happy in the company of small children, and very enthusiastic for the work done by the Federation of Childrens' Books Group, who are doing so much to see that the child gets to the book."

EICHNER, James A. 1927-

PERSONAL: Born November 30, 1927, in Rochester, N.Y.; son of Perry C. (a salesman) and Katharine (Adams) Euchner; married Dorothy Wade, January 6, 1951; children: Katharine, Richard, Patricia. *Education:* Cornell University, B.A., 1949; Columbia University, law study, 1949-50; University of Richmond, LL.B., 1956. *Religion:* Episcopalian. *Home:* 702 Seneca Rd., Richmond, Va. 23226.

CAREER: Richmond (Va.) *Times-Dispatch,* reporter, 1950-56; admitted to Virginia bar, 1956; assistant city attorney, Richmond, Va., 1956-65; Federal Reserve Bank of Richmond, assistant counsel, 1965-66; assistant attorney general of Virginia, 1966; Allen, Allen & Allen Professional Association, vice-president, 1966—. University of Richmond, Richmond, Va., instructor in business law at University College, 1963-66. *Military service:* U.S. Navy, 1945-46. U.S. Naval Reserve, 1946-71; retired as lieutenant commander. *Member:* American Bar Associa-

Every year control of automobile traffic becomes a more serious problem for major American cities. ■ (From *The First Book of Local Government* by James A. Eichner. Illustrated by Bruce Bacon.)

tion, American Trial Lawyers' Association, Virginia Bar Association, Virginia Trial Lawyers' Association, Richmond Bar Association.

WRITINGS: Law, Watts, 1963; *First Book of Local Government,* Watts, 1964; *Thomas Jefferson: The Complete Man,* Watts, 1966; *The Cabinet of the President of the United States,* Watts, 1969; *Courts of Law,* Watts, 1969. Author of various law review articles.

ELLISON, Virginia Howell 1910- (Virginia Tier Howell, Mary A. Mapes, Virginia T.H. Mussey, V.H. Soskin, Leong Gor Yung)

PERSONAL: Born February 4, 1910, in New York, N.Y.; daughter of William David (a builder and farmer) and Mary Augusta (Mapes) Howell; married William H. Soskin, April 9, 1941 (deceased); married James W. Ellison (an editor), April 11, 1955 (divorced); children: (first marriage) David Howell Soskin, Nicholas Howell Ellison. *Education:* Vassar College, B.A., 1932. *Politics:* Independent. *Religion:* Congregationalist. *Home and office:* Mather Rd., Stamford, Conn. 06903.

CAREER: Howell, Soskin Publishers, Inc., New York, N.Y., editor and part owner, 1940-48; editor with Crown Publishers, Inc. and Lothrop, Lee & Shephard Co., New York, N.Y., 1948-55; National Council of Churches, New York, N.Y., director of publications and promotion, Women's Division, 1961-64.

WRITINGS: (Under name Virginia T.H. Mussey) *The Exploits of George Washington* (postage stamp story and collectors album), Harper, 1933; (with Y.K. Chu under pseudonym Leong Gor Yun) *Chinatown Inside Out,* Barrows Mussey, 1936; (under name Virginia Howell) *Falla, a President's Dog,* Howell, Soskin, 1941; (under pseudonym Mary A. Mapes) *Fun with Your Child,* Howell, Soskin, 1943; (under pseudonym Mary A. Mapes) *Surprise!* (juvenile), Howell, Soskin, 1944; (under name

Cucumber or Mastershalum-Leaf Sandwiches

4 thin slices of peeled cucumber for each sandwich
or
4 small nasturtium leaves, if you live in the country and grow nasturtiums

Salt and pepper
Cream cheese or mayonnaise

Spread the sandwich bread with cream cheese or mayonnaise.
Arrange thin slices of cucumber or the nasturtium leaves on the mayonnaise on half the bread slices. Add salt and pepper to taste on the cucumber slices.
Put them together to make a sandwich.

"I thought they were called nasturtiums," said Piglet timidly, as he went on jumping.
"No," said Pooh. "Not these. These are called mastershalums."

The House at Pooh Corner

PROVISIONS FOR PICNICS AND EXPOTITIONS

(From *The Pooh Cook Book* by Virginia H. Ellison. Illustrated by Ernest H. Shepard.)

Virginia Howell) *Training Pants* (juvenile), Howell, Soskin, 1946; (under name Virginia Howell) *Who Likes the Dark?* (juvenile), Howell, Soskin, 1945; *The Pooh Cook Book* (juvenile), Dutton, 1969; *The Pooh Party Book* (juvenile), Dutton, 1971. Ghost-writer of other books.

WORK IN PROGRESS: Research on space, herbs, honey, and scented geraniums, with books expected to result on all those subjects.

HOBBIES AND OTHER INTERESTS: Music (especially jazz), beekeeping, inventing (four inventions in progress).

ENGDAHL, Sylvia Louise 1933-

PERSONAL: Born November 24, 1933, in Los Angeles, Calif.; daughter of Amandus J. and Mildred Allen (a writer for young people under her maiden name of Butler) Engdahl. *Education:* Attended Pomona College, 1950, Reed College, 1951, and University of Oregon, 1951-52; University of California, Santa Barbara, A.B., 1955; University of Oregon Extension, graduate study, 1956-57. *Religion:* Episcopalian. *Residence:* Portland, Ore.

CAREER: Teacher in elementary school near Portland, Ore., 1955-56; SAGE Air Defense System, programmer, then computer systems specialist, 1957-67, working in Lexington, Mass., Madison, Wis., Tacoma, Wash., and Santa Monica, Calif.; full-time writer, 1967—. *Awards, honors:* Newbery Honor Book Award, 1971, for *Enchantress from the Stars.*

WRITINGS—Novels for young people: *Enchantress from the Stars* (Junior Literary Guild selection, ALA Notable Book, *Horn Book* Honor List), Atheneum, 1970; *Journey between Worlds,* Atheneum, 1970; *The Far Side of Evil,* Atheneum, 1971; *This Star Shall Abide,* Atheneum, 1972; *Beyond the Tomorrow Mountains,* Atheneum, 1973. Contributor to *Horn Book* Magazine and *School Media Quarterly.*

WORK IN PROGRESS: A nonfiction book for young people presenting the views of both past philosophers and modern scientists on worlds of other solar systems.

SIDELIGHTS: "Since the age of twelve I have been fascinated by the concept of space travel. However, although I was always interested in writing, I never planned to become a professional writer; instead, I wanted to be a teacher. The basic ideas for the books I've written so far came to me in 1956, when I was doing graduate work in college, and I actually wrote short portions of the stories then. But at that time, before the first artificial satellites had been launched, space was not a topic of widespread interest as it is today; I had no thought of being able to publish such stories.

"The next year I left the field of education to enter the then-new profession of computer programming. I enjoyed the work immensely, but it left me neither the time nor the energy to write anything other than the technical papers it required, for I'm the kind of person who can concentrate on only one thing at a time. So when, after ten years, I left my position as a computer systems specialist to settle permanently in Portland, I decided to devote full time to writing. I feel very strongly that space exploration is vitally important to mankind's future, and that speculating about the future as related to the past— and about worlds elsewhere in the universe—helps to put the problems of our own time into perspective.

"My books aren't really aimed toward science fiction fans;

In spite of myself the thrill was taking hold of me: the music, the ceremonial torches— those things do something to you whether you've been sworn for five minutes or fifty years. ■ (From *The Far Side of Evil* by Sylvia Louise Engdahl. Illustrated by Richard Cuffari.)

SYLVIA LOUISE ENGDAHL

though I think science fiction fans will enjoy them, I hope other people will, too: people—girls as well as boys—who don't ordinarily read science fiction, and who perhaps aren't especially interested in science. They're directed primarily to older teenagers, but also appeal both to children who are advanced readers and to many adults. Their main emphasis is on what space exploration and the settlement of new worlds will mean to people of the future; and they deal less with technological progress than with human evolution and with the spiritual values I consider important. I believe that today's teenagers are seriously concerned about the question of man's place in the universe, and since I feel that a positive outlook is more valid than the gloomy one so prevalent in our society, I think there is great need for fiction that expresses hope."

HOBBIES AND OTHER INTERESTS: Collecting medals and postage stamps commemorating the Apollo flights and other space exploration achievements.

FOR MORE INFORMATION SEE: Horn Book, April, 1970, October, 1970, April, 1971, October, 1971, June, 1972; *New York Times Book Review,* May 3, 1970.

ERVIN, Janet Halliday 1923-

PERSONAL: Born May 29, 1923, in Muncie, Ind.; daughter of Everett Clayton and Lois (Kidnocker) Halliday; married Howard G. Ervin (a sales manager), July 3, 1946; children: Howard III, Dennis, David. *Education:* University of Chicago, Ph.B., 1946. *Religion:* Presbyterian. *Home:* 2450 North 97th St., Wauwatosa, Wis. 53226. *Agent:* Scott Meredith Literary Agency, Inc., 580 Fifth Ave., New York, N.Y. 10036.

CAREER: Muncie Evening Press, Muncie, Ind., reporter, 1941-44; free-lance writer. *Member:* Mensa, Council for Wisconsin Writers, Theta Sigma Phi, University of Chicago Alumni, Milwaukee Fictioneers. *Awards, honors: Vogue* Prix de Paris, 1946; *Mademoiselle* guest editor-in-chief, 1945; Friends of American Writers Juvenile Book Award, 1972.

WRITINGS: The White House Cook Book, Follett, 1964; *The Last Trip of the Juno* (juvenile), Follett, 1970; *More Than Half Way There* (juvenile), Follett, 1970.

Author of column, "Keeping Up with Janet," for the *Toledo Blade;* contributor of teen-age fiction and articles to women's magazines.

SIDELIGHTS: "At age nine I decided that I wanted to be a newspaper reporter. The years seemed to pass slowly until I finally reached that goal at age eighteen. I enjoyed the job as much as I had anticipated. After college and marriage and three sons, I wrote books and articles for adults. But for years I had been reading children's stories

JANET HALLIDAY ERVIN

JANET HALLIDAY ERVIN

(From *More Than Halfway There* by Janet Halliday Ervin. Book jacket by Ted Lewin.)

for my own pleasure. (When it comes to favorite books, I guess I am still about nine years old.) I decided to write for children instead of adults.

"Like most newspaper reporters, my favorite stories are true ones—interesting happenings from history or the present time. I like to 'dress them up' a bit and make them part-truth, part-imagination. *The Last Trip of the Juno* and *More Than Half Way There* are both more than half way true."

HOBBIES AND OTHER INTERESTS: Art, antiques, American history, conservation, the Head Start program.

ESTES, Eleanor   1906-

PERSONAL: Born May 9, 1906, in West Haven, Conn.; daughter of Louis and Caroline (Gewecke) Rosenfeld; married Rice Estes, December 8, 1932; children: Helena. *Education:* Pratt Institute Library School, 1931-32. *Politics:* Democrat. *Religion:* Episcopalian. *Residence:* New Haven, Conn.

CAREER: Free Public Library, New Haven, Conn.,

Here she loved to swing and dream. And here in the summertime—as it was now—she could watch the bees swarming in and out of their nests in the hard ground beneath her where the ivy did not grow. ■ (From *The Witch Family* by Eleanor Estes. Illustrated by Edward Ardizzone.)

children's librarian, 1924-31; New York Public Library, children's librarian, 1932-40; now full-time writer. *Member:* P.E.N., Author's Guild. *Awards, honors:* Herald-Tribune Spring Book Festival Award, 1951, Newbery Medal for distinguished contribution to children's literature, 1952, both for *Ginger Pye*.

WRITINGS: The Moffats, 1941, *The Middle Moffat,* 1942, *Rufus M.,* 1943, *The Sun and The Wind and Mr. Todd,* 1943, *The Hundred Dresses,* 1944, *The Echoing Green,* Macmillan, 1947, *The Sleeping Giant,* 1948, *Ginger Pye,* 1951, *A Little Oven,* 1955, *Pinky Pye,* 1958, *The Witch Family,* 1960, *The Alley,* 1964, *Miranda the Great,* 1967, *The Lollipop Princess: A Play for Paper Dolls in One Act,* 1967, The Tunnel of Hugsy Goode, 1972 (all published by Harcourt, unless otherwise noted). Has also contributed to magazines.

SIDELIGHTS: Books have been translated into many foreign languages.

FOR MORE INFORMATION SEE: Book Week, April 16, 1967; *Commonweal,* May 26, 1967; *Young Reader's Review,* June, 1967; *Book World,* February 25, 1968.

ELEANOR ESTES

EWEN, David   1907-

PERSONAL: Born November 26, 1907, in Lemburg, Austria; son of Isaac (an author) and Helen (Kramer) Ewen; married Hannah Weinstein (a teacher), September 10, 1936; children: Robert. *Education:* College of the

City of New York, student, two years; private instruction in piano, harmony, theory; Columbia University, courses in musicology. *Home:* 2301 Collins Ave., Apt. 1010-A, Miami Beach, Fla. 33139.

CAREER: Writer on music and musicians. *Cue,* New York, N.Y., music editor, 1937-38; *Stage,* New York, N.Y., record editor, 1938-39; *Musical Facts,* New York, N.Y., editor, 1940-41; Allen, Towne & Heath Publishing Co., New York, N.Y., director, 1946-50; script writer and co-producer of fifty-two Voice of America programs on history of popular music, 1961-62; University of Miami, Coral Gables, Fla., adjunct professor of music, 1966—. *Military service:* U.S. Army, 1944-45, as writer of authorized history of paratroopers.

WRITINGS: Unfinished Symphony: A Story-Life of Franz Schubert, Modern Classics, 1931; *Hebrew Music,* Bloch, 1931; *Wine, Women and Waltz; A Romantic Biography of Johann Strauss, Son and Father,* Sears, 1933; (editor) *From Bach to Stravinsky: The History of Music by Its Foremost Critics,* Norton, 1933; (editor) *Composers of Today,* Wilson, 1934, 2nd edition, 1936; (editor) *Composers of Yesterday,* Wilson, 1937; *Twentieth Century Composers,* Crowell, 1937; (with Frederic Ewen) *Musical Vienna,* McGraw, 1939; *Men and Women Who Make Music,* Crowell, 1939, revised edition, Merlin, 1949.

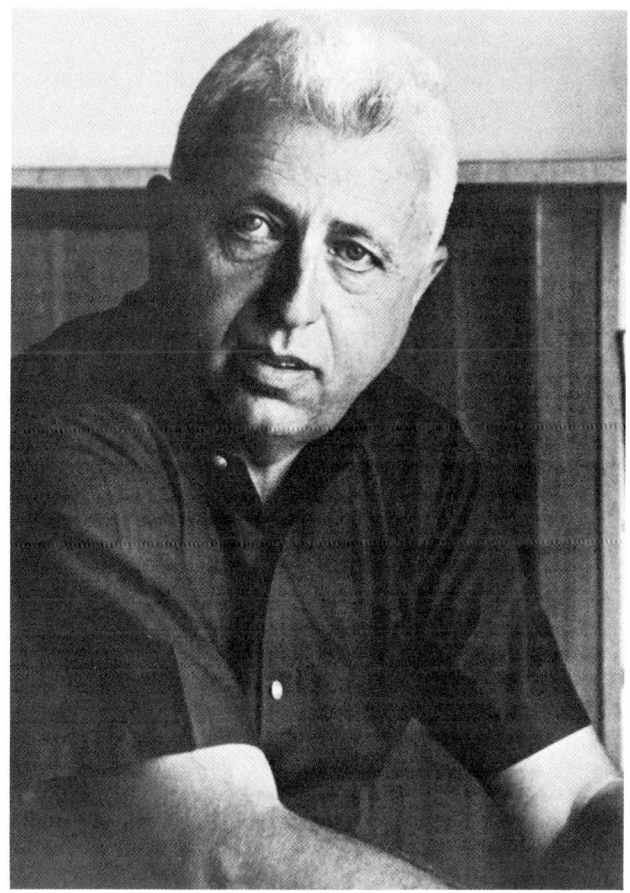

DAVID EWEN

(Editor) *Living Musicians,* Wilson, 1940, first supplement, 1957; *Pioneers in Music,* Crowell, 1940; *Music Comes to America,* Crowell, 1942, 2nd edition, 1947; (editor) *Book of Modern Composers,* Knopf, 1942, 3rd edition published as *New Book of Modern Composers,* 1961; *Dictators of the Baton,* Ziff-Davis, 1943, 2nd edition, 1948; *The Story of George Gershwin,* Holt, 1943; *Tales From Vienna Woods: The Story of Johann Strauss,* Holt, 1944; *Men of Popular Music,* Ziff-Davis, 1944; *Music for Millions,* Arco, 1944, new edition published as *Encyclopedia of Musical Masterpieces,* Grosset, 1950, another edition published as *Musical Masterworks,* Arco, 1956; (compiler) *Listen to the Mocking Words,* Arco, 1945; *Haydn: A Good Life,* Holt, 1946; (editor) *Songs of America,* Ziff-Davis, 1947; (editor) Romain Rolland, *Essays on Music,* Allen, Towne & Heath, 1948, revised edition, Dover, 1959; (editor) *Year in American Music,* Allen, Towne & Heath, 1948; (editor) *American Composers Today,* Wilson, 1949.

The Story of Irving Berlin, Holt, 1950; *The Story of Arturo Toscanini,* Holt, 1951; *The Complete Book of Twentieth Century Music,* Prentice-Hall, 1952, 2nd edition, 1959; (with Nicholas Slonimsky) *Fun With Musical Games and Quizzes,* Prentice-Hall, 1952; *The Story of Jerome Kern,* Holt, 1953; (with Milton Cross) *Encyclopedia of the Great Composers and Their Music,* 2 volumes, Doubleday, 1953; (editor) *European Composers Today,* Wilson, 1954; *Home Book of Musical Knowledge,* Prentice-Hall, 1954; *Encyclopedia of the Opera,* Hill & Wang, 1955, new edition, 1963; *A Journey to Greatness: The Life and Music of George Gershwin,* Holt, 1956; *Home Book of Twentieth Century Music,* Arco, 1956; *A Panorama of American Popular Music,* Prentice-Hall, 1957; *Richard Rodgers,* Holt, 1957; *Complete Book of the American Musical Theatre,* Holt, 1958, revised edition, 1959; *The Encyclopedia of Concert Music,* Hill & Wang, 1959.

The World of Jerome Kern, Holt, 1960; *Leonard Bernstein: A Biography for Young People,* Chilton, 1960; *History of Popular Music,* Barnes & Noble, 1961; *Lighter Classics in Music,* Arco, 1961; *The Story of America's Musical Theater,* Chilton, 1961; (editor) *Popular American Composers,* Wilson, 1962, new enlarged edition, 1968; (editor) *World of Great Composers,* Prentice-Hall, 1962; *David Ewen Introduces Modern Music,* Chilton, 1962, revised enlarged edition, 1969; *The Book of European Light Opera,* Holt, 1962; *With a Song in His Heart: The Story of Richard Rodgers,* Holt, 1963; *The Life and Death of Tin Pan Alley,* Funk, 1964; *Famous Instrumentalists,* Dodd, 1965; *The Cole Porter Story,* Holt, 1965; *The Complete Book of Classical Music,* Prentice-Hall, 1965; (editor) *Great Composers, 1300-1900,* H. W. Wilson, 1966; (editor) *American Popular Songs,* Random House, 1966; *Encyclopedia of American Popular Songs,* Random House, 1966; *Famous Modern Conductors,* Dodd, 1957; *World of 20th Century Music,* Prentice-Hall, 1968; *Composers Since 1900,* Wilson, 1969; (with Milton Cross) *The New Encyclopedia of the Great Composers and Their Music,* Doubleday, 1969.

George Gershwin: His Journey to Greatness, Prentice-Hall, 1970; *Great Men of American Popular Song,* Prentice-Hall, 1970; *New Complete Book of the American Musical Theater,* Holt, 1970; *New Encyclopedia of the*

On the Bowery they said a new song was more exciting to [Irving Berlin] than food or drink. ■ (From *The Story of Irving Berlin* by David Ewen. Illustrated by Jane Castle.)

Opera, Hill & Wang, 1971; *Composers of Tomorrow's Music,* Dodd, 1971; *Popular American Composers: First Supplement,* Wilson, 1972; *Opera,* Watts, 1972.

SIDELIGHTS: Ewen has written more books on music and has had wider circulation for them than any other writer on the subject past or present. His books, some of them book club selections, have been translated into seventeen languages, including Chinese, Japanese, Vietnamese and Hebrew. He was authorized by the estates of George Gershwin and Jerome Kern to write the definitive biographies of those late composers. He was also authorized by Richard Rodgers to write his definitive biography.

"Since 1931, when I published my first book, there has never been a year when at least one of my books wasn't on the lists, an achievement probably without precedent. Throughout my entire career I have divided my creative activities between serious and popular music with the aim of demonstrating that good music could be popular and that popular music could be good."

HOBBIES AND OTHER INTERESTS: Reading, the theatre, listening to music, record collecting and travel.

EYERLY, Jeanette Hyde 1908-
(Jeannette Griffith, a joint pseudonym)

PERSONAL: Born June 7, 1908, in Topeka, Kan.; daughter of Robert C. (railroad executive) and Mabel (Young) Hyde; married Frank Eyerly (managing editor, *Des Moines Register and Tribune*), December 6, 1932; children: Jane (Mrs. Lawrence Kozuszek), Susan (Mrs. Joseph Pichler). *Education:* Drake University, student, 1926-29; University of Iowa, A.B., 1930. *Politics:* Independent. *Religion:* Catholic. *Home*: 231 42nd St., Des Moines, Iowa. *Agent:* Curtis Brown Ltd., 60 East 56th St., New York, N.Y. 10022.

CAREER: Writer and lecturer. *Member:* American Association of University Women, League of Women Voters, Menninger Foundation, Authors Guild, Theta Sigma Phi. *Awards, honors:* Susan Glaspell Award for *Gretchen's Hill,* 1965; Christopher Awards, 1969, for *Escape from Nowhere; Ratigan Cares* was selected as one of the Child Study Association's Books of the Year, 1970.

WRITINGS: (With Valeria Winkler Griffith, under joint pseudonym Jeannette Griffith) *Dearest Kate,* Lippincott, 1961; *More Than a Summer Love,* Lippincott, 1962; *Drop-Out,* Lippincott, 1963; *The World of Ellen March,* Lippincott, 1964; *Gretchen's Hill,* Lippincott, 1965; *A Girl Like Me,* Lippincott, 1966; *The Girl Inside,* Lippincott, 1968; *Escape from Nowhere,* Lippincott, 1969; *Radigan Cares,* Lippincott, 1970; *The Phaedra Complex,* Lippincott, 1971; *Bonnie Jo, Go Home,* Lippincott, 1972. Contributor to *Ladies' Home Journal, McCall's,* and other women's magazines. Formerly wrote column, "Family Diary," with V.W. Griffith, for Hall Syndicate.

WORK IN PROGRESS: A young adult novel.

HOBBIES AND OTHER INTERESTS: Gardening, birdwatching, collecting prints and pictures of all periods.

FOR MORE INORMATION SEE: *Christian Science Monitor,* November 11, 1971.

JEANNETTE HYDE EYERLY

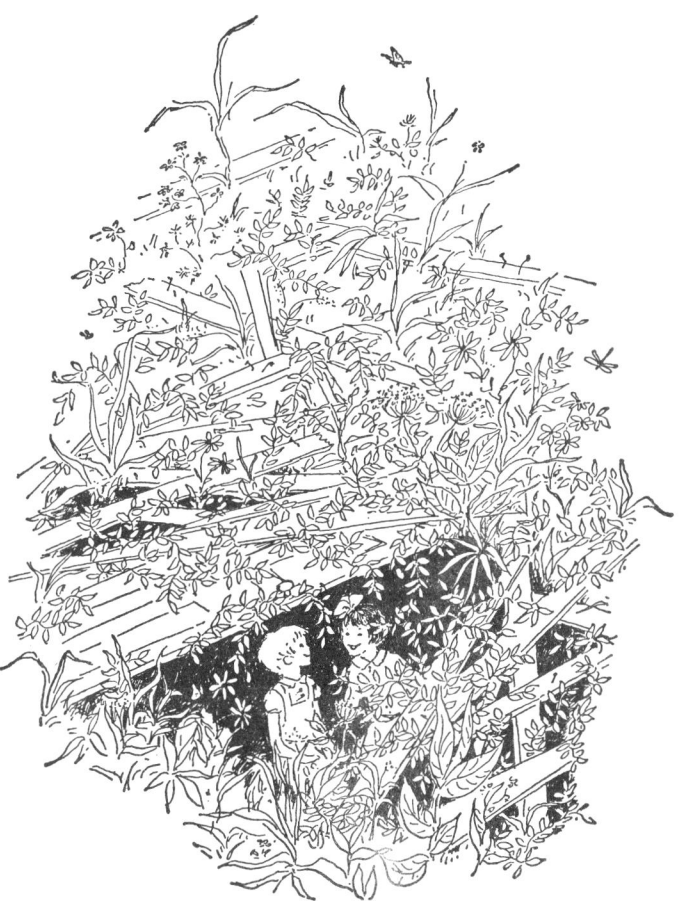

So here [they] stood, in a grassy sheltered place with sunlight trickling through. Yet it was almost invisible from above! ■ (From *Gretchen's Hill* by Jeannette Eyerly. Illustrated by Burmah Burris. Reprinted by permission of J. B. Lippincott Co.)

FARLEY, Carol 1936-
(Carol McDole)

PERSONAL: Born December 20, 1936, in Ludington, Mich.; daughter of Floyd (a laborer) and Thressa (Moreen) McDole; married Dennis Scott Farley (an officer, U.S. Army), June 20, 1956; children: Denise, Elise, Roderick, Jeannette. *Education:* Western Michigan University, Teacher's Certificate, 1956; Michigan State University, further courses in communication, 1968, 1969. *Address:* (permanent) 605 East Melendy St., Ludington, Mich. 49431.

CAREER: Has taught school, picked fruit, worked in an office, sold ladies wear, and worked in a library; as an army wife (with thirteen moves in fifteen years), her volunteer activities have centered on Boy Scouts, Girl Scouts, Red Cross, and Children's reading groups. *Member:* Authors Guild, Armed Forces Writers League. *Awards, honors:* Franklin Watts Medal Mystery Award, 1966, for *Mystery of the Fogman*.

WRITINGS—Juvenile: (Under name Carol McDole) *Yekapo of Zopoland*, Row, Peterson, 1958; *Mystery of the Fogman*, Watts, 1966; *Mystery in the Ravine*, Watts, 1967; *Sergeant Finney's Family*, Watts, 1969; *The Bunch on McKellahan Street*, Watts, 1971.

WORK IN PROGRESS: A book tentatively titled *That Question*, a juvenile *Pilgrim's Progress* in which the main characters are trying to find an answer to "What's the most important thing in the world?"

SIDELIGHTS: "My main purpose in writing books for children is to alleviate some of the tensions they feel in today's society. I want to illustrate that, although much of life is bad, most of it is good. I concentrate on using mystery and humor as a vehicle for my philosophy because this type of writing reaches the greatest number of readers.

"My book, *Sergeant Finney's Family*, shows another side to military life and was written in the hope that children in one-parent families could see that love, not proximity, is what matters."

The Farleys lived in Munich for four years and have been stateside residents of Kansas, Illinois, Michigan, Virginia, and New Jersey.

When I opened my eyes again, I was staring into the face of a witch: ■ (From *Mystery in the Ravine* by Carol Farley. Illustrated by Joseph Escourido.)

CAROL FARLEY

FENTEN, D.X. 1932-

PERSONAL: Born January 3, 1932, in New York, N.Y.; son of Harry J. and Ethel (Scheinwald) Fenten; married Barbara Doris Levy (an elementary school librarian), April 7, 1957; children: Donna Ruth, Jeffrey Allan. *Education:* New York University, B.A., 1953, M.A., 1954; Columbia University, further graduate study, 1956-57. *Home:* 27 Bowdon Rd., Greenlawn, Long Island, N.Y. 11740.

CAREER: Prior to 1965 held writing and editing positions with Grumman Aircraft Engineering Corp., Perfection on Long Island, Inc., McGraw-Hill Book Co., and other firms; *Progressive Grocer* (magazine), New York, N.Y., associate editor, 1965-70; Syosset High School, Syosset, Long Island, N.Y., teacher of creative writing, journalism, modern communications, and cinematography, 1970—. *Military service:* U.S. Army, 1954-56. *Member:* Garden Writers Association of America, American Horticultural Society.

WRITINGS—Adult books: *Better Photography for Amateurs*, Chilton, 1960; *Electric Eye Still Camera Photography*, Chilton, 1961; *Flower and Garden Photography*, Chilton, 1966; *Greenhorn's Guide to Gardening*, Grosset, 1969; *The Clear and Simple Gardening Guide*, Grosset, 1971; *The Organic Grow It, Cook It, Preserve It Guidebook*, Grosset, 1972.

Youth books: *Plants for Pots: Projects for Indoor Gardeners*, Lippincott, 1969; *Aviation Careers: Jobs in the Air and on the Ground*, Lippincott, 1969; *Harvesting the Sea*, Lippincott, 1970; *Sea Careers*, Lippincott, 1970; *Ins and Outs of Gardening*, Lion Press, 1972; *The Making of a Police Officer*, Westminster, 1972; *Ms.—M.D.*, Westminster, in press.

SIDELIGHTS: "I have been fortunate that my literary efforts always seem to be the result of 'one thing leading to another.' Because of this I always write in areas of great personal interest and enthusiasm. For example, the arrival of our photogenic daughter sparked my interest in photography. This lead to my first book, and then, two more. The purchase of our suburban home necessitated learning about gardening and after much trial, error, and enjoyment, I wrote *Greenhorn's Guide to Gardening* and *Organic Grow It*.

Because working in the garden is only feasible during warm months, I became interested in indoor gardening and, with the help of our children wrote my first children's book, *Plants for Pots*. The success of this lead my publisher to request career books, and now the same daughter's interest in medicine has me working on *Ms.—M.D.*

"In 1970, I became tired of hearing people (many near famous, well-educated, well-spoken, etc.), say they 'wished they too could write.' Determined to do something about it, I left my job on the magazine to teach at Syosset High School. I worked with students in courses on writing, modern communications, journalism and cinematography—all areas of both proficiency and interest. It is a most marvelous experience for me because the students are honest, willing and interested in working with a 'real' writer—one they know knows, teaches, and cares."

D. X. FENTEN

JEAN FIEDLER

FIEDLER, Jean

PERSONAL: Born in Pittsburgh, Pa.; daughter of Harry (a businessman) and Dina (Diness) Feldman; married Harold Fiedler (a painter), July 5, 1949; children: Judith, Joan. *Education:* University of Pittsburgh, B.A., 1945; graduate study at New York University, 1955-57, New School for Social Research, 1960-61, and Bank Street College of Education, 1962-65. *Politics:* Democrat. *Home:* 69-23 Bell Blvd., Bayside, N.Y. 11364.

CAREER: Children's Aid Society, Pittsburgh, Pa., social worker, 1945; high school teacher of English in Pittsburgh, Pa., 1946-48; Gimbel's Department Store, Pittsburgh, Pa., copywriter, 1948; Brooklyn Public Library, Brooklyn, N.Y., librarian, 1949-50; free-lance writer and editor in New York, N.Y., 1950 . Substitute teacher in high schools of New York, N.Y., 1961—; teacher in adult creative writing courses, Bayside, N.Y., 1964-67; Queens College, Flushing, teacher of writing for juveniles, 1964. *Member:* Authors League of America, Women's National Book Association.

WRITINGS—Children's and young adult books: *The Green Thumb Story*, Holiday House, 1952; *Big Brother Danny*, Holiday House, 1953; *Teddy and the Ice Cream Man*, Abelard, 1957; (with Carol Reuter) *The Last Year*, McKay, 1962; *A Yardstick for Jessica*, McKay, 1964; *Jill's Story*, McKay, 1965; *Lassie, Sand Bar Rescue*, Whitman Publishing, 1965; *New Brother, New Sister*, Golden Press, 1966; *Great American Heroes*, Hart Publishing, 1966; *Lassie and the Deer Mystery*, Whitman Publishing, 1967; *My Special House*, Whitman Publishing, 1967; *My Special Day*, Whitman Publishing, 1967; *Call Me Juanita*, McKay, 1968; *In Any Spring*, McKay, 1969; *I Know What a Farm Is*, Whitman Publishing, 1970; *A Break in the Circle*, McKay, 1971. Contributor to magazines.

WORK IN PROGRESS: A book about the "revolution in the high school."

SIDELIGHTS: "As for me as a writer and a person, I'm not sure it's possible to separate the two although I do many things besides write. I am a wife, a mother, a teacher as well as a writer. But since I have been writing since childhood and was first published at the age of eleven, the act of writing as well as planning the work, searching for ideas, taking notes wherever I may happen to be, is inextricably bound up with me as a person in any of my other activities.

"Most of my more serious books are autobiographical in some respect. *The Last Year* was based on my own last year in high school. Both *A Yardstick for Jessica* and *Jill's Story* were inspired by my own daughters who had urged me to write a book for the 'middle-aged' child. I used activities of theirs and ours to begin with, then took off and let my imagination do the rest. *Call Me Juanita* was born in Mexico; in Cuernavaca my husband and I visited friends who lived in the same kind of cottage that my heroine Johanna does and then later, Juanita. There is a great deal of me in *In Any Spring*, a novel for your adults. The setting is Pittsburgh, the University of Pittsburgh, the foreign students, are all based on real people who were my dear friends. My newest book, *A Break in the Circle*, takes place too in a city about the size of Pittsburgh, where I grew up and begins six months after the heroine's father dies. My own father died when I was twenty-one, and Julie's grief and longing for her father are very strongly reminiscent of my own. It took many years before I could use this personal tragedy in a book.

"I believe that I write because writing seems to be my way of interpreting and making sense out of the world in which I live. Everything I see, experience, long for, fear, hate, all contribute to what I write and the way I see the world. I love the act of writing and always have enjoyed filling a clean page with my own thoughts and ideas. I could never use a tape recorder as a substitute for the pen or typewriter. I like to see the sentences and idea take shape and form as I work.

"Although most of my work has been for young people of all ages (from three to the teenager) I hope to eventually finish a novel for adults on which I have been working with many interruptions for many years. I want to continue writing for young people too because I like and respect them very much. I enjoy their wit, their perception, their ideals, the fact that they have illusions. A good book for young people is one which never loses its appeal. I remember my own childhood and youth vividly, and for that reason, I suppose, I can actually feel what my heroine and the other characters experience; their fears and doubts are real to me, as well as their dreams.

"I write at all times and in all places; on buses, on

(From *A Break in the Circle* by Jean Fiedler. Book jacket by Genia.)

subways, on trains, on planes, in the library, in the dentist's office and of course, at home. My favorite place to write, however, is the beach. Many of my books have been written at least in rough draft on Jones Beach, one of the most beautiful beaches in the world and a short distance from my home. I prefer to write in the morning, but that isn't always possible, and I have been known to take out my notebook during a sleepless night and work on the current book."

HOBBIES AND OTHER INTERESTS: Music (plays piano and sings in a choir), travel, amateur theatre, transcendental meditation.

FISHER, Leonard Everett 1924-

PERSONAL: Born June 24, 1924, in New York, N.Y.; son of Benjamin M. and Ray (Shapiro) Fisher; married Margery R. Meskin, 1952; children: Julie Anne, Susan Abby, James Albert. *Education:* Yale University, B.F.A., 1949, M.F.A., 1950. *Home and office:* 7 Twin Bridge Acres Rd., Westport, Conn.

CAREER: Whitney School of Art, New Haven, Conn., dean, 1951-53; painter, illustrator and designer of more than 185 children's books, adult books, and educational materials, author, 1954—. Paintings exhibited in New York galleries and selected for national tours by American Federation of Arts and Emily Lowe Foundation; originals of book illustrations in public collections, including Library of Congress, University of Oregon, Mid-Fairfield County Youth Museum, Free Library of Philadelphia, University of Southern Mississippi, and University of Minnesota. Lecturer at art institutes and at academic seminars; speaker at children's book week programs in major cities of East and Midwest; faculty member, Paier School of Arts, 1966—, and Silvermine Guild School of the Arts, 1971—. *Military service:* U.S. Army, Corps of Engineers, 1942-46; became technical sergeant; participated in topographic mapping of five major campaigns in European and Pacific areas.

MEMBER: P.E.N., American Institute of Graphic Arts, Authors Guild, Authors League, Silvermine Guild of Artists (trustee, 1969—), New Haven Paint and Clay Club (president, 1968-70; trustee, 1969—), Westport-Western Arts Council (founding member; board of directors, 1969-72). *Award, honors:* William W. Winchester fellowships, 1949; Pulitzer Prize in Art, 1950; American Institute of Graphic Arts outstanding textbooks, 1958, outstanding children's books, 1963; Ten Best Illustrated Books Award of *New York Times*, 1964, for *Casey at the Bat*; American Library Association Notable Children's Book List, 1958, 1959, 1960, 1962, 1964; International Book Fair [Bologna, Italy], premio grafico, 1968; New Haven Paint and Clay Club, Carle J. Blenner Prize for painting, 1968.

WRITINGS—Author and illustrator: *Pumpers, Boilers, Hooks and Ladders*, Dial, 1961; *Pushers, Spads, Jennies and Jets*, Dial, 1961; *A Head Full of Hats*, Dial, 1962; *The Glassmakers*, Watts, 1964; *The Silversmiths*, Watts, 1964; *The Papermakers*, Watts, 1965; *The Printers*, Watts, 1965; *The Wigmakers*, Watts, 1965; *The Hatters*, Watts, 1965; *The Weavers*, Watts, 1966; *The Cabinetmakers*, Watts, 1966; *The Tanners*, Watts, 1966; *The Shoemakers*, Watts, 1967; *The Schoolmasters*, Watts, 1967; *The Peddlers*, Watts, 1968; *The Doctors*, Watts, 1968; *The Potters*, Watts, 1969; *The Linners*, Watts, 1969; *The Architects*, Watts, 1970; *Two If by Sea*, Random House, 1970; *Picture Book of Revolutionary War Heroes*, Stackpole, 1970; *The Shipbuilders*, Watts, 1971; *Death of Evening Star*, Doubleday, 1972; *The Westfall Warlock*, Doubleday, 1972.

Illustrator: Roger P. Buliard, *My Eskimos: A Priest in the Arctic*, Farrar, Straus, 1956; Richard B. Moris, *The First Book of the American Revolution*, Watts, 1956; L.D. Rich, *The First Book of New England*, Watts, 1957; Kenneth S. Giniger, *America, America, America*, Watts, 1957; Henry Steele Commager, *The First Book of American History*, Watts, 1957; James C. Bowman, *Mike Fink*, Little, Brown, 1957; Robert Payne, *The Splendor of Persia*, Knopf, 1957; Richard B. Morris, *The First Book of the Constitution*, Watts, 1958; Jeanette Eaton, *America's Own Mark Twain*, Morrow, 1958; Harry B. Ellis, *Arabs*, World Publishing, 1958; Robert Irving, *Energy and Power*, Knopf, 1958; Estelle Friedman, *Digging into Yesterday*, Putnam, 1958; Gerald W. Johnson, *America is Born*, Morrow, 1959; Richard B. Morris, *The First Book of the Indian Wars*, Watts, 1959; *Westward, Westward, Westward*, edited by Elizabeth Abell, Watts, 1959; Phillip H. Ault, *This is the Desert*, Dodd, 1959; Robert Irving, *Sound and Ultrasonics*, Knopf, 1959.

Gerald W. Johnson, *America Moves Forward*, Morrow,

LEONARD EVERETT FISHER

1960; Gerald W. Johnson, *America Grows Up*, Morrow, 1960; Robert Irving, *Electromagnetic Waves*, Knopf, 1960; *Declaration of Independence*, Watts, 1960; Trevor N. Dupuy, *Military History of Civil War Actions*, Watts, 1960; Trevor N. Dupuy, *Military History of Civil War Land Battles*, Watts, 1960; Edward E. Hale, *The Man Without a Country*, Watts, 1960; Natalia M. Belting, *Indy and Mrs. Lincoln*, Holt, 1960; Natalia M. Belting, *Verity Mullins and the Indian*, Holt, 1960; Richard B. Morris, *The First Book of the War of 1812*, Watts, 1961; Emma G. Sterne, *Vasco Nunez De Balboa*, Knopf, 1961; Harold W. Felton, *A Horse Named Justin Morgan*, Dodd, 1962; Charles M. Daugherty, *Great Archaeologists*, Crowell, 1962; Margery M. Fisher, *But Not Our Daddy*, Dial, 1962; Robert C. Suggs, *Modern Discoveries in Archaeology*, Crowell, 1962; Jean L. Latham, *Man of the Monitor*, Harper, 1962; Gerald W. Johnson, *The Supreme Court*, Morrow, 1962; Harold W. Felton, *Sergeant O'Keefe and His Mule, Balaam*, Dodd, 1962; Gerald W. Johnson, *The Presidency*, Morrow, 1962; Jack London, *Before Adam*, Macmillan, 1962; Eric B. Smith & Robert Meredith, *Pilgrim Courage*, Little, Brown, 1962; E. Hubbard, *Message to Garcia*, Watts, 1962; Charles Ferguson, *Getting to Know the U.S.A.*, Coward, 1963; Anico Surany, *Golden Frog*, Putnam, 1963; Gerald W. Johnson, *The Congress*, Morrow, 1963; Margery M. Fisher, *One and One*, Dial, 1963; Andre Maurois, *The Weigher of Souls*, Macmillan, 1963; Jack London, *Star Rover*, Macmillan, 1963; *Patriotism, Patriotism, Patriotism*, edited by Helen Hoke, Watts, 1963; Gerald W. Johnson, *Communism, An American's View*, Morrow, 1964; E. Brooks Smith & Robert Meredith, *Coming of the Pilgrims*, Little, Brown, 1964; Richard Armour, *Our Presidents*, Norton, 1964; Robert Meredith & E. Brooks Smith, *Riding with Coronado*, Little, Brown, 1964; Anico Surany, *Ride the Cold Wind*, Putnam, 1960; Robert C. Suggs, *Alexander the Great, Scientist-King*, Macmillan, 1964; Robert C. Suggs, *Archaeology of San Francisco*, Crowell, 1965; Martin Gardner, *Archimedes*, Macmillan, 1965; Florence Stevenson, *Aida*, Putnam, 1965; Lois P. Jones, *The First Book of the White House*, Watts, 1965; Ernest L. Thayer, *Casey at the Bat*, Watts, 1965; John Foster, *Rebel Sea Raider*, Morrow, 1965; Anico Surany, *The Burning Mountain*, Holiday House, 1965; Martha & Charles Shapp, *Let's Find Out about John*

"Enough man, enough!" his companion cried hoarsely, his face all but hidden behind the thick turns of a muffler. "Do you want the bloody King's Own here, to do our knocking for us?" ■ (From *Two If by Sea* by Leonard Everett Fisher. Illustrated by the author.)

Fitzgerald Kennedy, Watts, 1965; Robert C. Suggs, *Archaeology of New York,* Crowell, 1966; Clifford L. Alderman, *The Story of the Thirteen Colonies,* Random House, 1966; John Foster, *Guadalcanal General,* Morrow, 1966; Robert Silverberg, *Forgotten by Time,* Crowell, 1966; Gerald W. Johnson, *The Cabinet,* Morrow, 1966; Washington Irving, *The Legend of Sleepy Hollow,* Watts, 1966; Anico Surany, *Kati and Kormos,* Holiday House, 1966; Anico Surany, *A Jungle Jumble,* Putnam, 1966; Robert K. Meredith & E. Brooks Smith, *Quest of Columbus,* Little, Brown, 1966; Madeleine L'Engle, *Journey with Jonah,* Farrar, Straus, 1967; L. Sprague & Catherine C. De Camp, *The Story of Science in America,* Scribner, 1967; Nathaniel Hawthorne, *Great Stone Face and Two Other Stories,* Watts, 1967; Gerald W. Johnson, *Franklin D. Roosevelt,* Morrow, 1967; George B. Shaw, *The Devil's Disciple,* Watts, 1967; Anico Surany, *Covered Bridge,* Holiday House, 1967; Anico Surany, *Monsieur Jolicoeur's Umbrella,* Putnam, 1967; Washington Irving, *Rip Van Winkle,* Watts, 1967; James Playsted Wood, *The Queen's Most Honorable Pirate,* Seabury, 1967; Richard B. Morris, *The First Book of the Founding of the Republic,* Watts, 1968; Anico Surany, *Malachy's Gold,* Holiday House, 1968; Bret Harte, *The Luck of Roaring Camp,* Watts, 1968; (with Cynthia Basil) John Foster, *Napoleon's Marshal,* Morrow, 1968; Gerald W. Foster, *British Empire,* Morris, 1969; Robert Meredith & E. Brooks Smith, *Exploring the Great River,* Little, Brown, 1969; Anico Surany, *Lora Lorita,* Putnam, 1969; Julian May, *Why the Earth Quakes,* Holiday House, 1969; Victor B. Scheffer, *The Year of the Whale,* Scribner, 1969; Victor B. Scheffer, *The Year of the Seal,* Scribner, 1970; Berenice R. Morris, *American Popular Music,* Watts, 1970; Victor B. Scheffer, *Little Calf,* Scribner, 1970; Julian May, *The Land Beneath the Sea,* Holiday House, 1971; Loren Eisely, *The Night Country,* Scribner, 1971; Isaac B. Singer, *The Wicked City,* Farrar, Straus, 1972; Paul Engle, *Golden Child,* Dutton; *John F. Kennedy's Inaugural Address,* Watts; *Gettysburg Address,* Watts.

WORK IN PROGRESS: The Art Experience and *The Homemakers,* for Watts.

SIDELIGHTS: "I knew that someday someone would ask how I came to write my books. I am as ill-prepared to answer that query as I am to supply a satisfactory response to similar queries regarding my painting and illustrating. I have no idea how I came to do any of this except to say that I knew I would from the day I was born—give or take a few years. It never occurred to me to do anything else (encouraged as I was by proper parental applause).

"The first thing I drew was a bad portrait—in profile, no less—of Abraham Lincoln. That was in 1928. Soon after I began a long apprenticeship as a painter and that is what I am truly—a painter. Lately, I seem to be functioning more and more in three distinct artistic disciplines—simultaneously. I dare not look back to wonder over the converging paths that have led me to this point of artistic fusion. I am sure that if I did look back I should turn into a pillar of salt—or something like that.

"Thus far my writing has been confined to American history for the most part. I suppose this stems from seventeen years of illustrating the American theme. I have always had a yen for history—and whose history is better than one's own. Yet, I have illustrated an assortment of other subjects—world history, science, science fiction, general fiction, not-so-classical fiction, and informational books of all types. I have always had a thirst for knowing and a willing energy to pass on to others what I found out. Happily, this thirst was slaked by numerous publishers who dared to oblige.

"My painting is in another dimension which I cannot adequately summarize here. It neither looks like the illustration I do, nor does its ever-changing conceptual matter even approximate my writing interests at the moment. Nevertheless, these muses—painting, illustrating, writing (and I hesitate to mention my clumsy attempts at the piano or the teaching that I do ... but I shall)—are all one and indivisible to me, if to no one else. And they have been nourished by both overwhelming desire and various experiences that have left their mark."

Fisher's paintings are in the permanent collections of: The Butler Institute of American Art, The Norton Gallery of Art, Fairfield University, New Haven Paint and Clay Club, Housatonic Community College. He also painted wall decorations at St. Patrick's Church (Armonk, N.Y.) in 1970 and designed the 4 block 8" U.S. Postage Stamps Commemorating the Bicentennial. The stamps were issued on July 4, 1972, at Williamsburg, Virginia and went on National sale, July 5. His recent major exhibitions include: Silvermine Guild one man show, 1968, Artists of Southern New England, 1968, Pennsylvania State University, 1970, Mainstreams, 1971.

FOR MORE INFORMATION SEE: Design, November, 1945, June-July, 1952; *Milwaukee Journal,* November 17, 1960; Huck and Young, *Children's Literature in the Elementary Schools,* Holt, 1961; *Christian Science Monitor,* May 3, 1962; *American Artist,* September, 1966; *Illustrators of Children's Books: 1957-1966,* Horn Book, 1968; *Third Book of Junior Authors,* edited by de Montreville and Hill, Wilson, 1972.

FLOETHE, Louise Lee 1913-

PERSONAL: Surname is pronounced "flirta"; born March 13, 1913, in New York, N.Y.; daughter of Louis Franklin and Selma (Van Praag) Lee; married Richard Floethe, 1937; children: Stephen Lee, Ronald K. *Education:* Studied dramatics at Columbia University, and the Neighborhood Playhouse Studios. *Religion:* Unitarian Universalist. *Home and office:* 1391 Harbor Dr., Sarasota, Fla.

CAREER: Writer of children's books, illustrated by her husband, Richard Floethe. *Member:* Friends of the Library (Sarasota), Asolo Theatre Festival Association, Bignonia Garden Circle, Sarasota Yacht Club.

WRITINGS: If I Were Captain (Junior Literary Guild selection), Scribner, 1956; *The Farmer and His Cows,* Scribner, 1957; *The Winning Colt,* Sterling, 1957; *Terry Sets Sail,* Harper, 1958; *A Year To Remember,* Lothrop, 1958; *The Cowboy on the Ranch,* Scribner, 1959; *The Indian and His Pueblo,* Scribner, 1960; *Triangle X,* Harper, 1960; *The Fisherman and His Boat,* Scribner, 1961; *Sara,* Ariel Books, 1961; *Blueberry Pie,* Scribner, 1962;

LOUISE AND RICHARD FLOETHE

The Story of Lumber, Scribner, 1962; *Sea of Grass,* Scribner, 1963; *The Island of Hawaii,* Scribner, 1964; *Bittersweet Summer,* Ariel Books, 1964; *The New Roof,* Scribner, 1965; *Fountain of the Friendly Lion,* Scribner, 1966; *A Thousand and One Buddhas,* Ariel Books, 1967; *Floating Market,* Ariel Books, 1969; *Farming Around the World,* Scribner, 1970; *Jungle People,* Scribner, 1971; *Fishing Around the World,* Scribner, 1972. Scripts: "A day at the Beach," 1971; "Jeff Sets Sail," 1972, "Ranch Girl," 1972, "How About It," 1972, "Must We Have Noise," 1972, "Who Wants America Ugly," 1972 (all produced by Gordon-Kerckhoff Products and released by ACI Films—director, cameraman is son, Ronald Floethe.

SIDELIGHTS: "I draw on the many varied experiences of my life for the subjects of my books. (*A Year to Remember,* for example, deals with a year I spent in school in Switzerland.) Many of my books are based on experiences of my childhood and early married life. However in the past ten years my husband and I have travelled all over the world and the subject matter of our latest books reflect this.

"Our object is to produce beautiful children's books and we are never satisfied unless we give the best of ourselves to our work. We discuss subject matter in advance of starting a book and if we are doing on the spot research my husband makes sketches and takes movies while I take notes. Upon returning home I do follow up research and then write the entire manuscript before my husband begins his illustrations. He completes a dummy which includes the entire story and illustrations and this we send to the publisher. When they return the dummy, he begins work on the finished art work for which he does the color separations.

"For the past year I have become deeply involved in the making of our son's educational children's films for which I do the stories and also assist at the filming and cutting. This is a new form of collaboration for me which I enjoy very much and which calls on different facets of my talent—my early training for the theatre comes in handy now.

"Our older son, Stephen, who has been in TV news for the past eight years now joins his brother in the children's film production business. The Floethe family looks forward to exciting and creative years in our joint efforts producing books, illustrations and films."

HOBBIES AND OTHER INTERESTS: Tennis, sailing, riding.

FOR OTHER INFORMATION SEE: "Kid Stuff," film produced by Gordon-Kerckhoff Productions, 1970.

FLOETHE, Richard 1901-

PERSONAL: His surname formerly appeared in some sources as Flöthe (pronounced "Flirta"), but he has used the anglicized form for some years; born September 2, 1901, in Essen, Germany; son of Richard William (in civil service) and Anna Maria (Kerckhoff) Flöthe; married Louise Lee (a writer of children's books), June 24, 1937; children: Stephen Lee, Ronald Kerckhoff (producer of children's films). *Education:* Studied at art academies in Dortmund, 1920-22, Munich, 1922-23, and at the Bauhaus in Weimar, 1923-24. *Politics:* Republican. *Religion:* Unitarian Universalist. *Home and studio:* 1391 Harbor Dr., Sarasota, Fla. 33579.

CAREER: Painter, print maker, and book illustrator. First major commission as an artist was a mural for the International Exposition in Cologne, Germany, 1928; came to the United States in 1928; art director of Poster Division, Federal Art Project, New York, N.Y., 1936-39; instructor in commercial design at Cooper Union, New York, N.Y., 1940-41; art director of Poster Division, War Service of City of New York, N.Y., 1942-43; instructor in illustration at Ringling School of Art, Sarasota, Fla., 1954-67. His water colors and prints are in the collections of Library of Congress, Metropolitan Museum of Art, Philadelphia Museum of Art, New York Public Library, and a number of university collections. *Member:* Sarasota Yacht Club, Forest Lakes Country Club. *Awards, honors:* Winner of Limited Editions Club international competition for book illustration for *Glorious Adventures of Tyl Ulenspiegl,* 1934, and *The Adventures of Pinocchio,* 1937.

WRITINGS—Self-illustrated: *Summer Holiday,* limited edition, Brookdale Press (Middletown, N.Y.), 1939.

Illustrator: Allen Chaffee, *Wandy the Wild Pony,* Harrison Smith, 1932; George D. Parrish, *Hung for a Song,* Farrar & Rinehart, 1934; Myron Brinig, *Out of Life,* Farrar & Rinehart, 1934; Charles T.H. Coster, *Glorious Adventures of Tyl Ulenspiegl,* translated into English by Allan R. Macdougall, Limited Editions Club, 1934; Sterner St. Paul Meek, *The Monkeys Have No Tails in Zamboanga,* Morrow, 1935; Marjorie Fischer, *Street Fair,* Random House, 1935; Marjorie Fischer, *Palaces on Monday,* Random House, 1936; *Cupid's Horn Book,* Peter Pauper, 1936; Daniel Defoe, *Robinson Crusoe,* Peter Pauper, 1937; Nor Burglon, *The Gate Swings In,* Little, Brown, 1937; Noel Streatfeild, *Ballet Shoes,* Random House, 1937; Carlo Lorenzini, *The Adventures of Pinocchio,* translated into English by Walter S. Cramp, Limited Editions Club, 1937; Helen Follett, *Third Class Ticket to Heaven,* Winston, 1938; Noel Streatfeild, *Tennis Shoes,* Random House, 1938; Giovanni Boccaccio, *Decameron,* Peter Pauper, 1938; Noel Streatfeild, *Circus Shoes,* Random House, 1939; Heluiz C. Washburne, *Friedl, the Mountain Boy,* Winston, 1939; Caroline Cunningham, editor, *The Talking Stone,* Knopf, 1939.

Kathleen Coyle, *Brittany Summer,* Harper, 1940; Elizabeth Goudge, *Smoky House,* Coward, 1940; Noel Streatfeild, *The Secret of the Lodge,* Random House, 1940; William Shakespeare, *All's Well that Ends Well,* Limited Editions Club, 1940; Noel Streatfeild, *The Stranger in Primrose Lane,* Random House, 1941; Mary Treadgold, *Left Till Called For,* Doubleday, 1941; Jack Bechdolt, *Junior Air Raid Wardens,* Lippincott, 1942; Jerome K. Jerome, *Three Men in a Boat,* Scribner, 1942; *The Adventures of Baron Munchausen,* Peter Pauper, 1944; Jerome S. Meyer, *Picture Book of Astronomy,* Lothrop, 1945; Noel Streatfeild, *Theater Shoes,* Random House, 1945; Carlo Lorenzini, *Pinocchio,* World Publishing, 1946; Darwin L.O. Teilhet, *The Avion My Uncle Flew,* Appleton, 1946; Jerome S. Meyer, *Picture Book of Molecules and Atoms,* Lothrop, 1947; Charles Lamb, *Dissertation on Roast Pig and Other Essays,* Peter Pauper, 1947; Jerome S. Meyer, *Fun-To-Do,* Dutton, 1948; Noel Streatfeild, *Party Shoes,* Random House, 1948; Hester O'Neill, *Young Patriots,* Thomas Nelson, 1948; Jerome S. Meyer, *Picture Book of the Weather,* Lothrop, 1948; E.M. Orr and others, editors, *Stories Old and New,* Doubleday, 1948; Amy Hogeboom, editor, *Tales from the High Seas,* Lothrop, 1948; Lucy Sprague Mitchell, *A Year on the Farm,* Simon & Schuster, 1948; Walter Havighurst and M.M. Boyd, *Song of the Pines,* Winston, 1949; Jerome S. Meyer, *Picture Book of the Earth,* Lothrop, 1949; Hazel H. Wilson, *Island Summer,* Abingdon-Cokesbury, 1949.

Margaret Wise Brown, *The Dream Book,* Random House, 1950; Edna L. Sterling and others, *English Is Our Language,* Heath, 1950; Jerome S. Meyer, *Picture Book of Chemistry,* Lothrop, 1950; Noel Streatfeild, *Skating Shoes,* Random House, 1951; *The World's Best Limericks,* Peter Pauper, 1951; Elizabeth Goudge, *The Valley of Song,* Coward, 1951; Jerome S. Meyer, *Picture Book of Radio and Television,* Lothrop, 1951; Paul Witty and others, *Do and Dare* (reader), Heath, 1951; Katherine B. Shippen, *Mr. Bell Invents the Telephone,* Random House, 1952; Jerome S. Meyer, *Picture Book of Electricity,* Lothrop, 1953; Noel Streatfeild, *Family Shoes,* Random House, 1954; Frank R. Stockton, *Ting-A-Ling Tales,* Scribner, 1955; Lee Sutton, *Venus Boy,* Lothrop, 1955; Nancy Nash, *Wumpy's Christmas Gift,* Northrop, 1956; Jerome S. Meyer, *Picture Book of the Sea,* Lothrop, 1956; Noel Streatfeild, *Dancing Shoes,* Random House, 1957; Charles M. Purin, *Fortunatus,* Heath, 1958; Stella M. Hinz, *Das Geheimisvolle Dorf,* Heath, 1958; Peter Hagboldt, *Das Abenteur der Naujahrsnacht,* Heath, 1958; Arthur Schnitzler, *Der Blinde Geronimo und ein Bruder,* Heath, 1959.

Illustrator of books by his wife, Louise Lee Floethe: *If I Were Captain* (Junior Literary Guild selection), Scribner, 1956; *The Farmers and His Cows,* Scribner, 1957; *The Winning Colt,* Sterling, 1957; *Terry Sets Sail,* Harper, 1958; *The Cowboy on the Ranch,* Scribner, 1959; *The Indian and His Pueblo,* Scribner, 1960; *Triangle X,* Harper, 1960; *Sara,* Ariel, 1961; *The Fisherman and His Boat,* Scribner, 1961; *Blueberry Pie,* Scribner, 1962; *The Story of Lumber,* Scribner, 1962; *Sea of Grass,* Scribner, 1963; *The Islands of Hawaii,* Scribner, 1964; *Bittersweet Summer,* Ariel, 1964; *The New Roof,* Scribner, 1965; *Fountain of the Friendly Lion,* Scribner, 1966; *A Thousand and One Buddhas,* Ariel, 1967; *Floating Market,* Ariel, 1969; *Farming Around the World,* Scribner, 1970; *Jungle People,* Scribner, 1971; *Fishing Around the World,* Scribner, 1972.

Designer of jackets for *A Year to Remember,* also by

White elephants, tame leopards too,
And baskets filled with precious stones. ■ (From *If I Were Captain* by Louise Lee Floethe. Illustrated by Richard Floethe.)

Louise Lee Floethe, Lothrop, 1957, and many other books. Contributor to *Horn Book*.

HOBBIES AND OTHER INTERESTS: Tennis, sailing.

FOR MORE INFORMATION SEE: More Junior Authors, edited by Muriel Fuller, H.W. Wilson, 1963; "Kid Stuff," film produced by Gordon-Kerckhoff Productions, 1970.

FORMAN, Brenda   1936-

PERSONAL: Born August 1, 1936, in Hollywood, Calif.; daughter of Harrison (a writer) and Sandra (Carlyle) Forman. *Education:* Barnard College, B.A., 1956; City University of New York, Ph.D., 1969. *Home:* 301 North Beauregard St., Alexandria, Va. 22312.

CAREER: Mitre Corp., McLean, Va., analyst. *Member:* Phi Beta Kappa.

WRITINGS: (With father, Harrison Forman) *The Land and People of Nigeria,* Lippincott, 1964; "Famous First Name" series for children, published by Frommer-Pasmantier: *Is Your Name James?,* 1965; . . . *John?,* 1965; . . . *Richard?,* 1965; . . . *Robert?,* 1965; . . . *William?,* 1965; . . . *Michael?,* 1965; *The Story of Thailand,* McCormic-Mathers, 1965; *America's Place in the World Economy,* Harcourt, 1969.

SIDELIGHTS: "My writing aim is to make historical and political subjects interesting and stimulating to young readers, particularly the teen-age groups."

FOR MORE INFORMATION SEE: Saturday Review, August 16, 1969.

FRANKAU, Mary Evelyn Atkinson   1899-
(M. E. Atkinson)

PERSONAL: Born June 20, 1899, in Highgate, London, England; daughter of George Thomas (a schoolmaster) and Edith Jessie (Howard) Atkinson; married George Neuberg Frankau, April 16, 1951, (died, 1969). *Education:* Privately, and at Leeson House, Langton, Matravers, Dorsetshire, England. *Politics:* Conservative. *Religion:* Anglican. *Home:* The White Hart Hotel, Wiveliscombe, near Taunton, Somerset, England.

CAREER: Playwright and author of children's books. Red Cross nurse in both World Wars. *Member:* British Legion.

WRITINGS— Under name M.E. Atkinson: (Editor with Father, George Thomas Atkinson) *A Book of Giants and Dwarfs,* Dent, 1929; *August Adventure,* J. Cape, 1936; *Mystery Manor,* Bodley Head, 1937; *The Compass Points North,* John Lane, 1938; *Smugglers' Gap,* John Lane, 1939; *Going Gangster,* John Lane, 1940; *Crusoe Island,*

Bodley Head, 1941; *Challenge to Adventure,* Bodley Head, 1941; *The Monster of Widgeon Weir,* Bodley Head, 1943; *The Nest of the Scarecrow,* John Lane, 1944; *Problem Party,* John Lane, 1945; *Chimney Cottage,* Bodley Head, 1947; *The House on the Moor,* Bodley Head, 1948; *The 13th Adventure,* Bodley Head, 1949; *Steeple Folly,* Bodley Head, 1950; *Castaway Camp,* Bodley Head, 1951; *Hunter's Moon,* Bodley Head, 1952; *The Barnstormers,* Bodley Head, 1953; *Riders and Raids,* Bodley Head, 1955; *Unexpected Adventure,* Bodley Head, 1955; *Horseshoes and Handle Bars,* Bodley Head, 1958, A.S. Barnes, 1959; *Where There's a Will,* Nelson, 1961.

One-act plays: *Here Lies Matilda* (comedy), Baker Plays, 1931; *Beginner's Luck* (comedy), Baker Plays, 1932; *Patchwork,* Baker Plays, 1933; *The Chimney Corner,* Baker Plays, 1934; *The Day's Good Cause* (comedy), Baker Plays, 1935; *Crab-Apple Harvest,* Baker Plays, 1936; *Going Rustic* (comedy), Baker Plays, 1936; *Little White Jumbo* (comedy), J.B. Pinker, 1937; *Can the Leopard?* (comedy), Baker Plays, 1939; *The Lights Go Up* (comedy), H.F.W. Deane, 1945.

Contributor of stories to British Broadcasting Corp. "Children's Hour."

SIDELIGHTS: "I was brought up in a boy's preparatory school, learning to shoot a goal long before I acquired any lady-like accomplishments. Yet, with all this, I remained something of a milksop—afraid of the dark and demanding the night-light. Coats hanging on my bedroom door became bears and I would not go to sleep unless my nurse sat in the adjoining room. Altogether you could write me off as the sort of person who *will* look under her bed before getting into it.

"At the age of ten I was put on a cousin's little thoroughbred pony—and nothing would make me go off the leading-rein until he acquired a quieter pony. All the fears sprang from an over-active imagination, of course. An imagination that has stood me in good stead with writing.

"When my father retired we went to live at Beaconsfield and here I gave to golf the devotion that had previously been spent upon other games. I got into the county second team (Bucks) and sometimes played for the first. Here I also tried my hand at teaching. I was surprised to find that I could keep order in an advanced form. At my home my one attempt had led to red revolution! There, I was too much 'one with the boys.'

"It was my cousin at Jonathan Cape, who started me off on the long series of adventure stories. I think we were both surprised at my very first effort *August Adventure* proving worthy of publication. I had become tired of writing those one-act plays for women, and this new venture was enjoyable as well as remunerative. These books have now been translated into many languages."

HOBBIES AND OTHER INTERESTS: Golf.

GALLANT, Roy (Arthur) 1924-

PERSONAL: Born April 17, 1924, in Portland, Me.; children: Jonathan Roy, James Christopher. *Education:* Bowdoin College, B.A., 1948; Columbia University, M.S., 1949, and advanced courses. *Home:* P.O. Box 228, Rangeley, Me. 04970 and Orr's Island, Me. *Office:* American Museum-Hayden Planetarium, New York, N.Y.

CAREER: Science Illustrated and *Boys' Life,* New York, N.Y., staff writer, 1949-51; *Scholastic Teacher,* New York, N.Y., managing editor, 1953-56; Doubleday & Co., Inc., New York, N.Y., author-in-residence, 1956-58; executive editor of Aldus Books Ltd., London, England, 1959-62; editor-in-chief of Natural History Press, New York, N.Y., 1962-65. Columbia University, instructor at Teachers College, 1958; University of Illinois, guest lecturer, 1964, 1965, 1966; Hackley School, Tarrytown, N.Y., lecturer in astronomy, 1969-70; American Museum-Hayden Planetarium, New York, N.Y., member of the faculty, 1970—. Consultant (temporary appointment) to President's Committee for Scientists and Engineers. *Military service:* U.S. Army Air Forces, navigator, 1943-46; member of faculty and staff, Psychological Warfare School, Fort Riley, Kan., and psychological warfare officer, Tokyo, Japan, during Korean War. *Member:* P.E.N., Authors Guild of the Authors League of America, American Association for the Advancement of Science. *Awards: honors:* Co-recipient of Thomas Alva Edison Foundation Award for best children's science book of year, for *Exploring the Universe,* 1957; Boys' Clubs of America junior book award certificate, 1959.

WRITINGS: Exploring the Moon, 1955, revised edition, 1966, *Exploring the Universe,* 1956, revised edition, 1968, *Exploring Mars,* 1956, revised edition, 1968, *Exploring the Weather,* 1957, revised edition, 1969, *Exploring the Planets,* 1958, revised edition, 1966, *Exploring Chemistry,* 1958, *Exploring the Sun,* 1958, *Man's Reach into Space,* 1959, revised edition, 1965, *Exploring Under the Earth,* 1960, *The ABC's of Astronomy,* 1962, *The ABC's of Chemistry,* 1962, *Antarctica,* 1962, (with C.J. Schuberth) *Discovering Rocks and Minerals,* Natural History Press, 1967, *Man Must Speak,* Random, 1969, *Man's Reach for the Stars,* 1971, *Me and My Bones,* 1971, *Charles Darwin, the Making of a Scientist,* 1972, *Man, the Measurer,* 1972, *Elementary Science Program* (k-9), Ginn & Co., 1973, *Birth of the Earth,* Prentice-Hall, in press, *Explorers of the Atom,* in press, (co-author) *Biology: The Behavioral View,* Xerox College Publishers, in press (all published by Doubleday, except where otherwise noted).

Contributor of fourteen articles to new *Book of Knowledge;* some two hundred articles, mainly on science subjects, to magazines; occasional political articles to *Reporter.*

Editorial adviser: Doubleday "Pictorial Library" series in science, nature, world history, geography; *Discovery and Exploration,* Doubleday, 1960; *Men, Maps, and Seas,* Doubleday; eight other science books in an international edition, 1965-66; Prentice-Hall's high school biology textbook program; *Biology: The Behavioral View,* Xerox, in press.

SIDELIGHTS: Gallant's special interest in the physical sciences is astronomy. As a science writer, teacher, and editor he believes that no subject is too complex to present for children. "If a writer has command of the scientific concept he is dealing with, he can operate on the level of

ROY A. GALLANT

abstraction he chooses; and if he knows the capabilities of his audience, he can communicate with them. I feel that my writing is a more effective form of teaching than teaching exclusively in the classroom."

HOBBIES AND OTHER INTERESTS: Photography, oil painting, skiing, walking in the woods.

FOR MORE INFORMATION SEE: Horn Book, December, 1969.

GOODALL, John S(trickland) 1908-

PERSONAL: Born June 7, 1908, in Heacham, Norfolk, England; son of Joseph Strickland (a physician and surgeon) and Amelia (Hunt) Goodall; married Margaret Alison Nicol, March 25, 1933; children: Sarah Strickland (Mrs. H. Stead-Ellis). *Education:* Attended Harrow School, 1922-26; studied art privately under J. Watson Nicol, Sir Arthur Cope, and Harold Speed, and later at Royal Academy School of Art, London. *Politics:* Conservative. *Religion:* Church of England. *Home and studio:* Lawn Cottage, Tisbury, Wiltshire, England.

CAREER: Painter. Illustrator at first for books, periodicals, and advertising; after the war started landscape painting in water color and gouache and also doing "conversation groups," including one of the late Duchess of Kent and her family; has had exhibitions of his Victorian pastiche in London and Canterbury recently at Charles Howard Gallery and Foyles Gallery, 1969. *Military service:* British Army, Royal Norfolk Regiment, 1939-45; served in India and Burma. *Member:* Royal Institute of Water Colour Painters, Royal Society of British Artists, National Society of British Artists. *Awards, honors:* Boston Globe-Horn Book Award for excellence in illustration of a children's book, 1969, for *The Adventure of Paddy Pork.*

WRITINGS—Picture books: *Field Mouse House,* Blackie & Son, circa 1958; *Dr. Owl's Party,* Blackie & Son, circa, 1959; *The Adventures of Paddy Pork* (ALA Notable Book, *Horn Book* Honor List), Harcourt, 1968; *The Ballooning Adventures of Paddy Pork,* Harcourt, 1969; *Shrewbettina's Birthday,* Harcourt, 1971; *Jacko,* Macmillan, 1971; *Kelly,* Atheneum, 1971; *Dot and Esmerelda,* Atheneum, 1972.

Illustrator: Anthony Robertson, *How to Do and Say in England,* Dickson, 1936; Susan Dorritt, *Jason's Lucky Day,* Abelard, 1958; Edith N. Bland (E. Nesbit), *Five Children and It,* Looking Glass Library, 1959; Edith N. Bland, *Story of the Amulet,* Looking Glass Library, 1960; Edith N. Bland, *Phoenix and the Carpet,* Looking Glass Library, 1960; Barbara Ker Wilson, *Fairy Tales of England,* Dutton, 1960; Lewis Carroll, *Alice in Wonderland* (illustrations after John Tenniel), Blackie & Son, 1965. Also illustrated Miss Read, *All the Village School,* M. Joseph; Nancy Pense Britton, *The Insane Folly,* Basil Blackwood; Simon Dewes, *Suffolk Childhood,* Hutchinson; Simon Dewes, *Essex Schooldays,* Hutchinson; Simon Dewes, *When all the World was Young,* Hutchinson; R. Arkell, *Trumpets over Merriford,* M. Joseph; R. Arkell, *The Round House,* M. Joseph; Garrick Play Books, Blackie; two books by Chenvix Trench for Blackwood; a number of "Seekers and Finders" books by Amabel Williams-Ellis, for Blackie, and others.

Contributor to *Connoisseur, Radio Times* and other magazines and newspapers.

WORK IN PROGRESS: *Paddy at Theatre,* completion expected in 1974.

SIDELIGHTS: Goodall has painted in India, France, Italy, Yugoslavia, Portugal, Spain, Andorra, Greece, Netherlands, Switzerland, and Sweden. He made a leisurely trip around the world on a cargo ship, 1960-61.

FOR MORE INFORMATION SEE: *Connoisseur,* July, 1968, November, 1971, *Book World,* October 20, 1968; *Horn Book,* December, 1969, June, 1971; *Library Journal,* March 15, 1970; *Times Literary Supplement,* April 16, 1970; *Life,* December 17, 1971; *Graphis 155,* Volume 27, Graphis Press, 1971/72.

(From *The Ballooning Adventures of Paddy Pork* by John S. Goodall. Illustrated by the author.)

CHARLES P. GRAVES

GRAVES, Charles Parlin 1911-1972
(John Parlin)

PERSONAL: Born January 23, 1911, in Apalachicola, Fla.; son of John Ernest and May (Parlin) Graves; married Elizabeth Minot (an editor), April 11, 1953; children: Elizabeth Weld, John Parlin. *Education:* University of Florida, B.S. in Journalism, 1933. *Religion:* Episcopalian. *Home:* Peter Bont Rd., Irvington, N.Y. *Agent:* McIntosh & Otis, Inc., 18 East 41st St., New York, N.Y. 10017.

CAREER: Writer for advertising agencies, New York, N.Y., and Hollywood, Calif., 1938-58; free-lance writer. *Military service:* U.S. Army, World War II, Mountain Infantry and Transportation Corps; served in Aleutians and Philippines; became lieutenant.

WRITINGS: Benjamin Franklin—Man of Ideas, Garrard, 1960, Dell Yearling edition, 1968; *Annie Oakley—The Shooting Star,* Garrard, 1961; (under pseudonym John Parlin) *Andrew Jackson—Pioneer and President,* Garrard, 1962; (under pseudonym John Parlin) *Amelia Earhart—Pioneer in the Sky,* Garrard, 1962, Dell Yearling edition, 1968; *Mickey-Angelo,* Funk, 1962; *Marco Polo,* Garrard, 1963; (under pseudonym John Parlin) *Skeleton Creek* (boy's novel), Abelard, 1963; *Fourth of July,* Garrard, 1963; *Robert E. Lee: Hero for the South,* Garrard, 1964; *Paul Revere: Rider for Liberty,* Garrard, 1964; (under pseudonym John Parlin), *Patriot's Days,* Garrard, 1964; *John Smith,* Garrard, 1965; *John F. Kennedy: New Frontiersman,* Garrard, 1965, Dell Yearling edition, 1966; *Eleanor Roosevelt: First Lady of the World,* Garrard, 1966, Dell Yearling edition, 1968; *Henry Morton Stanley,* Garrard, 1967; (with Ruby L. Radford) *James Edward Oglethorpe,* Garrard, 1968; *William Tecumseh Sherman: Champion of the Union,* Garrard, 1968; *Grandma Moses: Favorite Painter,* Garrard, 1969; *William Bradford,* Garrard, 1969; *Robert F. Kennedy: Man Who Dared to Dream,* Garrard, 1970, Dell Yearling edition, 1972; *Frederick Douglass,* Putnam, 1970; *Nellie Bly: Reporter for the World,* Garrard, 1971; *Matthew Henson,* Putnam, 1971; *Father Flanagan: Founder of Boys Town,* Garrard, 1972; *Mark Twain,* Putnam, 1972; *John Muir,* Crowell, 1972.

SIDELIGHTS: "When I met my wife she was working as a children's book editor under the late May Massee at Viking Press. After we were married she persuaded me to try to write for children. With her help I sold the first book I wrote and have been writing for children ever since.

Ben was leaning out of a window of his family's house in Boston. ■ (From *Benjamin Franklin* by Charles P. Graves. Illustrated by Gerald McCann.)

"I do much more research than necessary for my books, but I do enjoy spending time in libraries. When I'm working on a book about a person who lived in this century I try to interview people who have known my subject—relatives, teachers, scout masters, roommates, etc. I find that most people are glad to help me."

(Died August 2, 1972)

GRAY, Genevieve S. 1920- (Jenny Gray)

PERSONAL: Born August 6, 1920, in Jonesboro, Ark.; daughter of Howard Charles and Bess (Graham) Stuck; married Paul Gray, Jr., October 31, 1941 (divorced, 1946); children: Paul Russell, Howard Axtell. *Education:* University of Arkansas, B.A., 1941; University of Arizona, M.Ed., 1961; University of Southern California, further study, 1963-64. *Politics:* Democrat. *Religion:* Methodist. *Home:* 4382 East Fort Lowell Rd., Tucson, Ariz. 85712.

CAREER: Public school teacher in Jonesboro, Ark., 1955-57, and Tucson, Ariz., 1957-63; Litton Industries, Adler-Westrex Division, multi-media education coordinator (in anti-poverty program), at Camp Atterbury, Ind., 1964-65; high school teacher in Sacramento, Calif., 1965-67; full-time writer, principally of educational materials, 1967—. *Member:* Authors League of America. *Awards, honors:* "Our Environment: Sound and Noise" received the Gold Camera Award at U.S. Industrial Film Festival, 1971.

WRITINGS: (Under name Jenny Gray) *Two-Too-To* (programmed instruction), Pak Donald, 1962; (under name Jenny Gray) *The Teacher's Survival Guide,* Fearon, 1967; (under name Jenny Gray) *Teaching Without Tears,* Fearon, 1967; (editor and abridger) Thomas W. Higginson, *Army Life in a Black Regiment,* Grosset, 1970; (editor and abridger) Frederick Douglass, *The Life and Times of Frederick Douglass,* Grosset, 1970; *The Yellow Bone Ring* (fiction for teens), Lothrop, 1971; *I Know a Bus Driver* (primary text), Putnam, 1972; *A Kite for Bennie* (juvenile), McGraw, 1972; *The Seven Wishes of Joanna Peabody* (juvenile), Lothrop, 1972; *Keep an Eye on Kevin* (juvenile), Lothrop, in press; *Send Wendell* (juvenile), McGraw, in press.

Other writings: "Composition and Language Activities" (series of supplementary booklets to accompany "Elementary School English" textbooks), Addison-Wesley, 1967; "People Are . . ." and "Operation Trek" (narration scripts for films), Aztec Film Productions, 1968, 1969; "Love, Rebellion, Conflict and Other Things" (tape self-instruction units on literature for high school and junior college students), EMC Corp. and Bantam, 1970; "Our Environment: Sound and Noise" (filmstrip), EMC Corp., 1970.

WORK IN PROGRESS: A series of beginning readers, for Benefic.

GENEVIEVE S. GRAY

In some schools, work-study programs or service clubs provide incentive for this kind of work by means of wages, service pins, or other recognition. ■ (From *Teaching without Tears* by Jenny Gray. Illustrated by Robert Haydock.)

SIDELIGHTS: "I'm one of those who switched careers after the children grew up and left home. From regular teaching, I sidled into multi-media teaching, then into writing multi-media materials *for* teachers, and finally into writing children's books. It's remarkable how similar they all are. All demand study and research, the more the better. Raw material must then be arranged to allow for the interests and language patterns of the target audience (for of course second grade children are not at all like fifth graders, who in turn are several light years younger than high school seniors). At whatever age, there must be adventure, always. And challenge. And fun. Especially must there be fun. That's what makes it all worthwhile."

FOR MORE INFORMATION SEE: *Sacramento Bee,* Sacramento, Calif., March 24, 1968; *Arizona Daily Star,* Tucson, November 5, 1971; *Leaders in Education,* 4th edition, Cattell-Bowker, 1971; *Christian Science Monitor,* November 11, 1971.

GRAY, Jenny
See GRAY, Genevieve S.

GRAY, Nicholas Stuart 1922-

PERSONAL: Born October 23, 1922, in Scotland; son of William Stuart and Lenore May (Johnson) Gray. *Education:* Educated at "various private grammar schools, names forgotten. No degrees, as never tried for any, and probably wouldn't have got them if had done so." *Politics:* None. *Religion:* None. *Home:* Castle House, Castle St., Bampton, Devonshire, England; and Langamull, Calgary, Isle of Mull, Scotland; and 20 Perrins Walk, Hampstead, London N.W.3, England. *Agent:* Samuel French, Inc., 25 West 45th St., New York, N.Y. 10036; and Lawrence Fitch, 113 Wardour St., London, England.

CAREER: Playwright, novelist, actor and stage director, and illustrator. Had his first play produced professionally when he was seventeen; actor and director in repertory in England and in London theaters; has directed many of his plays, and appeared in some, including "New Clothes for the Emperor," "The Imperial Nightingale," "The Tinder-Box," "The Marvellous Story of Puss in Boots," "The Wrong Side of the Moon," and "The Princess and the Swineherd"; has also played Hamlet, Richard II, and more recently, Iago in "Othello," at the Malvern Festival Theatre. *Member:* P.E.N., Societe des Auteurs (Paris).

WRITINGS—Novels: *Over the Hills to Fabylon,* Oxford University Press, 1954; *Down in the Cellar,* Dobson, 1961; *The Seventh Swan,* Dobson, 1962; *The Stone Cage,* Dobson, 1963; *Grimbold's Other World,* Faber, 1963, Meridith (Junior Literary Guild selection), 1972; *The Apple Stone,* Dobson, 1965, Meredith (Junior Literary Guild selection), 1968; *Mainly in Moonlight,* Faber, 1965, Meridith, 1966; *The Boys, or Cats with Everything,* Meridith, 1969; *The Further Adventures of Puss in Boots,* Faber, 1971.

Plays: *Beauty and the Beast,* 1951, *The Princess and the Swineherd,* 1952, *The Tinder-Box,* 1952, *The Hunters and the Henwife,* 1953, *The Marvellous Story of Puss in Boots,* 1955, *The Imperial Nightingale,* 1956, *New Clothes for the Emperor,* 1957, *The Other Cinderella,* 1958 (all published by Oxford University Press); *The Seventh Swan,* 1962, *The Stone Cage* (now titled *The Wrong Side of the Moon*), 1963, *Gawain and the Green Knight,* 1967, *New Lamps for Old,* 1967 (all published by Dobson). Also writer of television plays.

WORK IN PROGRESS: A novel based on the life story of Sir Gawain, involving research in early Celtic legends, Welsh legends, medieval writings and poems of England and France, and later works; full-length adaptation of "Tinder-Box" for T.V.

SIDELIGHTS: "I started writing stories and plays while still in the nursery for my younger brothers and sister. They all, very kindly, liked my stories and I compelled them to act in my plays, for a selected audience of parents, visiting relatives, Nanny, and the cook.

"At a much later stage, I decided to write some more short stories, this time just to amuse myself being far from home. I was working in the theatre and noticed how the cinema people were making special films for children, and giving Saturday morning matinees for them. And television was making special children's hour programs. The Theatre (this was immediately after the war) did nothing except *Peter Pan* which is boring for children over eight and under thirty, and pantomimes which are (were) no

NICHOLAS STUART GRAY, as Etienne, the wicked prince, in "The Princess and the Swineherd"

more than thinly disguised variety shows, mostly quite unfit for children with dirty jokes, silly popular songs, and no story. So I wrote a straight play, "Beauty and the Beast," aimed at both children and adults. It caught on, so I wrote some more.

"I wrote these plays on several levels, so that the younger tots—but not under an intelligent seven, they do *talk* right through the show!—could have a visual adventure to follow, and the older people could understand, according to their age and/or experience, the heights and depths of emotional tones. I hope it has worked.

"Most of the plays are based, loosely, on one of the traditional folk-tales of Hans Christian Andersen or Pereault. I find it fascinating to take a simple plot, and weave it into new shapes, and to explore the why of it, and what sort of people ever got themselves into such situations, and so on. To think 'What would a sensible person do if suddenly confronted by a Genii, or a demon, or a talking dragon?' The answer, to me, is mostly 'Run!' But I have had to make it logical, for theatrical purposes, that the meeter of the dragon does not run, at least not far. It's a challenge.

"Then the books. Again, I write to amuse myself. I like to read books of fantasy, so I like to write them. And for the adventures of various children, like those in *The Apple Stone* and *Down in the Cellar*, I bring back to mind very clearly, the way my brothers and sister and I adventured when we were all children together. As we all live very close to one another now, I can always get them talking about old days which reminds me of other funny things that happened. My eldest brother has a daughter, and she is only seven, but already reads some of my easier books. I don't know if she likes them, as she is very laconic about everything except art and 'sweeties.'

"I think it most important that people have a world of imagination into which they can escape from the turmoils of life. Myths used to provide this escape route. Now it is usual to hear people say they are not interested in 'fairytales,' and then proceed to weave themselves a fairytale based on what they would do if they suddenly became rich or famous. Materialism is no proper substitute, and I have been trying, in writing modern fantasies, to give children and adults some sort of temporary passport to a dream-world. It is interesting to find with what relief most of them take it."

HOBBIES AND OTHER INTERESTS: Archaeology history, art, literature, animals, mythology, gardening.

GREEN, D.
See CASEWIT, Curtis

GRIFFITH, Jeannette
See EYERLY, Jeannette

HAMILTON, Virginia 1936-

PERSONAL: Born March 12, 1936, in Yellow Springs, Ohio; daughter of Kenneth James (a musician) and Etta Belle (Perry) Hamilton; married Arnold Adoff (an an-

VIRGINIA HAMILTON

thologist and author), March 19, 1960; children: Leigh Hamilton (daughter), Jaime Levi (son). *Education:* Studied at Antioch College, 1952-55, Ohio State University, 1957-58, and at New School for Social Research. *Residence:* Yellow Springs, Ohio. *Agent:* Dorothy Markinko, McIntosh & Otis, Inc., 18 East 41st St., New York, N.Y. 10017.

CAREER: "Every source of occupation imaginable, from singer to bookkeeper." *Awards, honors:* Zeely received Nancy Block Memorial Award of Downtown Community School Awards Committee, New York; Edgar Allan Poe Award for best juvenile mystery and Ohioana Book Award, 1969, for *The House of Dies Drear*; *The Planet of Junior Brown* was a Newbery Honor Book, 1971, and nominated for the National Book Award, 1972.

WRITINGS—Children's novels: *Zeely* (ALA Notable Book), Macmillan, 1967; *The House of Dies Drear* (ALA Notable Book), Macmillan, 1968; *The Time-Ago Tales of Jadhu*, Macmillan, 1969; *The Planet of Junior Brown* (ALA Notable Book), Macmillan, 1971; *W.E.B. Dubois: An Anthology*, Crowell, 1972.

WORK IN PROGRESS: A children's novel about life along the Ohio River.

SIDELIGHTS: "I grew up in Yellow Springs, an Ohio

He had thick, white hair and a full white beard... and he was tall, taller than any elderly man Mrs. Small had ever seen. ■ (From *The House of Dies Drear* by Virginia Hamilton. Illustrated by Eros Keith.)

village that had been a station on the Underground Railroad. Some seventy miles from the Ohio River, it is home both for Antioch College and the descendants of abolitionists and fugitive slaves.

"I was the fifth child. My brothers and sisters were already intelligent, competitive and given to the family habit of staring off into space. Mother was the oldest daughter of a fugitive slave. My father was an outlander who ran gambling halls in mining towns. He was charming, talented, moody and forbidding. He and Mother were dollar poor in the thirties when I was born. Franklin Roosevelt's New Deal hadn't touched our household nor much of the Miami Valley where our village lay. But my parents turned acres of rich soil into a working farm with enough extra produce to sell by the bushel to the local grocer.

"By the time I was seven, I knew that life must be freedom; there was no better life than those acres and the surrounding farmlands. Being the 'baby' and bright, mind you, and odd and sensitive, I was left alone to discover whatever there was to find. I found all the neighbors and all my mother's Perry Clan—those cousins, aunts and uncles whose progenitor had lived in that corner of Ohio since before Emancipation.

"I learned early that the Perry Clan was more important than the house of Hamilton. My mother's 'people' were warm-hearted, tight with money, generous to the sick and the landless, close-mouthed and fond of telling tales and

gossip about one another and even their ancestors. They were a part of me from the time I understood that I belonged to all of them. My Uncle King told the best tall tales; my Aunt Leanna sang the finest sorrowful songs. My own mother could take a slice of fiction floating around the family and polish it into a saga. So could my father. He, having come from a Creole family that wandered the face of this country and Canada, was always a travelling man, if only in his mind.

"There was never any part of the world nor any incident in the black man's history that he didn't expound upon. He knew Jack London and Blind Lemon Jefferson, so he said. He was a superb mandolinist. He was bitter toward all unions because in his youth the musician's union would not give membership to blacks like him.

"I remember I could wake at any hour before dawn and hear the clear tones of his 1902 ivory inlaid Gibson mandolin. The sound was a comfort because I never liked the night. Daddy never liked it, either. He tried to conquer darkness through his haunting classic harmonies; I through the endless parade of figures that tramped across the reach of my mind.

"Ohio is surreal to me now. The past is fixed into symbol: my home is the warmth of clan and race. The fine valley soil is both freedom and internment. Like Zeely, I test my strength against darkness. In *The House of Dies Drear*, the scaring of the Darrows is as much a trial for me as it is for Thomas Small. Even now, I fear nothing so much as a silent, moonless Ohio night.

"After a leave of fifteen years when I lived in New York City, I return to that village. Knowing who and what I am, I can go home. With a bit of city style and humor I can claim what is left of the land. I am only reclaiming what was given to me without comment so long ago—that freedom and dependence which was partly happiness.

"There are new generations of the clan in the village. The cousins have children, as I do. So it is that the child of the outlander returns. With much of the gambler's instinct and something of the wanderer, I settle back with the coming of night to write in earnest. And that's happiness."

FOR MORE INFORMATION SEE: *Top of the News*, June, 1969; *Horn Book*, February, 1970, February, 1972; *Christian Science Monitor*, November 11, 1971.

HARPER, Wilhelmina 1884-

PERSONAL: Born April 21, 1884, in Farmington, Me.; daughter of William (an educator) and Bertha (Tauber) Harper. *Education:* Special courses at New York University, New York State Library School, and Columbia University. *Politics:* Democrat. *Religion:* Congregationalist. *Home:* 2385 Waverley St., Palo Alto, Calif. 94301.

CAREER: Queensboro Public Library, New York, N.Y., children's librarian and branch librarian, 1908-18; Pelham library assistant, 1918-19; Young Men's Christian Association, library organizer at Brest, France, 1919, assistant to director of Overseas Service, 1920; American Red Cross,

WILHELMINA HARPER

Chicago, Ill., field representative, 1920-21; Kern County Free Library, Bakersfield, Calif., organizer and supervisor of children's work, 1921-28; Redwood City Public Library, Redwood City, Calif., organizer and librarian, 1929-54. Instructor in children's literature at University of California and San Jose State College, 1929, and at Riverside Library School, 1929, 1932. Compiler of books for children. *Member:* American Library Association, California Library Association, Redwood City Woman's Club, Palo Alto Woman's Club.

WRITINGS—Anthologies compiled: *Story Hour Favorites*, Century, 1918; *Off Duty: A Dozen Yarns for Soldiers and Sailors*, Century, 1919; *Magic Fairy Tales*, Longmans, Green, 1926; *Fillmore Folk Tales*, Harcourt, 1926; *Stowaway and Other Stories for Boys*, Atlantic, 1928; *The Girl of Tiptop and Other Stories*, Altantic, 1928; (with A.J.

Such a ride does not come everybody's way, even on Halloween, and although Diccon's knees tried to knock together, he did as he was told.
■ (From *Ghosts and Goblins* by Wilhelmina Harper. Illustrated by William Wiesner.)

Hamilton) *Far Away Hills,* Macmillan, 1929; (with A.J. Hamilton) *Heights and Highways,* Macmillan, 1929; (with A.J. Hamilton) *Pleasant Pathways,* Macmillan, 1929; (with A.J. Hamilton) *Winding Roads,* Macmillan, 1929; *More Story Hour Favorites,* Century, 1929; *A Little Book of Necessary Ballads,* Harper, 1930; *Around the Hearthfire,* Appleton, 1931; *Mountain Gateways,* Macmillan, 1933; (with A.J. Hamilton) *Journey's End,* Macmillan, 1933; *Merry Christmas to You!* Dutton, 1935, new edition, 1965; *The Selfish Giant,* McKay, 1935; *Ghosts and Goblins,* Dutton, 1936, new edition, 1965; *The Gunniwolf and Other Merry Tales* (story collection; Junior Literary Guild selection), McKay, 1936; *The Lonely Little Pig* (Junior Literary Guild Selection), McKay, 1938; *The Harvest Feast,* Dutton, 1938, new edition, 1965; *Flying Hoofs,* Houghton, 1939; *Brownie of the Circus* (Junior Literary Guild selection), McKay, 1941; *Wings of Courage,* Appleton, 1941; *Easter Chimes,* Dutton, 1942, new edition, 1965; *For Love of Country,* Dutton, 1942; *Uncle Sam's Story Book,* McKay, 1944; *Yankee Yarns,* Dutton, 1944; *Where the Redbird Flies,* Dutton, 1946; (with Aimee M. Peters) *The Best of Bret Harte,* Houghton, 1947; *Down in Dixie,* Dutton, 1948; *Dog Show,* Hougton, 1950; *Gunniwolf* (picture book), Dutton, 1967.

School readers with Aymer J. Hamilton and Hollis P. Allen: *Pleasant Pathways, Winding Roads,* and *Far Away Hills,* three books, Macmillan, 1928, new editions, 1933; *Heights and Highways,* Macmillan, 1929, new edition, 1933; *Mountain Gateways* [and] *Journey's End* (two books), Macmillan, 1933.

School readers with Helen Heffernan and Gretchen Waulfing: *All Aboard for Story Land* and *Sails Set for Treasure Land,* Sanborn, 1941, new editions, 1953; *One to Adventure,* Sanborn, 1943, new edition, 1953.

WORK IN PROGRESS: Compiling more books for children.

SIDELIGHTS: "My anthologies have been the result of the long-felt need in schools and libraries for such books as my four holiday volumes for each season. Having worked with children in libraries east and west, and as a story-teller for many years, I came to know their needs and desires, also.

"My school readers, in collaboration with others, came about with the effort to provide a newer type of literature representing the works of leading authors for children.

"The whole idea in all my work has been to introduce boys and girls to the leading authors for young people, and with the hope of encouraging their reading habits."

FOR MORE INFORMATION SEE: Nancy Larrick, *A Teacher's Guide to Children's Books,* Merrill, 1966.

HARRIS, Janet 1932-

PERSONAL: Born April 17, 1932, in Newark, N.J.; daughter of Nathan (an attorney) and Ida (Lachow) Urovsky; formerly married to Martin Harris; children: Michael, Clint. *Education:* Ohio University, Athens, B.S.Ed., 1951. *Home:* 120 West Lena Ave., Freeport, N.Y. 11520. *Agent:* Dorothy Markinko, McIntosh & Otis, Inc., 18 East 41st St., New York, N.Y. 10017.

CAREER: Did fund raising and public relations work and wrote for radio during period, 1952-60; full-time writer, 1960—. Lecturer in English department, C.W. Post College, Long Island University, 1969, and Glen Cove Community College, State University of New York, 1970. Chairman for South Nassau, Women's Strike for Peace, 1964-65. *Member:* Authors League, Congress of Racial Equality (secretary of Long Island chapter, 1966-69). *Awards, honors:* Women's Press Club of New York City Award for "contribution to the literature of social protest."

WRITINGS: The Long Freedom Road: The Civil Rights Story (foreword by Whitney Young), McGraw, 1967; (with Julius Hobson) *Black Pride: A People's Struggle* (juvenile), McGraw, 1969; *Students in Revolt,* McGraw, 1970; *A Single Standard,* McGraw, 1971. Reviewer, *New York Times Book Review,* 1970-71.

WORK IN PROGRESS: Three books, one juvenile and two adult nonfiction.

SIDELIGHTS: "The theme of all my writing centers around my belief in the rights of the individual for freedom and self-expression, at the cost of non-violent revolution against authority. I am opposed to racism, sexism, to war, to the placing of property rights above human rights. I believe we are in the midst of a social revolution in which authoritarian values are being replaced with humane concepts and my work and my life are dedicated to this change in consciousness."

FOR MORE INFORMATION SEE: Newsday, April 22, 1969.

HARRIS, Leon A., Jr. 1926-

PERSONAL: Born June 20, 1926, in New York, N.Y.; son of Leon A. (a merchant) and Lucile (Herzfeld) Harris; married Marina Svetlova (a ballerina), September 10, 1963. *Education:* Phillips Academy at Andover, student, 1941-43; Harvard University, B.A., 1947. *Home:* 4512 Fairfax, Dallas, Tex. *Agent:* Harold Ober Associates, 40 East 49th St., New York, N.Y.

CAREER: A. Harris & Co. (department store), Dallas, Tex., executive vice-president, 1947-60.

Maurice thinks he might help her. ■ (From *The Great Picture Robbery* by Leon A. Harris. Illustrated by Joseph Schindelman.)

WRITINGS: The Night Before Christmas in Texas, Crown, 1952; *The Great Picture Robbery,* Atheneum, 1963; *Young France,* Dodd, 1964; *The Fine Art of Political Wit,* Dutton, 1964; *Only to God: A Biography of Godfrey Lowell Cabot,* Atheneum, 1967; *Maurice Goes to Sea,* Norton, 1968; *Young Peru,* Dodd, 1969; *The Moscow Circus School,* Atheneum, 1970; *The Russian Ballet School,* Atheneum, 1970; *Yvette,* McGraw, 1970; *Behind the Scenes in TV,* Lippincott, 1972; *Behind the Scenes in a Car Factory,* Lippincott, 1972; *Behind the Scenes in a Department Store,* Lippincott, 1972. Contributor to *Esquire, Harper's Bazaar, Good Housekeeping, McCall's,* and other American and foreign journals. Contributor of articles to *Encyclopedia Americana.*

WORK IN PROGRESS: A biography of Upton Sinclair, for Holt.

SIDELIGHTS: Competent in French.

HARRIS, Rosemary (Jeanne)

PERSONAL: Born in London, England; daughter of Arthur Travers (in Royal Air Force) and Barbara D.K. (Money) Harris. *Education:* Studied at Chelsea School of Art, London, and Courtauld Institute, London. *Politics:* Liberal. *Religion:* Church of England. *Home:* 33 Cheyne Court, Flood St., London SW3 5TR, England. *Agent:* Michael Horniman, A.P. Watt & Son, 26/28 Bedford Row, London, Eng.

CAREER: Writer and critic; one-time reader for Metro-Goldwyn-Mayer. *Member:* Society of Authors. *Awards, honors:* Carnegie Medal of Library Association (England) for outstanding children's book of 1968, *The Moon in the Cloud;* Arts Council grant for research, 1971.

WRITINGS—For adults: *The Summer House,* Hamish Hamilton, 1956; *Voyage to Cythera,* Bodley Head, 1958; *Venus with Sparrows,* Faber, 1961; *All My Enemies,* Faber, 1967, Simon & Schuster, in press; *The Nice Girl's Story,* Faber, 1968; *A Wicked Pack of Cards,* Faber, 1969, Walker & Co., 1970.

For pre-teens, except as noted: *The Moon in the Cloud,* Faber, 1968, Macmillan (ALA Notable Book, *Horn Book* Honor List), 1970; *The Shadow on the Sun,* Macmillan (New York), 1970; *The Seal-Singing,* Macmillan (New York), 1971; *The Child in the Bamboo Grove* (picture book for children based on Japanese legend; illustrated by Errol le Cain), Faber, 1971, S.G. Phillips, in press; *The Bright and Morning Star,* Macmillan (New York), 1972.

Contributor of reviews of children's books to *Times.*

WORK IN PROGRESS: Research on myths and legends for a book commissioned by Faber; also working on a new thriller.

SIDELIGHTS: "There are many, many different things which turn someone into a writer by profession, rather than someone who writes a book or two on the side as a relief from other activities. I always wrote—but equally I always painted, and was interested in music. Writing as a way of life is perhaps something that tends to happen instead of being deliberately chosen—unless one starts off with serious intentions as a journalist, and then gravitates to books.

"The turning point in my work was definitely my first book for children, *The Moon in the Cloud,* which got the Carnegie Medal. It was a book that almost seemed to write itself, everything fell into place with such ease; but, looking back, I see that it owed a great deal to my years of training as a painter in Chelsea. It was certainly there that I got a lot of my visual training which was a very strong element in that book, and one which the critics over here particularly noticed. And it was in the sculpture class with F.E. McWilliam and Henry Moore that I learned to love the Egyptians—particularly the sculpture of the Old Kingdom. Curiously enough, several people have asked me if I was influenced by Thomas Mann's *Joseph and His Brethren,* and the answer is 'Yes, I was,' but only *after* I'd written *The Moon in the Cloud*. I didn't read Mann's great work until later on; then I think it was a strong influence on my writing two other books to complete the trilogy—*The Shadow on the Sun* and *The Bright and Morning Star.*

(Jacket cover from *The Seal Singing* by Rosemary Harris. Illustrated by Emanuel Schongut.)

"*The Seal-Singing* owed a lot to my time in Scotland as a child, and later—and probably to some Scots ancestry. *The Child in the Bamboo Grove* is my first picture book; it's a gorgeous Japanese legend, retold, and has so far only been published over here. Errol le Cain has a terrific talent, and we're hoping to do some more work together."

HOBBIES AND OTHER INTERESTS: Theatre, music, photography.

FOR MORE INFORMATION SEE: Horn Book, April, 1970, October, 1970, February, 1972, April, 1972; *New York Times Book Review,* April 12, 1970; *Chicago Tribune Children's Book World,* November 8, 1970; *Books and Bookmen,* December, 1971; *Saturday Review,* May 20, 1972.

HARRISON, Harry (Max) 1925-

PERSONAL: Born March 12, 1925, in Stamford, Conn.; son of Leo and Ria (Kirjassoff) Harrison; married Joan Merkler, 1954; children: Todd, Moira. *Agent:* Robert P. Mills, Ltd., 156 East 52nd St., New York, N.Y. 10022.

CAREER: Free-lance commercial artist, 1946-55; free-lance writer, living in Mexico, England, Italy, Spain, and Denmark, 1956-66, California, 1967—. *Military service:* U.S. Army Air Corps, 1943-46, became sergeant.

WRITINGS: Deathworld, Bantam, 1960; *The Stainless Steel Rat,* Pyramid Books, 1961; *Planet of the Damned,*

ROSEMARY HARRIS

Bantam, 1962; *War with the Robots,* Pyramid Books, 1962; *Deathworld 2,* Bantam, 1964; *Bill, the Galactic Hero,* Doubleday, 1965; *Plague from Space,* Doubleday, 1965; *Make Room! Make Room!,* Doubleday, 1966; *The Technicolor Time Machine,* Doubleday, 1967; *The Man from P.I.G.* (juvenile), Avon, 1968; *Two Tales and 8 Tomorrows,* Bantam, 1968; *Deathworld 3,* Dell, 1968; *Captive Universe,* Putnam, 1969; (editor) *Tales of Wonder* (juvenile), Doubleday, 1969; *Spaceship Medic* (juvenile), Doubleday, 1970; *The Daleth Effect,* Putnam, 1970; *The Stainless Steel Rat's Revenge,* Walker, 1970; *Prime Number,* Berkley, 1970; *One Step from Earth,* Macmillan, 1970; *The Stainless Steel Rat Saves the World,* Putnam, 1972; *Tunnel Through the Deeps,* Putnam, 1972; (with L.E. Stover) *Stonehenge,* Scribner, 1972; *Montezuma's Revenge,* Doubleday, 1972; *Star Smashers of the Galaxy Rangers,* Putnam, 1973.

Editor: *The Collected Editorials of John W. Campbell,* Doubleday, 1966; (with Brian Aldiss) *Nebula Awards 2,* Doubleday, 1967; (with L.E. Stover) *Apeman, Spaceman,* Doubleday, 1968; *SF: Authors' Choice 1,* Berkley 1968; *Best SF: 1967,* Berkley, 1968; *Four for the Future,* Macdonald, 1969; *SF: Authors' Choice 2,* Berkley, 1970; *Best SF: 1969,* Putnam, 1970; *Nova 1,* Delacorte, 1970; *The Year 2000,* Doubleday, 1970; *SF: Authors' Choice 3,* Putnam, 1971; *The Light Fantastic,* Scribner, 1971; *Nova 2,* Walker, 1972; *Best SF: 1971,* Putnam, 1972; *SF: Authors' Choice 4,* Putnam, 1973. Editor, *SF Impulse,* 1966-67; co-editor and co-publisher, *SF Horizons,* 1966—.

(Jacket cover from *The Stainless Steel Rat's Revenge* by Harry Harrison. Illustrated by the author.)

HARRY HARRISON

SIDELIGHTS: "Drawing has always had a great affect on my writing, shaping it and aiding it. In New York City I did illustrations, book jackets, and comic books. Gradually I began to write and edit comics at the same time, sliding sidewise into editing other kinds of magazines—mostly science fiction for I have been a lifetime fan of SF. From editing, writing for the magazines was a next easy step that enabled me to leave art and move to Mexico to begin freelancing. But the visual sense that years of drawing gave me has always stood behind my stories enabling me to see scenes in all their color and detail and to then describe them to the reader.

"From Mexico I moved with my wife and two-year-old son to England and then to Italy, not only for the sheer pleasure of seeing different countries but for the background and inspiration of my work. Art indirectly supported these labors because, for the next ten years, I wrote the script for the 'Flash Gordon' comic strip. With our daughter just a few months old we then moved to Denmark where we stayed six years, learning to love the people, the country, even that strange language. While every summer we took the camper like other resident Europeans and traveled about visiting other countries, it must be forty in all. You'll find Yugoslavia in my short story 'Rescue Operation,' England in the novel *Stonehenge,* Denmark in the Viking adventures of *The Technicolor Time Machine.* You'll also find plenty about pigs in *The Man from P.I.G.* for they are fine animals and Denmark has plenty of large red ones.

"Though I have designed many of the covers of my books

I never drew one until I made a sketch for the layout of the jacket of the English edition of *The Stainless Steel Rat's Revenge* and was talked into doing the final drawing as well. Science fiction is popular around the world these days and my books have appeared in twenty languages including Japanese, German, Italian, Russian—even Latvian! This has helped me travel as well so that I have judged the science fiction film festival in Trieste, Italy, and have even flown to Rio de Janiero in Brazil for the SF festival there. Wonderful! And it all works for me. A camping trip all through Mexico produced the comic mystery of *Montezuma's Revenge* and a winter of solid skiing will be the background of another mystery novel. With a little effort a writer's life can be pure gold with every incident transmutable. Things have not always been easy; I can recall with a shiver that snowy winter on the Isle of Capri in Italy when sixteen cents was all we had to our name. But I also remember the next summer, swimming out a mile from shore to look back at that lovely island.

"Writing is very hard work. But I see no reason why there cannot be a lot of fun along the way."

HAUGAARD, Erik Christian 1923-

PERSONAL: Born April 13, 1923, in Frederiksberg,

ERIK CHRISTIAN HAUGAARD

He was seven years old, Dag of King's Acre; and he was alone. ■ (From *The Untold Tale* by Erik Christian Haugaard. Illustrated by Leo and Diane Dillon.)

Denmark; son of Gotfred Hans Christian (a professor of biochemistry) and Karen (Pedersen) Haugaard; married Myrna Seld (a writer), December 23, 1949; children: Mikka Anja, Mark. *Education:* Black Mountain College, student, 1941-42; New School for Social Research, student, 1947-48. *Home:* Veksebo, Pr. Fredensborg 3480, Denmark.

CAREER: Worked as farm laborer in Fyn, Denmark, 1938-40, and later as a sheep herder in Wyoming; now a writer of youth books, drama, and poetry. *Military service:* Royal Canadian Air Force, 1943-45; became flight sergeant; received War Service Medal from Christian X of Denmark. *Awards, honors:* John Golden Fund fellowship for play, "The Heroes," 1958; honorable mention, *New York Herald Tribune* Children's Spring Book Festival, 1962, for *Hakon of Rogen's Saga*, and 1967, for *The Little Fishes; Boston Globe* award, *Horn Book* award, 1967, Jane Addams Award, 1968, Danish Cultural Minister's Prize, 1970, all for *The Little Fishes*.

WRITINGS: Twenty-Five Poems, Squire Press, 1957;

Hakon of Rogen's Saga (ALA Notable Book), Houghton, 1963; *A Slave's Tale* (ALA Notable Book), Houghton, 1965; *Orphans of the Wind* (*Horn Book* Honor List), Houghton, 1966; *The Little Fishes* (*Horn Book* Honor List), Houghton, 1967; *Rider and His Horse* (*Horn Book* Honor List), Houghton, 1968; *The Untold Tale* (ALA Notable Book), Houghton, 1971; (translator) *Hans Christian Andersen's Fairy Tales,* Doubleday, 1973.

Plays: "The Heroes," "The President Regrets," "An Honest Man." Translator of Eskimo poetry, collected by Knud Rasmussen, for *American-Scandinavian Review*.

WORK IN PROGRESS: Translating all of Hans Christian Andersen's fairy tales and stories from Danish to English, for Doubleday.

SIDELIGHTS: "When I was a little boy, I used to tell myself stories, and in all of them I was the hero. I paid little attention to my own size, time, place, or even ideas. In the morning I could lead the French Revolution and in the afternoon be an aristocrat making a fine speech before my head was chopped off. But time catches all children in his net; some day they must grow up and lose their wings.

"Although I grew up and learned to distinguish between dreams and reality, the wish to tell stories remained. I was no longer the hero and a note of sadness had crept into my stories, for the purpose of telling them had changed. The stories I had told myself as a child had been dreams trying to explain an unknown world; now my stories dealt with a known world. I had grown up, been through a war, married and had children of my own. I had lived, experienced my share of happiness and sorrow, tested my strength and learned of my weakness.

"Man is forever lonely; but he has two friends whom he cannot lose, for though he may be unfaithful to them, they will never desert him. Nature and Art: ageless and eternal, they were there before we were born and will remain when we are gone. We are a part of nature which no end of scientific development can change, though it can distance us from it. Art: literature, music, painting, sculpture are the immortal parts of mortal man. This, too, we can deny; but only at the cost of greater loneliness. Hans Christian Andersen died long ago; but the fairy tales he wrote remain; if we do not read them the loss is not his but ours.

"No author can know whether his stories have enough truth in them to make them live forever. But if this is not his ambition, then I would not call him a humble man but a fraud. Once words are printed they take on a far greater importance than when they are spoken; therefore, especially when we write for children, we must only write what we consider to be the truth. Platitudes and lies are not harmless when they are disguised as truth and served to that audience which has the least experience with which to expose them.

"I have done my very best, knowing all the while that the greatest chance is that time will put away my books with a yawn. My hope has always been that my books will help some other human being—some other child—to feel a little less lonely, a little less lost, a little more comforted.

"To draw a portrait of yourself is difficult. I have as much vanity, pride, and foolishness within me as any other man. If I hadn't then I should not be able to write at all. But the private man—that mass of contradictions walking around on two legs—has always seemed less interesting to me than his work. It is the author's art, which should be our concern; it is that mirror we should reflect ourselves in."

Haugaard has long had a great interest in the Icelandic Sagas. He is fluent in Danish and Norwegian; knows some Swedish, Italian, and Spanish. His travels in the United States include a bicycle trip from San Francisco to Glacier Park, Mont., and a journey down the Yellowstone River in a Kayak.

FOR MORE INFORMATION SEE: Horn Book, June, 1971; *New York Times Book Review,* May 9, 1971, November 7, 1971; *Third Book of Junior Authors,* edited by de Montreville and Hill, Wilson, 1972.

HAUTZIG, Esther (Rudomin) 1930- (Esther Rudomin)

PERSONAL: Born October 18, 1930, in Vilno, Poland;

ESTHER HAUTZIG

daughter of Samuel and Chaja (Zunser) Rudomin; married Walter Hautzig (concert pianist), 1950; children: Deborah M., David R. *Education:* Hunter College, student, 1948-50. *Home:* 505 West End Ave., New York, N.Y. 10024. *Agent:* John Schaffner, 425 East 51st St., New York, N.Y.

CAREER: G.P. Putnam's Sons, New York, N.Y., secretary, 1950-52; Children's Book Council, New York, N.Y., publicity assistant, 1953; Thomas Y. Crowell Co., New York, N.Y., director of children's book promotion, 1954-59, consultant, 1961-68; free-lance children's book consultant, 1968—. *Awards, honors: Book World* Spring Book Festival Award and *Boston Globe* Honor Book Award, 1968, for *The Endless Steppe*; Synagogue, School and Center Division of Jewish Libraries named *The Endless Steppe* the "Best Jewish Novel," 1970; Jane Addams Book Award, 1969, and Lewis Carroll Shelf Award, 1971, for *The Endless Steppe*.

WRITINGS: *Let's Make Presents: 100 Easy-to-Make Gifts Under $1.00,* Crowell, 1962; *Redecorating Your Room for Practically Nothing,* Crowell, 1967; *The Endless Steppe: Growing Up in Siberia* (ALA Notable Book; *Horn Book* Honor list), Crowell, 1968; *In the Park: An Excursion in Four Languages,* Macmillan, 1968; *At Home: A Visit in Four Languages,* Macmillan, 1969; *In School: Learning in Four Languages,* Macmillan, 1969.

WORK IN PROGRESS: *Let's Make More Presents,* for Macmillan; a cookbook for Lothrop.

SIDELIGHTS: Ms. Hautzig wrote for *Horn Book* Magazine (October, 1970): "When we begin to write a book—and I use the word 'we' not in the royal or presidential manner, but merely as a reference to a group of people who spend their lives, or good parts of their

The school day is over.
Everyone goes home
with happy news of the first day
in school in San Francisco or San Sebastian,
Cherbourg or Odessa. ■ (From *In School* by Esther Hautzig. Illustrated by Nonny Hogrogian.)

lives, struggling with the typewriter—we do not, for the most part, say 'I am writing a book for children.' Some of us write with one person in mind only. Maia Wojciechowska said in one of her speeches that she wrote *Shadow of a Bull* for a girl she did not know but had seen on a bus one day. She just kept that girl in mind while she was writing her story.... A friend of mine says that you do not even have to know, or like, children to do books that will appeal to them or make them happy. All you have to do is write the book for yourself—thinking of yourself as the child you once were, and perhaps wish you were again, or still are. I personally cannot accept the notion that you do not have to like children to write books which they will read, but that is my problem, if problem it be. It seems to me that if one does not like children, one does not like people (for can one separate the two?), and then there is not any point in doing anything.

"I personally could no more write a book with a particular child in mind than I could climb Mount Everest; I would find it terribly intimidating. Nor do I think about 'writing a book for children' as if children were different

HAWES, Judy 1913-

PERSONAL: Born October 16, 1913, in New York, N.Y.; daughter of Edward Harris (a manufacturers' agent) and Lester (Baker) Mays; married John Hawes (a banker), June 6, 1936; children: John, Amanda (Mrs. David Fisher), Jane, Lester Ann. *Education:* Vassar College, A.B., 1934; Paterson State College (now William Paterson College), Teacher's Certificate, 1962. *Politics:* Democrat ("McCarthy delegate to Chicago"). *Religion:* Protestant. *Home:* 79 Abbington Ter., Glen Rock, N.J. 07452. *Office:* Coleman School, Pinelynn Rd., Glen Rock, N.J. 07452.

CAREER: Teacher of the handicapped, 1958—, presently at Coleman School, Glen Rock, N.J. *Member:* Council for Exceptional Children (chapter president, 1968-69). *Awards, honors:* New Jersey Association of English Teachers Book Award for each publication.

from adults, adolescents, octogenarians, or whatever. (I must exclude the writing of texts for picture books when making this statement.)

"When I started writing *The Endless Steppe* milleniums ago, I did not think of it as a book for children, nor did my agent. He sent the manuscript in its early stages to adult-trade editors. It did not sell to that audience, although I have a perfectly gorgeous collection of rejection letters. Begun in 1959, it was finally published in 1968 by a children's book department, but not one word in it was changed because it was published as a children's book instead of as an adult book. There were no parts to the story which would have been suitable for adults but not suitable for children. The cuts that were made, and over which I fought long and bitter battles, had nothing whatever to do with the fact that the book was being published for children and not for adults. (In England it is on both the adult and juvenile list of the same publisher.)

"It seems to me that some books we adults think are marvelous for children, the children themselves often reject. On the other hand, I often prefer reading children's books to reading the adult books published nowadays. Aside from the fact that I really do enjoy reading these books, they give me a most marvelous sense of sharing a special world with my children. It seems a pity to me that so many parents miss the pleasure of reading their children's books once they are past the picture-book age. Perhaps I have a case of arrested development. Or perhaps *for me* some children's books are better than some adult books. *For me* is, of course, a crucial point in discussing books. Books are like people, like friends, and one's chemical reactions to them cannot be really duplicated by anyone else's—much like fingerprints. A book may be universally liked but liked by a thousand people for a thousand different reasons and understood, or read, on a thousand different levels." (Copyright © 1970 by The Horn Book, Inc. Used with permission of the publisher and the author.)

FOR MORE INFORMATION SEE: *Publisher's Weekly*, February 17, 1969; *Horn Book*, December, 1969, October, 1970; *Third Book of Junior Authors*, edited by de Montreville and Hill, Wilson, 1972.

JUDY HAWES

Never forget that frogs are amphibians. They can live in the water or on land. But only so long as their skin stays wet! ■ (From *Why Frogs Are Wet* by Judy Hawes. Illustrated by Don Madden. Reprinted by permission of Thomas Y. Crowell Co.)

WRITINGS—"Let's-Read-and-Find-Out Science" series, published by Crowell: *Fireflies in the Night*, 1963; *Bees and Beelines*, 1964; *Watch Honeybees with Me*, 1964; *Shrimps*, 1967; *Ladybug, Ladybug, Fly Away Home*, 1967; *Why Frogs Are Wet*, 1968; *What I Like About Toads*, 1969; *The Goats Who Killed the Leopard*, Crowell, 1970; *Daddy Longlegs*, in press.

SIDELIGHTS: "I wrote and illustrated homemade books for my own children and for my first class of retarded children, which led to writing for T.Y. Crowell's science series.... For fun, I play tennis daily in summer, two and three times weekly in winter."

FOR MORE INFORMATION SEE: Horn Book, December, 1970.

HAWKINSON, John (Samuel) 1912-

PERSONAL: Born November 8, 1912, in Chicago, Ill.; son of John S. (a contractor) and Amy (Jackson) Hawkinson; married Lucy Ozone, September 20, 1954 (died December 6, 1971); children: Anne Miyo, Julia Eiko. *Politics:* Democrat.

CAREER: Painter; illustrator of four other books besides his own. Scoutmaster, thirteen years; Hyde Park Kenwood Community Conference, chairman of parks and recreation committee, one year. *Military service:* U.S. Army; awarded Bronze Star.

WRITINGS: (With wife, Lucy Hawkinson) *Winter Tree Birds*, A. Whitman, 1956; (with L. Hawkinson) *City Birds*, A. Whitman, 1957; *Robins and Rabbits*, A. Whitman, 1960; *Collect, Print and Paint from Nature*, A. Whitman, 1964; *More to Collect and Paint*, A. Whitman, 1964; *The Old Stump*, A. Whitman, 1965; *Birds in the Sky*, Childrens Press, 1965; *Where the Wild Apples Grow*, A. Whitman, 1966; *Our Wonderful Wayside*, A. Whitman, 1966; (with L. Ozone) *Little Boy Who Lives up High*, A. Whitman, 1967; *Pastels Are Great!*, A Whitman, 1968;

JOHN HAWKINSON

Music and Instruments for Children to Make, A. Whitman, 1969; *Rhythms, Music and Instruments to Make,* A. Whitman, 1969; *Paint A Rainbow,* A. Whitman, 1970; *Who Lives There?,* A. Whitman, 1970; *The Mouse that Fell Off the Rainbow,* A. Whitman, 1971; *Let Me Take You on a Trail,* A. Whitman, 1972.

SIDELIGHTS: "We now live in Michigan on a two-acre farm with two horses and a creek full of spearmint and watercress. We grind wheat for bread, eat wild foods, ski on the hills around us, and paddle down the river that flows near by. I am involved in 4-H and have a class in clay at the local library."

FOR MORE INFORMATION SEE: *Horn Book,* December, 1969.

tor, 1950-53; various jobs in industry, including production management and systems and procedures, 1953-56; General Precision Aerospace, Little Falls, N.J., technical writer, 1956-60, technical information manager, 1960-66; free-lance writer, 1966—. *Military Service:* U.S. Army, Medical Corps, 1945-47. *Member:* National Association of Science Writers, American Association for the Advancement of Science, World Future Society.

WRITINGS—For children or young adults, except as noted: *Navigation: Land, Sea and Sky,* Prentice-Hall, 1966; *The Art and Science of Color,* McGraw, 1967; *Controlled Guidance Systems* (adult), Howard W. Sams, 1967; *Light and Electricity in the Atmosphere,* Holiday House, 1968; *The Right Size: Why Some Creatures Survive and Others Are Extinct.* Putnam, 1968; *High*

Way up high in a tall pine tree
I saw a nest of sticks.
I wonder—
who lives up there? ■ (From *Who Lives There?* by John Hawkinson. Illustrated by the author.)

HELLMAN, Hal
See HELLMAN, Harold

HELLMAN, Harold 1927-
(Hal Hellman)

PERSONAL: Born September 15, 1927, in New York, N.Y.; son of Louis B. and Anna (Rosman) Hellman; married Sheila Almer (a dancer and teacher of dance), February 11, 1951; children: Jillana, Jennifer. *Education:* Hunter College, B.A., 1950; City College, New York, N.Y., M.A., 1955; Stevens Institute of Technology, M.S., 1961. *Home:* 100 High St., Leonia, N.J. 07605. *Agent:* Henry Morrison, Inc., 311 West 20th St., New York, N.Y. 10011.

CAREER: Free-lance photographer and interior decora-

Energy Physics, Lippincott, 1968; *Transportation in the World of the Future,* M. Evans, 1968; *Defense Mechanisms: From Virus to Man,* Holt, 1969; *Communications in the World of the Future,* M. Evans, 1969; *The City in the World of the Future,* M. Evans, 1969; *Energy and Inertia,* M. Evans, 1970; *Helicopters and Other VTOL's,* Doubleday, 1970; (with M. Klass) *The Kinds of Mankind* (*School Library Journal* Best Books list), Lippincott, 1971; *Biology in the World of the Future,* Evans, 1971; *The Lever and the Pulley,* Evans, 1971; *Feeding the World of the Future,* Evans, 1972; *Population,* Lippincott, 1972.

Author of booklets on lasers, spectroscopy, and nuclear particle detectors for U.S. Atomic Energy Commission, 1968, 1969, 1970. Contributor to *Journal of Navigation, Science Digest, Air Force, Popular Science, Coronet, Product Engineering,* and other scientific and popular periodicals.

HAL HELLMAN

WORK IN PROGRESS: A young-adult book, *Energy in the World of the Future,* for Evans.

SIDELIGHTS: "I am a full time, free-lance science writer. Although I have written for both specialists and the nontechnical public (especially young adults), I prefer to interpret science for the latter, believing that it is both more difficult and more rewarding.

"I came to science late in life, beginning my study at the age of thirty. When I decided to become a free-lance science writer I spent two years writing weekends and evenings to be sure that writing full time was what I wanted. It was."

FOR MORE INFORMATION SEE: *Bergen News,* Bergen, N.J., June 6, 1968.

HERRON, Edward A(lbert) 1912-

PERSONAL: Born June 5, 1912, in Philadelphia, Pa.; son of John F. and Margaret (Denney) Herron; married Loretta Martin, March 6, 1936; children: Dolores Herron Piper, David, Paul, Mark, Rosemary. *Education:* St. Joseph's College, Philadelphia, Pa., A.B., 1934. *Home:* 613 18th Ave., Manhattan Beach, Calif. *Agent:* August Lenniger, Lenniger Literary Agency, 11 West 42nd St., New York, N.Y. 10036.

CAREER: North American Rockwell, Pittsburgh, Pa., manager of executive speakers programs. *Awards, honors:* 1958 Commonwealth Club Award (San Francisco) for best juvenile book by a California author, for *First Scientist of Alaska.*

WRITINGS: *Life Returns to Die,* Benziger, 1934; *Alaska, Land of Tomorrow,* Whittlesey House, 1947; *The Big Country,* American Book Co., 1953; *Return of the Alaskan,* American Book Co., 1955; *Signal Hill,* Knopf, 1956; *Dimond of Alaska,* Messner, 1957; *First Scientist of Alaska,* Messner, 1958; *Wings Over Alaska,* Messner, 1959; *Alaska's Railroad Builder,* Messner, 1960; *Dynamite*

Johnny O'Brien, Messner, 1962; *Conqueror of Mt. McKinley: Hudson Stuck,* Messner, 1964; *Cobra in the Sky: The Supersonic Transport,* Collier, 1968; *Miracle of the Air Waves: A History of Radio,* Messner, 1969. Contributor of four hundred articles, the bulk of them on Alaskan subjects, to magazines.

SIDELIGHTS: "All my early recollections are of the oily Delaware River and the big-ocean-going ships my father's tug boat helped shove into a safe berth. I was supposed to be a school teacher, but immediately after graduation from St. Joseph's College in 1934 I shipped out as a merchant seaman on a freighter bound for South America.

"While still an undergraduate I had published my first book, *Life Returns,* and the arrival of my first royalty check on my return from South America was the perfect excuse for heading north to Alaska and the start of a long writing career involving that interesting part of the world!

"More than ten years ago I shifted to southern California and became directly involved as a writer in the space program, visiting and writing about practically every industrial and government space facility and activity in this nation and in many other countries throughout the world."

EDWARD A. HERRON

HESS, Lilo 1916-

PERSONAL: Born in 1916 in Erfurt, Germany. *Education:* Educated in European schools. *Home:* R.D. 2, East Stroudsburg, Pa. 18301.

CAREER: Animal photographer for magazines; writer and illustrator of children's books. *Awards, honors: Animals that Hide, Imitate and Bluff* was selected one of the Child Study Association's Books of the Year.

WRITINGS—Author and illustrator: *Christine, the Baby Chimp,* G. Bell, 1954; *Rabbits in the Meadow,* Crowell, 1963; *Easter in November,* Crowell, 1964; *Shetland Ponies,* Crowell, 1964; *The Timid Sheep,* Crowell, 1965; *Sea Horses,* Scribner, 1966; *Foxes in the Woodshed,* Scribner, 1966; *Pigeons Everywhere,* Scribner, 1967; *The Curious Raccoons,* Scribner, 1968; *The Remarkable Chameleon,* Scribner, 1968; *The Misunderstood Skunk,* Scribner, 1969; *Animals that Hide, Imitate and Bluff,* Scribner, 1970; *The Praying Mantis, Insect Cannibal,* Scribner, 1971; *Mouse & Co.,* Scribner, 1972; *Problem Pets,* Scribner, 1972; *Displaced Monkeys and Apes,* Scribner, 1973.

Illustrator: Dorothy C. Hogner, *Odd Pets,* Crowell, 1951; Irmengarde Eberle, *Fawn in the Woods,* Crowell, 1962.

SIDELIGHTS: "When I was a child I brought home a stray, mangy dog. Although my parents seldom objected to pets, I was forbidden to bring the dog into the house. I cried bitterly, emptied my piggybank, took the dog to a veterinarian and asked him to cure it and find a home for it. My interest in animals was genuine and persistent and every vacation I collected and observed small creatures. The wonder of a caterpillar changing into a butterfly or that of a tadpole and its metamorphosis into a frog held a fascination for me which never waned. Born in a small town in Germany, I grew up in Berlin. Zoology was my chief interest in school and after graduation, I continued to attend lectures and courses in that field. I attended finishing school in Switzerland and later studied photography at the Photographic School in Berlin and the Polytechnic School in London.

"For most people there is a sharp dichotomy between work and pleasure, but I succeeded in combining my profound and abiding interest in zoology with my special hobby of photography. Although I had studied commercial photography and had received several prizes for animal pictures which I had photographed at the zoo, it was not until I attended school in England that I began to do animal photography as a specialty. It was there that I met a commercial photographer who had been assigned to make a children's book about zoo animals. Although an excellent photographer, he lacked the patience required to take animal pictures and asked me to do the book for him. The event marked the inception of a career of challenge and fulfillment.

"In 1938 I came to America and began working as a volunteer for the American Museum of Natural History in New York City. The following year I joined the World's Fair, making animal postcards and publicity pictures for Frank Buck, a famous animal exhibitor. Before I began to get assignments from newspapers and magazines, I also

LILO HESS

served as a special assignment photographer at the Bronx Zoo. My articles and photographs have appeared in magazines in both Europe and America and many have been featured in *Life* Magazine.

"Today I divide my time between my home in Brooklyn and a farm in Pennsylvania. Most of the animals recorded in the picture stories and books which I created were found in the fields, woods and swamps surrounding the farm. I regard every book as a new challenge. In order to photograph a complete life history of one animal, I often have to raise two or three generations of this species to get the animals tame enough to allow me to approach them when they have young ones. Some books are three years in preparation. A lot of research has to be done, which brings me into contact with many scientists and other interesting people. The photographic technique has to be automatic so that all the time can be spent on watching the subject. I hope that my books will enable young people to see how important it is to preserve all the animals around them."

HIBBERT, Christopher 1924-

PERSONAL: Born March 5, 1924, in Enderby, Leicestershire, England; son of H.V. Hibbert (canon); married Susan Piggford, 1948; children: James, Tom, Kate. *Education:* Radley College, student, 1937-42; Oriel College, University of Oxford, M.A., 1948. *Home:* 64 St. Andrew's Rd., Henley-on-Thames, Oxfordshire, England. *Agent:* David Higham Associates Ltd., 5-8 Lower John St., Golden Square, London, W.1, England.

CAREER: Author. *Military service:* Royal Army, Infantry, four years; twice wounded, became captain; awarded the Military Cross. *Member:* Royal Society of Literature (fellow). *Awards, honors:* Royal Society of Literature award, 1962, for *The Destruction of Lord Raglan*.

WRITINGS: The Road to Tyburn, World Publishing, 1958; *King Mob,* World Publishing, 1959; *Wolfe at Quebec,* World Publishing, 1960; *Corunna,* Macmillan, 1961; *Il Duce,* Little, 1962; *The Destruction of Lord Raglan.* Little, 1962; *The Battle of Arnheim,* Macmillan, 1962; *The Roots of Evil,* Little, 1963; *Agincourt,* Dufour, 1964; *The Court at Windsor,* Harper, 1965; *Garibaldi and His Enemies,* Little, 1966; *Waterloo: Napoleon's Last Campaign,* New American Library, 1966; *The Making of Charles Dickens,* Harper, 1967; *Charles I,* Harper, 1968; *The Grand Tour,* Putnam, 1969; *The Search for King Arthur,* American Heritage Publishing, 1969; *London: The Biography of a City,* Morrow, 1970; *The Dragon Wakes: China and the West,* Harper, 1971; *The Personal History of Samuel Johnson,* Harper, 1972.

HOBBIES AND OTHER INTERESTS: Painting, gardening, collecting eighteenth- and early nineteenth-century caricatures.

CHRISTOPHER HIBBERT

This regal figure sat in the stern of the boat, holding a fishing line, while his companions tended the craft. ■ (From *The Sword and the Grail* retold by Constance Hieatt. Illustrated by David Palladini. Reprinted by permission of Thomas Y. Crowell Co.)

HIEATT, Constance B(artlett) 1928-

PERSONAL: Born February 11, 1928, in Boston, Mass.; daughter of Arthur Charles and Eleonora (Very) Bartlett; married A. Kent Hieatt (college professor), October 25, 1958. *Education:* Smith College, student, 1945-47; Hunter College, A.B., 1953, M.A., 1957; Yale University, Ph.D., 1959. *Religion:* Anglican. *Home:* 191 St. James St., London 11, Ontario, Canada. *Office:* The University of Western Ontario, London 72, Ontario, Canada.

CAREER: Held various positions of a secretarial or editorial nature, mostly in publishing, some teaching, 1948-57; City College of New York, lecturer in English, 1959-60; Queensborough Community College, assistant professor of English, 1960-64, associate professor, 1964-65; St. John's University, Jamaica, N.Y., associate professor of English, 1965-68, professor, 1968-70; University of Western Ontario, London, Ontario, professor of English, 1970—. *Member:* Modern Language Association, Mediaeval Academy of America, Association of Canadian University Teachers of English, International Arthurian Society, The Society for the Advancement of Scandinavian Study, Authors Guild of America.

WRITINGS: (With A. Kent Hieatt) *The Canterbury Tales of Geoffrey Chaucer* (adaptation for young readers), Golden Press, 1961; (translator) *Sir Gawain and the Green Knight* (adaptation for young readers), Crowell, 1967; (compiler) *Beowulf, and Other Old English Poems,* Odyssey, 1967; *The Realism of Dream Visions: The Poetic Exploitation of the Dream-Experience in Chaucer and His Contemporaries,* Mouton, 1967, Humanities, 1968; *The Knight of the Lion* (adaptation), Crowell, 1968; *Essentials of Old English,* Crowell, 1968; *The Knight of the Cart,* Crowell, 1969; (editor with A. Kent Hieatt) *Edmund Spenser: Selected Poetry,* Appleton, 1970; (editor) *The Miller's Tale of Geoffrey Chaucer,* Odyssey, 1970; (adaptor) *The Joy of the Court,* Crowell, 1971; (adaptor) *The Sword and the Grail,* Crowell, 1972.

SIDELIGHTS: "Most of my childhood memories are of my mother urging me to put down that book and go out and *play*. So no one was terribly surprised when I grew up to become a scholar and teacher of literature—except, probably, my high school classmates, among whom I carefully cultivated a reputation as a Dizzy Blonde. Combining more academic pursuits with writing for children came naturally to me, since my father also wrote for children as well as adults.

"It does not seem to me that adapting medieval literature for young people can be termed a 'sideline' or, much less, a distraction from my scholarly interests and professional duties: I love medieval literature, and enjoy reading it, studying it, contributing to scholarly understanding of it, teaching it, and, consequently, re-shaping it to make it available to a new generation of readers. Fortunately, my husband shares my interest in the period, and is even willing to sample occasional dishes prepared from recipes in medieval cookbooks."

FOR MORE INFORMATION SEE: New York Times Book Review, April, 1967; *Book Week,* May 21, 1967; *Horn Book,* December, 1969.

HAL HIGDON

HIGDON, Hal 1931-
(Lafayette Smith)

PERSONAL: Born June 17, 1931, in Chicago, Ill.; son of H.J. (an editor) and Mae (O'Leary) Higdon; married Rose Musacchio, April 12, 1958; children: Kevin, David, Laura. *Education:* Carleton College, B.A., 1953. *Politics:* Democrat. *Home:* 2815 Lake Shore Dr., Michigan City, Ind. 46360. *Agent:* Max Siegel & Associates, 154 East Erie, Chicago, Ill. 60611.

CAREER: The Kiwanis Magazine, Chicago, Ill., assistant editor, 1957-59; free-lance magazine writer, 1959—. *Military service:* U.S. Army, 1954-56. *Member:* Society of Magazine Writers.

WRITINGS: The Union vs. Dr. Mudd, Follett, 1964; *Heroes of the Olympics,* Prentice-Hall, 1965; *Pro Football USA,* Putnam, 1968, published as *Inside Pro Football,* Grosset, 1970; *The Horse that Played Center Field,* Holt, 1969; *The Business Healers,* Random House, 1970; *On the Run from Dogs and People,* Regnery, 1971; *Thirty Days in May: The Indy 500,* Putnam, 1971; *Champions of the Tennis Court,* Prentice-Hall, 1971; *The Electronic Olympics,* Holt, 1971.

WORK IN PROGRESS: The autobiography of Hank Stram, coach of the Kansas City Chiefs; a book of interviews with race drivers to be titled *Finding the Groove; Six Seconds to Glory: The Dragnationals,* for Putnam, "will probably spend several years in research before publishing."

SIDELIGHTS: "A long distance runner, I was the first American to finish in the 1964 Boston Marathon. I have won several national championships and set several national records (which no longer stand). In 1971 I placed first in the 10,000 meter run at the U.S. Masters Championships (for runners over forty) and also won the U.S. Masters cross country race.

"My running career and background has affected some of what I have written. Three of my books, for instance, have running backgrounds including my most recent, *The Electric Olympics,* which was described in a review for *School Library Journal* as the best sports novel of the year. I am interested in all sports, however.

"I enjoy watching the pro football games on Sunday and that was part of my motivation for doing *Pro Football USA.* I am currently in the midst of contract negotiations for another adult football book. One of my publishers asked me to do a book on the Indianapolis 500 and when I went down to see that race I became so fascinated by the sport that I became an autoracing fan, again. (I had gone to a lot of races when I was in high school, then had lost interest partly because my running career consumed so much of my time.)

"I am also motivated by my children, particularly my two boys, who are avid sports fans. When I wrote *The Horse that Played Center Field,* I named the main hero Kevin after my oldest son. In *The Electronic Olympics,* the hero was David, my second son. I am going to have to do at least one more sports novel with a girl as a heroine, otherwise my Laura will feel she is being cheated."

FLORENCE HIGHTOWER

HIGHTOWER, Florence (Cole) 1916-

PERSONAL: Born June 9, 1916, in Boston, Mass.; daughter of George Euart (lawyer) and Josephine (Sahr) Cole; married James Robert Hightower (sinologist), June 1, 1940; children: James Robert, Jr., Samuel Cole,

I don't know what they put into cookies now to make them taste so bad ... They tried again and again, sipping their tea, until Mrs. Wappinger found a cookie she liked. ■ (From *Mrs. Wappinger's Secret* by Florence Hightower. Illustrated by Beth and Joe Krush.)

Josephine, Thomas Denzil. *Education:* Vassar College, A.B., 1937. *Home:* 321 Central St., Auburndale, Mass.

WRITINGS: Mrs. Wappinger's Secret, 1955, *The Ghost of Follonsbee's Folly,* 1958, *Dark Horse of Woodfield,* 1962, *Fayerweather Forecast,* 1967, *The Secret of the Crazy Quilt,* 1972 (all published by Houghton).

FOR MORE INFORMATION SEE: Saturday Review, May 20, 1972; *Third Book of Junior Authors,* edited by de Montreville and Hill, Wilson, 1972.

HILL, Kathleen Louise 1917-
(Kay Hill)

PERSONAL: Born April 7, 1917, in Halifax, Nova Scotia, Canada; daughter of Henry and Margaret Elizabeth (Ross) Hill. *Education:* Attended schools in Halifax, Nova Scotia, Canada. *Religion:* Protestant. *Home:* Ketch Harbour, Nova Scotia, Canada. *Agent:* Collins-Knowlton-Wing, 60 East 56th St., New York, N.Y. 10022.

CAREER: Secretary and court reporter before becoming full-time free-lance writer, 1957—. *Member:* Association of Canadian Television and Radio Artists, Authors' Association. *Awards, honors:* Canadian Library Award, Book-of-the-Year-for-Children, 1969, for *And Tomorrow the Stars;* Vicky Metcalf Award ($1000), for a "body of work inspirational to Canadian youth."

WRITINGS—Under name Kay Hill: *Glooscap and His*

KAY HILL

He remembered every detail of that sail to Dini's, every breath of wind, every rock and shallow, every fishing cove they passed on the way. He wished the day would never end. ■ (From *And Tomorrow the Stars* by Kay Hill. Illustrated by Laszlo Kubinyi.)

Magic: Legends of the Wabanaki Indians, Dodd, 1963; *Three to Get Married* (three-act comedy), Samuel French, 1964; *Badger, the Mischief Maker,* Dodd, 1965; *Cobbler, Stick to Thy Last* (one-act play; produced in Ottawa at National Arts Centre, July 5, 1969), Dramatic Publishing, 1967; *And Tomorrow the Stars: The Story of John Cabot,* Dodd, 1968; *More Glooscap Stories: Legends of the Wabanaki Indians,* Dodd, 1970. Anthologized in *Beyond the Footlights,* edited by Hugh Duncan McKellar, Macmillan, 1963; children's stories and plays appear in other anthologies. Writer of radio and television plays, short stories, articles, serials, and documentaries.

WORK IN PROGRESS: A children's book on the modern Indian, for Dodd.

SIDELIGHTS: "There's not much to tell about myself. I've always liked writing, especially fiction, and had pieces published in Sunday school and school magazines to begin with. For years I wrote spasmodically, selling nothing, then I found a market in radio and later in television, and one television show for children 'Indian Legends' led to the writing of *Glooscap and his Magic* and the other two Glooscap books. *And Tomorrow the Stars,* the fictionized biography of John Cabot, the explorer, was written with the help of a Canada Council Grant. This paid for a long summer in Europe where I followed the trail of Cabot from Genoa where he was supposed to have been born, through the Mediterranean, to Spain and Portugal and England and finally across the ocean to North America, getting background material for the book.

"When I haven't been writing, I've been an office worker, private secretary and court stenographer in various businesses—oil company, trust company, rubber manufacturer, public library and an historic site. Whenever I could, I gave up my office job and took a few months or a year off just to write. When the money ran out, I went back to stenography. Gradually I was able to write full time.

"I write to earn my living in the way that I find most enjoyable—and I write to communicate, to make people laugh and cry (I hope) especially children. I use everyday experiences as well as history, present and past, for ideas and background. I read philosophy sometimes to get myself started on something—it works for some reason. I find that unless I am moved, even a little, by what I am writing, I cannot move others—so I wait for that little jolt in the interior that says 'yes, this is it—keep on.'

"There's not much money in writing, the way I write—perhaps I'm a bit lazy. I decided after the European trip that I had better move from high-priced city apartments and live *cheaply* in the country unless I wanted to increase my output to the point of exhaustion—I was lucky. I found a 120-year old house at Ketch Harbour, a fishing village near Halifax, once the home of fishermen, with low ceilings and a stone fireplace and a big roomy kitchen—and I've been living *richly* ever since! For two years and a half now. I got a cat the day I moved in, and this time last year a stray came to the door, so now the two of them and I are a family. Tinker is a big gray Maltese, Chris is a short plump tortoiseshell.

"The kitchen has a half door and, winter and summer, there's usually someone leaning over it. The village has a lot of children and I enjoy their visits—they wash my dishes, make my bed, use a corner of the kitchen for their 'art work,' (drawing and painting). They help me paper the walls and paint the woodwork and cook and make decorations for Christmas—and when I have to work and can't have company, I hang a fisherman's glass buoy in a net on the door and that's the notice I don't want to be disturbed—'Miss Hill's Busy Ball,' they call it.

"I'm learning to grow vegetables, organically, and I'm a disciple of the Euell Gibbons books—a grand excuse for roaming the countryside with the cats and the kids when I ought to be in my den working. I have too many visitors in summer for the good of my work too, but I can't close my door to a friendly face."

HOBBIES AND OTHER INTERESTS: Oil painting, Scottish country dancing.

FOR MORE INFORMATION SEE: Horn Book, August, 1970; *Profiles,* Canadian Library Association, 1971.

HILL, Kay
See HILL, Kathleen Louise

HILTON, Suzanne 1922-

PERSONAL: Born September 3, 1922, in Pittsburgh, Pa.; daughter of Edwin P. (an insurance broker) and Helen (McFeely) McLean; married Warren Mitchell Hilton (an insurance engineer), June 15, 1946; children: Edwin Bruce, Diana Lester. *Education:* Pennsylvaina College for Women (now Chatham College), student, 1940-43; Beaver College, B.A., 1945. *Religion:* Methodist. *Home:* 301 Runnymede Ave., Jenkintown, Pa. 19046.

CAREER: Public relations writer for a school district and researcher and copywriter for advertising department of Westminster Press, Philadelphia, Pa. *Member:* Philadelphia Children's Reading Round Table, Free Library of Philadelphia. *Awards, honors: How Do They Get Rid of It?* and *How Do They Cope With It?* were selected books of the year by the Child Study Association.

WRITINGS: How Do They Get Rid of It? (Junior Literary Guild selection), Westminster, 1970; *How Do They Cope with It?* (juvenile), Westminster, 1970; *It's Smart to Use a Dummy* (Junior Literary Guild selection),

SUZANNE HILTON

Westminster, 1971; *It's a Model World* (Junior Literary Guild selection), Westminster, 1972. Contributor of short stories and articles to periodicals.

SIDELIGHTS: "One rejection slip doesn't mean you're a hopeless case as a writer. But I wish I'd known that when my first rejection came—just after high school. It was many years before I tried writing again and sold my first story. By the time I sold my first book, I had an enviable collection of rejection slips.

"The years between were filled with a heap of living. Our children led my husband and me a merry chase through Scouts, camping, sailing, travel, and a houseful of exchange students from many countries. Our son is now married and in another year he will be a doctor. Our daughter spent a year as an exchange student to Japan and in another year she will be a teacher. Now my husband and I do together those fun things we used to do with the children.

"I enjoy researching for a book so much that it's hard to sit down at the typewriter and put the notes in some semblance of order. The basic information comes from libraries and fortunately Philadelphia has a good supply of them—medical libraries, maritime, art, natural history, science, historical, as well as the regular library. But nothing takes the place of a visit to the actual scene—sailing on an oil-slicked river, running your hand along the polished stainless steel wall of a supersonic wind tunnel, shaking hands with a dummy that has been battered from daily trips in a centrifuge.

"The nicest part about being a writer is that there is no experience in life that does not help you become a better one. From shopping at the local grocery (I once saw two policeman corner a car thief at the meat counter) to waggling an orange smoke flare and praying for the Coast Guard to come when your sailboat loses its rudder—all of living is the author's source of ideas."

HOBBIES AND OTHER INTERESTS: Camping, travel, reading, swimming, hiking, acting in local little theatre group, choral groups, photography, sailing around Chesapeake Bay.

FOR MORE INFORMATION SEE: Junior Literary Guild Catalogue, September, 1972.

HISER, Iona Seibert 1901-

PERSONAL: Born January 30, 1901, in Pemberville, Ohio; daughter of Frederick Wellington and Pearl (Bell) Seibert; married Noble M. Hiser (former school principal), June 13, 1922; children: Donald Howard, Leland Ladd. *Education:* Studied at Park College, 1919-21, Wooster College, 1922-23, watercoloring under Gerry Pierce, 1945, at University of Arizona Evening School, 1954, and Tucson Adult Evening School, 1957-58. *Politics:* Republican. *Religion:* Presbyterian. *Home and office:* 3019 East Drachman, Tucson, Ariz. 85716.

CAREER: Rural school, Carey, Ohio, teacher, 1921. Sunday school teacher, 1935-65. *Member:* Arizona

IONA SEIBERT HISER

Manuscripters, Tucson Writers' Workshop, Society of Southwestern Authors, Families for International Friendship, Civic Unity, P.E.O. Sisterhood, 49'ers Square Dance Club.

WRITINGS: (Author, illustrator) *Desert Drama,* Abelard, 1956; *From Scales to Fancy Feathers,* Rand, 1962; *The Coyote,* Steck, 1968; *The Mountain Lion,* Steck, 1970; *Collared Peccary—The Javelina,* Steck, 1971; *The Gila Monster,* Steck, 1972; *The Pronghorn,* Steck, 1973. Short stories and articles in magazines and newspapers.

WORK IN PROGRESS: More natural history books for young people, *The American Alligator, The California Condor,* and *The Bighorn Sheep;* "also hope to do further articles on natural history."

SIDELIGHTS: "My desire to write began in childhood, but it took me years to know which I liked best, watercol-

The mother coyote is very protective. ■ (From *The Coyote* by Iona Seibert Hiser. Illustrated by J. M. Roever.)

oring or writing. In school I enjoyed the classes associated with books: reading, literature, storywriting—even grammar and spelling! Since I have loved to read ever since childhood I began early in life to want to write. But because I also liked painting, I worked at that more during the first half of my life. I did not work very consistently at writing until my two sons were grown. Because they, as boys, had been very interested in animals—often bringing home from their desert wanderings horned toads, lizards, or ground squirrels—and since I too am an animal lover, writing about nature easily became my chosen subject. My first two books deal chiefly with my own and my family's experiences with the flora and fauna of the Arizona desert—our home country. The four later books are included in Steck-Vaughn's 'Wildlife' series, written for children in grammar school.

"Because of my deep interest in nature study, I have become an ardent advocate of conservation. I am very much opposed to industrial pollution of our land and waters, which kills our plants and wildlife; and am intensely interested in the battle to save endangered animal species. One of the pleasures which my husband and I enjoy is watching the birds that come to eat at the feeders outside our dining room picture window." Ms. Hiser has exhibited watercolors in Tucson Fine Arts Show.

HOBBIES AND OTHER INTERESTS: Photography, travel, reading, watercoloring, nature study, raising flowers, square dancing, and bicycling for miles at a trip.

HOFFMAN, Phyllis M. 1944-

PERSONAL: Born September 7, 1944, in New York, N.Y.; daughter of Morris and Bertha (Levine) Hoffman. *Education:* Harper College, B.A., 1965. *Politics:* Liberal/radical. *Religion:* Jewish. *Home:* 49 Eighth Ave., New York, N.Y. 10014.

CAREER: Harper & Row Publishers, Inc., New York, N.Y., children's book editor, 1965-70; Abelard-Schuman Ltd., New York, N.Y., children's book editor, 1970—. Teacher at New York City Vacation Day Camps.

WRITINGS: Steffie and Me, Harper, 1970; (editor of German translation) *The Ugly Duckling,* Abelard, 1972.

WORK IN PROGRESS: Several children's books.

HOBBIES AND OTHER INTERESTS: Art, dance, music, cooking, baking, movies, photography, anthropology, psychology.

PHYLLIS M. HOFFMAN

Our room is on the first floor. It has lots and lots of windows with stupid tulips on them. ■ (From *Steffie and Me* by Phyllis Hoffman. Illustrated by Emily McCully.)

HOGNER, Dorothy Childs

PERSONAL: Born in New York, N.Y.; daughter of Albert Ewing (a physician) and Amelia (McGraw) Childs; married Nils Hogner (an artist, illustrator, and mural painter), July 23, 1932 (died, 1970). *Education:* Wellesley College, student, 1923-24; University of New Mexico, B.A., 1936. *Politics:* Republican. *Home:* Hemlock Hill Herb Farm, Litchfield, Conn. 06759.

CAREER: Writer, principally of juvenile books illustrated by her husband. Runs Hemlock Hill Herb Farm in the Berkshires and sells herb plants. *Member:* Authors League of America, Garden Club of America, Herb Society of America.

WRITINGS—Adult: *South to Padre* (travel), Longmans, Green, 1936; *Westward: High, Low and Dry* (travel), Dutton, 1938; *Summer Roads to Gaspe* (travel), Dutton, 1939; *Herbs from the Garden to the Table,* Oxford University Press, 1953; *A Fresh Herb Platter,* Doubleday, 1961; *Gardening and Cooking on Terrace and Patio,* Doubleday, 1964.

DOROTHY CHILDS HOGNER

Juvenile—All except one book illustrated by her husband, Nils Hogner: *Navajo Winter Nights,* Thomas Nelson, 1935; *Education of a Burro,* Thomas Nelson, 1936; *Santa Fe Caravans,* Thomas Nelson, 1937; *Little Esther,* Thomas Nelson, 1937; *Lady Bird,* Oxford University Press, 1938; *Old Hank Weatherbee,* Oxford University Press, 1939; *Pancho,* Thomas Nelson, 1939.

Don't Blame the Puffins, Oxford University Press, 1940; *Stormy, the First Mustang,* Oxford University Press, 1941 (published in England as *Stormy, the First American Mustang,* Hutchinson, 1944); *Children of Mexico,* Heath, 1942; *The Animal Book: American Mammals North of Mexico,* Oxford University Press, 1942; *The Bible Story,* Oxford University Press, 1943; *Our American Horse,* Thomas Nelson, 1944; *Reward for Brownie,* Oxford University Press, 1944; *Farm Animals, and Working and Sporting Breeds of the United States and Canada,* Oxford University Press, 1945; *Unexpected Journey: The Story of a Dog,* Creative Age Press, 1945; *Winky, King of the Garden,* Oxford University Press, 1946; *Blue Swamp,* Oxford University Press, 1947; *Barnyard Family,* Oxford University Press, 1948; *Daisy: A Farm Fable,* Oxford University Press, 1949.

Dusty's Return, Oxford University Press, 1950; *Odd Pets* (illustrated with photographs by Lilo Hess), Crowell, 1951; *Wild Little Honker,* Oxford University Press, 1951; *Snowflake,* Oxford University Press, 1952; *Earthworms,* Crowell, 1953; *The Horse Family,* Oxford University Press, 1953; *The Dog Family,* Oxford University Press, 1954; *Wide River,* Lippincott, 1954; *Spiders,* Crowell, 1955; *Rufus,* Lippincott, 1955; *Frogs and Polliwogs,*

This big, distinctive, and odd-looking owl, with the heart-shaped facial disc and very long legs, has extremely keen hearing that enables it to catch prey on the darkest nights. ■ (From *Birds of Prey* by Dorothy Childs Hogner. Illustrated by Nils Hogner. Reprinted by permission of Thomas Y. Crowell Co.)

Crowell, 1956; *The Cat Family*, Oxford University Press, 1956; *Conservation in America*, Lippincott, 1958; *Snails*, Crowell, 1958.

Grasshoppers and Crickets, Crowell, 1960; *Water Over the Dam*, Lippincott, 1960; *Butterflies*, Crowell, 1962; *Water Beetles*, Crowell, 1963; *Moths*, Crowell, 1964; *A Book of Snakes*, Crowell, 1966; *Weeds*, Crowell, 1968; *Birds of Prey*, Crowell, 1969.

WORK IN PROGRESS: A children's book on insect control in the garden, field, pasture, and woods without the use of poisonous chemicals, for Crowell.

FOR MORE INFORMATION SEE: *Junior Book of Authors,* edited by Kunitz and Haycraft, 2nd edition Wilson, 1951.

HOLT, Margaret 1937-

PERSONAL: Born August 22, 1937, in Buffalo, N.Y.; daughter of Edward Henry (a contractor) and Estella (Bulkley) Holt; married Tat Parish (an attorney), May 30, 1965 (divorced May, 1970); children: Amy Randall, Tat David. *Education:* Elmira College, B.A., 1958; Simmons College, M.L.A., 1964. *Politics:* Democrat. *Religion:* Unitarian. *Address:* 1542I Spartan Village, East Lansing, Mich. 48823. *Office:* 301C Erickson Hall, Michigan State University, East Lansing, Mich. 48823.

CAREER: Boston (Mass.) Public Library, children's assistant and librarian, 1961-65; Niles (Mich.) Public Library, children's librarian, 1965-66; Lake Michigan College, teacher of children's literature, 1966-71. Currently graduate assistant at Michigan State University, working on a doctorate in children's literature. *Member:* American Association of University Women, National Council of Teachers of English.

WRITINGS: *David McCheever's 29 Dogs,* Houghton, 1963.

WORK IN PROGRESS: "Probably doctoral thesis on storytelling or folklore."

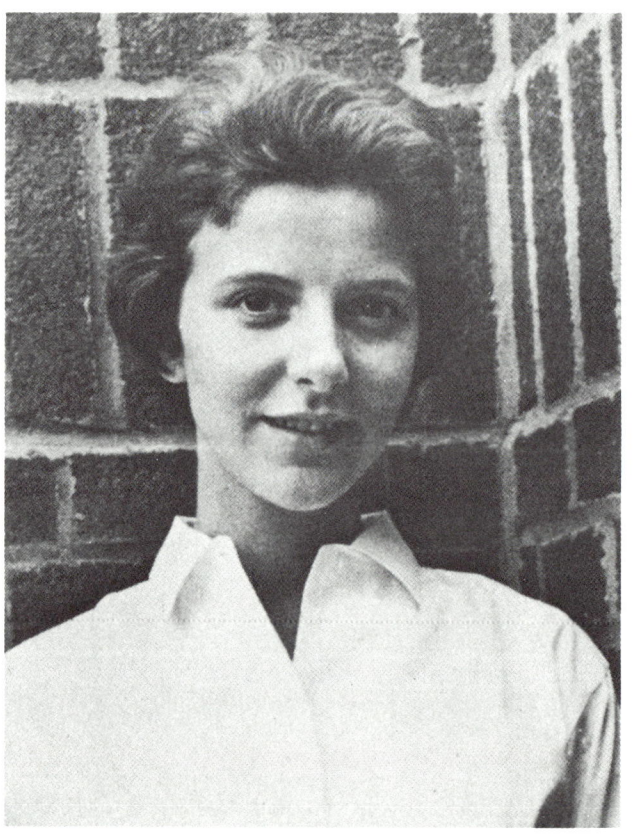

MARGARET HOLT

David McCheever's family had just moved into a new house. ■ (From *David McCheever's 29 Dogs* by Margaret Holt. Illustrated by Walter Lorraine.)

HOOD, Joseph F. 1925-

PERSONAL: Born August 12, 1925, in Philadelphia, Pa.; son of Joseph A. (an insurance broker) and Mary F. (McNally) Hood; married Helen Chopko (a department store executive), 1948. *Education:* "Proud High school grad. Preferred to continue flying career rather than college. Am a firm believer in education through osmosis. Prerequisite: An enduring love affair with books." *Politics:* Independent. *Home:* 704 Prospect Row, San Mateo, Calif. 94401. *Agent:* Curtis Brown Ltd., 60 East 56th St., New York, N.Y. 10022.

CAREER: Former commercial pilot, Pan American World Airways to 1964; free-lance writer and editor. *Military service:* U.S. Army Air Forces, 1943-46. *Member:* American Aviation Historical Society, Wingfoot Lighter-Than-Air Society, California Writers' Club.

WRITINGS: When Monsters Roamed the Skies: The Saga of the Dirigible Airship (juvenile), Grosset, 1968 (published in England as *The Story of Airships: When Monsters Roamed the Skies,* Arthur Barker, 1968); *Skyway Round the World: The Story of the First Global Airway,* Scribner, 1968; *The Sky Racers: Speed Kings of Aviation's Golden Age,* Grosset, 1969. Contributor of articles on aviation and American history to magazines, including *American West.* Consulting editor, Sunset Books.

WORK IN PROGRESS: Collaborating with Ralph A. O'Neill on book detailing origin and first operations of New York, Rio, and Buenos Aires Airline; collaborating with Jean Stoner Rieth on biographical novel set in American Revolution; individual research on two other historical books.

SIDELIGHTS: "Always interested in history—a fascination honed by worldwide travel during my flying career—I am especially enchanted by that shadow world of history peopled by character actors rather than stars. Martin Pinzon, captain of the 'Pinta' under Christopher Columbus, persuaded his commander to alter course from west to southwest, thereby heading the expedition toward the West Indies and away from mainland North America. Thus Pinzon—though little remembered today—made his dent in history. He is the sort of character I most enjoy writing about."

HOBBIES AND OTHER INTERESTS: Photography, music (theatre pipe organ buff).

JOSEPH F. HOOD

BETTY HORVATH

HORVATH, Betty 1927-

PERSONAL: Born May 20, 1927, in Jefferson City, Mo.; daughter of Brans Bolton (a railroader) and Augusta (Kapell) Ferguson; married John Anthony Horvath (a teacher), March 11, 1954; children: Sally, Polly, Jay. *Education:* Attended Jefferson City Junior College, and Phillips University. *Religion:* Episcopalian. *Home:* 2340 Waite Ave., Kalamazoo, Mich. 49008.

CAREER: Continuity writer for radio station in Jefferson City, Mo., 1946-48, and Enid, Okla., 1948-49; Girl Friday with Radio Station WIL, St. Louis, Mo., 1949-50, and Palan Advertising Co., St. Louis, 1950-52; secretary, Camp Nebagamon for Boys, Lake Nebagamon, Wis., 1952-54; now writer for children.

WRITINGS: Hooray for Jasper, Watts, 1966; *Jasper Makes Music,* Watts, 1967; *Will the Real Tommy Wilson Please Stand Up,* Watts, 1969; *The Cheerful Quiet* (Junior Literary Guild selection), Watts, 1969; *Be Nice to Josephine* (Junior Literary Guild selection), Watts, 1970; *Not Enough Indians* (Junior Literary Guild selection), Watts, 1971.

SIDELIGHTS: "People who know what they want to do are lucky. I've known ever since I was in third grade that I wanted to be a writer, though it took me a long time to discover that my special field was writing for children.

"Some of my books were inspired by events or small characters in and around our house. Others just seem to have materialized out of thin air.

"My husband is a teacher, and we have three children: Sally the musician, Polly the budding ballerina (also cheerleader, writer, political agitator, etc., etc.), and Jay who refuses to be labelled. We spend our winters in Kalamazoo and our summers in Lake Nebagamon, Wisconsin where we are all involved with a boys' camp.

"When I'm not writing, housekeeping, reading or listening to music, I'm daydreaming about walking the Appalachian Trail someday."

FOR MORE INFORMATION SEE: Junior Literary Guild Catalogue, March, 1971.

HOWELL, Virginia Tier
See ELLISON, Virginia Howell

HUGHES, (James) Langston 1902-1967

PERSONAL: Born February 1, 1902, in Joplin, Mo.; son of James Nathaniel (a lawyer) and Carrie (Langston) Hughes. *Education:* Columbia University, student, 1921-22; Lincoln University, Pa., A.B., 1929. *Agent:* Harold Ober Associates, 40 East 4th St., New York, N.Y. 10017.

CAREER: Author, playwright, song lyricist, and lecturer since 1926. Atlanta University, Atlanta, Ga., visiting professor in creative writing, 1947; University of Chicago, Laboratory School, poet-in-residence, 1949. *Member:*

LANGSTON HUGHES

Authors Guild, Dramatists Guild, American Society of Composers, Authors, and Publishers, P.E.N. Club, Omega Psi Phi, National Institute of Arts and Letters. *Awards, honors: Opportunity* literary contest, first prize in poetry, 1925, *Palms* Intercollegiate Poetry Award, 1927, Harmon Gold Medal for Literature, 1931, Guggenheim fellowship for creative work, 1935, Rosenwald Fellowship, 1941, Litt. D., Lincoln University, 1943, American Academy of Arts and Letters Grant, 1947, Anisfield-Wolfe Award, 1953, Spingarn Medal, 1960.

WRITINGS INCLUDE—Juvenile: *The Dream Keeper* (poems for young people), 1932; *The First Book of Negroes,* Watts, 1952; *The First Book of Rhythms,* Watts, 1954; *Famous American Negroes,* Dodd, 1954; *The First Book of Jazz,* Watts, 1955; *Famous Negro Music Makers,* Dodd, 1955; *The First Book of the West Indies,* Watts, 1956, republished as *The First Book of the Caribbean,* E. Ward, 1965; *Famous Negro Heroes of America,* Dodd, 1958; *The First Book of Africa,* Watts, 1950, revised edition, 1964.

Editor: *Four Lincoln University Poets,* Lincoln University Herald, 1930; (with Arna Bontemps) *The Poetry of the Negro, 1746-1949,* Doubleday, 1949; (with Waring Cuney

Good [bands] were often parading, their golden trumpets playing gay, syncopated rhythms as the trombones bassed for people to swing along by. ■ (From *The First Book of Jazz* by Langston Hughes. Illustrated by Cliff Roberts.)

and Bruce M. Wright) *Lincoln University Poets,* Fine Editions, 1954; (with Arna Bontemps) *The Book of Negro Folklore,* Dodd, 1958; *An African Treasury,* Crown, 1960; *Poems From Black Africa,* Indiana University Press, 1963; *New Negro Poets U.S.A.,* Indiana University Press, 1964; *The Book of Negro Humor,* Dodd, 1965; *The Best Short Stories by Negro Writers,* Little, Brown, 1967.

Collaborator: *Popo and Fifina,* Macmillan, 1941; *The Sweet Flypaper of Life,* Simon and Schuster, 1955; *A Pictorial History of the Negro in America,* Crown, 1956, revised edition, 1963.

Other books: *The Big Sea* (autobiography), Knopf, 1940; *The Ways of White Folks* (short stories), Knopf, 1940; *Laughing to Keep From Crying* (short stories), Holt, 1951; *I Wonder as I Wander* (autobiography), Rinehart, 1956; *Langston Hughes Reader* (anthology) Braziller, 1958; *The Best of Simple* (anthology), Hill and Wang, 1961; *Fight for Freedom: Story of the NAACP* (history), Norton, 1962; *Something in Common, and Other Stories,* Hill and Wang, 1963; *Five Plays,* edited by Webster Smalley, Indiana University Press, 1963; *Simple's Uncle Sam,* Hill & Wang, 1965. (For complete list of writings see *Contemporary Authors,* Volume 1-4).

SIDELIGHTS: "I was born in Joplin, Missouri, in 1902, but I grew up mostly in Lawrence, Kansas. My grandmother raised me until I was twelve years old. Sometimes I was with my mother, but not often. My father and mother were separated. And my mother, who worked, always traveled about a great deal, looking for a better job. When I first started to school, I was with my mother a while in Topeka. She was a stenographer for a colored lawyer and rented a room near his office, downtown. So I went to a 'white' school in the downtown district.

"At first, they did not want to admit me to the school, because there were no other colored families living in that neighborhood. They wanted to send me to the colored school, blocks away down across the railroad tracks. But my mother, who was always ready to do battle for the rights of a free people, went directly to the school board, and finally got me into the Harrison Street School—where all the teachers were nice to me, except one who sometimes used to make remarks about my being colored. And after such remarks, occasionally the kids would grab stones and tin cans out of the alley and chase me home.

"But there was one little white boy who would always take up for me. Sometimes others of my classmates would, as well. So I learned early not to hate *all* white people. And ever since, it has seemed to me that *most* people are generally good, in every race and in every country where I have been.

"When I was about five or six years old, my father and mother decided to go back together. They had separated shortly after I was born, because my father wanted to go away to another country, where a colored man could get ahead and make money quicker, and my mother did not want to go. My father went to Cuba, and then to Mexico, where there wasn't any color line, or any Jim Crow. He finally sent for us, so we went there, too.

"But no sooner had my mother, my grandmother, and I got to Mexico City than there was a big earthquake, and people ran out from their houses into the Alameda, and the big National Opera House they were building sank down into the ground, and tarantulas came out of the walls—and my mother said she wanted to go back home at once to Kansas, where people spoke English or something she could understand and there were no earthquakes.

So we went. And that was the last I saw of my father until I was seventeen.

"When I was in the second grade, my grandmother took me to Lawrence to raise me. And I was unhappy for a long time, and very lonesome, living with my grandmother. Then it was that books began to happen to me, and I began to believe in nothing but books and the wonderful world in books—where if people suffered, they suffered in beautiful language, not in monosyllables, as we did in Kansas. And where almost always the mortgage got paid off, the good knights won, and the Alger boy triumphed.

"My grandmother was a proud woman—gentle, but Indian and proud. I remember once she took me to Osawatomie, where she was honored by President Roosevelt—Teddy—and sat on the platform with him while he made a speech; for she was then the last surviving widow of John Brown's raid.

"I was twelve when she died. I went to live with a friend of my grandmother's named Auntie Reed. Auntie Reed and her husband had a little house a block from the Kaw River, near the railroad station. They had chickens and cows. Uncle Reed dug ditches and laid sewer pipes for the city, and Auntie Reed sold milk and eggs to her neighbors. For me, there have never been any better people in the world. I loved them very much, Auntie Reed let me set the hens, and Uncle Reed let me drive the cows to pasture. Auntie Reed was a Christian and made me go to church and Sunday school every Sunday. But Uncle Reed was a sinner and never went to church as long as he lived, nor cared anything about it. In fact, he washed his overalls every Sunday morning (a grievous sin) in a big iron pot in the back yard, and then just sat and smoked his pipe under the grape arbor in summer, in winter on a bench behind the kitchen range. But both of them were very good and kind—the one who went to church and the one who didn't. And no doubt from them I learned to like both Christians and sinners equally well.

"My mother sent for me to come to Lincoln, Illinois, where she was then living, not far from Chicago. I was going on fourteen. And the papers said the Great War had begun in Europe. She had married again—a chef cook named Homer Clark. But like so many cooks, as he got older he couldn't stand the heat of the kitchen, so he went to work at other things. Odd jobs, the steel mills, the coal mines. By now I had a little brother. I liked my stepfather a great deal and my baby brother, also; for I had been very lonesome growing up all by myself, the only child, with no father and no mother around.

"But ever so often, my stepfather would leave my mother and go away looking for a better job. The day I graduated from grammar school in Lincoln, he had left my mother, and was not there to see me graduate.

"I was the Class Poet. It happened like this. They had elected all the class officers, but there was no one in our class who looked like a poet, or had ever written a poem. There were two Negro children in the class, myself and a girl. In America most white people think, of course, that *all* Negroes can sing and dance, and have a sense of rhythm. So my classmates, knowing that a poem had to have rhythm, elected me unanimously—thinking, no doubt, that I had some, being a Negro.

"The day I was elected, I went home and wondered what I should write. Since we had eight teachers in our school, I thought there should be one verse for each teacher, with an especially good one for my favorite teacher. And since the teachers were to have eight verses, I felt the class should have eight, too. So my first poem was about the longest poem I ever wrote—sixteen verses, which were later cut down. In the first half of the poem, I said that our school had the finest teachers there ever were. And in the latter half, I said our class was the greatest class ever graduated. So at graduation, when I read the poem, naturally everybody applauded loudly.

"That was the way I began to write poetry."

In 1965, Hughes' 1940 autobiography inspired Harry Belafonte to do his television show, *The Big Sea*. Hughes, in consultation with Belafonte, wrote the script which recalled the nightlife of Harlem in the 1920's.

Hughes' poems have been translated into German, French, Spanish, Russian, Yiddish, and Czech. Many of them have been set to music.

FOR MORE INFORMATION SEE: New York Herald Tribune, August 1, 1926; Huck and Young, *Children's Literature in the Elementary School*, Holt, 1961; *Saturday Review*, November 22, 1958, September 29, 1962; *American Mercury*, January, 1959; *San Francisco Chronicle*, April 5, 1959; *New York Herald Tribune Books*, November 26, 1961; *Life*, February 4, 1966; Charlamae H. Rollins, *Black Troubador: Langston Hughes*, Rand, 1970.

(Died May 22, 1967)

HUTCHINS, Ross E(lliott) 1906-

PERSONAL: Born April 30, 1906, in Ruby, Mont.; son of Elliott J. (a rancher) and Hellen M. Hutchins; married Annie L. McClanahan, June 5, 1931. *Education:* Montana State College, B.S., 1929; Mississippi State University, M.S., 1932; Iowa State College, Ph.D., 1935. *Address:* Drawer EH, State College, Miss. 39762.

CAREER: Mississippi State College, State College, 1929—, became professor of entomology and entomologist, now professor emeritus. Executive officer of Mississippi Plant Board, 1951-68. *Military service:* U.S. Navy, epidemic disease control officer, 1942-45; became lieutenant commander. *Member:* American Entomological Society, Mississippi Entomological Society, Authors Guild, Sigma Xi, Phi Kappa Phi.

WRITINGS: Insects: Hunters and Trappers, Rand, 1957; *Strange Plants and Their Ways,* Rand, 1958; *Insect Builders and Craftsmen,* Rand, 1959 (published in England as *Insects: Builders and Craftsmen,* Burke Publishing, 1960); *Strange Ways of the Plant and Insect World* (contains *Strange Plants and Their Ways* and *Insects: Builders and Craftsmen*), Burke Publishing, 1960; *Wild Ways: A Book*

ROSS E. HUTCHINS

of *Animal Habits,* Rand, 1961 (published in England as *Wild Ways of the Animal World,* Burke Publishing, 1962); *Lives of an Oak Tree,* Rand, 1962; *This Is a Leaf,* Dodd, 1962; *This Is a Flower,* Dodd, 1963; *This Is a Tree* (ALA Notable Book), Dodd, 1964; *The Amazing Seeds,* Dodd, 1965; *Plants without Leaves: Lichens, Fungi, Mosses, Liverworts, Slim-Molds, Algae, Horsetails,* Dodd, 1966; *The Travels of Monarch X,* Rand, 1966; *Insects,* Prentice-Hall, 1966; *Caddis Insects: Nature's Carpenters and Stonemasons,* Dodd, 1969; *The Ant Realm,* Dodd, 1967; *The Last Trumpeters,* Rand, 1967; *Galls and Gall Insects,* Dodd, 1969; *The World of Dragonflies and Damselflies,* Dodd, 1969; *Adelbert the Penguin,* Rand, 1969; *Little Chief of the Mountains,* Rand, 1970; *The Mayfly,* Addison-Wesley, 1970; *Hop, Skim and Fly: An Insect Book,* Parents' Magazine Press, 1970; *Scaly Wings: A Book About Moths and their Caterpillars,* Parents' Magazine Press, 1971; *Saga of Pelorus Jack,* Rand, 1971; *Hidden Valley of the Smokies,* Dodd, 1971; *Cicadia,* Addison-Wesley, 1971. Contributor to *National Geographic.*

FOR MORE INFORMATION SEE: Christian Science Monitor, November 2, 1967, December 21, 1967; *New York Times Book Review,* November 5, 1967, November 3, 1968; *Book World,* January 7, 1968; *Commonweal,* May 23, 1969; *Library Journal,* October 15, 1970; *Third Book of Junior Authors,* edited by de Montreville and Hill, Wilson, 1972.

They hopped out of the water and landed on the deck of the submarine. ■ (From *Adelbert the Penguin* by Ross E. Hutchins. Illustrated by Jerome P. Connolly.)

INGRAHAM, Leonard W(illiam) 1913-

PERSONAL: Born June 6, 1913, in New York, N.Y.; surname legally changed, 1934; son of Frederick (an electrician) and Rose (Holtz) Israel; married Claire Rosenbloom (a free-lance writer), June 27, 1947. *Education:* City College, N.Y., B.S., 1933; Columbia University, M.A., 1934, Ed.D., 1957. *Home:* 190-19D 71st Crescent, Fresh Meadows, N.Y. 11365.

CAREER: Teacher of social studies in Richmond Hill, N.Y., 1937-54; chairman of social studies at high school in Brooklyn, N.Y., 1954-58; New York (N.Y.) Board of Education, acting assistant director of Bureau of Current Research, 1958-62, acting assistant supervisor of Division of Curriculum Development, 1962-64, director of Bureau of Social Studies, 1963—. Encyclopaedia Britannica Education Corp., educational consultant; Foreign Ministry of Japan, consultant, 1960. Queens Speech and Hearing Service Center, member of board of directors, 1960-69. *Military service:* U.S. Army, 1942-46; became technical sergeant. *Member:* National Council for the Social Studies, Association for Supervision and Curriculum Development, National Education Association. *Awards, honors:* Ford Foundation fellow, 1952-53; John Hay fellowship in humanities, 1961.

LEONARD W. INGRAHAM

WRITINGS—Youth books: *Slavery in the United States*, Watts, 1968; *An Album of Colonial America*, Watts, 1969; *An Album of the American Revolution*, Watts, 1971; *An Album of Women in American History*, Watts, 1972. Author of social studies courses and curriculum bulletins. Contributor to education journals.

SIDELIGHTS: "As a teacher of youth, I am anxious in my writings to 'grab' the young reader. Textbooks do not always reach our youth with *his*tory and *her*story. These books are an attempt to bring realism to the story of America."

JEFFRIES, Roderic (Graeme) 1926-

PERSONAL: Born October 21, 1926, in London, England; son of Graham Montague (a writer) and Lorna (Louch) Jeffries; married Rosemary Woodhouse, March 13, 1958; children: Xanthe Kathleen, Crispin John. *Education:* Attended Harrow View House, 1933-41; University of Southampton, navigation studies, 1942-43; Gray's Inn, Barrister-at-Law, 1953. *Home:* Bourne Farm, Aldington Frith, near Ashford, Kent, England. *Agent:* Mrs. G. Hughes, 68 Girdwood Rd., London S.W. 18, England.

CAREER: British Merchant Navy, 1943-49, becoming third officer; practiced law, 1953-54; now professional writer. *Member:* Crime Writers Association, Paternosters.

WRITINGS: Police and Detection, Brockhampton, 1962; *Against Time*, Harper, 1963; *Police Dog*, Harper, 1965; *Patrol Car*, Harper, 1967; *River Patrol*, Harper, 1969; *Trapped*, Harper, 1972.

SIDELIGHTS: "Writing books seemed a natural occupation for me because that was what my father has always done (he's now had well over 100 published): indeed, when young, I tended to think this was what most people did. As in most cases, all my early work ended up in the wastepaper basket, but eventually a very short story was accepted by a magazine. That restored my enthusiasm and quite soon afterwards I had a juvenile book accepted which was about a cadet at sea—naturally, I drew on my own experiences for background.

"I write mystery novels for both adult and young readers and have now had over sixty published, under several names. The background in each case is as factual as I can make it and I have always been greatly helped by the police in my researches. I made several visits to a police dog training school before writing *Police Dog* and went on a long patrol in a police launch before *River Patrol*. The police further help me by reading the scripts and pointing out any errors I have made so that these can be corrected before publication.

"I am one of those writers who keeps office hours even when I can't think what on earth to write: with me, inspiration only comes when I'm working and not, unfortunately, when I'm gardening. I write directly on the typewriter and when I've finished I then re-write the whole book and this usually takes longer than the original work. Finally, I type out the fair copy and usually there's still a little rewriting to do.

RODERIC JEFFRIES

"Because our house is an old Elizabethan farmhouse with many walls still of mud plaster, noise carries from one end to the other and so I work out in a field in a caravan I've rigged up as an office."

HOBBIES AND OTHER INTERESTS: Shooting, training gun-dogs, vintage Bentleys (he is rebuilding a 1924 three-litre Bentley).

JONES, Weyman 1928-

PERSONAL: Born February 6, 1928, in Lima, Ohio; son of Paul W. and Jewel (Beckett) Jones; married Marilyn Ann Blasio, February 6, 1954; children: Lynn, Paula. *Education:* Harvard University, A.B. (cum laude), 1950. *Home:* 41 Nubel Lane, New Canaan, Conn. 06840. *Agent:* Collins-Knowlton-Wing, Inc., 60 East 56th St., New York, N.Y. 10022. *Office:* Kennecott Copper Corp., New York, N.Y.

CAREER: International Business Machines Corp., sales.

There was always a well inside him where his nightmares lived. Some nights he could feel the lid stirring when he slipped into sleep and then, if he was lucky, he sat up in bed and slammed it back. ■ (From *Edge of Two Worlds* by Weyman Jones. Illustrated by J. C. Kocsis.)

WEYMAN JONES

public relations and management positions, 1955-70; Kennecott Copper Corp., New York, N.Y., director of public relations, 1970—. *Military service:* U.S. Navy, 1950-54; became lieutenant junior grade. *Awards, honors:* Western Heritage best juvenile, Child Study Association book of the year, 1968, Lewis Carroll Shelf Award, 1969, all for *Edge of Two Worlds.*

WRITINGS: *The Talking Leaf,* Dial, 1965; *Edge of Two Worlds* (ALA Notable Book), Dial, 1968; *Computer the Mind Stretcher,* Dial, 1969.

WORK IN PROGRESS: Novel with contemporary business setting for adult audiences.

SIDELIGHTS: Jones inherited an interest in the Cherokee as a descendent of early settlers in Oklahoma; his undergraduate honors thesis at Harvard was largely researched in his grandfather's library of Indian history and law.

Edge of Two Worlds was based on the account of an Indian named "The Worm," published in a Cherokee newspaper, of the search for a lost Cherokee band by Sequoyah, who had earlier designed a practical alphabet for the Cherokee language.

JORDAN, June 1936-
(June Meyer)

PERSONAL: Born July 9, 1936, in Harlem, New York, N.Y.; daughter of Granville I. (a post office clerk) and Mildred (Fisher) Jordan; children: Christopher David Meyer. *Education:* Studied at Barnard College and at University of Chicago for a total of three-and-one-half years. *Residence:* Long Island, N.Y. *Agent:* Wendy Weil, Julian Bach, Jr., 3 East 48th St., New York, N.Y. 10017.

CAREER: Assistant to Frederich Wiseman, producer of "The Cool World," New York, N.Y., 1963-64; research associate in technical housing department, Mobilization for Youth, Inc., New York, N.Y., 1965-66; teacher of English and literature at City College, New York, N.Y., 1966-68, and in S.E.E.K. program (Search for Education, Elevation and Knowledge) at Connecticut College, New London, Conn., 1967-69, and Sarah Lawrence College, Bronxville, N.Y., 1969-70. Founder and co-director, Voice of the Children, Inc., 1967-70. *Awards, honors:* Rockefeller Foundation grant in creative writing, 1969-70; Prix de Rome in environmental design, 1970-71. *His Own Where* was nominated for the National Book Award, 1967; Nancy Bloch Memorial Award, 1972, for *The Voice of Children.*

JUNE JORDAN

the tempering sweetness of a little girl who wears her first pair of earrings and a red dress ■ (From *Who Look at Me* by June Jordan. Painting by Colleen Browning, "Door Street." Collection, Milwaukee Art Center, Milwaukee, Wis. Gift of Mrs. Harry Lynde Bradley.)

WRITINGS: Who Look at Me (juvenile in free verse), Crowell, 1969; (poet-author) *Soulscript: Afro-American Poetry,* (ALA Notable Book), Doubleday, 1970; (editor) *The Voice of the Children* (anthology of Afro-American poetry), Holt, 1970; *Some Changes* (collection of poems), Dutton, 1971; *His Own Where* (ALA Young Adult Notable Book), Crowell, 1971; *Dry Victories* (history for young adults), Holt, 1972. Contributor to *Esquire, Nation, Evergreen, Village Voice, New York Times Magazine* and *Book Review, Essence, Ms., Encore, Black Creation,* and other publications.

WORK IN PROGRESS: A biography of Fannie Lou Hamer, for Crowell; a novel, *Okay Now,* for Simon & Schuster; also "trying to work into film."

SIDELIGHTS: "My work is one way I know how to try to love the world, and to ask for love."

FOR MORE INFORMATION SEE: Horn Book, February, 1960, December, 1971; *New York Times Book Review,* November 7, 1971; *Christian Science Monitor,* November 11, 1971; *Publishers' Weekly,* February 21, 1972; *Redbook,* August, 1972.

JUMPP, Hugo
See MacPEEK, Walter G.

KARK, Nina Mary (Mabey) 1925-
(Nina Bawden)

PERSONAL: Born January 19, 1925, in London, England; daughter of Charles Mabey and Ellalaine Ursula (Cushing) Mabey; married Austen Steven Kark (an executive in Overseas Department of British Broadcasting Corp.), 1954; children: (prior marriage) Nicholas Bawden, Robert Humphrey Felix Bawden; (present marriage) Perdita Emily Helena Kark. *Education:* Somerville College, Oxford, B.A., 1946, M.A., 1951; Salzburg Seminar in American Studies, student, 1960. *Agent:* Curtis Brown Ltd., 60 East 56th St., New York, N.Y. 10022.

CAREER: Writer. *Member:* P.E.N., British Ski Club.

WRITINGS—All under name Nine Bawden; adult novels: *Eyes of Green,* Morrow, 1953 (published in England as *Who Calls the Tune,* Collins, 1955); *The Odd Flamingo,* Collins, 1955; *Solitary Child,* Collins, 1956; *Devil by the Sea,* Collins, 1957, Lippincott, 1959; *Change Here for Babylon,* Collins, 1957; *Just Like a Lady,* Longmans, Green, 1960 (published in America as *Glass Slippers Always Pinch,* Lippincott, 1960); *In Honour Bound,* Longmans, Green, 1961; *Tortoise By Candlelight,* Harper, 1963; *Under the Skin,* Harper, 1964; *A Little Love, A Little Learning,* Harper, 1966; *A Woman of My Age,*

NINA MARY KARK

In spite of her funny hat and her bare feet and the kettle in her lap, Ben thought she looked grand and imperious, rather like a queen. ■ (From *The House of Secrets* by Nina Bawden. Illustrated by Wendy Worth. Reprinted by permission of J. B. Lippincott Co.)

Harper, 1967; *A Grain of Truth,* Harper, 1968. Contributor to *Evening Standard* and *London Mystery.*

Juveniles: *Secret Passage,* Gollancz, 1963 (published in America as *The House of Secrets,* Lippincott, 1964); *On the Run,* Gollancz, 1964 (published in America as *Three on the Run,* Lippincott, 1965); *The White Horse Gang,* Lippincott, 1966; *The Witch's Daughter,* Lippincott, 1966; *A Handful of Thieves,* Lippincott, 1967; *The Runaway Summer,* Lippincott, 1969; *Squib* (ALA Notable Book), Lippincott, 1971.

SIDELIGHTS: "I was born in London. My father was an engineer, my mother a schoolteacher. I was educated at a local school and then at Somerville College, Oxford. I have been writing all my adult life (I did write one novel, unpublished, when I was eight), but until *The House of Secrets,* not for children. My children suggested that I should write *The House of Secrets;* my eleven-year-old son read it, chapter by chapter, as it was written and was an extremely stern critic."

FOR MORE INFORMATION SEE: *Times Literary Supplement,* April 27, 1967; *Observer Review,* April 30, 1967, May 15, 1968; *Books and Bookmen,* June, 1967, January, 1968; *Christian Science Monitor,* July 10, 1967, November 6, 1969; *Young Reader's Review,* October, 1967; *Children's Book World,* November 5, 1967; *Commonweal,* November 10, 1967; *Punch,* May 22, 1968; *Book World,* September 1, 1968; *Horn Book,* October, 1969, October, 1971.

KAUFMAN, Mervyn D. 1932-

PERSONAL: Born November 30, 1932, in Los Angeles, Calif.; son of Max (a furrier) and Fannie (Jackson) Kaufman. *Education:* University of California, Los Angeles, A.B., 1954; Columbia University, M.S., 1959. *Home:* 305 West 86th St., New York, N.Y. 10024. *Agent:* Curtis Brown Ltd., 60 East 56th St., New York, N.Y. 10022. *Office:* Fifth Floor, 641 Lexington Ave., New York, N.Y. 10022.

CAREER: Scholastic Magazines, Inc., New York, N.Y., assistant editor of high school classroom periodical, 1959-61; American Heritage Publishing Co., New York, N.Y., associate editor, "Horizon Caravel Books," a world history series for teen-agers, 1961-64; *Automobile Quarterly,* New

Edison and his men had come to New York to set up an electric power system. They hoped it would provide enough electricity to light up a part of the city. ■ (From *Thomas Alva Edison* by Mervyn D. Kaufman. Illustrated by Cary.)

York, N.Y., managing editor, 1964-66; Silver Burdett Co., New York, N.Y., senior editor of "Illustrious Americans" series, 1966-68; *Reader's Digest* general books, New York, N.Y., staff editor, 1968-71; *American Home* Magazine, New York, N.Y., 1971—. *Military service:* U.S. Army, public information officer, 1955-56; served in Korea; became first lieutenant.

WRITINGS: Thomas Alva Edison, Miracle Maker, Garrard, 1962; *Christopher Columbus, a World Explorer*, Garrard, 1963; *The Wright Brothers, Kings of the Air*, Garrard, 1964; *No Holidays for Honeybees*, Coward, 1966; *Father of Skyscrapers: A Biography of Louis Sullivan*, Little, Brown, 1969; (with Richard Altman) *The Making of a Musical*, Crown, 1971; *Fiorello La Guardia*, Crowell, 1972.

WORK IN PROGRESS: A biography of Jesse Owens.

FOR MORE INFORMATION SEE: Saturday Review, May 20, 1972.

KEANE, Bil 1922-

PERSONAL: Born October 5, 1922, in Philadelphia, Pa.; son of Aloysius William and Florence R. (Bunn) Keane; married Thelma Carne, October 23, 1948; children: Gayle, Neal, Glen, Chris, Jeff. *Education:* Attended parochial schools in Philadelphia. *Religion:* Roman Catholic. *Home:* 5815 East Joshua Tree Lane, Paradise Valley, Ariz. 85253.

CAREER: Philadelphia Bulletin, Philadelphia, Pa., staff artist, 1945-59; free-lance artist doing cartoons for most major magazines, 1952-60; creator of syndicated newspaper cartoons, "Channel Chuckles," 1954—, and "The Family Circus," 1960—, both cartoons syndicated by Register & Tribune Syndicate to more than four hundred newspapers. *Military service:* U.S. Army, 1942-45; while in service drew cartoons for *Yank* and *Pacific Stars and Stripes;* became staff sergeant. *Member:* National Cartoonists Society, Newspaper Comics Council, Magazine Cartoonists Guild. *Awards, honors:* Named best syndicated panel cartoonist by National Cartoonists Society, 1967 and 1971; Ohioana Book Award, 1972, for *Just Wait Till You Have Children of Your Own*.

WRITINGS: Channel Chuckles, Scholastic Book Services, 1964; *The Family Circus*, Register & Tribune Syndicate, Volume I, 1965, Volume II, 1966; *Sunday with the Family Circus*, Judson, 1966; *Jest in Pun*, Scholastic Book Services, 1966; *The Family Circus*, Fawcett, 1967; *I Need a Hug*, Fawcett, 1968; *Pun-Abridged Dictionary*, Scholastic Book Services, 1968; *Peace, Mommy, Peace!*, Fawcett, 1969; *Through the Year with the Family Circus*, Judson, 1969; *Wanna Be Smiled At?*, Fawcett, 1970; *Peekaboo! I Love You!*, Fawcett, 1971; (with Erma Bombeck) *Just Wait Till You Have Children of Your Own*, Doubleday, 1971; *It's Apparent You're a Parent*, Doubleday, 1971; *More Channel Chuckles*, Scholastic Book Services, 1972; *Look Who's Here*, Fawcett, 1972.

SIDELIGHTS: "I was born the second clown in a family circus of four children in 1922, and grew up in Philadelphia, where the neighbors still claim that the Liberty Bell is not the only thing in Philly that was cracked. Until I was ten I drew nothing—except criticism. However my mother did encourage me to draw and she now appears as one of the grandmas in *The Family Circus*.

"When my daughter was five, she was the spittin' image of Dolly, the girl-type child in my feature. The other children in the cartoon are based on our boys when they were of similar age. Our dog is a Labrador which I draw as Barfy in my cartoons. Her best trick is playing dead, which she practices eight or nine hours each day in my air-conditioned studio.

"'I have never taken a formal art course, but taught myself to draw by imitating my favorite cartoonists in the newspapers and magazines while in my teens. I was art editor of the monthly magazine in high school and after three years in the Army, I joined the news art staff of the *Philadelphia Bulletin*. My cartoons went unnoticed by 'nearly everybody.' When television was coming into its own in 1954 I started a feature lampooning the boob tube and called it 'Channel Chuckles.' I still draw it daily for the *Register* and *Tribune* Syndicate. 'The Family Circus' first came to town on February 29th, 1960. Taking advantage of the leap year date I have determined that the characters in 'The Family Circus' are growing older at the rate of one year in every four. Now, if I could only

BIL KEANE

make that work for myself! The feature has grown in popularity and scores at the top of most readership surveys, for which I am thankful. It takes one day a week just to answer the fan mail. I am happy to get writer's cramp that way. American newspaper readers are the sincerest and most appreciative audience in the world and 'Family Circus' now appears in 385 leading newspapers throughout the U.S. and Canada.

"Speaking of audiences, I recently was one of six cartoonists selected to entertain the troops in Vietnam (ours, I think). The tour lasted twenty-four days and I was decorated for extreme precaution under cover.

"I am now residing in Arizona where I am studying to be a cactus. With five children in school, most of my best art work is done on mimeograph sheets for PTA announcements. Our youngest son, Jeffy's middle name is 'My Dad will do it.' My wife Thel, whom I met while hiding in a kangaroo's pouch during World War II in Australia, is my technical adviser, model for the 'Family Circus' mommy, and my editor. She is the most kissable editor I have ever met."

Keane says that the syndicate estimates his daily readers at fifty million and that "The Family Circus" is rated the ranking comic in readership by Nelson surveys.

HOBBIES AND OTHER INTERESTS: "When not at the drawing board, I'm playing tennis."

KEEN, Martin L. 1913-

PERSONAL: Born February 14, 1913, in Atlantic City, N.J.; married Laurel Hochstein, October 18, 1964; children: (wife's prior marriage) Rena Veith Shenk, Linda Veith Goukler. *Education:* Columbia University, B.S., 1953. *Politics:* Democrat. *Home and office:* 9 Brentwood Rd., Matawan, N.J. 07747. *Agent:* Curtis Brown Ltd., 60 East 56th St., New York, N.Y. 10022.

CAREER: Standard Brands, Inc., industrial chemist, prior to World War II; active politically, 1946-49; trade journal reporter, 1949—; edited and wrote for National Lexicographic Board, Dell, Grolier, Funk & Wagnalls, McGraw-Hill, New American Library, *New York Times*, Doubleday, and others, 1951—; *Collier's Encyclopedia*, New York, N.Y., senior science editor, 1961-64. *Military service:* U.S. Army, 1942-46; became technical sergeant. *Member:* Authors Guild, American Veterans Committee.

WRITINGS— "How and Why Wonder Book" series, published by Grosset: *How and Why Wonder Book of the Human Body*, 1961; . . . *of the Microscope*, 1961; . . . *of Chemistry*, 1961; . . . *of Wild Animals*, 1962; . . . *of Science Experiments*, 1962; . . . *of Sound*, 1962; . . . *of Prehistoric Animals*, 1962; . . . *of Magnets and Magnetism* 1963; . . . *of Electronics*, 1969; (with C.C. Cunniff) . . . *of Air and Water*, 1969.

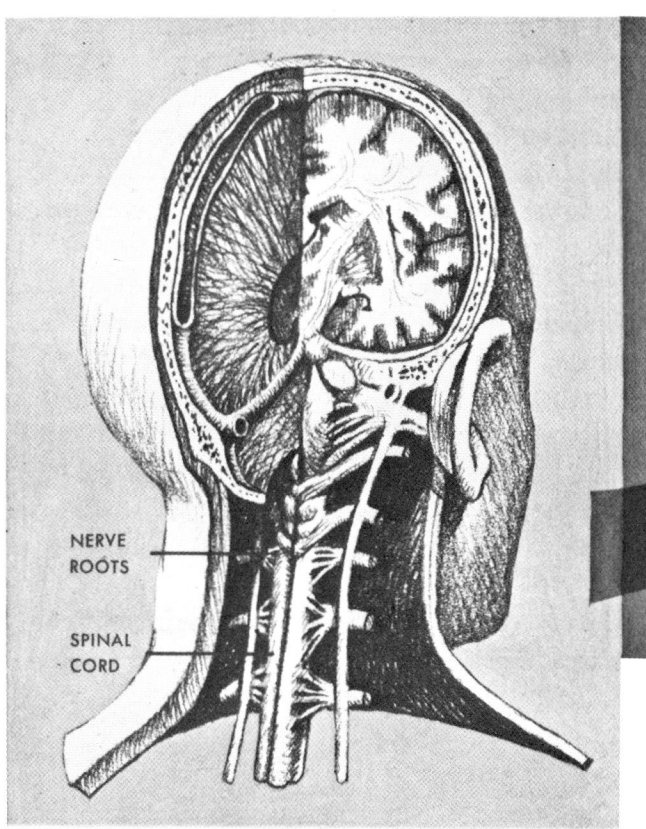
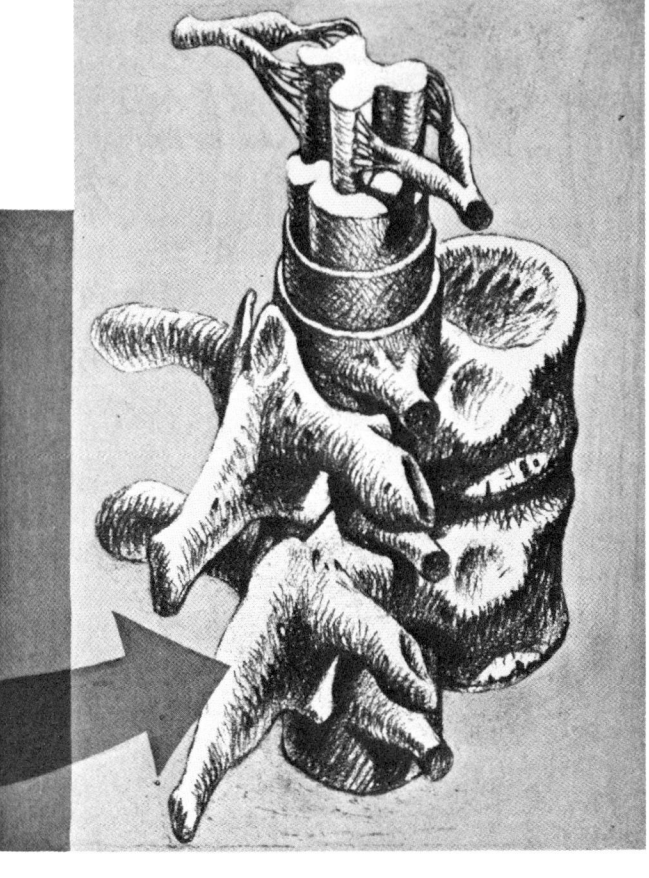

These nerve branches run to all the organs of the body, where they branch again and again, until the smallest branches are nerves which are so thin that they cannot be seen with the unaided eye. ■ (From *The Wonders of the Human Body* by Martin L. Keen. Illustrated by Darryl Sweet.)

Other juvenile books: *Weighing and Measuring,* Ohaus, 1964; *The Wonders of the Human Body,* Grosset, 1966; *The Wonders of Space: Rockets, Missiles and Spacecraft,* Grosset, 1967; *Let's Experiment,* Grosset, 1968; *Lightning and Thunder,* Messner, 1969; *Hunting Fossils,* Messner, 1967; *Soil: A World at Your Feet,* Messner, 1972; *Let's See How It Works,* Grosset, 1972.

Ghost-writer of about a dozen elementary science textbooks and teachers' manuals for several publishers. Major contributor to the *New York Times Encyclopedia Almanac,* 1970, 1971.

SIDELIGHTS: "I undoubtedly have written—as a signed or unsigned contributor, as a rewriter, and as a ghost-writer—more encyclopedia articles than anyone else in the world. They number in the thousands. This is my claim to fame."

KILREON, Beth
See WALKER, Barbara K.

KOHN, Bernice (Herstein) 1920-

PERSONAL: Born June 15, 1920, in Philadelphia, Pa.; daughter of Joseph B. and Sarah (Freedman) Herstein; married Morton Hunt (writer); children: Barbara (Mrs. Dan Isaac), Judith (Mrs. Richard Wolman), Eugene. Education: Attended University of Wisconsin. Home: 490 West End Ave., New York, N.Y. 10024.

CAREER: Writer.

WRITINGS: *Our Tiny Servants: Molds and Yeasts,* Prentice-Hall, 1962; *Computers at Your Service,* Prentice-Hall, 1962; *The Peaceful Atom,* Prentice-Hall, 1963; *Marvelous Mammals: Monotremes and Marsupials,* Prentice-Hall, 1964; *The Scientific Method,* Prentice-Hall, 1964; *Everything Has a Shape and Everything Has a Size,* Prentice-Hall, 1964; *Light,* Coward, 1965; *Koalas,* Prentice-Hall, 1965; *Light You Cannot See,* Prentice-Hall, 1965; *Echoes,* Coward, 1965; *One Day It Rained Cats and Dogs,* Coward, 1965; *Fireflies,* Prentice-Hall, 1966; *Telephones,* Coward, 1967; *Levers,* Coward, 1967; *The Bat Book,* Hawthorn, 1967; *Raccoons,* Prentice-Hall, 1968; *Secret Codes and Ciphers,* Prentice-Hall, 1968; *All Kinds of Seals,* Random House, 1968; *The Look-It-Up-Book of Transportation,* Random House, 1968; *Ferns: Plants without Flowers,* Hawthorn, 1968; *Ramps,* Hawthorn, 1969; *Chipmunks,* Prentice-Hall, 1969; *A First Look at Psychol-*

BERNICE KOHN

ogy, Hawthorn, 1969; *Talking Leaves: The Story of Sequoyah* (Junior Literary Guild selection), Hawthorn, 1969.

The Beachcomber's Book, Viking, 1970; *The Amistad Mutiny*, McCall's, 1971; *How High is Up?*, Putnam, 1971; *The Organic Living Book*, Viking, 1972; *The Gypsies*, Bobbs, 1972; *Out of the Cauldron: A Short History of Witchcraft*, Holt, 1972; *Honeybees*, Four Winds, 1972; (illustrated by daughter, Barbara Kohn Isaac) *One Sad Day*, Third Press, 1972.

SIDELIGHTS: "My husband and I divide our time about equally between our New York apartment and our waterfront house in East Hampton, Long Island where we are enthusiastic organic gardeners and bird watchers. My three children are now all grown and I have recently become a grandmother. One daughter is a book designer and illustrator; another daughter is a French teacher; my son is a promising young opera conductor and is on the faculty at Juilliard."

FOR MORE INFORMATION SEE: Best Sellers, June 1, 1968; *Library Journal*, May 15, 1970; *New York Times Book Review*, June 7, 1970, May 7, 1972; *Horn Book* October, 1972.

KONIGSBURG, E(laine) L(obl) 1930-

PERSONAL: Born February 10, 1930, in New York, N.Y.; daughter of Adolph (a businessman) and Beulah (Klein) Lobl; married David Konigsburg (a psychologist), July 6, 1952; children: Paul, Laurie, Ross. *Education:* Carnegie Institute of Technology, B.S., 1952; University of Pittsburgh, graduate study, 1952-54. *Religion:* Jewish. *Home and office:* Jacksonville, Fla.

CAREER: Shenago Valley Provision Co., Sharon, Pa., bookkeeper, 1947-48; Bartram School, Jacksonville, Fla., science teacher, 1954-55, 1960-62. *Awards, honors:* Jennifer, Hecate, Macbeth, William McKinley, and Me, Elizabeth was chosen as an honor book in *Book Week* Children's Spring Book Festival, 1967; Newbery Medal, 1968, for *From the Mixed-Up Files of Mrs. Basil E. Frankweiler;* Newbery Honor Book, 1968, for *Jennifer, Hecate, Macbeth, William McKinley, and Me, Elizabeth;* William Allen White Award, 1970, for *From the Mixed-Up Files of Mrs. Basil E. Frankweiler;* Carnegie-Mellon Merit Award, 1971.

WRITINGS: Jennifer, Hecate, Macbeth, William McKinley, and Me, Elizabeth (*Horn Book* Honor List), Atheneum, 1967; *From the Mixed-Up Files of Mrs. Basil E. Frankweiler* (*Horn Book* Honor List), Atheneum, 1967; *About the B'nai Bagels*, Atheneum, 1969; *(George)*, Atheneum, 1970; *Altogether, One at a Time*, Atheneum, 1971; *A Proud Taste for Scarlet and Miniver*, Atheneum, 1973.

SIDELIGHTS: "All my stories use the same things in different proportions: things that happen to me, to my family, to my friends; things that I read, that I see, that I hear about. When I stir all this together and write it down, the people become characters. All in all, I can tell you that my book people are more fun than molecules.

"That's what I started with: molecules. Long before I began writing, long before I had children, I was a chemist. Determined to push back the frontiers of science, I continued studying chemistry at the University of Pittsburgh Graduate School. After two years there I found that the only thing I had succeeded in pushing back was my hairline; I twice blew up the laboratory sink, losing my eyebrows and bangs in the flash.

"I was born in New York City, but I did most of my growing up in small towns in Pennsylvania. I remember always looking for myself in books and never finding either me or my town—even though the book jacket sometimes promised that I would be meeting children in a typical small town. When my own children started school, I realized that their growing up was very different from mine. I decided to write a book about what was happening to them in their towns, the suburbs. After they left for school each morning, I began writing. *Jennifer, Hecate, Macbeth, William McKinley, and Me, Elizabeth,* was the result. We were living in Port Chester, New York, at the time, and the story was based on something that happened to my daughter, Laurie, shortly after we had moved there.

E. L. KONIGSBURG

"My second book, *From the Mixed-Up Files of Mrs. Basil E. Frankweiler*, grew in part from a family picnic in Yellowstone National Park a few summers ago. I purchased bread, cold cuts, chocolate milk, and paper cups from the commissary and found a clearing where we could eat. There were no picnic tables, so my small group ate squatting slightly above the ground. This was hardly unseasoned buffalo meat and cooking over an open fire and chopping down wood to make that fire. But they groaned—about ants and flies and how could they keep the milk from tipping over.

"Laurie was somewhat independent, somewhat shy, and did not mix readily with other children. At first she walked to school with her brother, but when he found friends and boy interests this ceased and Laurie walked alone and played alone. The girls in her class, most of whom had lived in the neighborhood for some time, had their friends and did not go out of their way or interrupt their established routines to welcome a newcomer. It was only after a number of weeks had passed that Laurie came running into the house, asking to go play at the home of a friend. With enormous relief, I asked the friend's name and address and gave permission. Then I looked out the window to see a tall, proud Negro girl striking off down the street, with Laurie following with obvious respect. Two outsiders had found each other, and a friendship had begun. Laurie's friend became the pattern for Jennifer, although the two were not really alike in background, and the school situation was somewhat different. Laurie was not really Elizabeth, either, except as her one experience created the idea for the book.

The only real difference between them was that the cat wore tiny golden earrings and looked a trifle less smug. ■ (From *From the Mixed-Up Files of Mrs. Basil E. Frankweiler* by E. L. Konigsburg. Illustrated by the author.)

"I realized that if my children ever left home, they would never revert to barbarism. They would carry with them all the fussiness and tidiness of suburban life, and they would hold onto these habits. Where then would they go? Caution appears to come with the lease in middleclass suburban life. They would probably consider nothing less than the Metropolitan Museum of Art. How they love it! (And how do I!) Those wonderful beds and all that elegance, and maybe they could find some way to live with caution and compulsiveness and still satisfy their need for adventure.

"When the book was in the writing, all sorts of research was needed. When did they clean the museum? What kind of security was there at night? Was there a way the children could get their clothes into the museum without having to check them? Where could they hide in the morning and at night when the museum staff was around but the museum was closed? And for how long would they have to hide? The Museum was understandably reluctant to divulge most of this information. So I snooped. I spent hours tracking down my suspicions as to how all of this was really done and just how much my children could get away with. The results sound plausible, but of course, only the museum really knows, and no one there is telling.

"All three of my children are my first editors. I read them what I have written, and I watch their reactions. They also pose for me. I take pictures of them with a Polaroid camera, and then I make drawings from the pictures.

"Besides writing I enjoy painting, reading, gardening (in fair weather), taking long walks and chocolate. The things I hate most in the whole world are liver and phonies."

From the Mixed-Up Files of Mrs. Basil E. Frankweiler will be filmed by Westfall Productions and star Ingrid Bergman.

FOR MORE INFORMATION SEE: *Saturday Review*, November 9, 1968; *School Library Journal*, February, 1970; *Chicago Tribune Children's Book World*, November 8, 1970; *Horn Book*, December, 1970, August, 1971; Hoffman and Samuels, *Authors and Illustrators of Children's Books*, Bowker, 1972; *Third Book of Junior Authors*, edited by de Montreville and Hill, Wilson, 1972.

KRAUS, Robert 1925-

PERSONAL: Born June 21, 1925, in Milwaukee, Wis.; son of Jack and Esther (Rosen) Kraus; married Pamela Wong, December 11, 1946; children: Bruce, William. Education: Studied at Layton Art School, Milwaukee, 1942, and at Art Students' League of New York, 1945. Residence: Ridgefield, Conn. Office: Windmill Books, Inc., 201 Park Ave. S., New York, N.Y. 10003.

CAREER: Cartoonist for national magazines, and author and illustrator of children's books; president of Windmill Books, Inc., New York, N.Y., 1966—; Springfellow Books, Inc., president, 1972—. Had a cartoon published in the *Milwaukee Journal* when he was eleven; continued with cartoons for magazines, chiefly the *New Yorker*.

ROBERT KRAUS

WRITINGS—Author and illustrator: *Junior the Spoiled Cat*, Oxford University Press, 1955; *All the Mice Came*, Harper, 1955; *Ladybug, Ladybug*, Harper, 1956; *The Littlest Rabbit*, Harper, 1957; *I, Mouse*, Harper, 1958; *The Trouble with Spider*, Harper, 1962; *Miranda's Beautiful Dream*, Harper, 1964; *Penguin's Pal*, Harper, 1964; *Mouse at Sea*, Harper, 1964; "The Bunny's Nutshell Library," Harper, four books with titles of *The Silver Dandelion, Juniper, The First Robin,* and *Springfellow's Parade; Amanda Remembers*, Harper, 1965; *My Son, the Mouse*, Harper, 1967; *Little Giant*, Harper, 1967; *Hello Hippopotamus*, Windmill Books, 1969; *Daddy Long Ears*, Windmill Books, 1970; *How Spider Saved Christmas*, Windmill Books, 1970; *Vip's Mistake Book*, Windmill Books, 1970; *The Tale Who Wagged the Dog*, Windmill Books, 1971.

Author; all published by Windmill Books, except as noted: *Harriet and the Promised Land*, 1968; *Unidentified Flying Elephant*, 1968; *The Children Who Got Married*, 1969; *Animal Etiquette*, 1969; *Don't Talk to Strange Bears*, 1969; *Rumple-Nose Dimple and the Three Horrible Snaps*, 1969; *The Christmas Cookie Sprinkle Snitcher*, 1969; *I'm Glad I'm a Boy, I'm Glad I'm a Girl*, 1970; *Whose Mouse*

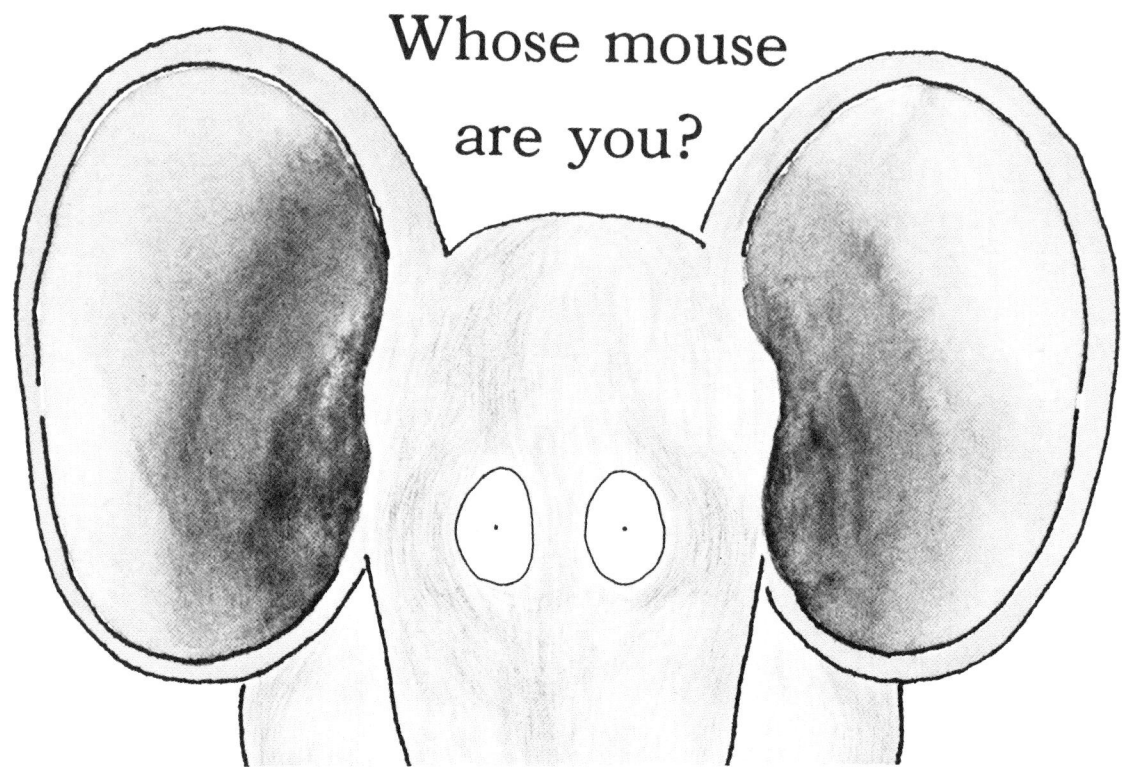

(From *Whose Mouse Are You?* by Robert Kraus. Illustrated by Jose Aruego.)

Are You? (ALA Notable Book), Macmillan, 1970; *Bunya the Witch,* 1971; *Shaggy Fur Face,* 1971; *Ludwig, the Dog Who Snored Symphonies,* 1971; *Pipsqueak, Mouse in Shining Armor,* 1971; *Lillian Morgan and Teddy Morgan,* 1971; *Leo the Late Bloomer,* 1971; *The Tree That Stayed Up Until Next Christmas,* 1972; *Milton the Early Riser* (Junior Literary Guild selection), 1972.

Author; all published by Springfellow Books, "The Night Light Library": *Good Night Little One,* 1972; *Good Night Little ABC,* 1972; *Good Night Richard Rabbit,* 1972.

Illustrator: Carla Stevens, *Rabbit and Skunk and the Scary Rock,* Scholastic Book Services, 1970.

SIDELIGHTS: "I always liked to draw. I read books about how to become a cartoonist. One suggested that drawing funny signs and selling them to barbershops was a way to get started. I was ten years old when I trudged through the streets of Milwaukee with my cartoon signs about shaves and shoeshines. I managed to sell one to my local barber and was thus launched into a career in art."

FOR MORE INFORMATION SEE: Junior Literary Guild Catalogue, September, 1972; *Third Book of Junior Authors,* edited by de Montreville and Hill, Wilson, 1972.

LAMPMAN, Evelyn Sibley 1907-
(Lynn Bronson)

PERSONAL: Born April 18, 1907, in Dallas, Ore.; daughter of Joseph E. and Harriet (Bronson) Sibley;

EVELYN SIBLEY LAMPMAN

married Herbert Sheldon Lampman, 1935 (deceased); children: Linda Sibley Lampman McIsaac, Anne Hathaway Lampman Knutson. *Education:* Oregon State University, B.S., 1929. *Religion:* Episcopalian. *Home:* 6810 Southeast Yamhill, Portland, Ore.

CAREER: Radio Station KEX, Portland, Ore., continuity writer, 1929-34, continuity chief, 1937-45; Radio Station KGW, Portland, Ore., educational director, 1945-52; full-time writer of children's books, 1952—. *Member:* Delta Delta Delta. *Awards, honors:* Award from Committee on Art of Democratic Living for *Treasure Mountain,* 1949; Dorothy Canfield Fisher Memorial Children's Book Award for *City Under the Back Steps,* 1962; Western Writers of America Spur Award, 1970, for *Cayuse Courage.*

WRITINGS—Juveniles: *Crazy Creek,* 1948, *Treasure Mountain,* 1949, *The Bounces of Cynthiann',* 1950, *Elder Brother,* 1951, *Captain Apple's Ghost,* 1952, *Tree Wagon,* 1953, *Witch Doctor's Son,* 1954, *The Shy Stegosaurus of Cricket Creek,* 1955, *Navaho Sister,* 1956, *Rusty's Space Ship,* 1957, *Rock Hounds,* 1958, *Special Year,* 1959, *City Under the Back Steps,* 1960, *Princess of Fort Vancouver,* 1962, *Shy Stegosaurus at Indian Springs,* 1962, *The Tilted Sombrero,* 1966, *Half-Breed,* 1967, *The Bandit of Mok Hill,* 1970, *Cayuse Courage,* Harcourt, 1970, *Once Upon the Little Big Horn,* Crowell, 1971, *The Year of Small Shadow,* Harcourt, 1971 (all published by Doubleday except where otherwise noted).

Under pseudonym Lynn Bronson: *Timberland Adventure,* Lippincott, 1950; *Coyote Kid,* Lippincott, 1951; *Rogue's Valley,* Lippincott, 1952; *The Runaway,* Lippincott, 1953; *Darcy's Harvest,* Doubleday, 1956; *Popular Girl,* Doubleday, 1957; *Mrs. Updaisy,* Doubleday, 1963; *Temple of the Sun,* Doubleday, 1964; *Wheels West,* Doubleday, 1965.

FOR MORE INFORMATION SEE: More Junior Authors, edited by Muriel Fuller, Wilson, 1963.

LARRICK, Nancy G. 1910-

PERSONAL: Born 1910, in Winchester, Va.; daughter of Herbert S. and Nancy (Nulton) Larrick; married Alexander L. Crosby, 1958. *Education:* Goucher College, A.B., 1930; Columbia University, M.A., 1937; New York University, Ed.D., 1955. *Home:* Box 20, R.R. 4, Quakertown, Pa.

CAREER: Public schools, Winchester, Va., teacher, 1930-42; U.S. Treasury Department, Washington, D.C., education director, War Bond Division, 1942-45; *Young America Readers* (weekly news magazines), New York, N.Y., editor, 1946-51; Random House, Inc., New York, N.Y., education director, children's books, 1952-59; Lehigh University, Bethlehem, Pa., visiting professor, 1963—. Held teaching posts at other periods at New York University Graduate School of Education, Indiana University, Bank Street College of Education; lectured at University of Chicago, University of Montana, University of Texas, and at other universities in the East. *Member:* International Reading Association (president, 1956-57), National Council of Teachers of English, National Conference on Research in English. *Awards, honors:* Edison Foundation Award, 1959; Carey-Thomas Award, 1959; New York University Founder's Day Achievement Award, 1955.

WRITINGS: (With Daniel Melcher) *Printing and Promotion Handbook,* McGraw, 1949, 3rd edition, 1966; *See for Yourself,* Dutton, 1952; *A Parent's Guide to Children's Reading,* Doubleday, 1958, 3rd edition, 1969; *Color ABC,* Platt, 1959; (with Alexander L. Crosby) *Rockets Into Space,* Random House, 1959; *A Teacher's Guide to Children's Books,* Merrill, 1960; *Junior Science Book of Rain, Hail, Sleet and Snow,* Garrard, 1961; *A Parent's Guide to Children's Education,* Trident, 1963; (editor) *Piper, Pipe That Song Again,* Random House, 1965; *First ABC,* Platt & Munk, 1965; (editor) *Poetry For Holidays,* Garrard, 1966; (compiler) *On City Streets: An Anthology of Poetry,* M. Evans, 1968; (compiler) *Piping Down the Valleys Wild: Poetry for the Young of All Ages,* Delacorte, 1968; (editor), *Green Is Like a Meadow of Grass,* Garrard, 1968; (editor with Charles J. Versacci) *Reading: Isn't It Really the Teacher,* Interstate, 1968; (editor) *On City Streets,* M. Evans, 1968; (editor) *I Heard a Scream*

"I brought you a cupcake," said Joan hastily . . . George swallowed (it) solemnly, then reopened his mouth, his beady eyes on the second cupcake. ■ (From *The Shy Stegosaurus of Indian Springs* by Evelyn Sibley Lampman. Illustrated by Paul Galdone.)

In the evening the city
Goes to bed
Hanging lights
About its head.
—Langston Hughes ■ (From *Piping Down the Valleys Wild* edited by Nancy Larrick. Illustrated by Ellen Raskin.)

in the Street: Poems by Young People in the City, M. Evans, 1970; (editor) *Somebody Turned on a Tap in These Kids,* Delacorte, 1971. Contributor to *Publishers' Weekly, This Week, Saturday Review, Young Homemakers, Parents' Magazine,* and education journals. Editor, *Reading Teacher,* 1950-54.

Le GUIN, Ursula K(roeber) 1929-

PERSONAL: Born October 21, 1929, in Berkeley, Calif.; daughter of Alfred L. (an anthropologist) and Theodora (Kracaw) Kroeber; married Charles A. Le Guin (a historian), December 25, 1953; children: Elisabeth, Caroline, Theodore. *Education:* Radcliffe College, B.A., 1951; Columbia University, M.A., 1952. *Home:* 3321 Northwest Thurman St., Portland, Ore. 97210.

CAREER: Writer of science fiction and fantasy. *Member:* Science Fiction Writers of America. *Awards, honors: Boston Globe-Horn Book* Award, 1968, for *A Wizard of Earthsea; The Left Hand of Darkness* was awarded the Nebula Award (best novel) by the Science Fiction Writers' Association, and the Hugo Award (best novel) by the International Science Fiction Association, 1970; *The Tombs of Atuan* was nominated for the National Book Award, 1971, and was a Newbery Honor Book.

WRITINGS: Rocannon's World, Ace Books, 1964; *Planet of Exile,* Ace Books, 1966; *City of Illusions,* Ace Books, 1967; *A Wizard of Earthsea, (Horn Book* Honor List; ALA Notable Book), Parnassus, 1968; *The Left Hand of Darkness,* Ace Books, 1969; *The Tombs of Atuan* (ALA Notable Book; *Horn Book* Honor List), Atheneum, 1971; *The Lathe of Heaven,* Scribner, 1971; *The Farthest Shore* (Junior Literary Guild selection), Atheneum, 1972.

SIDELIGHTS: "I have been writing ever since I was six, mostly fantasies and science fiction. As a science fiction writer I always get asked, 'Where do you get those weird

In the deep valley, in the twilight, the apple trees were on the eve of blossoming; here and there among the shadowed boughs one flower had opened early, rose and white, like a faint star. ■ (From *The Tombs of Atuan* by Ursula K. Le Guin. Illustrated by Gail Garraty.)

URSULA K. Le GUIN

ideas from?' As a fantasy writer I always get asked, 'Don't you ever want to write about the REAL world?' All I can answer is that I do write about the real world, and I get all my weird ideas from it, too. It is just that reality is much stranger than many people want to admit. After all, the real world is not made up only of the actual. If it were, it would stop right now. It is also made up of the possible and the probable: they are part of it now and always have been.

"It doesn't seem probable that one's grandfather was once an egg the size of a pinhead; that leaves eat light; that whales sing in choruses deep under the sea; that when you look at a distant star you are seeing the past: yet all these things are actual—are real. I could never invent anything so improbable, so unexpected. Indeed, I can't invent anything; none of us writers can. We can only take what we know and put it together in a different way. And that is the essential process of life itself, expressed in terms of the mind.

"Imagination is one of humanity's greatest tools. It can be badly used, just as an axe can. A writer can lie, or refuse to admit facts he doesn't like, just as a scientist can. But skillfully and honestly used, imagination is our best means of understanding reality, and the chief tool of both the scientist and the artist. What it produces may be theories about the origin of the universe, or stories about hobbits. That's the beauty of it. The human mind is as various, and as improbable, as the universe man is part of."

FOR MORE INFORMATION SEE: Horn Book, April, 1971, October, 1971; *Christian Science Monitor,* November 11, 1971; *Junior Literary Guild Catalogue,* September, 1972.

LEONG GOR YUN
See ELLISON, Virginia Howell

LEVITIN, Sonia 1934-

PERSONAL: Born August 18, 1934, in Berlin, Germany; daughter of Max (a manufacturer) and Helene (Goldstein) Wolff; married Lloyd Levitin (a corporate planning director), December 27, 1953; children: Daniel Joseph, Shari Diane. *Education:* University of California, Berkeley, student, 1952-54; University of Pennsylvania, B.S., 1956; San Francisco State College, graduate study, 1957-60. *Residence:* 41 Blaine Circle, Moraga, Calif. 94556.

CAREER: Elementary teacher in Mill Valley, Calif., 1956-57; adult education teacher in Daly City, Calif., 1962-64; Acalanes Adult Center, Lafayette, Calif., teacher, 1967—. *Member:* Moraga Historical Society (founder and past president). *Awards, honors:* Jewish Book Council of America, Charles and Bertie G. Schwartz Award, 1971, for *Journey to America.*

WRITINGS: Journey to America (Junior Literary Guild selection), Atheneum, 1970; *Rita the Weekend Rat* (juvenile), Atheneum, 1971. Contributor to *Parents' Magazine, San Francisco Magazine,* and other magazines and newspapers.

WORK IN PROGRESS: Who Owns the Moon, a picture book to be published by Parnassus in 1973.

"It seems to me that Rita is on-the-verge-of-a-nervous-breakdown." ■ (From *Rita the Weekend Rat* by Sonia Levitin. Illustrated by Leonard Shortall.)

SIDELIGHTS: "While I was quite young I began to imagine myself as a writer, and at the age of eleven I confessed this ambition in a letter to Laura Ingalls Wilder. She responded with a kind, encouraging note—I still treasure her letter. Although I wrote an occasional poem while I was growing up, being a student and then a teacher left little time for any serious writing. When my first baby was born, I began writing in earnest. I wrote every single day, and after eight months I sold an article to a baby magazine. I enrolled in night classes at San Francisco State College and had the good fortune to study with Walter Van Tilburg Clark who taught me to write about that which I feel most deeply—and then to *rewrite.*

"My life is about equally divided between the two things I love most: my family and home on the one hand, and writing on the other. Daniel and Shari help me more than they realize. I marvel at their curiosity and their ingenuity, two traits that every writer can use more of.

"To write well is my overriding ambition. The greatest influences are my inner need to communicate, my admiration of artistic achievement, and the great pleasure I have derived from reading good books."

Born in Germany, Mr. Levitin moved to the United States in 1938 when she was four years old, with her mother and two older sisters, where she was reunited with her father. *Journey to America* is the fictionalized account of their experences. She has subsequently travelled in Europe, and Hawaii and speaks German fluently.

HOBBIES AND OTHER INTERESTS: History, music, and books.

FOR MORE INFORMATION SEE: Horn Book, April, 1970, June, 1971; *Library Journal,* May 15, 1970; *Writer,* August, 1972.

LISS, Howard 1922-

PERSONAL: Born July 22, 1922, in Brooklyn, N.Y.; son of Benjamin (a builder) and Eva (Kimmel) Liss; married Anne M. Harris, July 5, 1952; children: Jodi Robin, Dana Jennifer. *Education:* Studied at School of American Music, 1951-52, and New York Musical Institute, 1952-53. *Residence:* New York, N.Y. *Agent:* Patricia Lewis, Room 620, 450 Seventh Ave., New York, N.Y. 10001.

CAREER: Former factory hand, shipping clerk, hand-truck pusher, and writer for radio (comedy material) and television; writer of books for young people and continuity for syndicated comic strips, 1960—. *Military service:* U.S. Army, 1943-46. *Awards, honors: Playoff!* was included on Child Study Association of America recommended reading list, 1966.

WRITINGS: (With Y.A. Tittle) *Pro Quarterback,* Argonaut Books, 1963; (with Tittle) *Quarterbacking To Win,* Argonaut Books, 1964; (with Curly Morrison) *Strategy of Pro Football,* McKim Advertising, 1965; (with Yogi Berra) *Baseball Guidebook,* McGraw, 1966; (with Adolph Rupp) *Basketball Guidebook,* McGraw, 1966; (with Penny Pitou) *Skiing Guidebook,* McGraw, 1966; *Playoff!,* Delacorte, 1966; *Willie Mays Album,* Hawthorn, 1966; *Mickey Mantle Album,* Hawthorn, 1966; *Sandy Koufax Album,* Hawthorn, 1966; *Heat* (science), Coward, 1966; (with Willie Mays) *Secrets of Baseball,* Viking, 1967; *The Mighty Mecong,* Hawthorn, 1967; *Soccer, International Game,* Funk, 1968; *The Making of a Rookie,* Random House, 1968; *Unidentified Flying Objects,* Hawthorn, 1968; *The Winners!: National Basketball Championship Playoffs,* Delacorte, 1968; *Friction* (science), Coward, 1968; *AFL Dream Backfield,* Cowles, 1969; *Father and Son Book of Baseball,* Harper, 1969; *The Triple Crown Winners,* Messner, 1969; *Football Talk for Beginners,* Messner, 1969; *Policeman's Handbook,* Popular Library, 1969; *Goal: The Stanley Cup,* Delacorte, 1970; *Asgeir of Iceland,* Messner, 1970; *Basketball Talk for Beginners,* Messner, 1970; *Great Moments in Football,* Cowles, 1970; (with Phil Moriarty) *The Father and Son Book of Swimming,* Harper, 1970; *Baseball's Zaniest Stars,* Random House, 1971; (with Finn Ronne) *The Ronne Antarctic Expedition,* Messner, 1971; *More Strange but True Baseball Stories,* Random House, 1972; *More Strange but True Hockey Stories,* Random House, 1972; *Strange but True Basketball Stories,* Random House, 1972.

Comic strips: (Writer) "Buck Rogers," 1960-67; (co-writer) "Ben Casey," 1965-67; (editor) "The Green Berets," 1966—.

SIDELIGHTS: "Since nearly all my books are nonfiction, more than half my working time is spent in research. Over the course of years my face has become familiar to various people at the New York Public Library, the National Football League, Madison Square Garden's Felt Forum, and at second-hand book shops, where I often hunt for an out-of-print biography or old magazines. Actually, I enjoy the research more than the writing. Putting the right words on paper can be hard work; research is often entertaining as well as informative.

"I'm most happy in the microfilm room of the library, especially when pouring over a *New York Times* of the 1930's. Sometimes a stray paragraph will give me an idea for a book, or a lead on where to find some obscure piece of information I've been hunting for. It's almost like detective work. Or, suddenly I'll stop at the real estate section, the A&P ads, a clothing store sale. Brick houses in Westchester County (very desirable today) were going begging at $15,000; now that house costs $85,000. Bread was a nickel a loaf. A two-trouser suit at a chain store sold for $22.50—and no tax!

"I do not try to assemble all my notes before starting to write the book. For me, the words come easier while the material is still fresh in my mind. My notes needn't be as extensive; a word or phrase can take the place of paragraphs, because I still remember what I read the day before. Otherwise, I tend to forget important meanings and nuances. So I'll research a section or chapter, write it, then go on to the next part of the book.

"Although I've written adult books, I vastly prefer to write for young people of various ages. It's far more challenging, infinitely more difficult. A good author can't write down to his young readers because they'll toss the book aside. Yet he can't go too far over their heads or the purpose of the book is defeated. I try to put on paper the words I would use to explain something to my own children or the children of friends. And if I'm describing a football game, I try to be as vivid as possible without splashing the page with purple prose. Make the youngster see the game through your eyes; and that is why there is so much very good but unappreciated work done by newspaper sportswriters. They know how to communicate.

"Most of my books are purchased by school and public libraries, although some, such as the Random House 'Punt, Pass and Kick,' or 'Little League' series sell primarily at book and department stores. Generally I write on assignment, although a number of my books were my own ideas.

"If there is anything at all I've learned about the book business—after almost fifty books—it is a healthy respect for all editors. A couple of disasters—by different authors—can cost an editor his job; the authors will go on to write other books.

"Therefore, I'll usually listen to an editor, and often follow his advice, reserving the right to disagree if I feel strongly enough, which sometimes does happen. No editor is omnipotent; neither is any single author. (I wonder who Shakespeare's editor was?)"

HOBBIES AND OTHER INTERESTS: Music, cooking; puttering around the family's weekend retreat, a 150-year-old house in northeastern Pennsylvania.

LUNN, Janet 1928-

PERSONAL: Born December 28, 1928, in Dallas, Tex.; daughter of Herman Alfred (a mechanical engineer) and Margaret (Alexander) Swoboda; married Richard Lunn (a teacher); children: Eric, Jeffrey, Alexander, Katherine, John. *Education:* Queen's University at Kingston, student, 1947-50. *Politics:* New Democratic Party. *Home:* R.R. 2, Hillier, Ontario, Canada. *Agent:* Matie Molinaro, Canadian Speakers and Writers, 44 Douglas Crescent, Toronto, Ontario, Canada.

AWARDS, HONORS: Canada Council grant, 1967.

WRITINGS: (With husband, Richard Lunn) *The County* (history of Prince Edward County, Ontario), County of Prince Edward, 1967; *Twin Spell* (juvenile), Harper, 1969. Has written scripts for Canadian Broadcasting Corp. and articles for Canadian periodicals; children's book reviewer for *Toronto Globe and Mail.*

All that afternoon Jane and Elizabeth sat under the cherry tree in the back garden. ■ (From *Twin Spell* by Janet Lunn. Illustrated by Emily McCully.)

JANET LUNN

WORK IN PROGRESS: A children's novel; a historical novel on Scottish immigration in Ontario; a picture book.

SIDELIGHTS: "I have always (still do) thought of raising children as a full-time job which makes writing an avocation. My youngest is now thirteen which makes writing more and more a full time job with interest firmly founded in human relations."

HOBBIES AND OTHER INTERESTS: Art, archeology, and history. "I expect to go on in university with courses in history and archeology."

FOR MORE INFORMATION SEE: *Horn Book,* December, 1969.

MacBETH, George (Mann) 1932-

PERSONAL: Born January 19, 1932, in a mining village in Scotland; son of George and Amelia Morton Mary (Mann) MacBeth; married Elizabeth Browell Robson (a geneticist), 1955. *Education:* New College, Oxford, Litt. Hum. (first class honours), 1955. *Office:* British Broadcasting Corp., Broadcasting House, London W.1, England.

CAREER: British Broadcasting Corp., London, 1955—, producer, Overseas Talks Department, 1957-58, producer, Talks Department, 1958—. *Awards, honors:* Co-recipient of Sir Geoffrey Faber Award, 1964.

Ho there, grass. / Are you dry behind the ears after all / that rain? ■ (From *Noah's Journey* by George MacBeth. Illustrated by Margaret Gordon.)

WRITINGS: A Form of Words (poems), Fantasy Press (England), 1954; *Lecture to the Trainees* (poems), Fantasy Press, 1962; *The Broken Places* (poems), Scorpion Press (England), 1963, Walker & Co., 1968; (editor) *The Penguin Book of Sick Verse,* Penguin (London), 1963, Penguin (Baltimore), 1965; (with Edward Lucie-Smith and Jack Clemo) *Penguin Modern Poets VI* (anthology), Penguin (London), 1964; *A Doomsday Book: Poems and Poem-Games,* Scorpion Press, 1965; (editor) *The Penguin Book of Animal Verse,* Penguin (London), 1965; *The Calf: A Poem,* Turret Books (London), 1965; *The Humming Birds: A Monodrama,* Turret Books, 1965; *Missile Commander,* Turret Books, 1965; *The Twelve Hotels* (poems), Turret Books, 1965; *Noah's Journey* (a long poem in four parts, for children; *Horn Book* Honor List), Viking, 1966; (editor) *Poetry 1900-1965,* Longmans, Green, 1967; *The Colour of Blood* (poems), Atheneum, 1967; *The Screens,* Turret Books, 1967; *The Night of Stones* (poems), Macmillan (London), 1968, Atheneum, 1969; (editor) *The Penguin Book of Victorian Verse,* Penguin (London), 1968; *A War Quartet* (poems), Macmillan (London), 1969; *Jonah and the Lord* (long poem for children; ALA Notable Book, *Horn Book* Honor List), Macmillan (London), 1969, Holt, 1970; (editor) *An Anthology of War Verse,* Penguin (London), 1970; *The Burning Cane* (poems), Macmillan, 1970; (editor), *The Falling Splendor,* Macmillan, 1970; *Collected Poems: 1958-70,* Macmillan, 1971, Atheneum, 1972; *The Orlando Poems,* Macmillan, 1971. Editor, *Poet's Voice,* 1958-65, *New Comment,* 1959-64, and *Poetry Now,* 1965—.

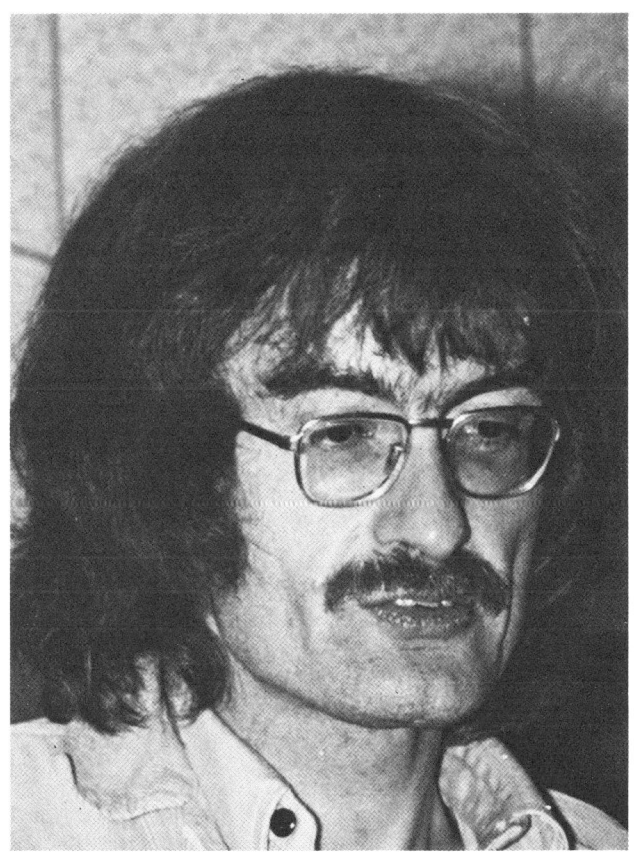

GEORGE MacBETH

SIDELIGHTS: "I live with a stuffed leather pig in a small house built before the French Revolution and while America was still a colony. My poems are written in pencil (and corrected in orange Pentel pen) on white quarto sheets pinned to an Art Nouveau board or sliding loose on the dust jacket of *The Architecture of Sir John Soane.* As I write I lie on my back on an early nineteenth century Sheraton settee upholstered in flowered green brocade. Sometimes I am interrupted by the beautiful tabby cat who gave his name and some of his adventures, to *The Orlando Poems.*"

FOR MORE INFORMATION SEE: New York Times Book Review, October 16, 1966; *Horn Book,* December, 1966, October, 1969, February 15, 1970; *London Magazine,* May, 1967, October, 1968; *Observer,* May 14, 1967; *Times Literary Supplement,* June 22, 1967; *Punch,* July 5, 1967; *Listener,* July 6, 1967; *Poetry Review,* summer,

1967; *Books and Bookmen,* November, 1967; *Kenyon Review,* November, 1967; *Book World,* December 24, 1967, November 9, 1969; *Hudson Review,* winter, 1967-68; *Virginia Quarterly Review,* winter, 1968, summer, 1969.

MacKELLAR, William 1914-

PERSONAL: Born February 20, 1914, in Glasgow, Scotland; brought to United States when he was eleven; son of Iohn (a blacksmith) and Mary (Justice) MacKellar; married Helen Mulcahy, April 10, 1954; children: John, Laurie, David. *Education:* Studied at New York University for three years and at University of Geneva. *Home:* 40 Mountain Rd., West Hartford, Conn. 06107. *Agent:* McIntosh & Otis, Inc., 18 East 41st St., New York, N.Y. 10017. *Office:* Royal Typewriter Co., Hartford, Conn. 06106.

CAREER: Royal Typewriter Co., International Division, Hartford, Conn., export manager, 1965—. Writer for children and teen-agers. *Military service:* U.S. Army, Signal Corps, 1942-45; served in North Africa and Europe. *Awards, honors:* Citation in Child Study Association of America Children's Book Awards, 1957, for *Wee Joseph.*

WRITINGS: The Mystery of the Ruined Abbey, Whittlesey House, 1954; *Kickoff,* Whittlesey House, 1955; *Danger in the Mist,* Whittlesey House, 1956; *The Team That Wouldn't Quit,* Whittlesey House, 1956; *Wee Joseph,* Whittlesey House, 1957; *Two for the Fair,* Whittlesey House, 1958; *A Goal for Gregg,* McKay, 1958; *Ghost in the Castle,* McKay, 1960; *A Dog Like No Other,* McKay, 1965; *A Place by the Fire,* McKay, 1966; *The Secret of the Dark Tower,* McKay, 1967; *Score: A Baker's Dozen Sports Stories,* McKay, 1967; *A Very Small Miracle,* Crown, 1969; *Mound Menace,* Follett, 1969; *The Smallest Monster in the World,* McKay, 1969; *Secret of the Sacred Stone,* McKay, 1970; *A Ghost Around the House,* McKay, 1970; *The Mystery of Mordach Castle,* Follett, 1970. Stories included in anthologies and school readers, and published in *Boys' Life* and other magazines.

SIDELIGHTS: MacKellar's books have a Scottish and European flavor, reflecting his own boyhood in Glasgow, Scotland, European service during World War II and a four-year business assignment in Switzerland. "I've always stuck to boys. I don't know how a girl's mind works. And it's a funny thing, girls will read stories about boys, but boys won't read stories about girls! And no kid likes to read about fellows younger than he. So you've got to hedge a bit about the age.

"Writers are just as much in the entertainment business as actors and television personalities—maybe more so. Certainly they are not in the education business, or social science or theology. I don't believe fiction writers should try to remold and somehow improve the child's mind with inspirational lessons and moralizing examples. Children are naturally idealistic and hopeful, at least until they grow up. Who was it said 'A grown-up is just an obsolete child?' I believe that.

"I try to preserve that special sense of innocence and fantasy that are so much a part of the imaginative child. Too often, in giving wisdom, we take away wonder. The child without a sense of marvel at the world around him, one who is incurious, unstirred by dreams, is an incomplete and cheated child."

MacKellar lived in Switzerland, 1958-62, and has travelled in all countries of western Europe, in Yugoslavia, and in Bulgaria, 1971.

FOR MORE INFORMATION SEE: Horn Book, February, 1970; *Hartford Times Sunday Magazine,* Hartford, Conn., September 26, 1971.

MacPEEK, Walter G. 1902-
(Hugo Jumpp)

PERSONAL: Born March 14, 1902, in Stockton, Ill.; son of Perry Oliver and Louisa Anna (Brunner) MacPeek; married Virginia Stevens, October 24, 1941; children: Walt L. *Education:* University of Chicago, Ph.B., 1924; graduate study at University of Michigan, 1939-40, New York University, 1953, and Rutgers University, 1960.

WALTER G. MAC PEEK

Politics: Republican. *Religion:* Presbyterian. *Home:* Apt. 5, Twin Oaks Villas, 11200 102nd. Ave. N., Seminole, Fla. 33540.

CAREER: Boy Scouts of America, New Brunswick, N.J., writer and editor, 1953-67, assistant to director of editorial service and associate editor of *Scouting,* 1953-67; *New Brunswick Sunday Home News,* New Brunswick, N.J., editor of book column, 1967—; *Boys' Life,* New Brunswick, N.J., stamp and coin editor, 1968—. American Humanities Foundation, consultant. *Member:* Sigma Delta Chi. *Awards, honors:* Gold Medal from Freedoms Foundation, 1960.

WRITINGS—Youth books: *George Washington: Real Boy,* Franklin Press (Washington, D.C.), 1932; *Glimpses into Boyland,* Franklin Press, 1933; *Stories Stamps Tell,* Franklin Press, 1933; *Fetching Up Fred,* Peak Press, 1940; *Celebrating Boy Scout Week,* Boy Scouts of America, 1955; *The Scout Law in Action,* Abingdon, 1966; *The Scout Oath in Action,* Abingdon, 1967; *Scout Leaders in Action,* Abingdon, 1969; *Resourceful Scouts in Action,* Abingdon, 1972. Contributing editor, *Quote,* 1967—.

WORK IN PROGRESS: A book on human relations; a book on stamps as aids to learning; other books, including one related to writing procedures.

SIDELIGHTS: 'As a youngster I delighted in going to the library, in owning books, and in writing small bits for publication. At fourteen, I was editing a Lone Scout publication which circulated throughout the country. I wrote for school and college papers and throughout a long career with the Boy Scouts of America, I wrote interpretive material for newspapers and training and other materials for parents and leaders.

"My work has been chiefly the interpreting of the qualities and potentials of boys to grown-ups. I stress the importance of boys learning from reality, even from mistakes. I interpret practical concepts of everyday life and the Ideal of Scouting in my *Oath* and *Law* books, the importance of leaders in my *Scout Leaders in Action,* and the promises of boys in my most recent book, *Resourceful Scouts in Action.*

"I am a believer in everyday greatness. I believe that great men and women and boys, live all around us, on Main Street, and in Center City. More than 100,000 copies of my books are in use today. I am proud that my books are not merely sold and read, but that they are USED."

HOBBIES AND OTHER INTERESTS: "Making friends; collecting stamps and autographs, and doing some painting."

FOR MORE INFORMATION SEE: Sunshine Magazine, April, 1970.

MALO, John 1911-

PERSONAL: Born April 11, 1911, in Ringo, Kan.; son of John (a farmer) and Helen (Kocol) Malo; married Renee B. Mier (a free-lance artist), November 24, 1935; children: Kenneth, Marcia. *Education:* Northwestern University, B.S. in Ed., 1934; DePaul University, M.A. in Ed., 1947; also studied at University of Warsaw, University of Chicago, Chicago Teacher's College, and the Art Institute. *Home:* 1230 Pinehurst Dr., Glenview, Ill. 60025.

CAREER: Foreman High School, Chicago, Ill., teacher and coach, 1941-56, counsellor, 1956-60, assistant principal, 1960-71, retired, 1971. Canoe instructor at summer camps. *Member:* Outdoor Writers Association of America, American Snowmobile Association, Association of Great Lakes Outdoor Writers, North Shore Writers Group, Glenview Historical Society, Evanston Bird Club, Phi Delta Kappa. *Awards, honors:* Coach of the Year Award of Chicagoland Prep Writers, 1953; Citation in annual competition sponsored by Evinrude Motors and Outdoor Writers Association of America, 1970, for *Canoeing;* Thermos Award ($1000), 1972, for "excellence in writing and personal endeavor on outdoor recreation."

WRITINGS: Canoeing (youth book), Follett, 1969; *Malo's Complete Guide to Canoeing and Canoe-Camping,* Quadrangle, 1969; *Wilderness Canoeing,* Macmillan, 1971; *Snowmobiling: The Guide,* Macmillan, 1971; *All-Terrain Adventure Vehicles,* Macmillan, 1972. Writer of magazine and newspaper articles on canoeing, snowmobiling, dune buggying, and off-road adventuring.

WORK IN PROGRESS: Tranquil Trail, a nature diary.

SIDELIGHTS: Malo first became interested in canoeing as a teen-ager and has been exploring wilderness streams and introducing young people to outdoor life ever since. He has traveled by canoe in unmapped areas of Canada, kayaked in Europe, and paddled a dugout canoe in British Honduras and Guatemala. He also has tried gold panning and uranium prospecting in the American West and fished in the sea, lakes, and streams. With the heightened interest in snowmobiling, he has done research on snowmobiles in six states.

Malo takes forty boys from a local high school club on scheduled trips each year; fishing, skiing, snowmobiling, canoeing, and visits to historical sites. "The philosophy of the club is wrapped up in the fact that boys will grow up into a society with a lot more leisure then ever before, a four-day work-week, and three-day weekend. Not enough people are learning skills and developing interests that will make their leisure stimulating and worthwhile. Leisure will become a curse instead of a blessing, unless they develop techniques and attitudes in youth that will enable them to extract the adventure out of their spare time activities. These young men have developed a real sensitivity to nature. They have shot deer and moose in Canada and gone deep-sea fishing in Florida, and became involved in the conservation movements. They have broadened their experiences and are happier people for it. They tie their own flies, make their own rods, seek out new vistas, and develop a sensitivity to the realms of nature."

FOR MORE INFORMATION SEE: Peacock North West Newspapers, July 12, 1970.

MAPES, Mary A.
See ELLISON, Virginia Howell

RICHARD J. MARGOLIS

MARGOLIS, Richard 1929-

PERSONAL: Born June 30, 1929, in St. Paul, Minn.; son of Harry Sterling (a rabbi) and Clara (Brunner) Margolis; married Diane Rothbard (a sociologist), April 3, 1954; children: Harry Sterling, Philip Eliot. *Education:* University of Minnesota, B.A., 1952, M.A., 1953. *Home and office:* R.D.1, Georgetown, Conn. 06829.

CAREER: Brooklyn Heights Press, Brooklyn, N.Y., editor and publisher, 1956-60; Lerner Newspapers, Chicago, Ill., editorial director, 1960-62; free-lance writer, 1962—. Rural Housing Alliance, national chairman; consultant at various times to Ford Foundation, Stern Fund, U.S. Civil Rights Commission, U.S. Office of Economic Opportunity, U.S. Bureau of Indian Affairs, and other government and private agencies. Member of Library Board, Wilton, Conn. *Awards, honors:* George Polk Memorial Award for achievement in journalism, 1959; National Editorial Association Award for editorial writing, 1962.

WRITINGS: Something to Build On (nonfiction), American Friends Service Committee, 1966; *Only the Moon and Me* (poems), Lippincott, 1968; *Looking for a Place* (poems for younger people), Lippincott, 1969; *The Upside-Down King* (children's story in rhyme), Windmill Books, 1971; *Wish Again, Big Bear* (children's fable), Macmillan, 1972; *Homer the Hunter* (children's fable), Macmillan, 1972. Contributor of articles and reviews to *Life, New Leader, Redbook, New York Times Magazine, Nation, Playboy, Dissent, The New Republic, Washington Monthly,* and many other periodicals.

WORK IN PROGRESS: Adult book on the cooperative movement in America; essays on rural housing; children's book on Indian poetry; more poems and stories.

SIDELIGHTS: "I began writing children's poetry when my two sons started talking back to me in uncanny ways. The things they said made me remember the things *I* had said when I was a child. So much of my poetry is based on the plain talk of children.

"I believe that poetry is the art of saying something important in a way that people won't forget. (It doesn't have to be Significant; it simply must mean a lot to the poet.)

"The stories and fables I write are simple ideas that occur to me from time to time, usually early in the morning. They are mostly about friendship and how hard it is to come by (*Wish Again, Big Bear*).

"I've been free-lancing articles and studies for a decade. When I had 'steady jobs,' I never got to work on time. So I took the easy way out."

FOR MORE INFORMATION SEE: *Junior Literary Guild Catalogue,* March, 1972.

MAY, Charles Paul 1920-

PERSONAL: Born November 23, 1920, in Bedford, Iowa; son of Harry E. and Alice (Chamberlin) May. *Education:* Northwest Missouri State Teachers College, student, 1938-40; Drake University, B.A., 1947; Oklahoma Agriculture and Mechanical College (now Oklahoma State University), M.A., 1948. *Home:* 260 West 72nd St., New York, N.Y. 10023. *Mailing address:* P.O. Box 548, Ansonia Station, New York, N.Y. 10023.

CAREER: Oklahoma Agriculture and Mechanical College, Stillwater, teaching fellow, 1947-48; Ohio University, Athens, instructor, 1948-49; Grolier Society, Incorporated, New York, N.Y., editor, 1949-62 (editorial staff of *Book of Knowledge, Book of Popular Science, Lands and Peoples, Book of Knowledge Annual, Encyclopedia Year Book*); free-lance writer of youth books, and photographer, 1962—. *Military service:* U.S. Army, 1940-45.

Contributor to *Book of Knowledge,* and of almost two hundred entries to *Encyclopedia International.* Contributor of articles and stories to *Jack and Jill, Child Life,* and about thirty other youth periodicals; reviewer of youth books for *New York Times,* and regular contributor of reviews to *Library Journal* and to various newspapers. Photographs have appeared in *New York Times, National Geographic,* and *Travel.*

WRITINGS: *Box Turtle Lives in Armor,* Holiday House, 1960; *Michael Faraday and the Electric Dynamo,* Watts, 1961; *A Book of Canadian Animals,* Macmillan (Canada), 1962; *James Clerk-Maxwell and Electromagnetism,* Watts, 1962; *Women in Aeronautics,* Nelson, 1962; *Pink Pig and the Nut Tree,* Barnes, 1962; *Little Mouse,* Barnes, 1962; *Veterinarians and Their Patients,* Nelson, 1964; *A Second Book of Canadian Animals,* Macmillan (Canada), 1964; *Animals of the Far North,* Abelard, 1964; *When Animals Change Clothes,* Holiday House, 1965; *Central America: Lands Seeking Unity,* Nelson, 1966; *High-Noon Rocket,* Holiday House, 1966; *Great Cities of Canada,* Abelard, 1967; *A Book of Canadian Birds,* Macmillan, 1967; *Book of American Birds,* St. Martins, 1967; *Chile: Progress on Trial,* Nelson, 1968; *A Book of Reptiles and Amphibians,* St. Martin's, 1968; *Bats,* Hawthorn, 1969; *Peru, Bolivia, Ecuador: The Indian Andes,* Nelson, 1969; *The Early Indians,* Nelson, 1971; *Stranger in the Storm,* Abelard, 1972; *A Book of Insects,* St. Martin's, 1972; *Oceania,* Nelson, in press. Former member of editorial staff, *Encyclopedia Canadiana.*

SIDELIGHTS: "Having grown up on a dairy farm in Iowa, I was around domestic and wild animals for about seventeen years, which helped me write on nature subjects. As a sixth grader, I won a prize in school for a 'story' and from then on I wanted to be a writer. I wrote a book-length adult novel the summer I graduated from high school, but editors failed to find it publishable. This didn't stop me from writing others, which proved equally unmarketable. When I turned to writing for young people, however, I sold the first piece I produced and knew I had discovered an exciting, satisfying field of endeavor.

"The first sale was an article, accepted by *Jack and Jill* when I was twenty-one. Books remained my main interest, but my first tries at novels for young readers lacked what editors wanted. In time, just as with shorter pieces, I turned to nonfiction, and when I was thirty-seven I got my first book contract. This factual work, *Box Turtle Lives in Armor,* led to a variety of other animal books.

"Next in number are my works on other countries, which grow out of my love of travel and my ability to take the photographs to help illustrate them. Since discovering the delights of writing for young people, I have never tried to produce an adult book again, yet several of my books on other lands as well as *Women in Aeronautics* and *Veterinarians and their Patients* turn up in the adult sections of libraries.

"I go to schools and libraries throughout the United States and Canada (where I lived for more than a year while helping edit *Encyclopedia Canadiana*), talking to young people and giving programs with my colored slides from various sections of the world I visited. In this way I keep in touch with the young audience for whom I write, since I am a foot-loose bachelor rather than a family man."

CHARLES PAUL MAY

McCARTHY, Agnes 1933-

PERSONAL: Born June 20, 1933, in New York, N.Y.; daughter of Daniel Charles and Agnes (Blandford) McCarthy; married Harold L. Wise (an educational consultant), September 4, 1965; children: Daniel. *Education:* Catholic University of America, A.B., 1954; State University of New York, New Paltz, M.A. (African Studies), 1972. *Residence:* Woodstock, N.Y. *Agent:* McIntosh & Otis, Inc., 18 East 41st St., New York, N.Y. 10017.

CAREER: Elementary teacher in Casper, Wyo., 1956-58; Scholastic Magazines, New York, N.Y., coordinating editor, 1960-62; Harcourt, Brace & World, Inc., New York, N.Y., language text editor, 1962-64; American Education Publications, Middletown, Conn., professional materials editor, 1964-65; Center for the Study of Instruction, San Francisco, Calif., research associate, 1966—; free-lance writer and editor of books for young people.

WRITINGS: Let's Go to Vote, Putnam, 1961; *Let's Go to a Court,* Putnam, 1962; *Giant Animals of Long Ago,* Prentice-Hall, 1963; *Creatures of the Deep,* Prentice-Hall, 1963; *New York State: Its Land and People,* Doubleday, 1963; (with Lawrence Reddick) *Worth Fighting For: A Story of the Negro in the Civil War,* Zenith Books, 1965; *Room 10* (juvenile fiction), Doubleday, 1966; *The Impossibles* (juvenile), Doubleday, 1968; (with others) *The Social Sciences: Concepts and Values,* (Books 1-6), Harcourt, 1970. Contributor of articles and short stories to elementary school publications.

Editor: *Language for Daily Use,* Book 5, Harcourt, 1965; *The Picture Story of Cape Cod,* Scrimshaw, 1965; *Around Cape Cod with Cap'n Goody,* Scrimshaw, 1965; *Cape Cod Seashore Life,* Scrimshaw, 1966.

WORK IN PROGRESS: Co-author of *The Humanities* (Book 1-6), for Harcourt; research on non-verbal communication and on cognitive styles, and comparative cultures.

SIDELIGHTS: "When I sit down to write, I think about two things—myself and the subject. As for myself, I want to enjoy what I am writing about. As for the subject, words-on-paper have to sound right when you whisper them to yourself. So, the words have to suit the subject; as, in a book about fish, you would want flowing words and gliding words, and in a book about war, you would want quick, loud, sharp words.

"One thing I hardly ever consider at all as I write is the reader. I don't think young people really want to be catered to, nor do they fall for fads and fashions in books. It seems to me that young people generally are more perceptive and more compassionate than older people, and because of these qualities they accept or reject books with sweet reason and amazing objectivity.

"If by happy chance someone enjoys reading a book that I have enjoyed writing, then some kind of bond of trust and understanding has been established. It does make me happy to think of invisible, spontaneous bonds like that. It does make me feel that perhaps there is no generation gap—no communication gap—between old writers and young readers."

Jimmy couldn't even spell his last name right on his picture. Miss Lavender had to spell it for him. We teased him about that quite a bit. ■ (From *Room 10* by Agnes McCarthy. Illustrated by Ib Ohlsson.)

McDOLE, Carol
See FARLEY, Carol

McHARGUE, Georgess
(Alice Chase, Margo Scegge Usher)

PERSONAL: Born in Norwalk, Conn.; daughter of W.R. (in advertising) and Georgess (Boomhower) McHargue. *Education:* Radcliffe College, B.A., 1963. *Politics:* Radical-Independent. *Religion:* None. *Home and office:* 339 East 82nd St., New York, N.Y. 10028. *Agent:* Ellen Levine, Curtis Brown Ltd., 60 East 56th St., New York, N.Y. 10022.

CAREER: Golden Press, New York, N.Y., various staff work, 1963-65; Doubleday & Co., Inc., New York, N.Y., associate editor, 1965-68, editor, 1968-70; free-lance writer, 1970—. *Member:* American Civil Liberties Union, Wilderness Society, Phi Beta Kappa, Lexington Dem-

GEORGESS McHARGUE

He was the most beautiful, the most noble, the most elusive of legendary creatures. He walked alone; he was gentle and proud, but would fight to the death if attacked. ■ (From *The Beasts of Never* by Georgess McHargue. Illustrated by Frank Bozzo.)

ocratic Club. *Awards, honors:* Book World's Spring Book Festival Award, 1972, for *The Impossible People.*

WRITINGS: The Beasts of Never: A History Natural and Un-natural of Monsters Mythical and Magical (juvenile), Bobbs, 1968; (compiler) *The Best of Both Worlds: An Anthology of Short Stories for All Ages,* Doubleday, 1968; *The Baker and the Basilisk* (Junior Literary Guild selection), Bobbs, 1970; *The Wonderful Wings of Harold Harrabescu* (Junior Literary Guild selection), Delacorte, 1971; *The Impossible People,* Holt, 1972; *Facts, Frauds, and Phantasms: A Survey of the Spiritualist Movement* (Junior Literary Guild selection), Doubleday, 1972. Author of mass-market juveniles under the pseudonyms Alice Chase and Margo Scegge Usher.

WORK IN PROGRESS: Private Zoo, for Delacorte; a book on mummies for Lippincott; a juvenile novel for Holt; *The Mermaid and the Whale,* for Holt; an anthology of science fiction, for Holt.

SIDELIGHTS: "I suppose I write books for children to read because I was a reading child. For some reason I had more than my share of childhood illnesses, from continuous colds to rheumatic fever, and, sick or well, I read everything I could get my hands on—children's classics, Nancy Drew, comic books, the *Reader's Digest* and *Saturday Evening Post,* Shakespeare, *The Golden Treasury,* my parents' mystery stories, and many supposedly 'adult' books such as *The Once and Future King,* Steinbeck, Hemingway, and a lot of anthropology.

"When I was looking for my first job with a publishing house, I suddenly realized that I had a good background for children's books: I had read everything. I also had some strong opinions about what I had *not read* because it wasn't available. Stories that showed families as real people who had problems with anger, jealousy, divorce, and other disruptions were totally non-existent among the books I read and when I turned to adult novels I often came upon things I simply didn't understand. As a result, I am convinced that children should be encouraged to read everything they feel a need for, with no taboos. Though my writings to date have been aimed more at the need for fantasy, which I also feel is very strong, I still see some gaps in the kind of books I would have wanted to read—gaps that I hope to help fill.

"As for the way I write, I do most of my work at home, but I can write and have written in all sorts of places, from beaches to bus stations. I guess I am blessed with the sort of Protestant conscience that won't let me rest until I've accomplished a modicum of work each day. I love freelancing but I know I've worked harder at it than I ever did in an office"

Ms. McHargue's vacations are usually spent in Scotland, Italy, or the wilderness areas of the far West.

HOBBIES AND OTHER INTERESTS: Falconry, mythical beings, monsters, politics, art, theater, arcana, conservation, Renaissance history, gardening, embroidery, hiking, and horseback riding.

FOR MORE INFORMATION SEE: Junior Literary Guild Catalog, March, 1972; *New York Times Book Review,* April 2, 1972.

MEYER, June
See JORDAN, June

MIKLOWITZ, Gloria D. 1927-

PERSONAL: Surname is pronounced *Mick*-lo-witz; born May 18, 1927, in New York, N.Y.; daughter of Simon (president of a steamship company) and Ella (Goldberg) Dubov; married Julius Miklowitz (a college professor), August 28, 1948; children: Paul S., David J. *Education:* Hunter College, student, 1944-45; University of Michigan, B.A., 1948. *Home:* 5255 Vista Miguel Dr., La Canada, Calif. 91011. *Agent:* Larry Sternig, 2407 North 44th St., Milwaukee, Wis. 53210.

CAREER: U.S. Naval Ordnance Test Station, Pasadena, Calif., scriptwriter, 1952-57; author. *Member:* P.E.N. International, California Writer's Guild, Southern California Council of Literature for Children and Young People.

WRITINGS: Barefoot Boy (juvenile), Follett, 1964; (contributor) *The Old Fashioned Ice-Cream Freezer,* Science Research Associates, 1967; *The Zoo That Moved* (juvenile), Follett, 1968; (with Wesley A. Young) *The Zoo Was My World,* Dutton, 1969; *The Parade Starts at Noon,* Putnam, 1969; (contributor) *Real and Fantastic,* Harper, 1970; *The Marshmallow Caper,* Putnam, 1971; *Turning Off,* Putnam, 1973; *Sad Song, Happy Song,* Putnam, 1973; *When the Earth Shakes,* Putnam, in press. Contributor to *Sports Illustrated* and other magazines.

SIDELIGHTS: "I write for children because the world of children interests me. I am curious, as they are, about everything: about insects and animals, people, and how things work and why, about what it feels like to walk in the rain, or touch the snow. I ask a lot of questions, which most adults are reluctant to do—either because they already know the answers, or because they are embarrassed to reveal that they don't. But *I* want to know. When I meet strangers, I like to know what they do, how they do it, and why and what they think about what they do. This curiosity, I think, is almost childlike, and maybe that's why I know what children might find interesting. If it interests me, it should interest them.

"The world of the imagination is sometimes more exciting than the real world because in the imagination we can manipulate the world. We can put ourselves in strange places and situations, do things we might not normally do, give villain roles to people we dislike—all in our imaginations. Sometimes, when I'm writing, the characters take on lives of their own. It's a kind of magic, a little like playing with dolls. Without conscious thought, the people you create on paper take on personalities and thoughts of their own, and their words flow out through your fingers to the paper.

Ivan, the polar bear, was sure the cooling system needed work. He was nearly always feeling the heat. ■ (From *The Zoo That Moved* by Gloria D. Miklowitz. Illustrated by Don Madden.)

GLORIA D. MIKLOWITZ

"How do ideas develop? The head is like a computer. Feed it with all kinds of information and experience, and it selects from the chaos, finding a shape or form for a story. As an example, when writing *Turning Off*, I did not have a story until three quite separate things fit together: a flood at an animal reserve that I had read about; a black boy I knew; and a conviction I had about life. The flood was interesting, and I had taken notes on it some two years before writing the book, but in itself it was only an interesting incident. The black boy was the son of a friend, a high school dropout, in a camp for drug addicts. The conviction was the long held belief that people who have something interesting to do with their time don't get into trouble.

"It was not until all three elements were present in my mind that the mental computer went to work, identified these three elements as belonging together, and showed me how a story might develop. The story is that of a black boy who has been on drugs and is still fearful that he could return to his old habits. His probation officer gets him a job at an animal reserve where animals are trained for television and movies. There he gradually discovers the pleasure in doing a job well and in gaining the respect of fellow workers. With responsibility comes self respect and the knowledge that he no longer needs drugs. He gets his kicks from life.

"Most of my books have dealt with animals, an interest which developed quite accidentally. About five years ago I read a news item about the proposed move of the Los Angeles Zoo. Curious about how an entire zoo might be moved, I went to the director and asked, and later observed the move over a period of months. From this experience I wrote *The Zoo That Moved* and *The Zoo Was My World.* If I had not been curious, I might not have written either book, nor *The Parade Starts at Noon,* based on something that had happened to the zoo director years before: he had saved a squirrel that was caught in a tuba.

"Because I had written amusingly about the zoo, my publisher suggested I write about seven adventuresome polar bears who had escaped from a Chicago zoo and were discovered eating marshmallows and ice cream at the snack bar the next day. *The Marshmallow Caper* grew from this news story.

"A friend sent me a news item which began: 'Can big city alligators find happiness in the swamps of Mississippi?' The rehabilitation of zoo alligators became *Sad Song, Happy Song,* about an alligator who is forceably taken from his home, sold as a pet, abused, donated to the zoo, and finally returned to the swamp."

Ms. Miklowitz spent eight months abroad in 1964-65, when her husband was on a National Science Foundation fellowship in Rome and in Rehovoth, Israel.

FOR MORE INFORMATION SEE: *Writer,* August, 1972.

MINTONYE, Grace

PERSONAL: Surname is pronounced Min-*tone*-ya; born in Kansas City, Mo.; daughter of Fred (an engineer) and Rose Belle (Turpin) Gabelman; married Byron Everhart Mintonye, October 21, 1926 (deceased). *Education:* Central Missouri State College, Warrensburg, student, 1924-26. *Politics:* Republican. *Religion:* Christian. *Home:* Oak Hall, 4550 Warwick Blvd., Kansas City, Mo. 64111.

CAREER: Former editor of house organ for chain of women's wear stores and writer-producer of daily homemaker program on KMBC and KMBC-TV, Kansas City, Mo.; William Rockhill Nelson Gallery of Art and Mary Atkins Museum of Fine Arts, Kansas City, Mo., children's librarian and assistant to James E. Siedelman, director of education, 1960-68; Living Arts and Science Center, Lexington, Ky., administrative assistant to director, 1968—. *Member:* National League of American Pen Women (past secretary of Kansas City branch; president of Kentucky branch, 1970-72), Woman's City Club (Kansas City; executive secretary, 1971—), Gamma Alpha Chi. *Awards, honors:* First award for juvenile plays in two contests sponsored by Kansas City branch of National League of American Pen Women.

WRITINGS—"Creating" series, with James E. Seidelman; all published by Crowell-Collier: *Creating with Clay,* 1967, *Creating with Paper,* 1967, *Creating with Paint,*

1967, *Creating Mosaics*, 1968, *Creating with Wood*, 1969, *Shopping Cart Art*, 1970, *Creating with Paper Mache*, 1971.

Other children's books with Seidelman: *The Rub Book*, Crowell-Collier, 1968; *The 14th Dragon*, Harlin Quist Books, 1968. The writing team also is responsible for four gallery films, "Treasures of Time" distributed by International Film Co., Chicago, and a monthly column in *Wee Wisdom* (children's magazine published by Unity School of Christianity).

Author with Bea Johnson of "Happy Home" series of cookbooks. Plays include "Explosion in a Glass Factory," produced by the Junior Curator Association of Corning Museum of Glass.

SIDELIGHTS: Ms. Mintonye began writing in Kansas City when a friend happened to mention that publishers in New York were looking for children's books. At the time James Seidelman was director of The Junior Gallery and Creative Arts Center at the William Rockhill Nelson Gallery of Art and Ms. Mintonye was children's librarian. "Seidelman asked me if I'd help him and I said, 'Sure'. The next day we sent a query three paragraphs long telling the publisher what we thought we could do. The editor immediately called and asked when we could start writing.

GRACE MINTONYE

"Jim and I are continuing our writing by sending tape recordings back and forth. He sends me recordings of his classroom projects with the children and I write them up as material for our books or for a monthly feature we do for *Wee Wisdom* magazine, published by the Unity School of Christianity. The feature 'Seidelman Says,' began in 1968."

FOR MORE INFORMATION SEE: *Kansas City Star*, September 25, 1967; *Pen Women*, November, 1967.

MUNZER, Martha E. 1899-

PERSONAL: Born September 22, 1899, in New York, N.Y.; daughter of Samuel and Stella (Stettheimer) Eiseman; married Edward M. Munzer, 1922 (deceased); children: Edward, Jr., Martha Munzer Glogau, Stella Munzer Loeb. *Education:* Ethical Culture School, student, 1918; Massachusetts Institute of Technology, B.S. in Electrochemical Engineering, 1922. *Home:* 517 Munro Ave., Mamaroneck, N.Y. 10543.

CAREER: Fieldston School, New York, N.Y., teacher of chemistry, director of community activities, 1930-54; Conservation Foundation, New York, N.Y., research, writing, 1954-68; Wave Hill Center for Environmental Studies, associate, Riverdale, N.Y., 1968-71; Environmental education consultant, 1971—. Ethical School Camp, Cooperstown, N.Y., sometime head counselor, 1931-55; Junior Work Camp, Netcong, N.J., director, 1938-41; European Work Camp, France, director, 1948; Science Work Camp, South Salem, N.Y., 1952; Riverdale Outdoor Laboratories, staff member; Town of Mamaroneck, member of conservation advisory committee. *Member:* Chemistry Teachers Club of New York (president, 1947), National Science Teachers Association, Conservation Education Association (board of directors, 1962-64), Student Conservation Association (board of directors, 1965—). *Awards, honors:* Honored by Governor Nelson Rockefeller in his 1966 "Salute to Women."

WRITINGS: (With Paul Brandwein) *Teaching Science Through Conservation*, McGraw, 1960; *Unusual Careers*, Knopf, 1962; *Planning Our Town: An Introduction to City and Regional Planning*, Knopf, 1964; *Pockets of Hope*, Knopf, 1967; *Valley of Vision: The TVA Years*, Knopf; 1970; (with Helen Vogel) *Block by Block: The Rebuilding of a City*, Knopf, in press. Contributor to professional journals.

SIDELIGHTS: "Conservation is where people are, as well as where they aren't. That's why my interest in conservation has focused more and more on the urban scene, and on city and regional planning. I've also become interested in what ordinary people—you and I—can do to improve the quality of our environment."

Ms. Munzer wrote *Unusual Careers* because she wanted children to know that "conservation isn't just for the birds." She writes outdoors "in sight and sound and feel of sky and sun" and doesn't go indoors to write in the winter but bundles in a sleeping bag and wears mittens. She travels to give lectures and to study conservation projects, examples of city and regional planning.

MARTHA E. MUNZER

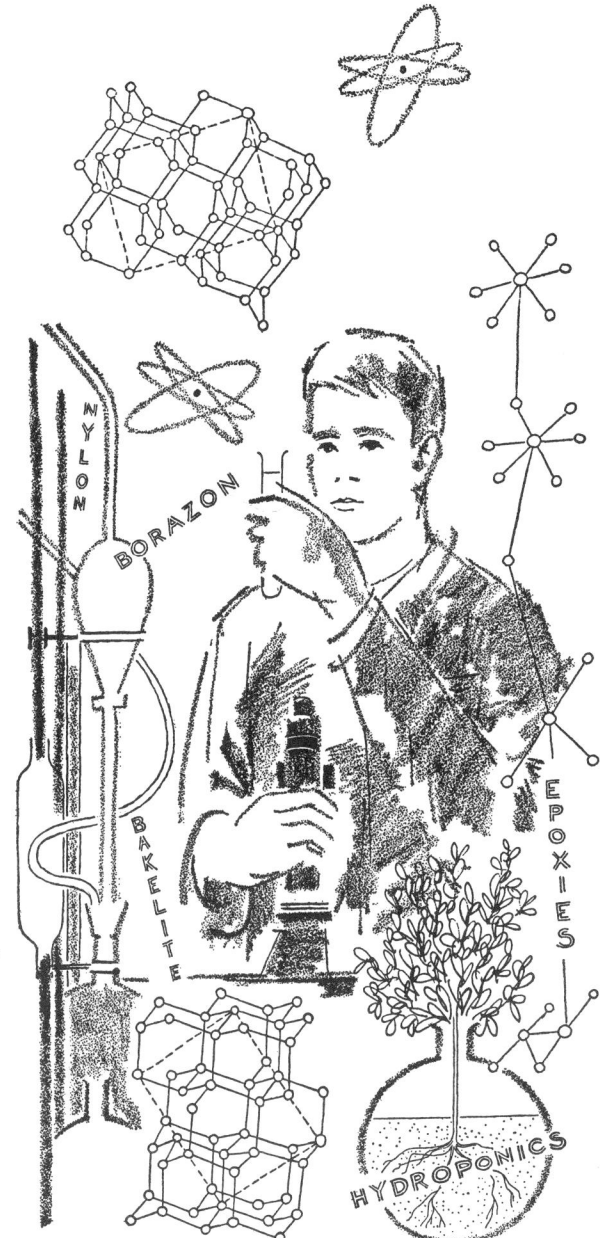

Scientists explore other more immediate methods of increasing our conventional food supply. ■ (From *Unusual Careers* by Martha E. Munzer. Illustrated by John Kaufmann.)

HOBBIES AND OTHER INTERESTS: Knitting, hiking, swimming and "basking," reading and grand-and-great-grandchildren.

FOR MORE INFORMATION SEE: Milwaukee Journal, February 11, 1962; *Daily Times,* Mamaroneck, N.Y., March 24, 1962, February, 1965; *Arkansas Democrat,* June 25, 1963; *Westport* (Conn.) *News,* December 3, 1964; *Standard Star,* New Rochelle, N.Y., November 15, 1967; *The Riverdale* (N.Y.) *Press,* April 4, 1968; *The Post Mail,* Port Washington, N.Y., May 21, 1970; *Herald Statesman,* Yonkers, N.Y., October 15, 1971.

MURPHY, E(mmett) Jefferson 1926-
(Pat Murphy)

PERSONAL: Born July 2, 1926, in Thomasville, Ga.; son of Emmett Jefferson (a dentist) and Gladys (Jeffers) Murphy; married Mildred Blackman (a real estate broker), March 7, 1957; children: Therese, Kathleen, Emmett Jefferson III. *Education:* Emory University, A.B., 1948, M.A., 1949; additional graduate study at University of North Carolina, 1950-51, University of Chicago, 1951-52, and University of Connecticut, 1971-72. *Home:* 15 Ferncliff Rd., Cos Cob, Conn. 06807.

CAREER: Emory University, Atlanta, Ga., instructor in sociology, 1950; University College of Fort Hare, Fort Hare, Union of South Africa, visiting lecturer in anthropology, 1952-53; African-American Institute, New York, N.Y., director of programs, Washington, D.C., 1954-57, regional representative in Accra, Ghana, 1957-61, in Dar es Salaam, Tanganyika, 1961-63, vice-president, Washington, 1963-65, executive vice-president, New York, N.Y., 1965-71. African Scholarship Program of American Universities, trustee, 1964-71; Museum of African Art, Washington, D.C., trustee, 1964—. *Military service:* U.S. Navy, 1943-46; became lieutenant junior grade. *Member:* Columbia University Faculty Seminar on Africa, African Studies Association.

WRITINGS: Understanding Africa (young adult), Crowell, 1969; *African Legacy: A History of African Civilization,* Crowell, 1972. Numerous articles and book reviews on Africa and educational exchange for journals and newspapers.

WORK IN PROGRESS: The Bantu Civilization of Southern Africa, for Crowell; *Teaching Africa Today,* a handbook for teachers, for Citation Press.

SIDELIGHTS: "I had written nothing, except a number of short book reviews and articles for various newspapers and specialized journals and newsletters, until age forty. At that time I began my first book, *Understanding Africa,* as a book for general readers who could be expected to know very little about Africa. I had just finished a course of lectures for adults, and decided to use my notes and background work as the basis for a book. After I had written several chapters Crowell's children's department bought it, and I suddenly and unexpectedly found myself writing for young people. It turned out to be both a challenge and a joy, and launched me on a writing career with young people as my special and favorite readership.

"Although I have found that I enjoy writing in general, it is the writing to bring Africa understandably and sympathetically to life for younger readers that turns me on—so much so that I have resigned an active career in order to finish my Ph.D. in Education, then to devote my life to teaching (both in high school and college) and to writing for schools, younger readers, and teachers.

"My many years of studying sociology and anthropology, plus my years in Africa, are more relevant for the kind of writing and teaching I do than I ever expected. But the most direct influence on both writing and teaching comes

A West African Ashanti King. ■ (From *Understanding Africa* by E. Jefferson Murphy. Illustrated by Louise E. Jefferson. Reprinted by permission of Thomas Y. Crowell Co.)

from a deep rooted liking for Africans, combined with a feeling that Africa has long been misunderstood, unappreciated, and often maligned and exploited."

HOBBIES AND OTHER INTERESTS: Sailing and skiing with his children; "I enjoy young people, both my own and others, and especially like teaching."

FOR MORE INFORMATION SEE: Horn Book, August, 1969.

MURPHY, Pat
See MURPHY, E. Jefferson

MUSSEY, Virginia T. H.
See ELLISON, Virginia Howell

NAZAROFF, Alexander I. 1898-

PERSONAL: Born February 21, 1898, in Kiev, Russia; son of Ivan S. (a physician) and Ludmilla (Tripolitoff) Nazaroff; married Barbara De Carriere, September 12, 1918. *Education:* University of Odessa, law student, 1916-19. *Religion:* Russian Orthodox [Greek Catholic] Church. *Home:* 12 East 97th St., New York, N..Y 10029.

CAREER: In earlier years was free-lance writer, chiefly on Russian literature, history, and politics, for various publications, including *New York Times Book Review*, 1923-35, and *New York Herald-Tribune Magazine* (later *This Week*), 1929-35; free-lance researcher, chiefly on Russia, for *Time, Fortune,* and other publications, 1935-47; U.S. Information Agency, New York, N.Y., broadcaster of reviews on American cultural life to the Soviet Union, 1947-54; United Nations Secretariat, New York, N.Y., translator, 1954-65; retired, 1965. *Member:* Association of Former International Civil Servants, United Nations Association of the United States of America.

WRITINGS: (Editor and translator) Nicholas Evreinoff, *The Theatre in Life,* Brentano, 1927; *Tolstoy: The Inconstant Genius* (biography), Stokes, 1929, reprinted, Books for Libraries, 1972 *The Land of the Russian People* (teen book), Lippincott, 1944, later editions published as *The Land and People of Russia,* 5th revised edition, 1972; *Picture Map Geography of the USSR* (teen book), Lippincott, 1969.

WORK IN PROGRESS: A biography of Peter the Great of Russia.

SIDELIGHTS: Nazaroff spent more than two years (1919-21) in Turkey, and has done a great deal of traveling since. He visits Europe for a few weeks almost every year—chiefly England, France, and Spain.

NEIMARK, Anne E. 1935-

PERSONAL: Born October 3, 1935, in Chicago, Ill.; daughter of Robert M. and Anita (Bronner) Loeb; married Paul G. Neimark (a writer), June 13, 1955; children: Jill, Todd, Jeff. *Education:* Attended Francis W. Parker School, Chicago, Ill., 1945-53, and Bryn Mawr College, 1953-55. *Home:* 920 Ridgewood Pl., Highland Park, Ill. 60035.

AWARDS, HONORS: Friends of American Writers first prize for a juvenile, 1970, for *Touch of Light.*

WRITINGS: Touch of Light: The Story of Louis Braille (juvenile), Harcourt, 1970. Contributor of articles and stories to juvenile magazines, including *Highlights for Children* and *Jack and Jill;* writer of articles for teachers' manuals and educational publishers, including *Encyclopaedia Britannica* and Science Research Associates.

WORK IN PROGRESS: A young people's biography of Sigmund Freud, for Harcourt.

SIDELIGHTS: "I first came upon a mention of Louis

Braille in an article—and was both inspired and moved by his personal story. I subsequently wrote an article of my own about him, which was published in *The Sign* Magazine. However, I found that Louis, as a courageous and indomitable human being, lingered so strongly in my thoughts that I began my book about him.

"At the present time, I am in the midst of my Freud biography—having done a year of research—and I find that my interests seem to focus on figures who have met with supposedly insurmountable obstacles, and who have triumphed over them.

"I write for young people, mainly between eight and sixteen years of age, because I feel that they are not as closed to feeling, to *being,* as are so many adults. I strive, in my work, to bring to life the figures who are the subjects of my biographies, to show them as people with real feelings and needs of their own."

FOR MORE INFORMATION SEE: Horn Book, June, 1970.

... and then at last, in the orange glow from the torches, was the welcome sight of a small boy lying with wide, blank eyes and rain-soaked clothes. ■ (From *Touch of Light: The Story of Louis Braille* by Anne E. Neimark. Illustrated by Robert Parker.)

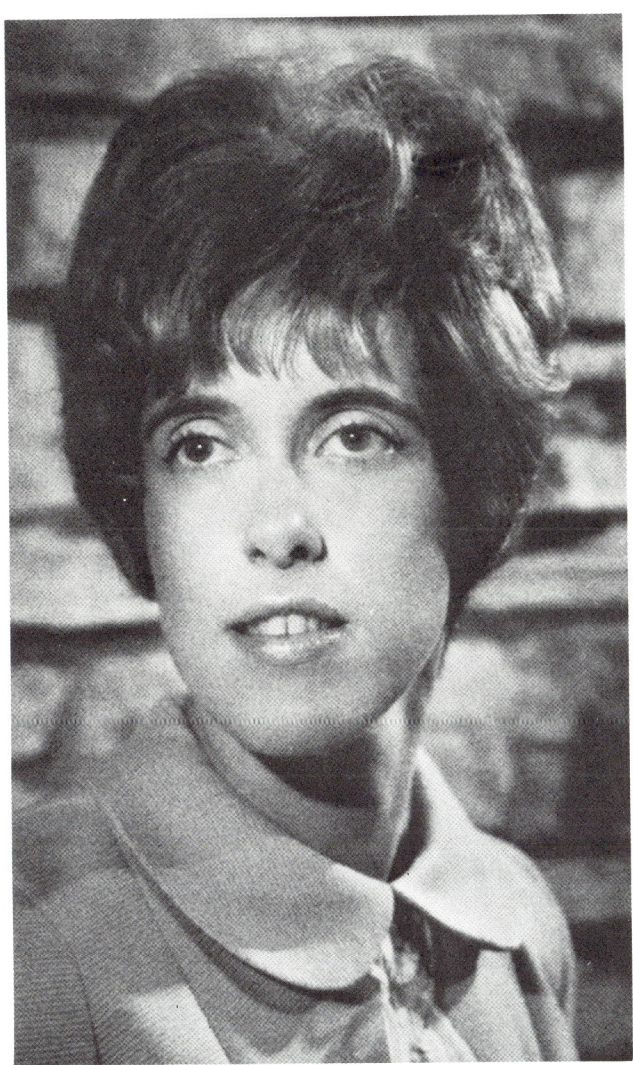

ANNE E. NEIMARK

NEWMAN, Robert (Howard) 1909-

PERSONAL: Born June 3, 1909, in New York, N.Y.; son of Samuel Jerome and Nance (Ortman) Newman; married Dorothy Crayder (a writer), 1936; children: Hila Feil (a writer). *Education:* Brown University, student, 1927-28. *Agent:* Harold Ober Associates, 40 East 49th St., New York, N.Y. 10017.

CAREER: Free-lance writer. Office of War Information, overseas branch, New York, chief, radio outpost division, 1942-44. *Member:* Radio Writers Guild (vice-president of eastern region, 1945, council member, 1942-49), Authors Guild, P.E.N., Writers Guild East.

WRITINGS: The Enchanter, Houghton, 1962; *The Japanese: People of the Three Treasures,* Atheneum, 1964; *Corbie,* Harcourt, 1966; *The Boy Who Could Fly,* Atheneum, 1967; *Grettir the Strong,* Crowell, 1968; *Merlin's Mistake,* Atheneum, 1970; *The Twelve Labors of Hercules,* Crowell, 1972. Verse, short stories, radio and television scripts, movie originals, plays, and industrial films.

WORK IN PROGRESS: A sequel to *Merlin's Mistake.*

SIDELIGHTS: "I began in radio in 1936. Previously I had written verse and short stories. I have done two daytime programs and five or six mystery shows. I also originated and wrote a program called 'City Hospital', before 'Medic' and long before 'Ben Casey' and 'Dr. Kildare'.

"Though I began writing books for young people fairly late it is now the field I am most interested in. I think I first became interested in it when my daughter was quite young and I used to read aloud to her. I have never forgotten her response to and involvement in the books we were reading and when I write a book today I am, in a sense, writing it for her as she was then.

It was still a great feat for Grettir to stand against them, for they were ten and all of great strength, and he was only one and not yet a grown man.
■ (From *Grettir the Strong* retold by Robert Newman. Illustrated by John Gretzer. Reprinted by permission of Thomas Y. Crowell Co.)

ROBERT NEWMAN

"An interesting sidelight is that, after working in film for several years, she has herself written her first children's book, *The Windmill Summer*. My wife has also been writing young people's books, the most recent of which, *The Pluperfect of Love,* has been receiving a great deal of well-deserved attention. Obviously I cannot speak for anyone but myself, but I suspect that all three of us are concentrating on books for young people for the same reason. Because we feel that it is the most rewarding kind of writing one can do today.

"I generally write for children between the ages of eleven and fourteen and all my books so far—the fiction, at least—have been fantasies of one sort or another; not because I am unaware of today's problems but because I do not feel I have any simple or satisfactory answers to them So instead of attempting social commentary—of which we already have a good deal, not all of it particularly valuable—I tell stories: stories which I hope will stimulate the imagination by introducing children to places that no longer exist or never existed and to characters and situations that they are not likely to meet in real life but which have some qualities which are recognizable and timeless."

HOBBIES AND OTHER INTERESTS: Field archery, travel.

FOR MORE INFORMATION SEE: *New York Times Book Review,* April 17, 1966; *Horn Book,* June, 1970.

NOONAN, Julia 1946-

PERSONAL: Born October 25, 1946, in Brooklyn, N.Y.; daughter of Francis M. (an engineer) and Mary (Richardson) Noonan; married Russell G. Poggensee (an accountant), October 2, 1971. *Education:* Pratt Institute, graduate in graphic arts (with honors), 1968. *Address:* 12 Dalton Dr., Naugatuck, Conn. 11215.

CAREER: Free-lance illustrator, 1968—. Illustrations have appeared in *Seventeen, Ladies' Home Journal, Town and Country, Redbook, New York Magazine,* and other magazines; also has done posters, calendars, and book work for Scholastic Book Services.

WRITINGS—Author and illustrator: *The Best Thing to Be* (juvenile), Doubleday, 1971.

Illustrator: Charles Perrault, *Puss in Boots* (adapted by Arthur Luce Klein from *Les Contes de fees*), Doubleday, 1970; John Langstaff, *Gather My Gold Together: Accumulative Songs for Four Seasons,* Doubleday, 1971; *The Pied Piper of Hamlin,* Scholastic, 1972.

WORK IN PROGRESS: Working on a series of children's "readers" (illustrations), for D.C. Heath.

He curled up on his bed and thought and thought. ■ (From *The Best Thing to Be* by Julia Noonan. Illustrated by the author.)

JULIA NOONAN

SIDELIGHTS: "After my brief exposure to publishing, I've become discouraged by the unwillingness of publishers to invest in higher quality production. There is a definite absence of four color process printing which limits the artist and cheats the child of the beauty that better reproduction affords."

HOBBIES AND OTHER INTERESTS: Animals; "would also enjoy hearing from children if any wish to write."

**PARLIN, John
    See GRAVES, Charles Parlin**

**PATON WALSH, Gillian 1939-
    (Jill Paton Walsh)**

PERSONAL: Born April 29, 1939, in London, England; daughter of John Llewellyn (an engineer) and Patricia (Dubern) Bliss; married Antony Paton Walsh (a chartered secretary), August 12, 1961; children: Edmund Alexander, Margaret Ann, Aden Clare. Education: St. Anne's College, Oxford, B.A. (honors), 1959. Politics: Liberal. Religion: None. Home: 60 Mount Ararat Rd., Richmond, Surrey, England. Agent: Bruce Hunter, David Higham Associates Ltd., 5-8 Lower John St., Golden Sq., London, England.

CAREER: Teacher of English in London, England, 1959-62. Awards, honors: Book World Children's Spring Book Festival award, 1970, for Fireweed.

WRITINGS—Juvenile books under name Jill Paton Walsh: Hengest's Tale, Macmillan (London), 1966, St. Martin's, 1967; The Dolphin Crossing, St. Martin's, 1967; (with Kevin Crossley-Holland) Wordhoard: Anglo-Saxon Stories, Farrar, Straus, 1969; Fireweed (Horn Book Honor List; ALA Notable Book), Macmillan, 1969, Farrar, Straus, 1970; Farewell Great King (historical novel), Coward, 1972; Goldengrove, Farrer, Straus, 1972.

SIDELIGHTS: "I am interested in nearly everything—the 'butterfly mind' syndrome. I don't understand my motivation, nor do I want to—it might switch off if I understood it." Ms. Paton Walsh is fluent in French, "adequate" in Latin, can read Old English, Icelandic, Italian, and is learning Greek.

HOBBIES AND OTHER INTERESTS: Cooking, carpentry.

FOR MORE INFORMATION SEE: Horn Book, December, 1969, June, 1970, February, 1972.

**PATON WALSH, Jill
    See PATON WALSH, Gillian**

PEPPE, Rodney 1934-

PERSONAL: Surname is pronounced Peppy; born June 24, 1934, in Eastbourne, Sussex, England; son of Lionel Hill (a lieutenant commander, Royal Navy) and Winifred Vivienne (Parry) Peppe; married Tordis Tatjana Tekkel,

July 16, 1960; children: Christen Rodney, Jonathan Noel. *Education:* Attended St. Edward's School, Oxford, England, 1948-51, and Eastbourne School of Art, 1955-57; London County Council Central School of Art and Craft, National Diploma in Design, 1958, Central School Diploma in Illustration, 1959. *Religion:* Church of England. *Home and studio:* 21 Denmark Ave., Wimbledon, London SW19 4HF, England. *Agent:* Curtis Brown Ltd., 13 King St., Covent Garden, London W.C.2, England.

CAREER: S.H. Benson Ltd. (advertising agency), London, England, art director, 1960-64; J. Walter Thompson Co. Ltd. (advertising agency), London, England, art director for television accounts, 1964-65; Ross Foods Ltd., London, England, design consultant, 1965—; also design consultant to other firms and groups. *Military service:* British Army, Intelligence Corps, 1953-55; served in Malaya. *Awards, honors:* Royal Humane Society Award for saving a life, 1952.

WRITINGS—Self-illustrated: *The Alphabet Book*, Four Winds, 1968; *Circus Numbers*, Delacorte, 1969; *The House That Jack Built* (Child Study Association Book List), Delacorte, 1970; *Hey Riddle Diddle!*, Holt, 1971; *Simple Simon*, Holt, 1972.

Illustrator: Ralph and Jill Marchant, *The Little Painter*, Thomas Nelson, 1971, Lerner, in press.

RODNEY PEPPE

The collages of *Hey Riddle Diddle!* were created by pasting down various materials, from tissue paper to gingham. ■ (From *Hey Riddle Diddle!* by Rodney Peppe. Illustrated by the author.)

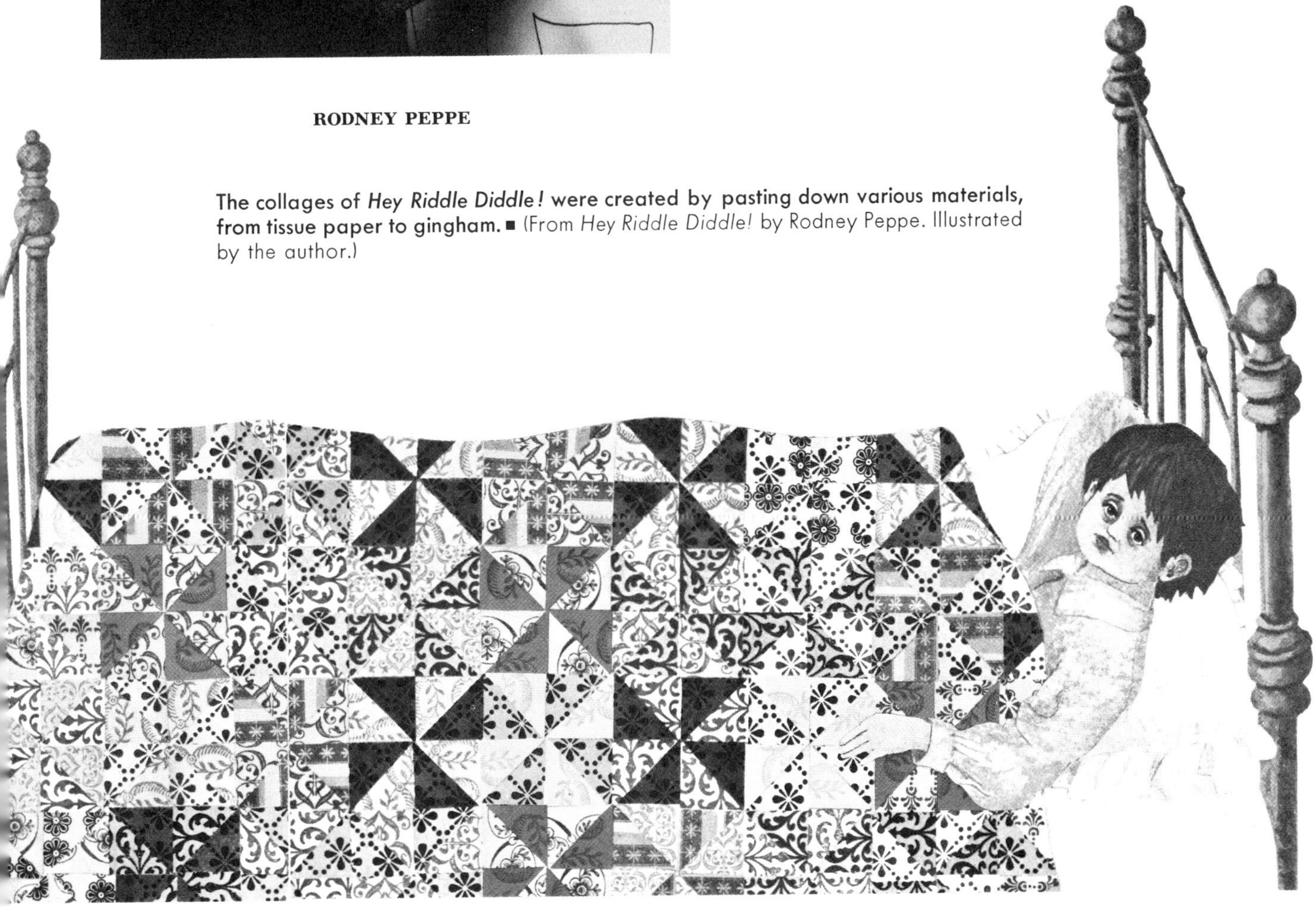

WORK IN PROGRESS: Cat and Mouse (Mother Goose rhymes), publication by Holt in America and by Longmans Young Books in England, expected in 1973.

SIDELIGHTS: Peppe trained as a wood engraver, but now works in color only—"a reaction against the wood block! I visited New York in 1970 to study the children's book market. I love 'Sesame Street'! and the Smithsonian Institute in Washington, was a revelation. Would love to see more of the U.S.A. . . . .

"It is easy for me to like young children en masse and individually. I have drawn for them publicly at children's book shows and find them polite and mercifully, appreciative! From these public appearances I learn what children like to see drawn. I try to apply this knowledge to my picture books. It's a feed-back which I appreciate." All of Peppe's books have been published in England. He also makes cartoon films using a simple cut-out technique by moving figures frame by frame.

HOBBIES AND OTHER INTERESTS: Collecting antique furniture, clocks, netsuke (miniature Japanese carvings used to fasten a pouch or purse to a kimono sash), Victorian children's books and other juvenilia; the cinema.

PERCY, Charles Henry
See SMITH, Dodie

SUSAN BETH PFEFFER

PFEFFER, Susan Beth 1948-

PERSONAL: Surname is pronounced Feffer; born February 17, 1948, in New York, N.Y.; daughter of Leo (a lawyer and professor) and Freda (a librarian; maiden name, Plotkin) Pfeffer. *Education:* New York University, B.A., 1969. *Home:* 17 Benton Ave., Middletown, N.Y. 10940.

CAREER: Orange County Community College, Middletown, N.Y., English instructor, 1972—. New Country Theatre, Ridgebury, N.Y., board of directors, 1972—.

WRITINGS: Just Morgan (novel for young teens), Walck, 1970; *Better Than All Right,* Doubleday, 1972.

WORK IN PROGRESS: A Witch in Time, a play for children.

SIDELIGHTS: "My interests range from baseball to medieval art, with stops at movie history, the lives of innumerable writers, and local theatre. I've been writing since age six, when I completed my first novel, *Dookie the Cookie* (as yet unpublished)."

FOR MORE INFORMATION SEE: Library Journal, July 1, 1970; *New York Times Book Review,* November 12, 1972.

PILKINGTON, Francis Meredyth 1907-

PERSONAL: Born June 16, 1907, in Kingstown Co., Dublin, Ireland; daughter of Guy Brabazon (a solicitor) and Charlotte Edith (Cotton-Walker) Pilkington. *Education:* Attended French School, Bray, Ireland. *Religion:* Church of England. *Home:* Brookleaze, Nettlebridge, Oakhill, near Bath, Somersetshire, England. *Agent:* A.M. Heath & Co., 35 Dover St., London, W.1, England.

AWARDS, HONORS: Three Sorrowful Tales of Erin was listed among the best books of 1966 by the School Library Section of American Library Association.

WRITINGS: Three Sorrowful Tales of Erin (youth Book), Bodley Head, 1965, Walck, 1966; *Shamrock and Spear: Tales and Legends from Ireland* (youth book), Bodley Head, 1966, Holt, 1968.

SIDELIGHTS: "I spent part of my childhood in Kingstown, and the second half in Dublin. Kingstown was on the coast—the royal mail steamers from England landed there—and there was a beautiful view of Dublin Bay. I can still remember standing at a window in my Aunt Alice's house after dark, and watching the lights of the trams running like glow-worms all along up to Dublin.

"I do not know that there is very much I can tell you about myself. I came to write in a rather odd way. The late E.M. Almedingen, whose books, especially for the young, are so well known, shared this house with me. She was as convinced that I could write as I was that I couldn't. I had always liked the story of Deidre. So one day I sat down with a pad, and started to write it. It took me a week. When it was done I handed it to Miss

So the marriage day was fixed and the invitations were sent out, and the wedding lasted for a year and a day. ■ (From *Shamrock and Spear* by F. M. Pilkington. Illustrated by Leo and Diane Dillon.)

Almedingen to read, and when she gave it back I was just about to throw it in the fire, when she snatched it from me, and said, 'You will send that to the Bodley Head tomorrow.' I was quite astonished, but she was so certain that I did so, and had the great good fortune to have it accepted at once.

"I am a very ordinary person, and enjoy best to be here in this lovely little house with the country all around me."

HOBBIES AND OTHER INTERESTS: Music, reading, gardening.

FOR MORE INFORMATION SEE: New York Times Book Review, September 15, 1968.

PITRONE, Jean Maddern 1920-

PERSONAL: Born December 20, 1920, in Ishpeming, Mich.; daughter of William Courtney (a clerk) and Gladys (Beer) Maddern; married Anthony Peter Pitrone (a landscaper in civil service), October 26, 1940; children: Joseph, Jill, Anthony, Jr., Joyce, John, Janet, Julie, Jane, Cheryl. *Education:* Educated in public schools of Ishpeming, Mich. *Politics:* Democrat. *Religion:* Roman Catholic. *Home:* 8244 Riverview, Dearborn Heights, Mich. 48127.

CAREER: Teacher of piano, 1950, and church organist, 1955, both in Dearborn Heights, Mich.; teacher of magazine-writing in adult education classes, Dearborn, Mich., 1963; associate editor, *Writer's Digest,* 1968—. Staff member, annual writers' conference at Oakland University, 1962—. *Member:* Women's National Book Association, Detroit Council of Catholic Women (race relations chairman, Western deanery), 1962-64, Detroit Women Writers, Theta Sigma Phi. *Awards, honors:* Friends of American Writers Award, 1970, for *Trailblazer.*

WRITINGS: The Great Black Robe, Daughters of St. Paul, 1964; *Trailblazer: Negro Nurse in the American Red Cross,* Harcourt, 1969; *The Touch of His Hand* (biography), Alba House, 1970; *Chavez: Man of the Migrants* (biography), Alpha House, 1971. Monthly columnist in *Detroit Purchasor;* contributor of articles and short stories to newspapers and magazines, including *Extension, Columbia, Family Digest, Adult Teacher, Presbyterian Life, Catholic Digest,* and *Detroit News Sunday Magazine.*

WORK IN PROGRESS: Presently working on a biography of the Horace and John Dodge families in collaboration with Joan Potter Elwart [see Volume 2].

PITZ, Henry C(larence) 1895-

PERSONAL: Born June 16, 1895, in Philadelphia, Pa.; son of Henry William (a manufacturer) and Anna (Stiffel) Pitz; married Molly Wheeler Wood, June 10, 1935; children: Julia Learning (Mrs. Edward Handy), Henry William II. *Education:* Studied at Philadelphia Museum College of Art, 1914-18, and Spring Garden Institute, Philadelphia, 1917, 1920. *Politics:* Independent. *Religion:* Episcopalian. *Home:* 3 Cornelia Pl., Philadelphia, Pa. 19118.

CAREER: Artist and illustrator, 1920—. Philadelphia Museum College of Art, Philadelphia, Pa., director of department of illustration and decoration, 1937-60, now professor emeritus; Pennsylvania Academy of Fine Arts, Philadelphia, instructor in water color, 1939-46; *American Artist,* New York, N.Y., associate editor, 1942—. Visiting lecturer in fine arts, University of Pennsylvania; visiting instructor, Cleveland Institute of Art. Work exhibited in national and international exhibitions; represented in permanent collections in museums, schools, and libraries throughout United States, including Library of Congress, Philadelphia Museum of Art, Cleveland Museum of Art, Los Angeles Museum; painted three murals for Government Building, Century of Progress, Chicago. *Military service:* U.S. Army, American Expeditionary Forces, 1918-19.

MEMBER: National Academy of Design (academician); American Water Color Society (director), Society of Illustrators (life member), Philadelphia Art Alliance (vice-president, 1938-61; director), Philadelphia Sketch Club (vice-president, 1938-40; president, 1940-42), Philadelphia Water Color Club (director), Newcomen Society, Audubon Artists, Salmagundi Club (New York), Franklin Inn Club (Philadelphia). *Awards, honors:* Bronze Medal, International Print Exhibition, 1932; Bronze Medal, Paris International Exposition, 1938; Hans Obst Prize, American Water Color Society Annual, 1952; Obrig Prize, National Academy, 1953, 1956; Alumni Gold Medal, Philadelphia Museum College of Art, 1956, Silver Star Cluster, 1957; National Academy Prize for Water Color, 1962; Pennational Artists Gold Medal, 1968; Philadelphia Atheneaum Literary Award, 1969; D.L., Ursinus College, 1971; and more than thirty other awards, 1932—.

WRITINGS: (Author and illustrator with Edward Warwick) *Early American Costume,* Century Co., 1929, revised edition (with Warwick and Alexander Wyckoff) published as *Early American Dress: The Colonial and Revolutionary Periods,* Benjamin Blom, 1965; (editor) *A Treasury of American Book Illustration,* Watson-Guptill and American Studio Books, 1947; *The Practice of Illustration,* Watson-Guptill, 1947; *Pen, Brush and Ink,* edited by Arthur L. Guptill, Watson-Guptill, 1949; (editor) Norman Kent and Others, *Watercolor Methods,* Watson-Guptill, 1955; *Drawing Trees,* Watson-Guptill, 1956; *Ink Drawing Techniques,* Watson-Guptill, 1957; *Sketching with the Felt-Tip Pen: A New Artist's Tool,* Studio Publications, 1959; (editor and reviser) Arthur L. Guptill, *Drawing with Pen and Ink,* revised edition, Reinhold, 1961; *Illustrating Children's Books: History, Technique, Production,* Watson-Guptill, 1963; *Drawing Outdoors,* edited by Susan E. Meyer, Watson-Guptill, 1965; *How to Use the Figure in Painting and Illustration,* Watson-Guptill and Reinhold, 1965; *The Brandywine Tradition,* Houghton, 1969; *Charcoal Drawing,* Watson-Guptill, 1971; (contributor) *Greek and Roman Civilization,* New American Library, in press. Writer of more than one hundred articles for *Encyclopaedia Britannica,* and for *American Artist, Horn Book, Studio, Print, American Heritage,* and other periodicals.

Illustrator: John Bennett, *Master Skylark,* Century Co., 1922; Conan Doyle, *Micah Clarke,* Harper, 1922; Robert Shackleton, *The Book of Washington,* Penn Publishing, 1923; Allen French, *The Story of Rolf and the Vikings Bow,* Little, Brown, 1924; Bertha Evangeline Bush, *A Prairie Rose,* Little, Brown, 1925; Francis S. Drake, *Indian History for Young Folks,* Harper, 1927; Ula

"The Last Tribe," by Henry C. Pitz. Lithographic crayons, both medium and hard grades, were used for this drawing. In the sky, the curving cloud shapes circle back to the center of interest.

Echols, *Knights of Charlemagne,* Longmans, Green, 1928; John Buchan, *Prester John,* Houghton, 1928; Robert Leighton, *Olaf, the Glorious,* Macmillan, 1929.

Robert W. Chambers, *Cardigan,* Harper, 1930; Rodrigo Diaz De Bivar (El Cid) *The Tale of the Warrior Lord* (translated by Merriam Sherwood), Longmans, Green, 1930; Washington Irving, *Voyages of Columbus,* Macmillan, 1931; *The Story of Beowulf* (retold by Strafford Riggs), Appleton, 1933; Ernest P. Mitchell, *Deep Water: The Autobiography of a Sea Captain,* Little, Brown, 1933; Charles J. Finger, *Dog at His Heels,* Winston, 1936; Geoffrey Household, *Spanish Cave,* Little, Brown, 1936; Daniel Defoe, *The Life and Strange Surprising Adventures of Robinson Crusoe* (edition adapted for young readers by Edward L. Thorndike), Appleton, 1937; Paul L. Anderson, *Pugnax the Gladiator,* Appleton, 1939.

Elizabeth Jane Coatsworth, *You Shall Have a Carriage,* Macmillan, 1941; Phyllis Reid Fenner, compiler, *There Was a Horse: Folktales from Many Lands,* Knopf, 1941; Albert L. Stillman, *Jungle Haven,* Winston, 1942; Sydney Greenbie, *Three Island Nations: Cuba, Haiti, Dominican Republic,* Row, Peterson, 1942; Frederic A. Krummer, *For Flag and Freedom,* Morrow, 1942; Phyllis Reid Fenner, editor, *Time to Laugh: Funny Tales from Here and There,* Knopf, 1942; Patricia F. Ross, *In Mexico They Say,* Knopf, 1942; Catherine Cate Coblentz, *Falcon of Eric the Red,* Longmans, Green, 1942; Robert Davis, *Hudson Bay Express,* Holiday House, 1942; Hope Brister, *Cunning Fox and Other Tales,* Knopf, 1943; Charles J. Finger, *High Waters in Arkansas,* Grosset, 1943; Phyllis Reid Fenner, compiler, *Giants and Witches, and a Dragon or Two,* Knopf, 1943; Phyllis Reid Fenner, compiler, *Princesses and Peasant Boys: Tales of Enchantment,* Knopf, 1944; Mildred A. Jordan, *Shoo-fly Pie,* Knopf, 1944; Mary Regina Walsh, *Molly, the Rogue,* Knopf, 1944; Mildred A. Jordan, *Apple in the Attic: A Pennsylvania Legend,* Grosset, 1944; David Loring MacKaye and J.J.G. MacKaye, under pseudonym Loring MacKaye, *Twenty-Fifth Mission,* Longmans, Green, 1944; William W. Theisen and G.L. Bond, compilers, *Living Literature for Supplementary Reading,* five books, Macmillan, 1945-48; Phyllis Reid Fenner, compiler, *Adventure, Rare and Magical,* Knopf, 1945; Rosita Torr Forbes, *Henry Morgan: Pirate,* McKay, 1946 (published in England as *Henry Morgan: Pirate and Pioneer,* Cassell, 1948); Andre Maurois, *Washington: The Life of a Great Patriot* (translated by Eileen Lane Kinney), Oxford University Press, 1946; David W. Moore, *The End of Long John Silver,* Crowell, 1946; Mary Regina Walsh, *The Mullingar Heifer,* Knopf, 1946; Elizabeth Hough Sechrist, editor, *One Thousand Poems for Children,* (based on the selections of Roger Ingpen), new edition, Macrae Smith, 1946; Charlie May Simon, *Joe Mason, Apprentice to Audubon,* Dutton, 1946; Phyllis Reid Fenner, compiler, *Demons and Dervishes: Tales with More-than-Oriental Splendor,* Knopf, 1946; Mildred Houghton Comfort, *Children of the Mayflower,* Beckley-Cardy, 1947; Phyllis Reid Fenner, compiler, *Fools and Funny Fellows: More "Time to Laugh" Tales,* Knopf, 1947; David Loring MacKaye and J.J.G. MacKaye, under pseudonym Loring MacKaye, *John of America,* Longmans, Green, 1947; Kathleen Monypenny, *Young Traveler in Australia,* Phoenix House, 1948, Dutton, 1954; Phyllis Reid Fenner, *With Might and Main,* Knopf, 1948; Charlie May Simon, *Royal Road,* Dutton, 1948; Mildred Houghton Comfort, *Children of the Colonies,* Beckley-Cardy, 1948; Enid LaM. Meadowcraft, *By Secret Railway,* Crowell, 1948; Margaret Carver Leighton, *Judith of France,* Houghton, 1948; Georgii Skrebitskii, *White Bird's Island* (translated from the Russian by Zina Voynow), Knopf, 1948; Phyllis Reid Fenner, compiler, *With Might and Main: Stories of Skill and Wit,* Knopf, 1948; Jeanette Eaton, *That Lively Man, Ben Franklin,* Morrow, 1948; Mary Regina Walsh, *The Widow Woman and Her Goat,* Knopf, 1949; David W. Moore, *End of Black Dog,* Crowell, 1949; Jan Juta, *Look Out for the Ostriches: Tales of South Africa,* Knopf, 1949; Sir Thomas Malory, *Book of King Arthur and His Noble Knights* (stories from *Morte d'Arthur* selected by Mary Macleod), Lippincott, 1949.

Mrs. Stockton V. Banks, *Washington Adventure,* Whittlesey House, 1950; David W. Moore, *Scarlet Jib,* Crowell, 1950; David W. Moore, *Sacramento Sam,* Crowell, 1951; Phyllis Reid Fenner, compiler, *Magic Hoofs: Horse Stories from Many Lands,* Knopf, 1951; Opal Wheeler, *Hans Andersen: Son of Denmark,* Dutton, 1951; Elizabeth Hall Janeway, *Viking,* Random House, 1951; Nathan Reinherz, *Quest of the Sage's Stone,* Crowell, 1951; Jakob Ludwig Grimm and Wilhelm Karl Grimm, "What Happened to Hansel and Gretel" in *Evergreen Tales,* Limited Editions Club, 1952; Armstrong Sperry, *River of the West,* Winston, 1952; Mabel Watts, *Over the Hills to Ballypog,* Aladdin Books, 1954; Robert Louis Stevenson, *Treasure Island,* Doubleday, 1954; Jules Verne, *Mysterious Island,* World Publishing, 1957; Catherine Owens Peare, *William Penn,* 1958.

Henry Frith, *King Arthur and His Knights,* Doubleday, 1963; James Fenimore Cooper, *The Spy,* Limited Editions Club, 1963; Thomas Fall, *Edge of Manhood,* Dial, 1964; Thomas Fall, *Wild Boy,* Dial, 1965.

His illustrations have appeared in *Scribner's, Cosmopolitan, Harper's, Saturday Evening Post, Gourmet, Jack and Jill, Reader's Digest,* and other national magazines.

WORK IN PROGRESS: Book for Clarkson Potter on life and works of Howard Pyle.

SIDELIGHTS: "I began my professional career as a picture-maker and was nudged into writing. Since I spent a large part of my growing years drawing, it was almost inevitable that I should find myself in an art school upon graduation from high school. In my junior year I found myself illustrating stories for the weekly Sunday School papers for children and that lead me into many busy years of picture-making for magazines, books, and advertising pages.

"One day an editor called me to ask if he could interview me for an article in his magazine. We spent a talking day together and when he left he asked me if I would jot down some of the things I had told him and send it to him. I hadn't counted on this chore but obeyed. When the article appeared it was my jottings with only a few additions. I felt cheated and told him so, but he smoothed me down and asked if I would have lunch with him, the next time I was in New York. When that came about he said, 'You are a writer and we would like you to write some articles for us.'

HENRY C. PITZ

"So the writing began, always at night after the days' stint in the studio. Soon I was talked into a book and the list began to grow. An appointment as professor in charge of the department of illustration at the Philadelphia College of Art directed my writing toward the developing student of art. I now had a three-sided professional life, illustrating, writing, and teaching and for recreation, an occasional spree of painting.

"With my retirement from my professorship, my life became more simplified, particularly as I gave less time to illustration. But writing and painting had more room and there were the unexpected assignments such as being official artist for N.A.S.A. at the Apollo 10 launching and at present an official artist for the government's Environmental Agency. Also visiting lecturer, at the recent conference on all phases of children's books at the University of Utah.

"One thing leads to another, and a chain is established but one has choices and there is a comforting sense of freedom—freedom from the confines of a routine job."

FOR MORE INFORMATION SEE: Forty Illustrators, Watson-Guptill, 1946; Albert Reese, *American Prize Prints of the 20th Century,* American Artists Group, 1949; Richard Ellis, *Book Illustration,* Kingsport Press, 1952; Norman Kent, *Watercolor Methods,* Watson-Guptill, 1955; *Illustrators of Children's Books: 1946-1956,* Horn Book, 1958; David Bland, *A History of Book Illustration,* World, 1958; *More Junior Authors,* edited by Muriel Fuller, Wilson, 1963; Diana Klemin, *The Art of Art for Children's Books,* Clarkson Potter, 1966; Elinor W. Field, *Horn Book Reflections,* Horn Book, 1969; Diana Klemin, *The Illustrated Book,* Clarkson Potter, 1970.

PRINGLE, Laurence 1935-

(Sean Edmund)

PERSONAL: Born November 26, 1935, in Rochester, N.Y.; son of Laurence Erin (a realtor) and Marleah (Rosehill) Pringle; married Judith Malanowicz, June, 1962; married second wife, Alison Newhouse (a free-lance editor), July 14, 1971; children: (first marriage) Heidi Elizabeth, Jeffrey Laurence, Sean Edmund. *Education:* Cornell University, B.S., 1958; University of Massachusetts, M.S., 1960; Syracuse University, further graduate courses. *Residence:* Cresskill, N.J.

CAREER: High school teacher of science in Lima, N.Y., 1961-62; *Nature and Science* (magazine of American Museum of Natural History), New York, N.Y., associate editor, 1963-65, senior editor, 1965-67, executive editor, 1967-70 (magazine ceased publication, 1970); free-lance writer, editor, and photographer, 1970—. Tenafly (N.J.) Nature Center Association, former vice-president and chairman of land use and publicity committees. *Member:* Outdoor, nature, and environmental organizations.

WRITINGS—Juvenile, except as noted: *Dinosaurs and Their World,* Harcourt, 1968; *The Only Earth We Have,* Macmillan, 1969; *From Field to Forest,* World Publishing, 1970; *In a Beaver Valley,* World Publishing, 1970; *One

LAURENCE PRINGLE

Earth, Many People: The Challenge of Human Population Growth,* Macmillan, 1971; *Ecology: Science of Survival,* Macmillan, 1971; *Cockroaches: Here, There, and Everywhere,* Crowell, 1971; *This is a River,* Macmillan, 1972; *From Pond to Prairie,* Macmillan, 1972; (self-illustrated with color photographs) *Wild River* (adult nonfiction), Lippincott, 1972.

Editor: *Discovering the Outdoors: A Nature and Science Guide to Investigating Life in Fields, Forests, and Ponds* (Child Study Association Book List), Natural History Press, 1969; *Discovering Nature Indoors: A Nature and Science Guide to Investigations with Small Animals,* Natural History Press, 1970.

Contributor to children's magazines, including *Highlights for Children* and *Ranger Rick's Nature Magazine,* sometimes under the pseudonym Sean Edmund.

WORK IN PROGRESS: More juvenile books.

SIDELIGHTS: "Writing is incredibly hard and unpleasant work much of the time. I would prefer to devote most of my time to photography.... In my limited spare time, I enjoy reading, movies, sports, and being with my children."

FOR MORE INFORMATION SEE: New York Times, November 9, 1969; Library Journal, October 15, 1970; Horn Book, April, 1972.

PRYOR, Helen Brenton 1897-1972

PERSONAL: Born July 31, 1897, near Green Mountain Falls, Colo.; daughter of William Henry and Mary C. (Foster) Brenton; married Roy Jay Pryor, December 1, 1922; children: Dorothy Elizabeth (Mrs. George L. Bartlett), Richard Brenton. Education: University of Oregon, B.A., 1919; University of Minnesota, M.D., 1924. Politics: Republican. Religion: Protestant. Home: 350 Sharon Park Dr., Apt. G-4, Menlo Park, Calif. 94025. Office: Department of Pediatrics, Medical School, Stanford University, Stanford, Calif. 94305.

CAREER: University of Minnesota Hospital, Minneapolis, intern, 1923-24; Rockefeller Foundation Hospital, Peiping, China, resident, 1924-25; Nanking University Hospital, Nanking, China, visiting physician in pediatrics and obstetrics, 1925-29; University of California Medical School, San Francisco, assistant in pediatrics, 1929-35, research associate, Institute of Child Welfare, 1931-39; Children's Hospital, San Francisco, Calif., visiting pediatrician, 1930-35; Stanford University, Stanford, Calif., professor of hygiene and director of Women's Health Service, 1935-45; Redwood Medical Clinic, Redwood City, Calif., pediatrician and partner in clinic, 1945-65; Stanford University Medical School, clinical professor of pediatrics, 1966—. Sequoia Hospital, chief of staff for pediatrics, 1952-64. American Board of Pediatrics, diplomate. President of board of directors, San Mateo County Heart Association, 1957-59, Volunteer Bureau, 1958-60, Mid-Peninsula YWCA, 1960-62, and Palo Alto Neighbors Abroad, 1966; chairman of Senior Division, Community Welfare Council, 1963-65.

MEMBER: American Academy of Pediatrics (fellow), American Student Health Association (national secretary-treasurer, 1942-44), Society for Research in Child Development, American Medical Association, National League of American Pen Women, California Congress of Parent-Teacher Association (honorary life member), Sigma XI, Palto Alto Quota Club (president, 1956-58).

AWARDS, HONORS: Medallions for distinguished achievement and distinguished service, American Heart Association, 1964; American Association of University Women Creative Living Award for contributions toward better health for the world's children, 1968; Matrix Award of Theta Sigma Phi, 1970, for Lou Henry Hoover: Gallant First Lady and other writings; California Commission on Aging Award for work in behalf of senior citizens.

WRITINGS: (With Wilson and Almack) Five books in "American Health" series published by Bobbs, Health at Home and School, 1942, Health at Work and Play, 1942, Growing Healthfully, 1943, Health Progress, 1943, Modern Ways to Health, 1943; As the Child Grows, Silver Burdett, 1943; Lou Henry Hoover: Gallant First Lady (teen book), Dodd, 1969.

Contributor to Encyclopedia of Sport Sciences and Medicine, World Book Encyclopedia, medical journals, and magazines.

FOR MORE INFORMATION SEE: Pen Woman, November, 1969.

(Died July 7, 1972)

HELEN B. PRYOR

REED, Betty Jane 1921-

PERSONAL: Born August 6, 1921, in Pittsburgh, Pa.; daughter of Charles August and Barbara (Miller) Reed. Education: University of Minnesota, B.S., 1951, M.A., 1954. Politics: Independent. Religion: Lutheran. Home: 4401 Columbus Ave. S., Minneapolis, Minn. 55407.

CAREER: Minneapolis (Minn.) public schools, first grade teacher, 1951-65, director of community resource volunteers, 1965—. Member: Association for Childhood, Association for Childhood Education (vice-president; Minneapolis branch), Education International, National Education Association, National Council of Teachers of English, Women in Education, Minnesota Association for Childhood Education, Minnesota Education Association,

BETTY JANE REED

Minneapolis Area Council of Teachers of English, University of Minnesota College of Education Alumni Association, Pi Lambda Theta.

WRITINGS—"Early Reading" series: *Golfin' with a Dolphin*, 1968, *Are You a Kangaroo?*, 1969, *A Horse of Course*, 1969, *Flyin' with a Lion*, 1969, *More Mom for Tom*, 1969, *Laugh with a Giraffe*, 1969, *Mouse in the House*, 1971, *Rabbit with a Habit*, 1972, *They Left the Moon too Soon*, 1972, *Such a Fuss for a Hippopotamus*, in press, *Wish for a Fish*, in press, *A Knapsack for Jack*, in press (all published by Denison).

WORK IN PROGRESS: *A Hullabalo in the Zoo*, *This Cat is Like That*, *Thinkin' about Lincoln*, *A Ghost for a Host*, *Double Trouble with a Bubble*, and *Zoom on Mr. Gloom's Broom*.

SIDELIGHTS: "My story writing began when I was a full-time television teacher for the Minneapolis Public Schools and was doing a series on mental health for first graders. At that time I wrote a poem-story called 'Tommy's Problem.' There were so many requests from teachers after the telecast asking where they could get a copy of the poem-story that I decided if it were in book form it might sell. That book is now called *More Mom for Tom* and was the first one written in the series. *Golfin' with a Dolphin*, however, was the first one to sell and the others followed shortly after. Most of my stories are purely from my imagination, but one of the newest, *This Cat is Like That*, is a true story of a cat belonging to some people I know. *Thinkin' about Lincoln*, of course, is a rhyming biography. Two of the latest ones, *A Ghost for a Host* and *Zoom on Mr. Gloom's Broom* are Halloween stories.

"You asked how I write my books. They are written in so many different ways it is difficult to answer that question. Since my series has rhyming titles, I start with the title and the rest of the story evolves from there. Sometimes I sit down and go through the first draft of the story in its entirety at one time, but more frequently I write the first one or two verses and then jot down some ideas, putting the material aside and not returning to it perhaps for a month or more when some specific verses come to mind using the ideas I have previously jotted down. The first part of *Golfin' with a Dolphin* was written in the middle of the night—a night when I was unable to sleep and the idea for that book just came to me then.

"The first draft of *Flyin' with a Lion* was written when I was in an airplane going from Minneapolis to Los Angeles. *Mouse in the House* was actually written with my five-year-old nephew who crawled in bed with me one morning in Los Angeles while his mother was still sleeping. This was just after *Golfin' with a Dolphin* had been published (which was dedicated to him) and he wanted to help me write a book. It is the only book that starts 'Once upon a time' because that is the way children generally seem to start their stories.

"I guess the only generalization to make is that I write whenever the ideas come and wherever I happen to be. I always carry paper and pen with me so that when the ideas are there I can get them down quickly because I have learned that if I don't they are lost forever."

HOBBIES AND OTHER INTERESTS: Reading, traveling, making rock jewelry, bowling, attending plays and musicals.

We put her in the attic
Where she sat and sat and sat. ■ (From *A Mouse in the House* by Betty Jane Reed. Illustrated by June Talarczyk.)

REEDER, Colonel Red
See REEDER, Russell P., Jr.

REEDER, Russell P., Jr. 1902-
(Colonel Red Reeder)

PERSONAL: Born March 4, 1902, at Fort Leavenworth, Kan.; son of Russell P. Reeder and Narcissa (Martin) Reeder Whitehouse; married Dorothea Darrah, 1934; children: Ann Reeder Riggs, Dorothea W. Hruby, Julia Reeder McCutchen, Russell P. III. *Education:* U.S. Military Academy, B.S., 1926. *Religion:* Episcopalian. *Home:* Garrison, N.Y. 10524.

CAREER: Regular Army officer, from second lieutenant to colonel, 1926-45; assistant director of athletics at West Point where he spent a quarter-century of his life. Attended Infantry School, Fort Benning, Ga., following commissioning; assistant football coach at West Point, 1929-37; Army director of athletics in Canal Zone, 1939-41. During World War II served as General George C. Marshall's personal representative on Guadalcanal early in Pacific fighting; commanded 12th Regiment of 4th Infantry Division in Normandy invasion, 1944; wounded in action shortly after D-Day, leading to retirement from active duty in 1945. *Member:* West Point Fishing Club (honorary). *Awards, honors:*—Military: Distinguished Service Cross, Legion of Merit, Silver Star, Bronze Star, Purple Heart, Combat Infantry Badge, Croix de Guerre with Palm, French Legion d'Honneur. Civilian: Congressional Silver Lifesaving Medal for saving a playmate from drowning when he was eleven; Freedom Foundation National Recognition Award, 1963.

WRITINGS: West Point Plebe, Duell, Sloane & Pearce, 1955; *West Point Yearling,* Duell, 1956; *Whispering Wind,* Duell, 1956; (with sister, Nardi Reeder Campion) *The West Point Story,* Random House, 1956; *The Mackenzie Raid,* Ballantine; *The Sheriff of Hat Creek,* Duell, 1957; *West Point Second Classman,* Duell, 1957; *West Point First Classman,* Duell, 1958; *The Story of the Civil War,* Duell, 1958; *The Story of the Revolutionary War,* Duell, 1959; *Attack at Fort Lookout,* Duell, 1959; *The Story of the War of 1812,* Duell, 1959; *2nd Lieutenant Clint Lane,* Duell, 1960; *Clint Lane in Korea,* Duell, 1961; *Sheridan,* Duell, 1962; *The Story of World War I,* Duell, 1962; *Pointers on Athletics,* Duell, 1962; *U.S. Grant,* Garrard, 1964; *The Northern Generals,* Duell, Sloan & Pearce, 1964; *The Southern Generals,* Duell, Sloan & Pearce, 1965; *Heroes of the Medal of Honor,* Landmark, 1966; *Born at Reveille* (autobiography), Duell, 1966; *On the Mound,* Garrard, 1966; *The Story of the Spanish American War,* Duell, 1966; *The Story of the Mexican War,* Hawthorn, 1967; *Dwight D. Eisenhower,* Garrard, 1968; *The Story of World War II* (two volumes), Hawthorn, 1969-70; *Omar N. Bradley,* Garrard, 1969; *Heroes and Leaders of West Point,* Nelson, 1970; *French and Indian War,* Nelson, 1972. Writer of U.S. Army training pamphlet, *Fighting on Guadalcanal,* 1942.

WORK IN PROGRESS: Ten Bold Men of the Revolutionary War, for Little, Brown.

SIDELIGHTS: A letterman in both football and baseball at West Point, Reeder had a tryout with the New York Giants baseball team in 1928 but elected to remain in the Army. More than a million copies were printed of the training pamphlet he wrote about Guadalcanal. The extraordinary impact of this pamphlet gave him the idea that if he worked he could become an author.

RINKOFF, Barbara (Jean Rich) 1923-

PERSONAL: Born January 25, 1923, in New York, N.Y.; daughter of John J. and Sophia B. (Frank) Rich; married Herbert Rinkoff (a dentist); children: Robert, Richard, June. *Education:* New York University, B.A., 1943. *Home:* Langland Dr., Mount Kisco, N.Y. 10549.

CAREER: Beeckman-Downtown Hospital, New York, N.Y., medical social worker, 1943-47; professional writer. Teacher of after-school course in creative writing for fifth and sixth grades, Mount Kisco; member of curriculum council, Bedford Central School District 2, 1960—. *Member:* American Association of University Women, Alpha Kappa Delta. *Awards, honors: The Member of the Gang, A Guy Can Be Wrong, Name: Johnny Pierce,* and *Rutherford T. Finds 21B* all cited by the Child Study Association as books of the year.

RUSSELL P. REEDER, JR.

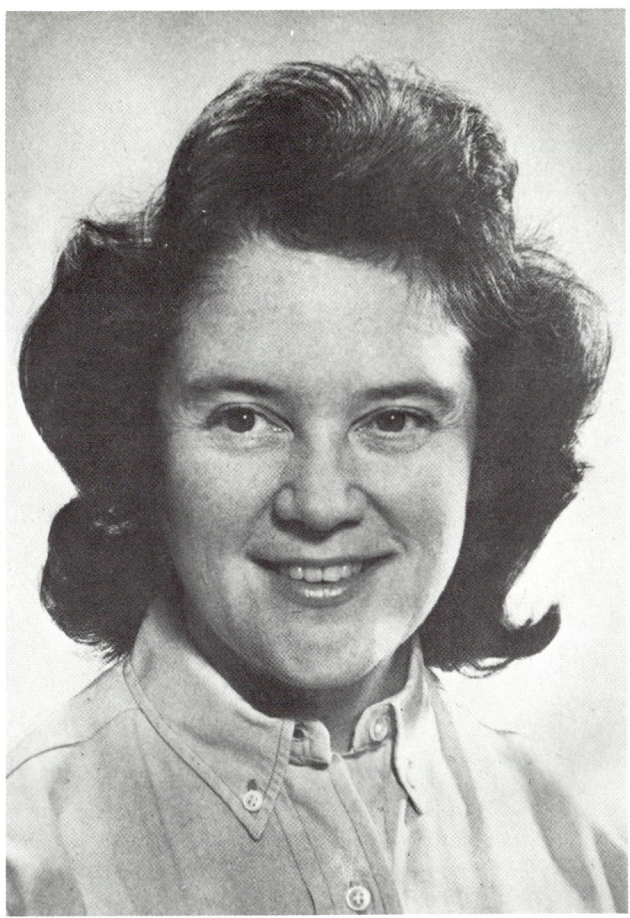

BARBARA J. RINKOFF

WRITINGS: *A Map Is a Picture*, Crowell, 1965; *The Remarkable Ramsey*, Morrow, 1965; *The Dragon's Handbook*, Nelson, 1966; *Birthday Parties Around the World*, Barrows, 1967; *The Troublesome Tuba*, Lothrop, 1967; *Elbert, the Mind-Reader* (ALA Notable Book), Lothrop, 1967; *Birthday Parties around the World*, Barrows, 1967; *Member of the Gang* (ALA Notable Book), Crown, 1968; *The Family Christmas Book*, Doubleday, 1969; *Sandra's View*, McGraw, 1969; *Name: Johnny Pierce*, Seabury, 1969; *Harry's Homemade Robot*, Crown, 1969; *Headed for Trouble*, Knopf, 1970; *The Pretzel Hero*, Parents' Magazine Press, 1970; *A Guy Can Be Wrong*, Crown, 1970; *I Need Some Time*, Scabury, 1970; *Tricksters and Trappers*, Abelard, 1970; *Rutherford T. Finds 21B*, Putnam, 1970; *The Case of the Stolen Code Book*, Crown, 1971; *Guess What Grasses Do*, Lothrop, 1972; *The Watchers*, Knopf, 1972; *Let's Go to an Airport*, Putnam, 1972. Contributor of stories and travel articles to a number of national magazines.

WORK IN PROGRESS: A book for eight-to-twelve, for Garrard.

SIDELIGHTS: "My first book, *Map is a Picture*, was written for my daughter June. She was in second grade at the time, and had many questions to ask about a family trip we were planning. I thought I would get her a book explaining map reading, but none were in print for younger readers. Going to school for guidance, I discovered that each teacher had to organize and bring in her own materials for teaching map reading, and that a simple text on the subject would be most welcome. Returning home, I devised a method for introducing and explaining different types of maps to June. This project became the book, which is used today as a text in many elementary schools throughout the United States and Canada.

"Although I was a sociology, not an English major in college, I have had my hand in writing since I was a child. Early efforts produced cards and verses for birthdays and anniversaries. At eleven, I began a book on my view of world history as it was taking place at the time. A project I soon discovered was way beyond my ability! During my high school years, I was a reporter for the school newspaper. I continued to write poetry which analyzed people I knew, and at camp I helped write shows. I was always an avid reader.

"After graduation from college, I worked as a medical case worker, dealing with chiildrens' behavioral problems at home and in school, and with children in trouble with the law. Writing featured heavily in my work in the form of writing comprehensive case histories, and also submitting some of the famous '100 Neediest Cases' featured at Christmas each year in the *New York Times*.

"When we moved to Mt. Kisco in the early 1950's, I was persuaded to write publicity copy for the local chapter of the American Red Cross. All this time I had never thought of becoming a professional writer. But after the experience with *A Map is a Picture*, my horizons broadened. I wrote some travel articles, which my husband illustrated with photographs, and found I was able to place them in national magazines. I had always invented stories for my children, now encouraged by success, I decided to write fiction.

"My first efforts were humorous books. *The Remarkable Ramsey*, based loosely on a dog we had who thought he was a person and acted accordingly. *The Troublesome Tuba*, inspired by the amusing incidents I observed when my son Richard played French horn and his friend played the tuba in the school band. *Birthday Parties around the World* resulted from June's questions about how children of today celebrated their birthdays in other countries. And then I combined my writing experience with my social work background for *Member of the Gang*.

"When I write, I try to create three dimensional characters that readers can identify with, and care about. The plot must move along and grab the reader with its action so that he will want to read on. My goal is to make the reader feel he really knows each person in the story, and has actually happened in on their lives.

"I write about what interests me. My feeling is that I must care and be enthusiastic about the material, then the reader will be caught up in my presentation. When you aren't totally involved, it shows. When I write fiction it is always about things I know personally, from experience, or observation. In nonfiction, I usually write about material I am curious about. Then I present it from my special point of view, which I hope will pique the interest of the

Matt made his decision that night. He was going to run away. ■ (From *Headed for Trouble* by Barbara Rinkoff. Illustrated by Don Bolognese.)

reader to delve further into more scholarly works on the subject.

"Books are important as sources of fun, and for learning. By learning I mean, learning about life. It is important to know that you are not the only one in the world beset by problems . . . that you are not isolated. By reading, you can be exposed to ways of coping. By becoming involved with a story, you can learn to empathize with someone you might be prejudiced against in real life. If an author can reach and move even one reader, it is an accomplishment.

"My fiction ideas come from experience or observation. Once I have the nucleus of an idea, I decide on an ending.

Endings may change along the way, the story may become more complex than planned, but I must know where I am headed and what I want to say to my reader before I begin to write a word. Without this framework a story rambles like a poorly told joke whose punchline is dissipated before the teller gets to the point. Timing is all important for pace and readability. As soon as I name my characters, they take shape as human beings. They take over the direction of the story. I can see them doing or saying this, but not that. They have personalities and must be true to themselves if they are to be real people. I do make a general outline of chapters—a sentence or two to indicate what I expect to be the highpoint of the chapter. My characters often vary this for me. Sometimes it takes longer for a piece of action to develop, sometimes it is more complex than I had planned and I must divide the chapter or I will have an anticlimax.

"I mull a lot before I write. I enact scenes in my head while driving-cooking-making beds. As I mull it over, the urgency to write it down mounts. All that remains is getting the opening sentence onto paper and characters and plot take over.

"I often speak to large groups of children in school or at libraries, and I find the question-answer period stimulating. We all seem to have a good time. In these days when the work week grows shorter and shorter, and free time often hangs heavy, the person who has not learned to enjoy reading has cut himself off from a world of stimulation, growth and pleasure. So, if I have stimulated one child to develop the reading habit, it was worth the effort."

FOR MORE INFORMATION SEE: *Christian Science Monitor*, November 6, 1969; *Saturday Review*, May 20, 1972; *New York Times Book Review*, September 3, 1972.

ROBINSON, Joan (Mary) G(ale Thomas) 1910- (Joan Gale Thomas)

PERSONAL: Born 1910, in Gerrard's Cross, Buckinghamshire, England; daughter of George Gale (a barrister-at-law and solicitor) and Beatrice Amy (a barrister-at-law; maiden name, Cuff) Thomas; married second husband, Richard Gavin Robinson (a writer and illustrator), 1941; children: Deborah, Susanna. *Education:* Educated in private schools in England; also studied at Chelsea Illustrators Studio. *Home:* Unicorn House, Burnham Market, King's Lynn, Norfolk, England and 39 South Hill Park, London N.W.3, England.

CAREER: Writer and illustrator of children's books, 1939—. *Member:* Society of Authors, National Book League, P.E.N.

WRITINGS—Under name Joan Gale Thomas, all self-illustrated: *A Stands for Angel*, Mowbray, 1939 (published in America as *A Is for Angel*, Lothrop, 1953); *Our Father*, Mowbray, 1940; *If Jesus Came to My House*, Mowbray, 1941, Lothrop, 1951; *Christmas*, Mowbray, 1946; *My Garden Book*, Mowbray, 1947; *God of All Things*, Mowbray, 1948; *One Little Baby*, Mowbray, 1950, Lothrop, 1956; *Ten Little Angels*, Mowbray, 1951; *The Happy Year*, Mowbray, 1953; *If I'd Been Born in Bethlehem*, Mowbray, 1953; *I Ask a Blessing*, Mowbray, 1955; *Where Is God?*, Mowbray, 1957, Lothrop, 1959; *The Christmas Angel*, Mowbray, 1961; *Seven Days*, Mowbray, 1964.

Under name of Joan G. Robinson, all self-illustrated: *Debbie Robbie's Day Nursery*, University of London

Press, 1950; *Susie at Home*, Harrap, 1953; *Teddy Robinson*, Harrap, 1953; *More About Teddy Robinson*, Harrap, 1954; *Teddy Robinson's Book*, Harrap, 1955; *Dear Teddy Robinson*, Harrap, 1956; *Mary-Mary*, Harrap, 1957; *More Mary-Mary*, Harrap, 1958; *Another Teddy Robinson*, Harrap, 1960; *Madam Mary-Mary*, Harrap, 1960; *Keeping Up with Teddy Robinson*, Harrap, 1964; *Mary-Mary Stories* (includes *Mary-Mary*, *More Mary-Mary*, and *Madam Mary-Mary*), Harrap, 1965, Coward, 1968.

Author only: (With Gale Young) *Monsieur Charbon*, Harrap, 1962; *When Marnie Was There*, Collins, 1967, Coward, 1968; *Charley* (ALA Notable Book), Collins, 1969, Coward, 1970; *The House in the Square*, Collins, 1972.

Illustrator only: *Carol Book*, Mowbray, 1959.

WORK IN PROGRESS: Another children's novel.

SIDELIGHTS: "There must be some advantages in not being good at school—I went to seven and was hopeless in each. One reason might be that nothing is expected of you. Another that one develops some small line of one's own which somehow sidesteps the competitive world. I drew. I painted Christmas cards. In time I wrote simple verses for very small children so as to have something to illustrate. These developed into a whole series of little books. I illustrated other people's stories, and when these did not please me, I wrote my own.

"Not wanting to aspire too high, I wrote about a teddy bear. It was not easy—I was very slow, putting a lot into it. Then came another series about a little girl, the smallest and most insignificant of a large family, who always came out on top. By this time illustrating seemed a mug's game. Writing was everything. Dare I write a novel I did for ten-to-twelve-year olds. Much went into it of the solitary child, for some of us are always solitary children, even though we are of four, as I was. Two more books about loners followed, not I hope without their humor, and this brings me up to the present time. Now . . ."

Ms. Robinson prefers writing to illustrating. She writes slowly, aiming in secular books at striking a balance between entertaining the children and not boring the parents to death if they read aloud. Her major concern in religious books is "no guilt—no strings attached to God's love," the result she believes of her own non-conformist childhood. "I never passed an exam, never mastered long division, and am still inclined to discover platitudes with great enthusiasm thinking I've invented them. I can also sit up all night talking."

FOR MORE INFORMATION SEE: Boris Ford, *Young Writers, Young Readers*, Hutchinson, 1960; Margery Fisher, *Intent Upon Reading*, Brockhampton Press, 1961; Brian Doyle, *The Who's Who of Children's Literature*, Schocken, 1968; *Horn Book*, August, 1970.

ROSENBERG, Nancy Sherman 1931- (Nancy Sherman)

PERSONAL: Born June 21, 1931, in New York, N.Y.; daughter of Monroe and Gertrude (Horn) Sherman; married Lawrence C. Rosenberg, 1951; children: Eric, Constance and Mark (twins), Elizabeth. *Education:* Bryn Mawr College (class of '52), B.A., 1958. *Home:* 28 Fanshaw Ave., Yonkers, N.Y. 10705.

CAREER: Free-lance writer. *Awards, honors:* First prize, *New York Herald Tribune* Children's Spring Book Festival, for *Gwendolyn the Miracle Hen*, 1961.

WRITINGS—Under name Nancy Sherman: *The Boy Who Ate Flowers*, Platt, 1960; *Gwendolyn the Miracle Hen*, Golden Books, 1961; *Gwendolyn and the Weathercock*, Golden Books, 1963; *Miss Agatha's Lark*, Bobbs, 1968.

Under name Nancy Rosenberg: (With Lawrence C. Rosenberg) *The Story of Modern Medicine*, Norton, 1966; (with Reuven K. Snyderman) *New Parts for People*, Norton, 1969; *How to Enjoy Mathematics with Your Child*, Stein & Day, 1970; (with Louis Z. Cooper) *Vaccines and Viruses*, Norton, 1971.

ROTHKOPF, Carol Z. 1929-

PERSONAL: "H" in surname is silent; born September 16, 1929, in New York, N.Y.; daughter of Frederic David (a physician) and Madeleine (Arnold) Zeman; married Ernst Z. Rothkopf (a psychologist), August 28, 1952; children: David, Paul, Marissa. *Education:* Goucher College, B.A., 1951; Columbia University, M.A., 1952. *Residence:* Summit, N.J.

CAREER: Dalton Schools, Inc., New York, N.Y., teacher, 1951-52; University of Illinois Press, Urbana, clerk, 1952-53; Spencer Press, Champaign, Ill., editor, 1953-56; Grolier, Inc., Grolier Council, New York, N.Y., Europe editor of *The New Book of Knowledge*, 1961-65,

CAROL Z. ROTHKOPF

1968-71, senior editor, *Lands and People,* 1968-71. Mobil Travel Guides, editorial consultant, 1961-64; free-lance consultant to several American and Italian publishers.

WRITINGS—Juvenile, except as noted: *Leo Tolstoy,* Watts, 1968; *Jean-Henri Dunant: Father of the Red Cross,* Watts, 1969; (co-editor) *Learning from Written Instructional Materials* (adult book), Teachers College Press, 1971; *The First Book of the Red Cross,* Watts, 1971; *The First Book of Yugoslavia,* Watts, 1971; *East Europe,* Watts, 1972. Writer of a number of Study-Master guides to classics, published by American R.D.M., 1962-66.

WORK IN PROGRESS: The Suez Canal, and *Czechoslovakia,* for Watts.

SIDELIGHTS: "The most important facts about me as a writer and a person are embodied in four other persons—my husband and my three children. All share and encourage my interest in history, politics, and literature. They are wonderful about getting me to my desk and being silent once they have succeeded. Each of my books has been a family adventure in discovery and learning; perhaps because the research that goes into the books is the most fun for me. In sum, I consider myself enormously fortunate because I am doing the work I most enjoy."

FOR MORE INFORMATION SEE: New York Times Book Review, May 12, 1968.

RUDOMIN, Esther
See HAUTZIG, Esther

RUSSELL, Patrick
See SAMMIS, John

RUTHIN, Margaret

PERSONAL: Born in England. *Home:* 31 Parkgate Dr., Bolton, Lancashire, England. *Agent:* Hope Leresche & Steele, 11 Jubilee Pl., London S.W. 3, England.

CAREER: Professional writer.

WRITINGS—All youth books: *Wings for a Gull,* Warne, 1951; *White Horse of Hungary,* Warne, 1952; *Secret Pagoda,* Warne, 1953; *Strange Safari,* Warne, 1953; *The Ring of the Prophet,* Warne, 1954; *Kidnapped in Kandy,* Blackie & Son, 1955; *Jungle Nurse,* Watts, 1960; *Reindeer Girl,* Dobson, 1961, published in United States as *Elli of the Northland* (Junior Literary Guild selection), Farrar, Straus, 1968; *Lapland Nurse,* Dobson, 1964; *Katrina of the Lonely Isles,* Dobson, 1964, Ariel Books, 1965; *Secret of the Shetlands,* Dobson, 1965; *Kidnapped on Stromboli,* Dobson, 1967; *Jungle Gipsy,* Dobson, 1968; *Hungarian Rebel,* Dobson, 1969.

FOR MORE INFORMATION SEE: Books and Bookmen, September, 1968.

Textbooks: Book 5 (*I Earn, Explore, Excel*) in American Book Co.'s "Triple I" collateral reading series for multi-ethnic elementary students, 1970, and units in Books 4 and 6; more than 150 short stories for various other reading series.

Filmstrips: "Image Makers" and "Black Image Makers," Eye-Gate House, 1969; "Afro-American Heritage," Eye-Gate House, 1970; "Families in Action," Eye-Gate House 1971; "They Came to America," Avna, 1971; "Living in the Other America," Avna, 1971; "Strangers in Their Own Land," Avna, 1972; "It's Up to You," Eye-Gate House, 1972. Writer of forty short cassettes dealing with science and social studies at the elementary level.

WORK IN PROGRESS: A series of brief sports biographies, tentatively titled *The Name of the Game: Football,* and similarly titled books for basketball and baseball; two filmstrip sets, "The Community in Action," for Eye-Gate House, and "The Price of Prejudice," for Avna.

HOBBIES AND OTHER INTERESTS: Painting and sculpture ("with great enthusiasm and little talent"), sewing and decorating, sports of all kinds ("mostly as a spectator").

RYDELL, Wendell
See RYDELL, Wendy

RYDELL, Wendy
(Wendell Rydell)

PERSONAL: Born in Perth Amboy, N.J.; daughter of Abraham and Sadie (Gottesman) Wilner; married Chester Rydell (president of Noble-Rydell, Inc.), April 6, 1952; children: Susan, David. *Education:* Ohio State University, B.A., 1947; Mexico City College, M.A., 1949. *Home:* 51 Wintercress Lane, East Northport, N.Y. 11731.

CAREER: Former beat reporter for *Newark Evening News,* Newark, N.J., and copywriter for several department stores in New York, N.Y.; sporadic columnist for small New Jersey weeklies. Member of board of trustees, East Northport Library. *Member:* Theta Sigma Phi, Chi Delta Phi, Alpha Lambda Delta.

WRITINGS: (Under pseudonym Wendell Rydell) *Abelard Sports Books: Basketball* (juvenile), Abelard, 1971, and similarly titled books, *Football,* 1971, *Baseball,* 1972; (with Steven Schepp) *Pot, Pills and Powders: The Truth About Drugs,* Western Publishing, in press; *The Instant Home Fashion Sewing Encyclopedia,* Career Institute, in press.

SAMMIS, John 1942-
(Patrick Russell)

PERSONAL: Born June 22, 1942, in New York, N.Y.; son of Fred Rutledge (a publisher) and Mary Ruth (Townsend) Sammis; married Susan Field (a free-lance editor and writer), August 26, 1966. *Education:* Bowdoin College, A.B., 1964. *Politics:* Independent. *Religion:* "Same as politics." *Home:* 6 Rebel Rd., Westport, Conn. 06880. *Office:* Rutledge Books, Inc., 17 East 45th St., New York, N.Y. 10017.

CAREER: Rutledge Books, Inc., New York, N.Y., associ-

JOHN SAMMIS, with Coach Billy Hunter

ate publisher, 1965—. *Member:* American Contract Bridge League, Bowdoin Club of New York, Briard Club of America.

WRITINGS: (With Earl Weaver) *Winning* (adult), Morrow, 1972.

Under pseudonym Patrick Russell: *Going Going Gone* (juvenile), Doubleday, 1967; *The Tommy Davis Story* (juvenile), Doubleday, 1969.

SIDELIGHTS: "I was never interested in English and took as few courses as the minimum would allow, through my school career. After college I entered the Peace Corps, but I was a little flamboyant for their tastes and was asked to leave training after eight weeks. I returned to New York where I took a job at Rutledge Books (family owned) until I could find a good paying job or a job which I would like. I've been at Rutledge ever since.

"I began editing books using common sense. Authors, especially those writing sports for juveniles, can be fairly bad writers. Since I love sports and was going to be a professional baseball player (contracts from Phillies and Orioles) but chose college instead, I have developed a number of sports books for our company including *The First 50 Years* (105,000 in print), *This Great Game* (65,000 in print), *Hockey* (40,000 in print), *The Other League, Playback, Basketball: The American Game, Clyde,* and *Mr. Cub* (four weeks on *Times* bestseller list).

"All the writing I have done has been involved with sports. There is a definite lack of good writers in this area, thus there is more opportunity available for prospective sports writers. Also, when you get involved in writing sports, you get to numerous super bowl games, world series, hockey playoffs, etc."

HOBBIES AND OTHER INTERESTS: Platform tennis (nationally ranked), baseball, softball, tennis, football, ice hockey, bowling, basketball, golf, bridge, dogs, especially his own champion Briards.

SANDERLIN, George 1915-

PERSONAL: Born February 5, 1915, in Baltimore, Md.; son of George Bismarck (a translator) and Charlotte (Brady) Sanderlin; married Owenita Harrah (now a teacher and writer), May 30, 1936; children: Frea Sanderlin Sladek, Mary Sanderlin Buska, David, Johnny (deceased). *Education:* The American University, B.A., 1935; Johns Hopkins University, Ph.D., 1938. *Office:* California State University, San Diego, Calif.

CAREER: University of Maine, Orono, associate professor of English, 1938-55; San Diego State College (now California State University), San Diego, Calif., professor of English, 1955—. San Diego Tennis Patrons, member. *Member:* American Association of University Professors, Mediaeval Academy of America, Modern Language Association.

WRITINGS: College Reading: A Collection of Prose, Plays and Poetry, Heath, 1953, revised edition, 1958; *St. Jerome and the Bible,* Farrar, Straus, 1961; (with J.I. Brown) *Effective Writing and Reading,* Heath, 1962; *St. Gregory the Great, Consul of God,* Farrar, Straus, 1964; *First Around the World: A Journal of Magellan's Voyage,* Harper, 1964; *Eastward to India: Vasco da Gama's Voyage,* Harper, 1965; *Effective Writing,* Heath, 1966; *Across the Ocean Sea: A Journal of Columbus's Voyage,* Harper, 1966; *1776: Journals of American Independence,* Harper, 1968; *The Sea-Dragon: Journals of Francis Drake's Voyage Around the World,* Harper, 1969; *Benjamin Franklin: As Others Saw Him,* Coward, 1971; (editor and translator) *Bartolome de Las Casas: A Selection of His Writings,* Knopf, 1971. Contributor to *Speculum, English Literary History, Woman's Day, Parents' Magazine, Classical World, Modern Language Notes, College English, Author and Journalist,* other journals. Also contributor to *Britannica Junior Encyclopedia.*

SIDELIGHTS: "It is a little difficult to think of something to say about myself. I like to try to write good English, to tell a story—particularly a story based on history. I like foreign languages—I learned to speak as well as read Spanish in order to work on Bartolome de Las Casas, one of the great early champions of the oppressed in the Americas.

"My favorite poet is Virgil. I teach medieval literature—Chaucer, the Gawain-poet, etc. I have now served as an examiner on Spanish M.A. examinations. I also teach medieval Latin from time to time—whenever I can corral a few students.

"I play tennis three days a week—our older son, David,

GEORGE SANDERLIN

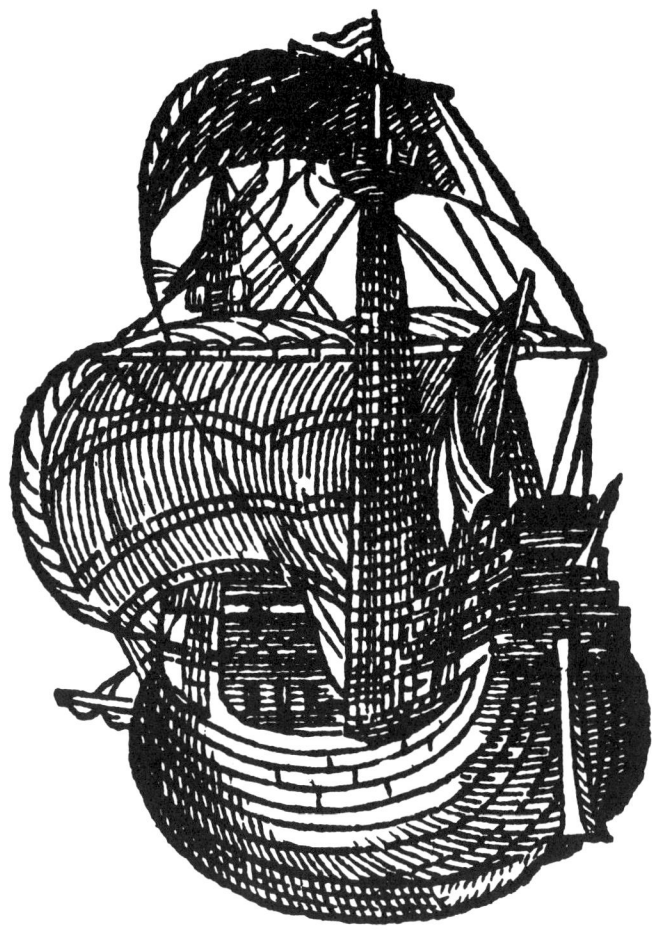

(From *The Sea-Dragon* by George Sanderlin.)

now a Ph.D. and assistant professor of history, comes down frequently to play with me and his mother. A few years ago, in addition to winning the men's singles for himself at La Jolla, he won the father and son and mother and son events in the same tournament, I think an unprecedented 'triple crown'. Our sons were both national junior champions—David went on to the top dozen or so men players in a career cut short by his work for the Ph.D. We lost our second son to leukemia—my wife's book about him, *Johnny*, is widely read (she is the author of several books).

"We live in the country on several acres in an old ranch-type house. I enjoy living in southern California even though the big fire last fall missed the house by about twenty-five feet—I watched it go by."

Caedmon issued the recording "Christopher Columbus, Chronicle of 1492" based on Sanderlin's *Across the Ocean Sea*.

SATTLER, Helen Roney 1921-

PERSONAL: Born March 2, 1921, in Newton, Iowa; daughter of Louie Earl (a farmer) and Hazel (Cure) Roney; married Robert E. Sattler (a chemical engineer), September 30, 1950; children: Richard, Kathryn. *Education:* Southwest Missouri State College, B.S., 1946; Famous Artist's School, Certificate in Commercial Art, 1960. *Politics:* Democrat. *Religion:* Christian. *Residence:* Bartlesville, Okla. 74003.

CAREER: Elementary teacher in Aldrich, Mo., 1941-42, Norwood, Mo., 1942-45, and Marshfield, Mo., 1945-48; Kansas City Public Library, Kansas City, Mo., children's librarian, 1948-49; Standard Oil of New Jersey, elementary teacher at company school on Aruba (Dutch Island off Venezuelan coast), 1949-50. *Member:* Oklahoma Writer's Association, Bartlesville Artist's Association (treasurer, 1960), Bartlesville Writer's Association (chairman).

WRITINGS: (Self-illustrated) *Kitchen Carton Crafts*, Lothrop, 1970; (self-illustrated) *A Beginning to Read Book of Puzzles*, Denison, 1971; (self-illustrated) *Holiday Gifts, Favors and Decorations*, Lothrop, 1971; *The Eggless Cookbook*, Barnes, in press; (self-illustrated) *Sockcraft*, Lothrop, in press (self-illustrated) *Jewelry from Junk*, Lothrop, in press. Contributor of puzzles, how-to articles, stories, and verse to more than twenty-five magazines, including *Child Life, Junior Discoveries, Jack and Jill, Boys' Life, Wee Wisdom* and *Instructor*.

WORK IN PROGRESS: Biography.

SIDELIGHTS: "Many years of experience working with children as a teacher, mother, and Scout leader led to my creating crafts and puzzles, first for magazine publication then in books. I believe that puzzles stimulate their minds and that most children can be taught to work with their hands and be creative if shown a few basic designs to get them started. A toy or gift made by themselves is more valuable than an expensive one bought in a store. Creative work need not be expensive. This is what I try to show in my craft books."

Ms. Sattler has lived most of the fifty states, Canada, Mexico, Haiti, Cuba, and Aruba.

HOBBIES AND OTHER INTERESTS: Painting, drawing, cooking, crafts, and puzzle solving.

SCHLOAT, G. Warren, Jr. 1914-

PERSONAL: Born July 15, 1914, in Mexico, Mo.; son of G. Warren (a builder) and Bessie (Thompson) Schloat, married Virginia Wilson, February 13, 1937; children: G. Warren III, Anson Wilson. *Education:* Otis Art Institute, Los Angeles, Calif., student, 1935-37. *Home:* Palmer Lane West, Pleasantville, N.Y. 10570. *Office:* Warren Schloat Productions, Inc., 115 Tompkins Ave., Pleasantville, N.Y. 10570.

CAREER: Walt Disney Productions, Burbank, Calif., animator and story director, 1939-45; Compton Advertising, Inc., New York, N.Y., vice-president and creative director, 1955-62; Warren Schloat Productions, Inc. (publishers of audiovisual materials for schools; now a subsidiary of Prentice-Hall, Inc.), Pleasantville, N.Y., president, 1962—.

G. WARREN SCHLOAT, JR.

WRITINGS—All photographic picture books: *What Shall I Do?* 1949, *Adventures of a Letter,* 1949, *Playtime for You,* 1950, *Milk for You,* 1951, *The Wonderful Egg,* 1952, *Your Wonderful Teeth,* 1954, *The Magic of Water,* 1955, *Andy's Wonderful Telescope,* 1958 (all published by Scribner).

The Haunted Forest, 1961, *Duee, A Boy of Libia,* 1962, *Kwaku, A Boy of Ghana,* 1962, *Prapan, A Boy of Thailand,* 1963, *Naim, A Boy of Turkey,* 1963, *Johnnyshah, A Boy of Iran,* 1963, *Uttam, A Boy of India,* 1963, *Fay Gow, A Boy of Hong Kong,* 1964, *Junichi, A Boy of Japan,* 1964, *Conchita and Juan, A Girl and Boy of Mexico,* 1964, *Maria and Ramon, A Girl and Boy of Puerto Rico,* 1966, *Marta and Fernando, A Girl and Boy of Spain,* 1970, *Four Fukoto's,* in press (all published by Knopf).

SIDELIGHTS: "I try and write about one book for children a year but most of my writing efforts now go into films and sound filmstrips for the school market and I concentrate on the area of human relations. My special kick is trying to help eliminate prejudice.

"This is like trying to fill up a sieve with water but since prejudice is learned perhaps it can be eliminated through education. My titles in current release through Warren Schloat Productions, Inc. are: 'Exploding the Myths of Prejudice,' 'Black Rabbits and White Rabbits,' 'Punishment Fits the Crime.' 'The Cluster Buster' is in production.

"Warren Schloat Productions, Inc. won the 1971 American Film Festival's Blue Ribbon; the 1971 Cine Golden Eagle, and the 1971 Columbus Film Festival's, 'Chris,' for the 54-minute documentary, 'The Fayette Story.' This examines prejudices of both blacks and whites in the town of Fayette, Mississippi where Charles Evers is the black mayor."

Schloat has traveled in Africa, Europe and Asia, photographing material and gathering stories for his books, which are used in many school systems throughout America.

SCHWARTZ, Alvin 1927-

PERSONAL: Born April 25, 1927, in Brooklyn, N.Y.; son of Harry (a taxi-driver) and Gussie (Younger) Schwartz; married Barbara Carmer, August 7, 1954; children: John, Peter, Nancy, Elizabeth. *Education:* City College, New York, N.Y., student, 1944-45; Colby College, A.B., 1949; Northwestern University, M.S. in Journalism, 1951. *Politics:* Independent. *Home and office:* 50 Southern Way, Princeton, N.J. 08540; Summer: R.D. Reach Rd., Deer Isle, Me. 04627. *Agent:* Marilyn Marlow, Curtis Brown Ltd., 60 East 56th St., New York, N.Y. 10022.

CAREER: Newspaper reporter, 1951-55; writer for nonprofit and commercial organizations, 1955-59; Opinion Research Corp., Princeton, N.J., director of communications, 1959-64; free-lance writer, 1964—; Rutgers University, New Brunswick, N.J., part-time teacher of English

ALVIN SCHWARTZ

composition, 1962—. *Military service:* U.S. Navy, 1945-46. *Member:* Boy Scouts of America (National Council).

WRITINGS: A Parent's Guide to Children's Play and Recreation, Collier, 1963; *How to Fly a Kite, Catch a Fish, Grow a Flower,* Macmillan, 1965; *America's Exciting Cities,* Crowell, 1966; *The Night Workers* (young people), Dutton, 1966; *What Do You Think? An Introduction to Public Opinion* (young people), Dutton, 1966; *The City and Its People* (young people), Dutton, 1967; *Museum* (young people), Dutton, 1967; *The People's Choice* (young people), Dutton, 1968; *Old Cities and New Towns* (young people), Dutton, 1968; *To Be a Father,* Crown, 1969; *The Rainy Day Book,* Trident, 1969; *University,* Viking, 1969; *Going Camping,* Macmillan, 1970, revised edition, 1972; *The Unions* (young people), Viking, 1972; *Hobbies,* Simon & Schuster, 1972; *A Twister of Twists* (young people), Lippincott, 1972. Also author of booklet on attitude research for social agencies. Contributor of articles to *Redbook, Coronet, Parade, Parent's Magazine, Public Opinion Quarterly, Journal of Marketing, New York Times,* and *New York Herald Tribune.*

WORK IN PROGRESS: Four books on folklore, two books on urban problems, a group of books on crafts.

SIDELIGHTS: "My work actually falls into several categories: books for young people ranging from eight

It is a quarter to seven. Night has begun to fade. This carrier boy has only a few more of his sixty papers to deliver. ■ (From *The Night Workers* by Alvin Schwartz. Photographs by Ulli Steltzer.)

through high school on urban problems, other social problems, American institutions, and folklore; books for families on recreation.

"I write books because it provides me with a rather remarkable opportunity to explore in depth what interests me without organizational ties that inevitably hamper a writer.

"I write in a small out building, a salt box my wife designed, which is 8X8 but almost all window. However, I spend a good deal of time traveling wherever need be to do my research, much of which is conducted on a first-hand basis through taped interviews. I also am learning to take photographs rather than relying on others for my material. Among my books in preparation are a number of picture books of the more traditional type involving folklore, which for one who is essentially a reporter and an interpreter is a new medium and an exciting one."

SEARS, Stephen W. 1932-

PERSONAL: Born July 27, 1932, in Lakewood, Ohio; son of John F. (a chemist) and Josephine (Ward) Sears; married second wife, Sally Tyson, September 26, 1970; children: (first marriage) Jeffrey Alan, Kathryn Grace. *Education:* Oberlin College, B.A., 1954. *Home:* 9 South Huckleberry Dr., Norwalk, Conn. 06850. *Office:* American Heritage Publishing Co., 1221 Avenue of the Americas, New York, N.Y. 10020.

CAREER: American Heritage Publishing Co., New York, N.Y., assistant editor, *American Heritage* (magazine), 1954-57, assistant editor, Major Books Division, 1957-61, editor, American Heritage Junior Library, 1961-64, executive editor, Education Division, 1964-71, project editor, Book Division, 1971—.

WRITINGS—All youth books: (With Marvin W. McFarland as consultant) *Air War Against Hitler's Germany,* American Heritage Press, 1964; (with E.M. Eller as consultant) *Carrier War in the Pacific,* American Heritage Press, 1966; (with I.S.O. Playfair as consultant) *Desert War in North Africa,* American Heritage Press, 1967; (with S.L.A. Marshall as consultant) *The Battle of the Bulge,* American Heritage Press, 1969.

STEPHEN W. SEARS

The GI used his wits and his initiative and his independence of mind with an effectiveness that few soldiers in any of the world's armies could match. ■ (From *The Battle of the Bulge* by Stephen W. Sears. Photo by the U.S. Signal Corps.)

... and he took the stroller from the front seat and unfolded it on the sidewalk and took Jacob out and put him in the stroller and took Mitzi out and put her on the sidewalk and walked around to his side and got in and drove away. ■ (From *Tell Me a Mitzi* by Lore Segal. Illustrated by Harriet Pincus.)

SEGAL, Lore 1928-

PERSONAL: Born March 8, 1928, in Vienna, Austria; daughter of Ignatz (an accountant) and Franzi (Stern) Groszmann; married David I. Segal (an editor), November 3, 1961 (deceased); children: Beatrice, Jacob. *Education:* Bedford College, University of London, B.A. (honors), 1948. *Religion:* Jewish. *Home:* 280 Riverside Dr., New York, N.Y. 10025. *Agent:* Lynn Nesbit.

CAREER: Teacher in the Dominican Republic, 1948-51; Columbia University, New York, N.Y., adjunct associate professor in the department of writing, school of the arts, 1969—. *Awards, honors:* Guggenheim fellowship in creative writing, 1965-66; National Council on the Arts and Humanities grant, 1967-68; *Book World* Children's Spring Book Festival First Prize, 1970, for *Tell Me a Mitzi*.

WRITINGS: Other People's Houses (autobiography; originally appeared in the *New Yorker*), Harcourt, 1964; (with W.D. Snodgrass) *Gallows Songs* (a translation from Christian Morgenstern), Michigan University Press, 1967; *Tell Me a Mitzi* (ALA Notable Book), Farrar, Straus, 1970. Contributor of short stories to *New Yorker, Saturday Evening Post, New Republic, Epoch, Commentary*, and other periodicals; reviews to *New York Times, New Republic,* translations of poetry have appeared in *Mademoiselle, Atlantic, Hudson Review, Poetry* and *Tri-Quarterly*.

WORK IN PROGRESS: Two children's books and a translation of twenty Grimm fairy tales (to be illustrated by Maurice Sendak), for Farrar, Straus; a novel.

SIDELIGHTS: "I was born in Vienna and came to England in 1938 at the age of ten years. I went to school in England and graduated from college. In 1948 I moved to the Dominican Republic where I taught English for the next three years. I have lived in New York since 1951. I am widowed and have two young children.

"All I can tell you about the writing of *Mitzi* is that I told these stories to my children and then spent a couple of years writing them over and over until all the sentences sounded right."

FOR MORE INFORMATION SEE: Reporter, November 19, 1964; *New York Review of Books*, November 19, 1964; *Book Week*, November 29, 1964; *New Republic*, December 12, 1964; *Commonweal*, January 29, 1965; *Commentary*, March, 1965; *New Statesman*, March 19, 1965; *Horn Book*, August, 1970; Selma G. Lanes, *Down the Rabbit Hole*, Atheneum, 1971; *Time*, April 24, 1972.

LORE SEGAL

SELDEN, George
See THOMPSON, George Selden

SHARMAT, Marjorie Weinman 1928-

PERSONAL: Born November 12, 1928, in Portland, Me.; daughter of Nathan (a wholesaler and manufacturer of dry goods and mens furnishings) and Anna (Richardson) Weinman; married Mitchell Brenner Sharmat (a realtor), February 24, 1957; children: Craig Lynden, Andrew Richard. Education: Attended Lasell Junior College, 1946-47; Westbrook Junior College, graduate, 1948. Home: 51 Sycamore Lane, Irvington-on-Hudson, N.Y. 10533.

CAREER: Yale University, New Haven, Conn., circulation staff of university library, 1951-54, circulation staff of law library, 1954-55. Writer of greeting card verse and advertising copy.

WRITINGS—Juveniles: Rex, Harper, 1967; Goodnight Andrew, Goodnight Craig, Harper, 1969; Gladys Told Me to Meet Her Here, Harper, 1970; A Hot Thirsty Day, Macmillan, 1971; 51 Sycamore Lane, Macmillan, 1971; Getting Something on Maggie Marmelstein, Harper, 1971; A Visit with Rosalind, Macmillan, 1972; Nate the Great, Coward, 1972; Sophie and Gussie, Macmillan, 1973. Contributor to magazines.

SIDELIGHTS: "In a story I recently wrote, a boy describes his writer-father as follows: 'His brain is like an enormous litter basket, and from time to time he dumps everybody and everything he knows into it. I think there's some sort of machine in there that goes around and around and it mixes and blends everyone and everything, and pretty soon out comes a story.'

"I suppose that very few, if any, writers would care to have their brains even remotely compared to litter baskets, but stories do represent the coming together of the diverse and often disparate experiences, emotions and people that are part of the life of the writer. The writer sorts them out, and gives them shape and substance and meaning. The writer feels the need to do this—to explore the variations and richness of human experience—to say that this is the way it is or was or could be or never could be. There is an almost relentless desire to communicate. It is, perhaps like a sore tooth or a nagging headache, conspicuously and unremittingly there. I have felt this compulsion ever since I can remember.

"I started writing when I was eight. I 'published' a newspaper 'The Snooper's Gazette' with a friend, and it achieved a circulation of about four—her parents and mine. At that time I also wrote my first poem. It was about a neighborhood dog, and I still have the memory of my mother supplying the last line when I was stuck. From then on I wrote and wrote—diaries, music, more poems, stories and one chapter of a mystery novel—and I sometimes drew illustrations to go with my words. Then I began to write for school magazines and newspapers.

"My parents gave me tremendous encouragement, and I have been forever grateful that they did. However, it wasn't until I started high school and began sending my stories to national magazines, and the magazines began sending them back, that I realized my parent's enthusiasm was not universally shared. But I continued to submit stories from time to time because I couldn't break the habit of unreasonable optimism.

"My first commercially published 'work' was a national advertising slogan for the W.T. Grant Company for their spring promotion. It consisted of four words. I used to enjoy walking into Grant stores and reading my four words. Eventually I had my first story—a short story for adults—published while I was working at the Yale Library. This unfortunately caused me to break out in hives. I have since regarded a collection of red spots on the skin as a hallmark of literary achievement, and never the result

MARJORIE SHARMAT

"My reading books, *A Hot Thirsty Day*, *Nate the Great*, and *Sophie and Gussie*, were stimulating to write. There is a certain precision and rhythm involved in writing any book, but a reading book seems to offer a special challenge in combining art with simplicity.

"In my novels, my inspiration comes from a variety of sources. I particularly enjoy the blending and contrasting of seemingly incongruous and unlikely elements—such as a chicken and a law firm in *51 Sycamore Lane* and my father's bread pudding recipe and Cary Grant in *Getting Something on Maggie Marmelstein*—allowing them either to interact or to coexist meaningfully between the same covers. I'm more interested in writing about people than about changing seasons, sunsets and nature in general. I think there is so much that is inherently funny and touching in human behavior, and I like to show contemporary children and adults humorously caught up in their often conflicting aspirations and priorities.

"I also draw upon my own basic family situations for ideas for my novels. My book *A Visit with Rosalind* which has Portland, Maine for a setting resulted from my visits in Portland with my sister Rosalind and my parents. I enjoy using family names in my books. In addition to my sons and sister already mentioned, my father, my mother, my husband—as well as other family members and friends—have appeared in various roles.

"I deeply care about the reactions of my readers. However, while I'm working on a book, I often have the feeling that I'm writing for the satisfaction and ultimate approval of my typewriter. The physical presence of this machine has an immediacy that seems to preclude any

of eating too much chocolate. My second published story, an article about Yale, became a part of the Yale Memorabilia Collection. (More hives)

"I now write children's books exclusively—picture books, readers, and novels. I became interested in them after my two children were born. All of my picture books were inspired by my children. My first book *Rex* is the story of a boy who runs away from home to the house of an old man in his neighborhood and pretends to be a dog. This book grew out of two unrelated happenings. My older boy, Craig, used to visit adult neighbors, and my other son, Andrew, sometimes pretended he was a dog. This book, incidentally, touches upon the subject of loneliness, a theme which perhaps above all others appeals to me as a writer. *Goodnight Andrew, Goodnight Craig* came about when my two boys were going to sleep, and Craig wished Andrew 'Pleasant nightmares.' *Gladys Told Me to Meet Her Here* had its inspirational origin in a supermarket where Craig met a friend, but its literary culmination was in Central Park.

"Well, goodnight. And I really mean it this time." ■ (From *Goodnight Andrew, Goodnight Craig* by Marjorie Sharmat. Illustrated by Mary Chambers.)

competitive company. I do manage, though, to ask my husband for his comments on my manuscripts, and they are objective and helpful. And after a book is published, I enjoy being on the receiving end of the kind of manuscript that begins, 'Dear Mrs. Sharmat, I've just read-------.' "

HOBBIES AND OTHER INTERESTS: "Playing piano, drawing, and writing to my political representatives hoping to receive a non-political reply."

SHAW, Arnold 1909-

PERSONAL: Born June 28, 1909, in New York, N.Y. Education: Columbia University, M.A., 1931. Home: 2288 Gabriel Dr., Las Vegas, Nev. 89109.

CAREER: Robbins Music Corp., New York, N.Y., advertising and publicity manager; Swank Magazine, New York, N.Y., editor; Leeds Music Corp., New York, N.Y., advertising and publicity director; Duchess Music Corp., New York, N.Y., vice-president and general professional manager; Edward B. Marks Music Corp., New York, N.Y., general professional manager; Hill and Range Songs, vice-president and general professional manager. Member: American Society of Composers, Authors and Publishers, Authors Guild, American Musicological Society, American Guild of Authors and Composers, Las Vegas Press Club.

WRITINGS: (With lyrics by Rosemary and Stephen Vincent Benet) "Sing a Song of Americans," 1941; (co-editor) Schillinger System of Musical Composition, Carl Fischer, 1946; (editor) Mathematical Basis of the Arts, Philosophical Library, 1948; Lingo of Tin Pan Alley, Broadcast Music, 1950; The Money Song, Random House, 1953; Belafonte, Chilton, 1960; Sinatra: 20th Century Romantic, Holt, 1968; The Rock Revolution: What's Happening in Today's Music, Crowell Collier, 1969; The World of Soul: Black America's Contribution to the Pop Music Scene (ALA Notable Young Adult Book), Regnery, 1970; The Street That Never Slept: New York's Fabled 52nd St., Coward, 1971. Author of numerous articles and book reviews in magazines and newspapers; a television adaptation, jazz liners; composer of many songs and collections of piano music. Producer, narrator, writer, composer of "Curtain Time," a series of eight TV shows on the great musicals of the 30's.

WORK IN PROGRESS: The Sound and Fury of the 1950's.

SHAY, Arthur 1922-

PERSONAL: Born March 31, 1922, in New York, N.Y.; son of Hyman (a tailor) and Mollie (Schesten) Shay; married Florence Gerson, November 30, 1944; children: Jane (Mrs. Jay Lynch), Harmon, Richard, Lauren, Steven. Education: Brooklyn College, student, 1939-42. Home: 618 Indian Hill Rd., Deerfield, Ill. 60015.

CAREER: Time, Inc., New York, N.Y., reporter and bureau chief for Life and Time, 1947-50; free-lance photographer and writer in Chicago, Ill., and vicinity, 1951—. Public relations director, Deerfield Citizens for Human Rights. Military service: U.S. Army Air Forces, 1946; served in European and Pacific theaters; became first lieutenant; received Distinguished Flying Cross and Air Medal (five) for aerial destruction of FW 190. Member: American Society of Magazine Photographers (secretary, 1968—). Awards, honors: Numerous photographic awards.

WRITINGS—Self-illustrated with photographs: "What Happens" series, published by Reilly & Lee: What Happens When You Put Money in the Bank, 1967; ... When You Mail a Letter, 1967; ... When You Travel by Plane, 1968; ... When You Make a Telephone Call, 1968; ... When You Go to the Hospital, 1969; ... in a Car Factory, 1969; ... at a Television Station, 1969; ... When You Build a House, 1970; ... When You Spend Money, 1970; ... at the Zoo, 1971.

ARNOLD SHAW

"What It's Like" series, published by Reilly & Lee: *What It's Like to be a Doctor,* 1971; . . . *to be a Fireman,* 1971; . . . *to be a Pilot,* 1971.

Other: *How a Family Grows* (sex education book; introductory notes by Morris Fishbein and Ner Littner), Reilly & Lee, 1968; (with Mort Leve) *Inside Handball,* Reilly & Lee, 1970. Author of play, "A Clock for Nikita," produced in Chicago at Stagelight Theater, 1964. More than 16,000 photographs have been published in *Time, Life, Fortune, Sports Illustrated,* and in books, brochures, and annual reports he has prepared or helped prepare for business and industrial firms.

WORK IN PROGRESS: A book, *Shooting the Mafia and Other Camera Exposures.*

SIDELIGHTS: "I am interested in the use of pictures and text to make clear to children processes and institutions that have previously defied teaching."

Shay was bugle champion of East Bronx in 1937, navigated the first non-stop low-level weather flight from California to Alaska, also the first non-stop transport flight from Guam to Tokyo in 1945, and was defeated in handball exhibition by World Champion, Paul Haber, in Chicago, 1971.

SHEMIN, Margaretha (Hoeneveld) 1928-

Amy, Elly, and Jos were sitting at the top of the stoop, waiting. Like the stoops of all the other houses that stood along both sides of the canal, theirs was ten stone steps high. ■ (From *Mrs. Herring* by Margaretha Shemin. Illustrated by Robert Quackenbush.)

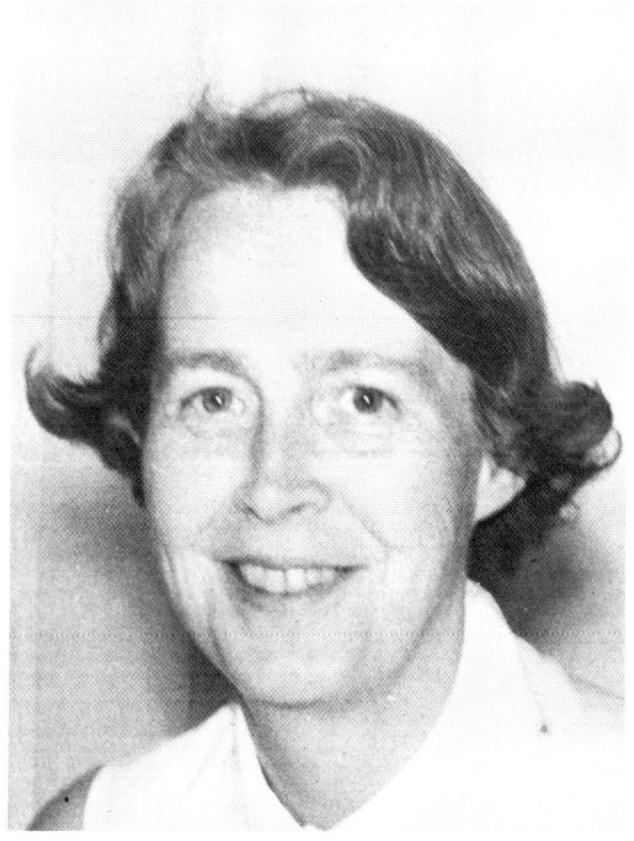

MARGARETHA SHEMIN

PERSONAL: Born November 23, 1928, in Alkmaar, Netherlands; daughter of Gabe (a physician) and Jantje (Toxopeus) Hoeneveld; married Elias Ralph Shemin (a physician), January 5, 1954; children: Douglas, Barbara, Frances. *Education:* University of Leiden, law degree; Columbia University, M.L.S. (with honors), 1971. *Religion:* Unitarian-Universalist. *Home:* 17 Otsego Rd., Pleasantville, N.Y. 10570.

CAREER: Writer. White Plains Public Library, White Plains, N.Y., part-time children's librarian. *Awards, honors:* Children's Book Award of the Child Study Association of America, 1969, for *The Empty Moat.*

WRITINGS: The Little Riders, Coward, 1963; *Mrs. Herring,* Lothrop, 1967; *The Empty Moat,* Coward, 1969.

WORK IN PROGRESS: A children's book.

SIDELIGHTS: "All my books take place in my native country, the Netherlands, and two of my books take place during World War II, one of the darkest periods in the history of my people.

"In American children's books, Holland is often pictured

as a quaint country, below sea level, where people wear wooden shoes and grow tulips. But Holland has much more to offer to American children than those stereotypes. The Americans and the Dutch have much in common. Both are freedom loving nations who have sacrificed much to obtain and preserve their freedom.

"It is out of this desire to break away from this stereotyped version of the Netherlands that I decided to write my books. I hope I have succeeded."

Ms. Shemin speaks and reads German, French and Dutch. She came to the United States right after she received her law degree and has never practiced as an attorney.

FOR MORE INFORMATION SEE: *Horn Book,* December, 1969.

SHEPHERD, Elizabeth

PERSONAL: Born in Boston, Mass.; daughter of Donald F. (a manufacturer) and Emma (a botanist; maiden name, Couch) Cameron; married Peter Shepherd (a literary agent), 1960; children: Ann, Adam. *Education:* Bryn Mawr College, B.A., 1948; also studied at University of Bordeaux and Harvard University. *Residence:* New York, N.Y.

CAREER: Dalton Schools, New York, N.Y., teacher of English, 1954-55; Oxford University Press, New York, N.Y., assistant trade editor, 1955-60; Dell Publishing Co., New York, N.Y., trade editor, 1960-63; Grolier Publications, New York, N.Y., science editor, 1963-66; writer for children. *Member:* Authors Guild.

WRITINGS—Juvenile: *Jellyfishes,* Lothrop, 1969; *In a Pygmy Camp,* Lothrop, 1969; *The Discoveries of Esteban the Black,* Dodd, 1970; *In Our Carib Indian Village,* Lothrop, 1971; *Tracks Between the Tides,* Lothrop, 1972. Contributor of articles on subjects concerned with children's welfare to magazines.

WORK IN PROGRESS: *Estuaries.*

SIDELIGHTS: "I read much anthropology and natural science. I try to write on subjects that expand my own knowledge about the way men live together and use their surroundings. An intense dislike of waste—whether human or material—motivates much of what I do. I seek to share with children certain life-affirming values."

HOBBIES AND OTHER INTERESTS: Hiking, sailing.

SHERMAN, Nancy
See ROSENBERG, Nancy Sherman

SHERROD, Jane
See SINGER, Jane Sherrod

SIMON, Seymour 1931-

PERSONAL: Born August 9, 1931, in New York, N.Y.; son of David and Clara (Liftin) Simon; married Joyce Shanock (a travel agent), December 25, 1953; children: Robert Paul, Michael Alan. *Education:* City College, New York, N.Y., B.A., 1953, graduate courses, 1955-60. *Home:* 4 Sheffield Rd., Great Neck, N.Y. 11020.

CAREER: New York (N.Y.) public schools, science teacher, 1955—, currently at Hawthorne Intermediate School, Long Island. *Military service:* U.S. Army, 1953-55. *Member:* United Federation of Teachers, National Science Teachers Association, Authors Guild of the Authors League of America. *Awards, honors:* The Paper Airplane Book was a Children's Book Showcase title, 1972.

WRITINGS—Youth books: *Animals in Field and Laboratory: Projects in Animal Behavior,* McGraw, 1968; *The Look-It-Up Book of the Earth,* Random House, 1968; *Motion,* Coward, 1968; *Discovering What Earthworms Do* (Child Study Association book list), McGraw, 1969; *Soap Bubbles,* Hawthorn, 1969; *Weather and Climate,* Random House, 1969; *Exploring With a Microscope,* Random House, 1969; *Weather and Climate,* Random House, 1969; *Let's Try It Out: Wet and Dry,* McGraw, 1969; *Discovering What Frogs Do,* McGraw, 1969; *Discovering What Goldfish Do,* McGraw, 1970; *A Handful of Soil,* Hawthorn, 1970; *Let's Try It Out: Light and Dark* (Child Study Association Book list), McGraw, 1970; *Science in a Vacant Lot* (Child Study Association book list), Viking,

SEYMOUR SIMON

A chorus of frogs will usually stop croaking when they see you moving toward them. ■ (From *Discovering What Frogs Do* by Seymour Simon. Illustrated by Jean Zallinger. Reprinted by permission of McGraw-Hill Book Co.)

1970; *Science at Work: Easy Models You Can Make,* Watts, 1971; *Chemistry in the Kitchen,* Viking, 1971; *Let's Try It Out: Finding Out Your Senses,* McGraw, 1971; *Discovering What Gerbils Do,* McGraw, 1971; *The Paper Airplane Book,* Viking, 1971; *Science at Work: Projects in Space Science,* Watts, 1971; *Science Projects in Ecology,* Holiday House, 1972; *Science Projects in Pollution,* Holiday House, 1972; *Let's Try It Out: Hot and Cold,* McGraw, 1972.

WORK IN PROGRESS: Other books in a series on the behavior of a single animal (the book on earthworms was the first in this series); science books using the process method for primary grades to be published by Holiday House; a series of project books to be published by Watts; a book on rock collecting to be published by Viking.

SIDELIGHTS: "Taking a walk and really looking, listening, and feeling the world around you can be a strange experience. You begin to observe things you never paid much attention to. You've seen clouds, trees, rocks, and machines thousands of times before, but now you begin to wonder about them. Does that dark cloud mean it's going to rain? Why do some leaves turn red while others turn yellow in the fall? What kind of rock has glittery little specks in it? How can a heavy thing like an airplane fly?

"It's questions like these that occur to me and that have been asked of me by children (both my own and in my science classes) that make me want to write science books. The books I write are full of such questions. Sometimes I'll provide an answer, but more often I'll suggest an activity or an experiment that will let a child answer a question by trying it out.

"To me, science is a way of finding out about the world. It's easy enough to read what an authority says about a particular subject, but it's so much more satisfying and rewarding to find out the answer to a question by working at it yourself. Many of the books I write are really in the nature of guidebooks to unknown territories. Each territory has to be discovered again by a child venturing into it for the first time.

"I like to try out the investigations and projects I write about. I've kept fishes, earthworms, gerbils, ants, crickets, and a host of other animals in my home. I've collected rocks, dug under rotting logs, tramped through swamps, made dozens of scientific models, experimented with chemicals, used microscopes to observe the world in a drop of water and telescopes to observe distant galaxies of other worlds.

"Finally, what I really enjoy is getting a letter from a child (or an adult sometimes) who tried out an experiment from one of my books and is writing to tell me about his discovery. When I can share his experience, it's as much fun as the first time I found something out for myself."

HOBBIES AND OTHER INTERESTS: Reading history and poetry, collecting books, breeding tropical fish, playing chess and tennis, traveling.

SINGER, Jane Sherrod 1917-(Jane Sherrod)

PERSONAL: Born May 26, 1917, in Wichita Falls, Tex.; daughter of St. Clair and Nina (Bean) Sherrod; married Kurt D. Singer (author, lecturer, and director of B.P. Singer Features), January 21, 1955. *Education:* Fullerton Junior College, A.A., 1936; University of California, Los Angeles, B.E., 1938; University of California, Berkeley, M.A., 1954. *Home:* 8357 Carnation Dr., Buena Park, Calif. 90620. *Office:* B.P. Singer Features, 3164 West Tyler Ave., Anaheim, Calif. 92801.

CAREER: University of California, Berkeley, master teacher in elementary education, 1940-45; supervisor of elementary education in Piedmont, Calif., 1942-45; instructor in elementary education at San Francisco State College, San Francisco, Calif. 1946-49, and Whittier College, Whittier, Calif., 1951; B.P. Singer Features, Anaheim, Calif., managing editor, 1955—. John C. Winston Co., Pasadena, Calif., educational consultant, 1946-54.

WRITINGS—With husband, Kurt Singer; juveniles, except as indicated: *Spies for Democracy,* Denison, 1960; *Great Adventures in Crime,* Denison, 1962; *Great Adventures of the Sea,* Denison, 1962; *Ernest Hemingway, Man of Courage,* Denison, 1963; *Albert Schweitzer, Medical Missionary,* Denison, 1963; *Lyndon Baines Johnson, Man*

JANE SHERROD SINGER

SLICER, Margaret O. 1920-

PERSONAL: Born January 5, 1920, in Baltimore, Md.; daughter of Gustav H. (a forester for U.S. Government) and Margaret (Kummer) Lentz; married J. Samuel Slicer (a fire protection engineer), September 23, 1941; children: James Sargent. *Education:* Student at Milligan College, 1936-37, Agnes Scott College, 1937-39, and Washington School for Secretaries, Washington, D.C., 1939-40. *Politics:* Republican. *Religion:* Episcopalian. *Home:* 542 High Rock St., Needham, Mass. 02192.

CAREER: U.S. Department of Justice, Washington, D.C., secretary, 1940-41; nursery school teacher in a private school, Needham, Mass., 1954-55; Welcome Wagon hostess, Needham, Mass., 1966-68. Free-lance writer. Secretary of Needham Republican Town Committee, 1952-56. *Member:* Needham Historical Society (publicity chairman).

WRITINGS—Juvenile: *The Balloon Farm,* Abingdon, 1968. Stories included in: *Jack and Jill Book,* Winston, 1948; *This Is Our Parish,* Ginn, 1962; *Friends Old and New,* two editions, Scott, 1963, 1965; *Reading for Little Ones,* Book 2 and Book 12, Research Council of Cleveland, 1967. Stories have been published in most children's magazines, including *Humpty Dumpty, Instructor, Child Life,* and *Children's Friend,* and in Sunday school maga-

of Reason, Denison, 1964; *Weird Tales of the Supernatural* (adult book), W.H. Allen, 1967; *Folktales from Mexico,* Denison, 1969.

Other books: (With Zel Thayer) *Folktales from the South Pacific,* Denison, 1966; (editor) *Cooking with the Stars* (adult book), A.S. Barnes, 1969; *What You Should Know About Yourself* (adult book), Meredith, 1969, Volume II, Peacock Press, 1972. Writer of column, "Pathways to Success," syndicated to about fifty newspapers.

WORK IN PROGRESS: Zany Grey Western Cookbook; Mini-Mysteries.

SIDELIGHTS: "The books I have written were done because I like young people and feel a need to talk with them via the printed word. I enjoy curiosity, and who is more investigative than youngsters? Too, because of my international experience, I wish to share some of my knowledge. My husband is a great help and we put our heads together and share ideas. It could all be summed up that the books we have written were with the idea to stimulate and educate."

The Singers have traveled worldwide, "latitudinally and longitudinally from Micronesia to Africa, from Australia to Greenland."

MARGARET O. SLICER

zines and children's pages of newspapers; poems, stories, and articles for adults have appeared in *Woman's Day, Boston Globe, Canadian Home Journal, Marriage, Wormwood Review, Catholic Home Journal, Presbyterian Life,* and about twenty other periodicals and newspapers; also has compiled literary quizzes for *Saturday Review,* and done Sunday school materials for David C. Cook Publishing Co. Editor of "The Visitor" (local church publication).

WORK IN PROGRESS: Several children's books: one laid in Austria, one entitled *The Hole in the Roof,* a book of children's poems about Cape Cod, and a compilation of short stories.

SIDELIGHTS: "My early writing was the outgrowth of sheer boredom, brought on by a traveling husband and a small boy eager for stories. The writing I do now is aimed at the four-to-eight age group and this is the age for whom I have always written, except when I did an adult item or two. They are imaginative and love humor, yet are willing to take a well-disguised moral without being upset by it. I always hope I teach a little as I entertain.

"I now have two grandsons, one of whom is already an avid listener, and I suspect he will turn into a first class audience before long. I have always used things that happened to me, to my child, to the children of others, and a great deal of themes from nature as bases for my stories. The years we have spent on Cape Cod have resulted in dozens of stories of all sorts." Ms. Slicer's great-uncle, Frederic Arnold Kummer, also wrote children's books.

HOBBIES AND OTHER INTERESTS: Reading, crafts (knitting, crewel embroidery, painting), gardening, and antiques.

SMITH, Dodie
(C. L. Anthony, Charles Henry Percy)

PERSONAL: Formal name, Dorothy Gladys; born in Whitefield, Lancashire, England; daughter of Ernest Walter and Ella (Furber) Smith; married Alec Macbeth Beesley, 1939. *Education:* Attended Manchester School and St. Paul's Girls' School, London; studied for the stage at Royal Academy of Dramatic Art, London. *Home:* The Barretts, Finchingfield, Essex, England.

CAREER: Wrote a screenplay, "Schoolgirl Rebels," under the pseudonym Charles Henry Percy while a student at Royal Academy of Dramatic Art; actress, 1915-22, appearing first at Tottenham Palace in "Playgoers," then mainly touring and playing with repertory companies; left the stage to become a buyer at Heal & Son, London; gave up business after the success of her first professionally produced play, "Autumn Crocus," 1931; playwright using the pseudonym C.L. Anthony up to 1935; since then has been writing under her own name.

WRITINGS—Plays under pseudonym C.L. Anthony: *British Talent,* first produced in London at the Three Arts Club, 1924; *Autumn Crocus* (three-act comedy; first produced in London at Lyric Theatre, April, 1931; first produced on Broadway at Morosco Theatre, 1932), Gollancz and Samuel French, 1931; *Service* (three-act comedy; first produced in London at Wyndham's Theatre, 1932), Gollancz, 1932, Samuel French, 1937; *Touch Wood* (three-act comedy; first produced in London at Theatre Royal, Haymarket, 1934), Gollancz and Samuel French, 1934.

Plays under name Dodie Smith: *Call It a Day* (three-act comedy; first produced in London at Globe Theatre, 1935; first produced on Broadway at Morosco Theatre, 1936), Gollancz and Samuel French, 1936; *Bonnet Over the Windmill* (three-act comedy; first produced in London at New Theatre, 1937), Heinemann, 1937; *Dear Octopus* (three-act comedy; first produced in London at Queen's Theatre, 1938; revived in London at Theatre Royal, Haymarket, 1967; first produced on Broadway at Broadhurst Theatre, 1939), Heinemann, 1938, Samuel French, 1939; *Three Plays: Autumn Crocus, Service, Touch Wood,* Heinemann, 1939; *Lovers and Friends* (three-act comedy; first produced on Broadway at Plymouth Theatre, 1943), Samuel French, 1944; *Letter from Paris* (three-act comedy adapted from Henry James's novel, *The Reverberator;* first produced in London at Aldwych Theatre, 1952), Heinemann, 1954; *I Capture the Castle* (two-act romantic comedy adapted by the author from her novel of the same title; first produced in London at Aldwych Theatre, 1953), Samuel French, 1953, Heinemann, 1954; *These People: Those Books* (three-act comedy first produced in Leeds at Grand Theatre, 1958);

DODIE SMITH

[The Badduns had] their eyes fixed on the screen. Behind them were ranged row after row of puppies, small pups at the front, large pups at the back. Those who did not care for television were asleep round the kitchen fire... A figure [entered] in a long white cloak. It was Cruella de Vil.
■ From the movie "One Hundred and One Dalmatians," © MCMLXI by Walt Disney Productions.

Amateur Means Lover (three-act comedy first produced in Liverpool at the Liverpool Playhouse, 1961), Samuel French, 1962.

Novels under name Dodie Smith: *I Capture the Castle* (Literary Guild selection), Atlantic-Little, Brown, 1948, reissued, 1962, (Book Society choice), Heinemann, 1949; *The New Moon with the Old,* Atlantic-Little, Brown, 1963, Heinemann, 1963; *The Town in Bloom,* Atlantic-Little, Brown, 1965, Heinemann, 1965; *It Ends with Revelations,* Atlantic-Little, Brown, 1967, Heinemann, 1967; *A Tale of Two Families,* Walker & Co., 1970, Heinemann, 1970.

Juvenile books under name Dodie Smith: *The Hundred and One Dalmatians,* Heinemann, 1956, Viking, 1957; *The Starlight Barking,* Heinemann, 1967, Simon & Schuster, 1968.

SIDELIGHTS: The Hundred and One Dalmatians was filmed as Walt Disney's "101 Dalmatians," and both that book and its sequel, *The Starlight Barking,* have also been issued in paperback editions in England and America—and altogether have been published in twelve countries. *Service* was filmed by MGM in 1944 as "Looking Forward," *Autumn Crocus* was filmed in England, 1934, *Call It a Day* was made into a movie by Warner Brothers, 1937, and *Dear Octopus* was filmed in England, 1945. Although Miss Smith's first novel, *I Capture the Castle,* was written for adults, she says that it has "largely been taken over by teenagers." She and her husband spent fifteen years in America, 1939 to 1953, but returned to England to live in a three-hundred-year-old country house where their current menage consists of two dalmatians, two donkeys, fantail pigeons, and a colony of wild ducks on the pond.

SMITH, Lafayette
See HIGDON, Hal

SNYDER, Anne   1922-

PERSONAL: Born October 3, 1922, in Boston, Mass.; daughter of Nathan (a manufacturer of key blanks) and Marsha (Borochowitz) Reisner; married Louis Snyder (a plant manager), June 15, 1941; children: Sherri Snyder Stevens, Mari-Beth Snyder Goldy, Nathalie. *Education:* Has taken courses at El Camino College, Valley College,

University of California, Los Angeles, University of Portland, and Maren Elwood College of Writing, Los Angeles. *Home:* 13937 Wyandotte St., Van Nuys, Calif. 91405. *Agent:* Michael Hamilburg, 1104 South Robertson Blvd., Los Angeles, Calif. 90035.

CAREER: Television writer: "C.B.S. Repertoire Theatre," "I Love Lucy Show," "Hollywood Squares" (staff writer), also wrote for several months for a national daytime TV series. Teacher of creative writing for Gifted Children's Association of San Fernando Valley, 1970, 1971. *Member:* Authors Guild, Writers Guild of America, West. *Awards, honors:* Child Study Association selected *50,000 Names for Jeff* as one of the ten best children's books of 1969.

WRITINGS: 50,000 Names for Jeff, Holt, 1969.

WORK IN PROGRESS: Editor with Helen Landgarten of *Art and Writing of Gifted Children;* a novel for young adults, *House with the Attic Bedroom:* two children's game shows for television; with Louis Pelletier, screenplays titled "The Scheme" and "Child's Play," and a pilot television program, "Nobody's Family."

SIDELIGHTS: "I was motivated to write *50,000 Names for Jeff* because each of us has a responsibility to help create better understanding between the races. My purpose was to reach the kids—white and black—*before* they became infected with prejudice."

Slowly, carefully, his hand guiding hers, they wrote: Mrs. J. Toller. ■ (From *50,000 Names for Jeff* by Anne Snyder. Illustrated by Leo Carty.)

ANNE SNYDER

SONNEBORN, Ruth (Cantor) A. 1899-

PERSONAL: Born October 14, 1899, in New York, N.Y.; daughter of Jacob A. and Lydia (Greenebaum) Cantor; married Lawrence H. Sonneborn, March 1, 1929; children, John Andrew, Eve Sonneborn Kiraly. *Education:* Ethical Culture Normal School, Teacher's Certificate, 1920. *Politics:* Democrat. *Home:* 45 Barrow St., New York, N.Y. 10014. *Office:* Bank Street College of Education, 610 West 112th St., New York, N.Y. 10025.

CAREER: Bank Street College of Education, New York, N.Y., member of publications staff and director of bookstore, 1944—, now special consultant.

WRITINGS: (Contributor) *Know Your Children in School,* Macmillan, 1954; (contributor) *Believe and Make Believe,* Dutton, 1956; *Question and Answer Book of Everyday Science,* Random House, 1961; *Question and Answer Book of Space,* Random House, 1965; *The Lollipop Party* (illustrated by Brinton Turkle), Viking, 1967; *Seven in a Bed* (illustrated by Don Freeman), Viking, 1968; *Friday Night is Papa Night* (illustrated by Emily McCully; Junior Literary Guild selection), Viking, 1970; *I Love Gram,* Viking, 1971. Editor of book page, *Journal of Nursery Education.*

SIDELIGHTS: "I have always been interested in writing.

"Never mind the talk," Mama said. "We have work to do. Everyone gets a job."
■ (From *Friday Night Is Papa Night* by Ruth A. Sonneborn. Illustrated by Emily A. McCully.)

RUTH SONNEBORN

When I joined Bank Street, Lucy Sprague Mitchell, the pioneer children's author in the 'Here and Now' was conducting a writer's workshop for people interested in writing for children. From Writer's Lab such famous people as Margaret Wise Brown, Ruth Krauss, Irma Simonton Black emerged. I learned a lot from Ms. Mitchell and the writers she collected.

"I ran the Bank Street bookstore. In a way this was a unique store. We made careful selections and carried no so-called junk. Because of this we were patronized by nursery school people, child care centers, etc. They talked to me and told me what they wanted and couldn't find. This is what led me to write for Puerto Rican children.

"I may add that my books have universal themes which apply to all children. It is only the illustrations and superficial trimmings—dress, food, etc. that give them a national character."

FOR MORE INFORMAITION SEE: Lee Bennett Hopkins. *Books Are by People,* Citation Press, 1969.

SOSKIN, V. H.
See ELLISON, Virginia Howell

SPIER, Peter (Edward) 1927-

PERSONAL: Born June 6, 1927, in Amsterdam, the Netherlands; son of Joseph E.A. (a journalist, illustrator) and Albertine (van Raalte) Spier; married Kathryn M. Pallister, July 12, 1958; children: Thomas Pallister, Kathryn Elizabeth. *Education:* Ryksacademie voor beeldende kunsten, student, 1945-47; attended Willems Park School, Amsterdams Lyceum. *Religion:* Reformed Church of America. *Home:* 5 Hillside Ave., Port Washington, Long Island, N.Y.

CAREER: Illustrator of about fifty other books besides his own. *Military service:* Royal Netherlands Navy, 1947-51; became lieutenant. *Member:* Netherlands Club (New York). *Awards, honors:* Christopher Award, 1971, for *The Erie Canal;* New York Academy of Science children's science book award, 1972, for *Gobble, Growl, Grunt; Gobble, Growl, Grunt* was selected as one of *New York Times* outstanding books of the year.

WRITINGS: The Fox Went out on a Chilly Night (ALA Notable Book), Doubleday, 1961; *Of Dikes and Windmills,* Doubleday, 1970; *The Erie Canal* (Junior Literary Guild selection), Doubleday, 1970; *Gobble, Growl, Grunt* (Junior Literary Guild selection), Doubleday, 1971; *Crash! Bang! Boom!,* Doubleday, 1972; *Fast-Slow, High-Low: A Book of Opposites* (Junior Literary Guild selection), Doubleday, 1972. Contributor to *Reader's Digest* and to Time/Life Books.

"Mother Goose Library" series: *London Bridge is Falling Down!,* Doubleday, 1967; *To Market! To Market!,* Doubleday, 1967; *Hurrah, We're Outward Bound!,* Doubleday, 1968; *And So My Garden Grows,* Doubleday, 1969.

Illustrator: Margaret G. Otto, *Cocoa,* Holt, 1953; Phyllis Krasilovsky, *The Cow Who Fell in the Canal,* Doubleday, 1957; Mary Mapes Dodge, *Hans Brinker or the Silver Skates,* Scribner, 1958; Ardo Flakkeberg, *The Sea Broke Through,* Knopf, 1960; *One Hundred More Story Poems,* edited by Elinor Parker, Crowell, 1960; Margaretha Shemin, *Little Riders,* Coward, 1963; *Here and There: One Hundred Poems about Places,* edited by Elinor Parker, Crowell, 1967; Frieda K. Brown, *Last Hurdle,* Apollo, 1970. Also illustrated *Ford Almanac* for the Ford Motor Co., 1956-72; and approximatey 60 other titles.

SIDELIGHTS: "I was born in Amsterdam but grew up in Broek-in-Waterland, a small romantic village which Americans know as the birthplace of Hans Brinker.

"My brother and sister and I went to school in Amsterdam. A trip in an ancient swaying train filled with the smoke of cigars and clay pipes, Volendam fishermen wearing huge wooden shoes and baggy pants, and the unforgettable aroma of herring and smoked eel, stacked in baskets in the aisles as it was taken to market. After the train a short boatride, some walking, and the city tram. It was a varied and wonderful trip, offering us a multitude of plausible and implausible excuses for being late. All this to the intense envy of our friends.

PETER SPIER

"Weekends and vacations were spent sailing the old Zuyderzee, great sections of which have now been reclaimed, and it is a strange and nostalgic sensation to drive past freshly ploughed fields on the old seabottom, when you sailed only eighteen years ago where the swallows fly now.

"I cannot remember a time when I did not dabble with clay, draw, or watch someone draw, for my father, the illustrator and journalist, Jo Spier, worked at home. So I grew up with it all. But it was not until I was eighteen that I decided to make it my career, and went to the Rijksacademie (an art school) in Amsterdam. Following that I was drafted and became an officer in the Royal Netherlands Navy, serving part of that time in the West Indies and South America.

"Once that was out of the way I went to work for *Elseviers Weekly,* the largest Dutch weekly newspaper, and was stationed in Paris for the first year. In 1952 I

They never ate such a dinner in their life. ■ (From *The Fox Went Out on a Chilly Night* by Peter Spier. Illustrated by the author.)

came to the United States where Elsevier Publishing then had a branch in Houston, Texas.

"Soon I moved to the New York area and have lived there ever since. It was then that I began illustrating magazines and children's books—almost a hundred of them. Later I began doing my own books.

"There is very little I can say about 'how I draw' beyond the mystery of putting a nice, white piece of paper on my table, picking up a pen (Gillot 192), dipping it in India ink and making a start. And the last, alas, I often find the most difficult. But before I get to that point a great deal of work has already been done.

"Since most of my picture books have some sort of historical setting—as in the case of *London Bridge is Falling Down*—or a very defined local setting like New England in *The Fox Went Out on a Chilly Night*. I first find out as much as possible about subject or region. Then I go there, sketchbook in hand, to collect the myriad details that go into the making of these books. The result of these trips is a stack of hundreds of sketches with notes on the color. It is then that the actual work of combining those sketches and details begins. Since I like to retain the effect of a colored pen drawing, I first make the black key and then use only blue, red, and yellow watercolors on non-photo blues of the black key. In this way there is no black halftone in the books at all, which I believe helps the impression of crispness.

"I am often asked whether I think of my own children, or of the reactions of children in general, while working on a book. I hope that I am not offending anyone by admitting that I do it initially for only one person in the world—myself. The worry about what others will think comes soon enough after the work is done."

HOBBIES AND OTHER INTERESTS: "I am one of those few fortunate people who earn their living with their hobby. My pleasure away from the drawing table is sailing and, in winter when it's raining, the building of models of old ships."

FOR MORE INFORMATION SEE: Lee Bennett Hopkins, *Books Are By People*. Citation, 1969; *New York Times Book Review*, January 23, 1972; *Junior Literary Guild Catalogue*, March, 1972, September, 1972; *Horn Book*, October, 1970; *Third Book of Junior Authors*, edited by de Montreville and Hill, Wilson, 1972.

When you dug by one of the holes, soon you'd see either the clam shell or a funny, long-necked, leathery thing that was the gooeyduck's neck. ■ (From *Polliwog* by Arthur D. Stapp. Illustrated by Charles Geer.)

STAPP, Arthur D(onald)   1906-1972

PERSONAL: Born December 26, 1906, in Seattle, Wash.; son of Orrill V. (a piano teacher) and Frances (Bailey) Stapp; married Eleanor Blakkestad (a children's librarian), August 6, 1949; children: Marilyn. *Education:* Attended New York University, 1945-46, Rand School, 1947-48. *Home and office:* 171 South Buckhout St., Irvington, N.Y.

CAREER, North Central Outlook, Seattle, Wash., co-publisher, 1923-41; writer of juvenile books, 1946-72. *Military service:* U.S. Army Air Forces, 1942-45, became sergeant. *Member:* Authors Guild, Washington Alpine Club.

WRITINGS: Mountain Tamer, Morrow, 1948; *Escape on Skis,* Morrow, 1949; *Captive of the Mountains,* Morrow, 1951; *Five Who Disappeared,* Sterling, 1958; *Polliwog,* Harper, 1962; *Too Steep for Baseball.* Harper, 1964; *The Fabulous Earthworm Deal,* Viking, 1969; *Ordeal by Mountains,* Viking, 1970.

SIDELIGHTS: "My interest in writing grew out of weekly newspaper reporting, column writing and editing. But why write at all? A Persian poet wrote, 'If you and I could but conspire to change this sorry scheme of things entire. . . .' I think that wish is at the base of good writing. It led me to sell my interest in the paper and took me to New York, where my literature of protest metamorphosed into a teenage novel with a mountain climbing background.

"Can you change the world with juvenile books as a fulcrum? Perhaps as much that way as any. It has been said that a good book is like an iceberg: what you see is only one-eighth of the whole. If the seven-eighths that is felt rather than seen enriches the philosophy of an occasional reader, progress has been made. As a pivotal example, what is the feeling about success I would like to see young readers elect? That its measure can be found in one question, self-asked: Is the world better off because of me? Or worse?"

FOR MORE INFORMATION SEE: More Junior Authors, edited by Muriel Fuller, Wilson, 1963.

(Died January 10, 1972)

STEINBERG, Fred J.   1933-

PERSONAL: Born August 9, 1933, in New York, N.Y.; son of Philip (a dentist) and Freda (Korins) Steinberg; married Elizabeth Cohen (a teacher), June 11, 1961; children: Stacy, Suzan. *Education:* Cornell University, B.S., 1955; Columbia University, M.S., 1956. *Home:* 198 Glen Ave., Glen Rock, N.J. 07452. *Office:* IBM, Parson's Pond Dr., Franklin Lakes, N.J. 07417.

CAREER: Editorial work for Prentice-Hall Inc., Englewood Cliffs, N.J., 1957-58, and McGraw-Hill Book Co., New York, N.Y., 1958-59; International Business Machines Corp., writer in New York, N.Y., 1959-68, information manager in Franklin Lakes, N.J., 1968—. Instructor in economics at New York Institute of Technology, 1964-66, and at Adelphi University, 1966-68.

WRITINGS: Computers (juvenile), Watts, 1969. Contributor to magazines.

SIDELIGHTS: Steinberg dictated his book and does all of his other "writing" via dictation equipment.

FRED J. STEINBERG

SUBA, Susanne

PERSONAL: Born in Budapest, Hungary; daughter of Miklos (a painter and architect) and May Suba. *Education:* Graduate of Pratt Institute. *Home:* 1019 Third Ave., New York, N.Y. 10021.

WRITINGS—Self-illustrated: *The Man with the Bushy Beard and Other Tales* (juvenile), Viking, 1969; *The Monkeys and the Pedlar,* Viking, 1970.

Illustrator: Gladys Malvern, *Dancing Star,* Messner, 1942; Carl A. Withers, *A Rocket in My Pocket,* Holt, 1948; Mary Mian, *The Merry Miracle,* 1949; John Mason Brown, *Morning Faces,* McGraw, 1949; Helen McLean, *There's No Place Like Paris,* Doubleday, 1951; Gerald Heard, *Gabriel and the Creatures,* Harper, 1952; Virginia Haviland, *Favorite Fairy Tales Told in Germany,* Little, Brown, 1959; Peggy Mann, *That New Baby,* Coward, 1967; Robert Burch, *The Hunting Trip,* Scribner, 1971.

FOR MORE INFORMATION SEE: Diana Klemin, *The Art of Art for Children's Books,* Clarkson Potter, 1966; *Library Journal,* July, 1969; Diana Klemin, *The Illustrated Book,* Clarkson Potter, 1970; *Horn Book,* December, 1970.

SULLIVAN, George E(dward) 1927-

PERSONAL: Born August 11, 1927, in Lowell, Mass.; son of Timothy J. (a salesman) and Cecilia (Shea) Sullivan; married Muriel Moran, May 24, 1952; children: Timothy. *Education:* Fordham University, B.S., 1952. *Home:* 330 East 33rd St., New York, N.Y. 10016. *Agent:* Lurton Blassingame, 10 East 43rd St., New York, N.Y. 10017.

CAREER: American Machine and Foundry Co., Inc., New York, N.Y., public relations manager, 1955-62; free-lance writer, 1962—. *Military service:* U.S. Navy,

He began to think of all he had eaten. ■ (From *The Man with the Bushy Beard* by Susanne Suba. Illustrated by the author.)

1945-48. *Member:* Authors Guild of Authors League of America.

WRITINGS: (With Frank Clause) *How to Win at Bowling*, Fleet, 1961; (with Dick Weber) *The Champions Guide to Bowling*, Fleet, 1963; (with Frank Clause and Patty McBride) *Junior Guide to Bowling*, Fleet, 1963; *The Story of the Peace Corps*, Fleet, 1964; (with Irving Crane) *The Young Sportsman's Guide to Pocket Billiards*, Nelson, 1964; *The Story of Cassius Clay*, Fleet, 1964; *Harness Racing*, Fleet, 1964; (with Luther Lassiter) *The Modern Guide to Pocket Billiards*, Fleet, 1964; *The Champions Guide to Golf*, Fleet, 1965; *Better Ice Hockey for Boys*, Dodd, 1965; (with Finn Larsen) *Skiing for Boys and Girls*, Follett, 1965; *How Do They Make It?*, Westminster, 1965; (with Larry Scott) *Teenage Guide to Skin and Scuba Diving*, Fell, 1965; *The Modern Guide to Softball*, Fleet, 1965; *Seven Wonders of the Modern World*, Putnam, 1966; *Pro Football's Unforgettable Games*, Putnam, 1966; *Complete Book of Family Skiing*, Coward, 1967; *Better Track and Field Events for Boys*, Dodd, 1967; *How Do They Grow It?*, Westminster, 1967; *The Boom in Going Bust*, Macmillan, 1968; *Better Swimming and Diving for Boys and Girls*, Dodd, 1968; *Pro Football's All-Time Greats*, Putnam, 1968; *They Flew Alone*, Warne, 1968; *More How Do They Make It?*, Westminster, 1968; *Better Horseback Riding for Boys and Girls*, Dodd, 1969; *The Dollar Squeeze and How to Beat It*, Macmillan, 1969; (with Earl Morrall) *In the Pocket*, Grossett, 1969.

How Do They Run It?, Westminster, 1970; *The New World of Robots*, Dodd, 1970; *Understanding Architec-

GEORGE SULLIVAN

Phlebitis, a disease that causes inflammation of the veins, had affected his legs, causing him agonizing pain. ■ (From *Knute Rockne* by George Sullivan. Illustrated by Dom Lupo.)

ture, Warne, 1970; *This is Pro Football*, Dodd, 1970; *Tom Seaver of the Mets*, Putnam, 1971; (with Edward Zegarowicz) *Inflation-Proof Your Future*, Walker, 1971; *The Complete Book of Autograph Collecting*, Dodd, 1971; *The Gamemakers*, Putnam, 1971; *Pro Football: Passing and Passers*, Dodd, 1972; *How Do They Build It?*, Westminster, 1972; *Understanding Photography*, Warne, 1972; *By Chance a Winner: The History of Lotteries* (Junior Literary Guild selection), Dodd, 1972.

SIDELIGHTS: Because many of Sullivan's books concern sports, professional football in particular, he spends most of his fall and winter weekends taking football action photos both at practice sessions and at games. "In the summer I do the same with baseball, but it's mostly to keep me proficient with my cameras until fall and football arrive."

FOR MORE INFORMATION SEE: *New York Times Book Review*, November 23, 1971; *Junior Literary Guild Catalogue*, March, 1972.

THOMAS, John Gale
See ROBINSON, Joan G.

THOMPSON, George Selden 1929-
(George Selden)

PERSONAL: Born May 14, 1929, in Hartford, Conn.; son of Hartwell Green (a doctor) and Sigrid (Johnson) Thompson. *Education:* Loomis School, student, 1943-47; Yale University, B.A., 1951. *Politics:* Independent. *Religion:* Independent. *Agent:* James Oliver Brown, 22 East 60th St., New York, N.Y.

CAREER: Free-lance writer. *Awards, honors:* Fulbright scholarship to Italy, 1951-52; Newbery Honor Book award, 1961, for *The Cricket in Times Square;* Christopher Award, 1969, for *Tucker's Countryside.*

WRITINGS—All under name George Selden: *The Dog that Could Swim Under Water*, Viking, 1956; *The Garden Under the Sea*, Viking, 1957; (contributor) *Best TV Plays of 1957*, Ballantine, 1958; *The Cricket in Times Square* (ALA Notable Book), Farrar, Straus, 1960, Dell Yearling, 1970; *I See What I See!*, Farrar, Straus, 1962; *The*

GEORGE SELDEN THOMPSON

"When I'm calling youuuuuuuu
Oooo-oooo-oooo
Oooo-oooo-oooo—" ■ (From *The Cricket in Times Square* by George Selden. Illustrated by Garth Williams.)

Mice and the Monks and the Christmas Tree, Macmillan, 1963; *Heinrich Schliemann, Discoverer of Buried Treasure,* Macmillan, 1964; *Sir Arthur Evans: Discoverer of Knossos,* Macmillan, 1964; *Sparrow Socks,* Harper, 1965; *Oscar Lobster's Fair Exchange,* Harper, 1966; *Dunkard,* Harper, 1968; *Tucker's Countryside* (sequel to *Cricket in Times Square*), Farrar, Straus, 1969. Television play, "The Genie of Sutton Place," for Westinghouse "Studio One." Film script of "The Genie of Sutton Place," Spoleto Productions.

WORK IN PROGRESS: A novel and some children's books.

HOBBIES AND OTHER INTERESTS: Archaeology and music.

FOR MORE INFORMATION SEE: Horn Book, August, 1969.

TOOZE, Ruth (Anderson) 1892-1972

PERSONAL, Born June 29, 1892, in Chicago, Ill.; daughter of Ernest Victor (a business executive) and Amanda (Seidel) Anderson; married William C. Tooze (U.S. Navy captain), September 2, 1920 (deceased); children, Nancy (Mrs. Richard Howard Hansen). *Education:* Oberlin College, A.B., 1914; Columbia University, special graduate certificate, 1917; Stanford University, graduate student, 1928-30. *Religion:* Presbyterian. *Home:* 946-A Avenida Carmel, Laguna Hills, Calif. 92653.

CAREER: Young Women's Christian Association, executive secretary in New York and California, 1917-22; Peninsula School, Palo Alto, Calif., faculty member, 1927-36; Book Box (bookstore), Evanston, Ill., owner and operator, 1936-48; Children's Book Caravan, operator, 1948-58; U.S. State Department, International Cooperation Administration, education adviser in Phnom Penh, Cambodia, 1958-60; Children's Book Caravan, operator, 1960-1972. Lecturer and visiting summer instructor at University of Maine, Indiana University, University of North Carolina, Temple University, Bowling Green State University, other universities, 1938-1972. *Member:* International Reading Association, National Council of Teachers of English, Children's Reading Round Table, Association for Childhood Education, Association for Supervision and Curriculum Development, Phi Beta Kappa, Delta Kappa Gamma (honorary member).

WRITINGS: Tim and the Brass Buttons, Messner, 1953, revised edition published as *Policeman Mike's Brass Buttons,* Melmont, 1964; *Wires Up!,* Messner, 1955, revised edition published as *Telephone Wires Up!,* Melmont, 1964; (with B.R. Krone) *Literature and Music as Resources for Social Studies,* Prentice-Hall, 1955; *America,* Viking, 1956; *Your Children Want to Read,* Prentice-Hall, 1957; *Story Telling,* Prentice-Hall, 1959; *Silver from the Sea,* Viking, 1962; *Cambodia: Land of Contrasts,* Viking, 1962; *Our Rice Village in Cambodia,* Viking, 1963; *Nikkos and the Pink Pelican,* Viking, 1964; *Three Tales of Monkey,* John Day, 1967; *Three Tales of Turtle,* John Day, 1968; *Dragon Tree,* John Day, 1969; *Wonderful Wooden Peacock Flying Machine, and Other Tales of Ceylon,* John Day, 1969. Contributor to education journals.

SIDELIGHTS: Ms. Tooze's Children's Book Caravan, carrying about eight hundred books, toured thirty states, stopping for two or three days at a time at schools and colleges where Ms. Tooze talked about reading, told stories to youngsters and let them see and read the books. She started collecting folk tales from other lands because she believed that better world understanding could best begin with children. In 1963 she conducted a group of a dozen or so persons on an "adventure in world understanding tour" of the Far East. She stayed on to collect folk tales, with Colombo, Ceylon, as her headquarters for some months.

"I live here in beautiful Laguna Hills (a leisure world community) full of fascinating professional people who have travelled widely and done exciting things. I lead our Foreign Policy study group of the American Association of University Women; am active in People to People, the Foreign Policy Great Decisions study group; speak at nearby colleges and universities on folklore of the Far East and storytelling—so my life is rich and full. I have a wide-open guest room door!"

Ms. Tooze taped four cassettes, three on storytelling, one

He grabbed it up quickly, but he was so out of breath he could not start back. ■ (From *Silver from the Sea* by Ruth Tooze. Illustrated by Kurt Wiese.)

Awards, honors: Runner-up for the Carnegie Medal, 1963, for *Hell's Edge,* 1969, for *The Intruder;* International P.E.N. Silver Pen Award, *Boston Globe*-Horn Book Award, "Edgar" award from Mystery Writers of America, all for *The Intruder,* 1970; delivered May Hill Arbuthnot Honor Lecture, Atlanta, Ga., 1971.

WRITINGS—Juvenile, except as noted: *Gumble's Yard,* Hutchinson, 1961, published in America as *Trouble in the Jungle* (*Horn Book* Honor List; ALA Notable Book), Lippincott, 1969; *Hell's Edge,* Hutchinson, 1963, Lothrop, 1969; *Widdershins Crescent,* Hutchinson, 1965, published in America as *Good-Bye to the Jungle* (ALA Notable Book), Lippincott, 1967; *Written for Children: An Outline of English Children's Literature* (adult), J. Garnet Miller, 1965, Lothrop, 1967; *The Hallersage Sound,* Hutchinson, 1966; *Pirate's Island* (ALA Notable Book), Lippincott, 1968; *The Intruder* (ALA Notable Book; *Horn Book* Honor List), Oxford University Press, 1969, Lippincott, 1970; *Good-Night, Prof, Love,* Oxford University Press, 1970, published in America as *Good Night, Prof, Dear* (ALA Best Young Adult Book), Lippincott, 1971; *A Sense of Story: Essays on Contemporary Writers for Children* (adult; *Horn Book* Honor List), Lippincott, 1971; (editor) *Modern Poetry: A Selection for Young People* (adult), Oxford University Press, 1971, Lippincott, in press; *The Summer People,* Lippincott, 1972. Contribu-

JOHN ROWE TOWNSEND

on poetry for children—for the Listening Corporation of Los Angeles.

HOBBIES AND OTHER INTERESTS: Music, writing poetry, rock-collecting, cooking.

(Died June 15, 1972)

TOWNSEND, John Rowe 1922-

PERSONAL: Born May 10, 1922, in Leeds, England; son of George Edmund Rowe and Gladys (Page) Townsend; married Vera Lancaster, July 3, 1948; children: Alethea Mary, Nicholas John, Penelope Anne. *Education:* Attended Leeds Grammar School, 1933-40; Emmanuel College, Cambridge, B.A., 1949, M.A., 1954. *Home:* Little Orchard, Hayton St., Knutsford, Cheshire, England.

CAREER: *Manchester Guardian* (now *Guardian*), Manchester, England, sub-editor, 1949-54, art editor, 1954-55, editor of the weekly international edition, 1955-69, children's books editor (part-time) 1968—; professional writer since 1969. Member of Harvard International Seminar, 1956; visiting lecturer, University of Pennsylvania, 1965, University of Washington, 1969, 1971: *Military service:* Royal Air Force, 1942-46; became flight sergeant.

tor to (London) *Times Literary Supplement, New York Times Book Review,* and many other publications.

SIDELIGHTS: "Five years ago I was talking to a very bright young man who'd just come back from postgraduate work at Yale, after previously taking a double first at Cambridge. Somebody came up and mentioned that I'd written books for children. The bright young man looked at me down his nose, as if he'd just been told that I practised some rather pathetic form of vice. 'I suppose,' he said, 'you do it under a pseudonym?'

"His attitude was almost universal at that time. To the British public, even the educated British public, a writer for children wasn't a *real* writer. He was a churner-out of kids' stuff, the literary equivalent of iced lollies [popsicles] and toffee-bars. Any prestige attached to the trade of authorship did not extend to him.

"Today, though many still take the same view, there are signs of rapidly increasing awareness of the value of children's books among teachers and parents and perhaps even a few general readers. Its beginning to be realized that the standard of the best modern children's books is high: higher now, I believe, than ever before. Plenty of publishers have novels in their children's lists that are every bit as good as those they're bringing out for adults. The new generation of [British] children's writers that emerged in the 1950's, headed by Rosemary Sutcliff, William Mayne, and Philippa Pearce, has been joined by an equally able group of writers of the sixties, among them Alan Garner, Leon Garfield, K.M. Peyton. Now the writers of the seventies are beginning to make themselves known, and I do not believe they will be inferior to their elders.

"What makes a man (or woman) write books for children? Should books be written 'for' children at all? Some people who are regarded as children's writers have declared emphatically that they shouldn't. The late Arthur Ransome, for instance, said: 'You write not for children but for yourself, and if by good fortune children enjoy what you enjoy, why then, you are a writer of children's books.' This was true for Ransome, and to some extent it must be true for anyone who has any of the instincts of the artist in him; you *do* write for yourself, the first person you must please is always *you.*

"All the same, I think that for most of us it can only be partly true. The question whether you write 'for' children is the same basic question as whether you write 'for' anybody. A book is a communication; an act of communication has two ends; and just as a play is not complete until it is performed before an audience, so a book is only completed by being read. To write for yourself alone, if it were possible, would not be praiseworthy. You must have a reader in mind. And if you are writing a book that will appear on a publisher's children's book list, you must be aware of a potential audience of children.

"It's sometimes said that children don't 'need' books these days—either because of the telly and all that, or because children are people like the rest of us and it's wrong to have a separate category of books for them. I can't see much force in either of these arguments. Clearly there just *are* large numbers of children who love reading (and there'd be many more if they were properly introduced to it). The case for recreational reading on general educational grounds is too obvious to need restating. And adult novels are not enough; they go too far beyond the child's field of experience; they put too stiff a tax on his patience and perhaps his grasp of language.

"Myself, I think an audience of children is a splendid and stimulating one. You can expect at least as much imagination, and a good deal more readiness to enter into things and live the story. You can take up your theme afresh as if the world was new, rather than picking it up where the last practitioner let it drop and allowing for the weariness and satiety of readers. True, you can't expect the child, as a busy creature, to put up with longwindedness or pomposity, or to be impressed by emperors' clothes. But that should concentrate your mind wonderfully.

"Still, there are at least three problems that arise out of writing specifically for children. One is that of style and vocabulary. This doesn't worry me, or authors I know, as much as people seem to expect. I believe in writing plainly and simply anyway, but I don't believe in using any but the best word, and if the child has to skim over it or look it up I don't care. The second problem is harder. There are times when you could cheat—by simplifying character, stepping up action—and much of your audience would prefer the cheat. I know of no answer to this except to resist temptation in the hope that you'll thereby be giving your readers more in the long run. My own rule, more easily stated than observed, is that characters must only do what they *would* do and that action must arise naturally out of the situation.

"The third problem is tricky, too: how far can you go into certain areas of experience? The child who dips into adult novels does it, so to speak, at his own risk. But a book that's on the children's list of a respectable publisher, offered for sale to schools and libraries and parents and aunts, carries with it a strong implication that it will be 'suitable.' And just what, at any given point in time, is suitable?

"Ideas on the subject change quite rapidly. When my own first book, *Gumble's Yard* [*Trouble in the Jungle*] was published, it was thought to be rather shocking. It's a story about a family of children in a very poor slum home. The (unmarried) couple who are supposed to be looking after them walk out, and the children set up house on their own in a deserted warehouse by a canal bank. It was rejected by one leading house because of its distasteful background; a headmaster who read it for another firm thought it would be disgraceful to put such a story into children's hands; and when eventually it did get published a young lady who interviewed me about it began accusingly: 'Mr. Townsend, you have written a *sordid* book for children. Why?'

"Today *Gumble's Yard* is available in a schools edition and as a Penguin paperback, and I haven't heard a complaint about it for years. And no one objected to its successor, *Widdershins Crescent* [*Good-bye to the Jungle*] in which the same family, with the grownups still unmarried, moved out to a bright new housing estate and got into a fresh tangle of problems. In the last decade there's been a total change of climate.

The rubber wheels of the cart made no noise, and our sneakers were just as quiet, so all should have been well. But we turned the corner too quickly. ■ (From *Trouble in the Jungle* [*Gumble's Yard*] by John Rowe Townsend. Illustrated by W. T. Mars. Reprinted by permission of J. B. Lippincott Co.)

"I can see now that my approach to *Gumble's Yard* was author-centered and audience-centered alternately. It began with the audience. I had come to the conclusion, broadly true then but not true now, that children's books were too harmless, hygienic and middle-class, too comfortably padded with nannies and ponies and boarding-schools, to little engaged with things that really mattered. I'd been writing some articles that involved going round on the beat with the NSPCC [National Society for the Prevention of Cruelty to Children] inspectors, and I felt that children should be able to read about this other side of childhood.

"But there was something growing in myself that hadn't much to do with any deliberate aim. I had a visual obsession with a certain industrial district where a tangle of grimy streets sloped down to a canal bank, ugly and beautiful together in a Lowryish way [L. S. Lowry, British painter]; I started wandering round it, putting imaginary people into it. Eventually I was writing a book; and it was (I think) only because these different preoccupations happened to coincide that it turned out to be a book for children.

"So I believe, and have tried to act on the belief, that one does indeed write 'for' children, but that there isn't really any Great Divide. I wouldn't claim to have solved for myself the problem of satisfying both the child's demands and one's own aspirations. But I think I know where to look for the solutions. One lies in universality. Children are part of mankind; there must be themes, and great themes, that have meaning for all.

"I think at this point of J.R.R. Tolkien; though I don't feel he has exhausted or even fully demonstrated the possibilities. The other lies in making different layers of meaning accessible to different readers—as for instance in Alan Garner's novel *Elidor,* where an apparently straightforward adventure story for children can be read quite differently by older readers in the light of the grail legend and the Golden Bough. As C.S. Lewis said, 'A children's story which is enjoyed only by children is a bad children's book.' The first-class book for children is never grown out of at all."

FOR MORE INFORMATION SEE: New Society [London] December 7, 1967; *Horn Book,* August, 1970, June, 1971, August, 1971, October, 1971; *New York Times Book Review,* May 2, 1971, November 19, 1972.

TRAVERS, P(amela) L(yndon) 1906-

PERSONAL: Born in 1906, in Queensland, Australia.

P. L. TRAVERS

"Now, quick March into the Park!" snapped [Mary Poppins]. "And no meandering!" ... The sun spread over Cherry Tree Lane like a bright enormous umbrella. ■ From the movie "Mary Poppins," © MCMLXIII by Walt Disney Productions.

Education: Privately educated. *Home:* Chelsea, London, England.

CAREER: Writer, journalist, dancer, and actress in Australia and England; full-time writer in England, 1930—. Writer-in-residence, Radcliffe College, Cambridge, Mass., 1965-66, Smith College, Northampton, Mass., 1966-67, and Scripps College, Claremont, Calif., 1970.

WRITINGS: Mary Poppins, Reynal & Hitchcock, 1934, Harcourt, 1962; *Mary Poppins Comes Back,* Reynal & Hitchcock, 1935 (previous two titles appeared in one volume, *Mary Poppins* and *Mary Poppins Comes Back,* Reynal & Hitchcock, 1937, Harcourt, 1963); *Moscow Excursion,* Reynal & Hitchcock, 1935; *Happy Ever After,* Reynal & Hitchcock, 1940; *I Go By Sea, I Go By Land,* Harper, 1941, new edition, Norton, 1964; *Mary Poppins Opens the Door,* Reynal & Hitchcock, 1943, Harcourt, 1962; *Mary Poppins in the Park,* Harcourt, 1952; *The Fox at the Manger,* Norton, 1962; *Mary Poppins from A to Z,* Harcourt, 1962; *Friend Monkey,* Harcourt, 1971.

Stories taken from *Mary Poppins*—all published by Simon & Schuster: *The Gingerbread Shop,* 1952; *Mr. Wiggs Birthday Party,* 1952; *Stories from Mary Poppins,* 1952; *The Magic Compass,* 1953.

SIDELIGHTS: Ms. Travers prefers not to be photographed, believing these likenesses to be too inaccurate, although she said she does "like the bronze head by Gertrude Herries, famous English sculptor ... and the pen drawing by the English artist, Agar. "I am a writer who likes anonymity, believing that all that concerns the general public is the books themselves which are, in the truest sense, any author's biography. It doesn't matter if an author exists. It matters only if the work lives."

P.L. Travers began to write before she was seven years old. When she arrived in Ireland, while still very young, George Russell, using the famed pseudonym "AE," published Travers' poetry in his paper, the *Irish Statesman,* and continued his interest in her work until his death. The writing of *Mary Poppins* began as an amusement for the author while she was recovering from an illness, and a friend's interest in the sketches convinced her to allow them to grow into a book. Although *Mary Poppins* came

Out of the glowing core of light emerged a curious figure—a figure in a black-straw hat and a blue coat trimmed with silver buttons—a figure that carried in one hand something that looked like a carpet bag, and in the other—oh, could it be true?—a parrot-headed umbrella. ■ (From *Mary Poppins Opens the Door* by P. L. Travers. Illustrated by Mary Shepard.)

to be considered a classic children's story, *Library Journal* reported that Travers prefers the term "books children like" to "children's books," believing that "all children's books are for grownups, and all adult books are for children."

In 1964, Walt Disney produced the tremendously popular film of *Mary Poppins,* about which *Library Journal* quotes Travers as saying: "The movie and the books are not the same thing and you mustn't muddle them. The movie is very glamorous if you take it on its own. But it has very little to do with the books." Several books based on the film itself have been published.

To commemorate Travers' delightful character, Mortimer Browning wrote "Mary Poppins Suite for Orchestra," and a dramatization of *Mary Poppins,* written by Sara Spencer, was published by Children's Theatre Press, c. 1940. The horticultural world, too, has responded to Mary Poppin's appeal by bringing out two different "Mary Poppins" roses, and one rose has been named "Pamela Travers." *Mary Poppins* has been translated into more than twenty languages, and sales of the book have run into the millions.

Travers told an interviewer for *Publishers Weekly:* "I was brought up on fairy tales and I have been intensely interested and enchanted by myths, legends, and folklore all my life. I feel strongly that this is what underlies everything—all our so-called real life is based on this so-called unreal world—but it is infinitely more real than anything that happens externally."

P.L. Travers once lived in a 900-year-old, small, thatched manor house which is mentioned in the Doomsday Book, and is of interest to archeological scholars. She now has a late Georgian house in Chelsea and a house in Dublin, Ireland. She has traveled to the United States and Russia, and made her home in this country during World War II.

FOR MORE INFORMATION SEE: Junior Book of Authors, edited by Kunitz and Haycraft, Wilson, 2nd edition, 1951; *Library Journal,* March 15, 1966; *New York Times,* October 4, 1966, October 15, 1966; *Quarterly Journal of the Library of Congress,* October, 1967; Roy Newquist, *Conversations,* Rand McNally, 1967; Brian Doyle, *The Who's Who of Children's Literature,* Schocken Books, 1968; Eleanor Cameron, *The Green and Burning Tree,* Atlantic-Little, Brown, 1969; *Time,* December 27, 1971; *New York Times Book Review,* November 7, 1971, May 7, 1972; *Publishers Weekly,* December 13, 1971; *Horn Book,* February, 1972.

TRIPP, Eleanor B(aldwin) 1936-

PERSONAL: Born May 27, 1936, in Boston, Mass.; daughter of William V., Jr. (in investment business) and Nell (Baldwin) Tripp; married Robert S. November (director of Development Planning, *New York Times*), August 17, 1969. *Education:* Smith College, B.A., 1958; London School of Economics and Political Science, further study, 1958-59; Columbia University, M.A., 1966. *Home:* 73 Walworth Ave., Scarsdale, N.Y. 10583.

CAREER: Teacher in Corte Madera, Calif., 1960-61, and Cambridge, Mass., 1961-64; Columbia University, New York, N.Y., lecturer on American immigration, periodically, 1966—; New York State Museum and Science Service, script writer, 1968-69; New Lincoln School, New York, N.Y., seventh grade teacher, 1969—. *Member:* American Historical Association, Authors Guild, Appalachian Mountain Club.

WRITINGS: To America (teen book), Harcourt, 1969.

HOBBIES AND OTHER INTERESTS: Reading, travel, the theater, photography; outdoor activities, including tennis and skiing.

UBELL, Earl 1926-

PERSONAL: Born June 21, 1926, in Brooklyn, N.Y.; son of Charles Abraham and Hilda (Kramer) Ubell; married Shirley Leitman (executive director of Modern Dance Education), February 12, 1949; children: Lori Ellen, Michael Charles. *Education:* City College, New York, N.Y., B.S., 1948. *Religion:* Ethical Culture. *Home:* 482

EARL UBELL

The crayfish held by the boy in this picture probably looks very much as crayfish did 100,000 years ago. ∎ (From *The World of the Living* by Earl Ubell. Photographs by Arline Strong.)

Summit Ave., Hackensack, N.J. 07601. *Agent:* Curtis Brown Ltd., 60 East 56th St., New York, N. Y. 10022.

CAREER: New York Herald Tribune, New York, N.Y., messenger, 1943, secretary, 1943-48, reporter, 1948-53, science editor, 1953-66; WCBS-TV, New York, N.Y., science editor, 1966-72; WNBC-TV, New York, N.Y., news director, 1972—; New York University, College of Liberal Arts, New York, N.Y., adjunct associate professor of journalism, 1971—. Mutual Broadcasting System, science editor, 1961-62; WNEW, special science editor, 1964-65. Plenum Publishing Corp., member of board of directors, 1971—. Council for Advancement of Science Writing, president, 1960-66; Foundation for Modern Dance Education, chairman, 1962—. North Jersey Cultural Council, president, 1966-72; Young Men's Hebrew Association of Bergen County, member of board of directors, 1968—. *Military service:* U.S. Navy, 1944-46.

Member: National Association of Science Writers (president, 1960-61), American Crystalographic Association, Phi Beta Kappa. *Awards, honors:* Albert and Mary Lasker Medical Journalism Award, 1957; American Association for the Advancement of Science-Westinghouse Science Writing Award, 1960; Empire State Award for excellence in medical reporting, 1963; Science Writers Award of American Psychological Foundation, 1965; New York State Associated Press Broadcasters Award for excellence in reporting, 1969, 1970; Emmy Award (for New York area) of National Academy of Television Arts and Sciences, 1970.

WRITINGS—Juveniles illustrated by Arline Strong: *The World of Push and Pull,* Atheneum, 1964; *The World of the Living,* Atheneum, 1965; *The World of Candle and Color,* Atheneum, 1969. Consultant, *Encyclopedia of Russia and the Soviet Union,* McGraw, 1961. Co-author of children's play, "Dirty Air is Everywhere" (produced by the Merry-Go-Rounders). Contributor of more than fifty popular and several scientific articles to magazines, and of more than two thousand articles to newspapers.

WORK IN PROGRESS: A book on health for adults.

SIDELIGHTS: As a newsman Ubell has traveled throughout the world and covered such notable events as the first Sputnik flight, 1961, and the first U.S. manned space flight, 1962. He has done scientific research on summer projects at various laboratories—Weizmann Institute, California Institute of Technology, and Jackson Laboratory. All of his spare time is devoted to the development of arts organizations in his home community.

UDRY, Janice May   1928-

PERSONAL: Surname pronounced *Yoo*-dri; born June

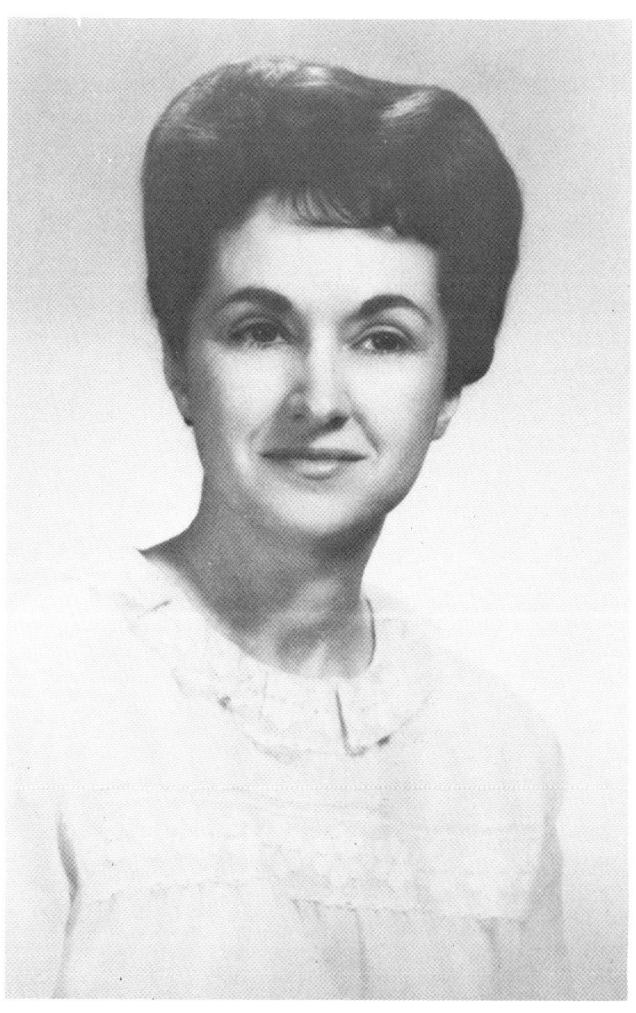

JANICE MAY UDRY

A tree is nice for a house to be near. ■ (From *A Tree is Nice* by Janice May Udry. Illustrated by Marc Simont.)

14, 1928, in Jacksonville, Ill.; daughter of Harold and Louise (Southwell) May; married Richard Udry (a teacher), August, 1950; children: Leslie, Susan. *Education:* Northwestern University, B.S., 1950. *Home:* Chapel Hill, N.C.

CAREER: Free-lance writer. *Member:* American Association of University Women.

WRITINGS: A Tree Is Nice, (Caldecott Award), Harper, 1956; *Theodore's Parents,* Lothrop, 1958; *Moon-Jumpers,* Harper, 1959; *Danny's Pig,* Lothrop, 1960; *Alfred,* A. Whitman, 1960; *Let's Be Enemies,* Harper, 1961; *Is Susan Here?,* Abelard, 1962; *The Mean Mouse, and Other Mean Stories,* Harper, 1962; *The End of the Line,* A. Whitman, 1962; *Betsy-Back-In-Bed,* A. Whitman, 1963; *Next Door to Laura Linda,* A. Whitman, 1965; *What Mary Jo Shared,* A. Whitman, 1966; *If You're a Bear,* A. Whitman, 1967; *Mary Ann's Mud Day,* Harper, 1967; *What Mary Jo Wanted,* A. Whitman, 1968; *Glenda,* Harper, 1969; *The Sunflower Garden,* Harvey House, 1969; *Emily's Autumn,* A. Whitman, 1969; *Mary Jo's Grandmother* (Junior Literary Guild selection), A. Whitman, 1971.

FOR MORE INFORMATION SEE: Chicago Daily News, February 3, 1962; *Newbery and Caldecott Medal Books: 1956-1965,* edited by Lee Kingman, Horn Book, 1965; Lee Bennett Hopkins, *Books Are By People,* Citation Press, 1969; *Third Book of Junior Authors,* edited by de Montreville and Hill, Wilson, 1972.

UNCLE RAY
See COFFMAN, Ramon Peyton

UNKELBACH, Kurt 1913-

PERSONAL: Born November 21, 1913, in New Britain, Conn.; son of Max J. (an architect) and Louise (Gunther) Unkelbach; married Evelyn Haskell; children: Evelyn P. and L. Cary (daughters). *Education:* Williston Academy, graduate, 1932; student at Wesleyan University, Middletown, Conn., 1932-34, and Pasadena Playhouse, 1934-36. *Religion:* Protestant. *Home:* Starks Rd., R.F.D. 3, Winsted, Conn. 06098. *Agent:* Knox Burger Associates Ltd., 39½ Washington Sq. S., New York, N.Y. 10012.

KURT UNKELBACH

CAREER: Radio writer for various independent stations and networks, 1936-41; account executive with advertising and public relations agencies in New York, N.Y., 1947-64; full-time writer, 1965—. *Military service:* U.S. Army, 1941-46; served in South Pacific; became captain. *Member:* Dramatist Guild of the Authors League of America.

WRITINGS: Love on a Leash, Prentice-Hall, 1964; *The Dog in My Life,* Four Winds, 1966; *The Winning of Westminster,* Prentice-Hall, 1966; *Murphy,* Prentice-Hall, 1967; *Ruffian: International Champion,* Prentice-Hall, 1967; *The Dog Who Never Knew,* Four Winds, 1968; *Both Ends of the Leash,* Prentice-Hall, 1968; *A Cat and His Dogs,* Prentice-Hall, 1969; *Catnip: Selecting and Training Your Cat,* Prentice-Hall, 1970; *The Pleasures of Dog Ownership,* Prentice-Hall, 1971; *You're A Good Dog, Joe,* Prentice-Hall, 1971; *The Love That Shook the World,* C & B Book House, 1971; *How to Bring Up Your Pet Dog,* Dodd, 1972; *Winning Ways,* Watts, 1972; *Albert Payson Terhune* (biography), Charterhouse, 1972. Ghost writer of other books.

Author of "Straw Hat," play produced on Broadway, 1937, and of 150 radio plays, 1936-41; also wrote scripts for twenty commercial films, 1948-56. Columnist and free-lance contributor to dog magazines, including *Dog World, Dogs in Canada,* and *American Kennel Gazette.* Contributing editor for *Dogs Magazine,* world's largest canine journal, and canine editor for *On the Sound,* the Eastern monthly.

WORK IN PROGRESS: "Three novels: one about a poodle I owned as a boy in the early Twenties, one about a contemporary feral dog, and one about a social theme. A biography about America's first lady of letters, Marion Harland, the mother of Albert Payson Terhune; a kitten training book for very young readers; a juvenile novel about an English setter; a collection of original dog stories and articles."

SIDELIGHTS: "Several reviewers have called me a Madison Avenue refugee. True, but not quite that simple. To my own surprise, I had achieved success as a businessman, but it was a hollow success. I was seeing less and less of my family, commuting to and from the city amounted to 120 miles per day, the years were slipping away, and so were my hopes of becoming a full-time writer. Finally, in 1965, when I was over fifty, I took the plunge.

"Looking back, I don't think I would repeat the gamble. I knew very little about publishing except that thousands of books were published each year, some of them were about dogs, and most of the dog books did not contain the truth. They contained beasts with too much intelligence and too many capabilities. To really know canines, one has to live with them over a long period of years, observe them and enjoy them. I had.

"I did not know that the vast majority of books do not make money, nor that ninety-five percent of the authors held salaried jobs and wrote books on the side. Very few editors had much knowledge about canines and fewer publishers are aware that the dog lover market is a huge one, and that some of the lovers buy books. I assumed that many authors made a living writing about dogs, but later I learned that only one man had: Albert Payson Terhune, whose books were very popular from 1920-35, when dog lovers were more naive and believed that a dog could do almost anything.

"Whereas I used to write all night and during the early morning hours, I am no longer a 'night person.' My health failed a few years ago, and my work hours are now restricted. While I try to write at least a few hundred words every day, my hours at the desk depend pretty much upon the weather. If it is a sunny day, I am outdoors, working with the dogs or walking in the woods or fishing. I spent too many years in the office to waste any more of nature's fine hours. So, on sunny days, I write for about three hours after dinner. On foul days, I probably get in another hour or two.

"Since the health problem developed, I am known as the 'Director of Labor' around here. I suggest and observe, and my wife does most of the work with the dogs. We usually have four or five old timers living in the house. Pups and young adults stay in the kennel.

"Some of my time is spent keeping up with animal research. And then, as time permits, I do answer my mail, which is rather heavy at times. Terhune, who wrote for adults, discovered that about half of his readers were youngsters. I write both adult and juvenile books about dogs, and find that each age group reads the books intended for the other. When it comes to dog lovers, there are no age restrictions.

"Still, about seventy-five percent of my mail comes from

young readers in about the 7-to-16 age range. From the beginning, when I received about ten letters a month, I have answered every letter from young readers, although once in a great while there has been an exception: a letter from a youngster who is an obvious egomaniac and makes impossible requests. These days, the letters amount to several hundred a month, and I am always months behind in answering them. While I do like the idea of corresponding with my readers, I also wish that more school teachers would practice wisdom and not assign an entire class to write letters to a single author. While there is merit in establishing the fact that books are not written by machines, teachers could assign two or three students to each of twenty authors. My oldest daughter is now a high school teacher, if she ever assigns an entire class to write to just one author, I think I'll disclaim her.

"The letters I enjoy the most are the spontaneous ones written at home. Erasures indicate that at least one parent has checked out the letter, or that the writer has gone to a dictionary. Often, these letters are instructive, in that I learn that dog lovers really want to know about dogs. Indeed, such letters have resulted in an entire book, *How to Bring Up Your Pet Dog.*

"Obviously, I have neither a writing system or schedule. I do try to keep about three things going, each fitting a different mood and writing style. My typewriter is an old friend and about ten years younger than I am. Several keys keep coming off, and no repairman has ever been able to keep them on for more than a week. So I use a special glue that my wife orders from Germany, and this glue keeps a key in place for about six months.

"I don't know how it is with others, but when I'm awake, my mind is usually on writing: the best way to phrase something, a new idea, where to find some needed information, or how to meet a deadline. This is fine for a writer, but tough on his wife. Mine never knows when I'm listening, and I am constantly in deep water for not doing something that I promised to do, although I seldom remember promising anything.

"My books have won a few awards, but the one I prize the most is a knighthood conferred by the *Mark Twain Journal,* a literary quarterly, for my novel about a beagle, entitled *Murphy.* The late William Faulkner was the only American author to be named a Knight of Mark Twain. It's nice to be called Sir Kurt, although my wife, daughters and dogs refuse to do so.

"I don't know how to describe myself as a 'person,' but I am six feet tall, bearded, an avid gardener, a lover of seafood, and consider applejack to be the world's finest tonic. And I just could be the only writer with the secondary vocation of professional dowser, although that's no way to make a living these days. I get about three jobs a year." Unkelbach breeds, trains, and exhibits Labrador retrievers.

UNSWORTH, Walt(er) 1928-

PERSONAL: Born December 16, 1928, in Littleborough, Lancashire, England; married Dorothy Winstanley (a teacher), 1952; children: Gail, Timothy Duncan. *Education:* Attended Wigan Technical College, 1942-47, and Chester College, 1949-51; Licentiate of the College of Preceptors (L.C.P.), 1956. *Home:* 16 Briarfield Rd., Worsley, Manchester M28 4GQ, England.

CAREER: Previously taught in Wednesfield, Staffordshire, and Horwich, Lancashire, England; Worsley Walkden Secondary School, Worsley, Lancashire, England, head of physics department, 1957—. Former professional mountain-climbing instructor during summer months; Cicerone Press (publishers of specialist mountaineering booklets), managing editor and partner. *Military service:* British Army, Royal Artillery, 1947-49; served in Malta and Libya. *Member:* Alpine Club, Association of British Members of the Swiss Alpine Club, Wayfarer's Club.

WRITINGS: The Young Mountaineer, Hutchinson, 1959; *A Climber's Guide to Pontesford Rocks,* Wilding & Son, 1962; *The English Outcrops,* Gollancz, 1964; *Matterhorn Man: The Life of Edward Whymper,* Gollancz, 1965; *Tiger in the Snow: The Life and Adventures of A.F. Mummery,* Gollancz, 1967; *Because It Is There: Famous Mountaineers 1840-1940,* Gollancz, 1968; *The Devil's Mill* (juvenile novel), Gollancz, 1968; *The Book of Rock-Climbing,* Arthur Barker, 1968; (compiler) *Otztal Alps* (climbing guide), West Col Productions, 1969; *North Face: The Second Conquest of the Alps,* Hutchinson, 1969; *Whistling Clough* (juvenile), Gollancz, 1970; (with R.B. Evans) *The Southern Lakes,* Cicerone Press, 1971; *Portrait of River Derwent* (travel), Robert Hale, 1971; *The High Fells of Lakeland* (travel), Robert Hale, 1972. Also author of *Everest 72,* the official booklet of the British Mount Everest Expedition, 1972.

Stories included in the anthologies, *The Mountainer's Companion,* Eyre & Spottiswoode, 1966, and *Miscellany Four,* Oxford University Press, 1967. Regular contributor to *Climber & Rambler;* also has contributed articles and reviews to magazines, mountaineering journals, and newspapers, including some in the United States and Australia.

WORK IN PROGRESS: Encyclopedia of Mountaineering for Robert Hale.

SIDELIGHTS: "I had my first piece published when I was seventeen—a true adventure story based on an old seaman's diary. The initial success kept me going because I had nothing else published for some time, and anyway I was serving in the Army, doing my college stint, etc.

"Brought up to walk in the beautiful Lakeland fells during the vacations, I eventually became a rock climber. The delights of mountain climbing stirred me to pass on the experience to young people, both as an instructor and writer and so I became well known as a climber-writer. My book on the smaller rocks of England, *The English Outcrops,* caused quite a stir in British climbing circles when it was published: a reviewer called it 'a seminal book of post-war climbing.' Finally, in this vein, I wrote *The Book of Rock Climbing* which is probably the best selling climbing book for youngsters in England.

"Meanwhile I was becoming more and more engrossed in our industrial heritage, especially as I live in the area where the Industrial Revolution started (I live only a couple of hundred yards from the entrance to James Brindley's famous canal, for example). Much of the industry has gone, of course, and what is left is in the care of preservation societies: it is ironical that what were once the cradles of heavy industry are now highly sought after residential areas! But living in such a place stimulated me into research about the past industries and led to the two Derbyshire novels: one about the lives of mill apprentices, *The Devil's Mill,* which is recommended by the History School Inspectorate as background reading for the period and was translated into German, and the second, *Whistling Clough,* which is about the old lead mines.

"I find the stimulus for the novels from the places themselves. These old mills and mines seem to speak of the long lost dead and the misery of the people who worked there. I can never walk down Miller's Dale in Derbyshire (which is an extremely beautiful limestone gorge) without hearing the moans of the hundreds of pauper children who slaved and died in the dreadful mill there.

"I work in an office in my home, usually for only two or three hours a day. Short pieces I draft straight on the typewriter, but longer work I rough out in longhand first because it gives me more time to think.

"My books, especially the novels, are written just because I want to write them. They seem to attract most age groups: schools have turned them into projects and one school is at the moment turning *The Devil's Mill* into a musical, with a professional score. That should really be something!"

Unsworth has climbed all over the Alps, where he still spends five or six weeks of every summer. His youth books are mainly for older children but he says that they "are not beyond the understanding of a reasonably intelligent adult, as well."

HOBBIES AND OTHER INTERESTS: Philately and industrial archaeology.

USHER, Margo Scegge
See McHARGUE, Georgess

Van der VEER, Judy 1912-

PERSONAL: Born October 17, 1912, in Oil City, Pa.; daughter of Tunis Herbert and Alice (Case) Van der Veer. *Education:* "I am a high school drop-out." *Home:* Star Route, Ramona, Calif. *Agent:* Ruth Aley, Maxwell Aley Associates, 145 East 35th St., New York, N.Y. 10016.

CAREER: Grew up in San Diego but "escaped from schools and cities at an early age" to live in the country; writer, for young people and adults.

WRITINGS: River Pasture, Longmans, Green, 1936; *Brown Hills,* Longmans, Green, 1938; *November Grass,* Longmans, Green, 1940; *A Few Happy Ones,* Appleton, 1943; (contributor) J.H. Jackson, editor, *Continent's End,*

Suddenly the rain turned to small, hard flakes of snow that stung against the face. A sharp wind swirled them around. ■ (From *Higher than the Arrow* by Judy Van der Veer. Illustrated by F. Leslie Matthews.)

Whittlesey House, 1944; (contributor) Roderick Peattie, editor, *Pacific Coast Ranges,* Vanguard, 1946; *My Valley in the Sky,* Messner, 1959; *Hold the Rein Free,* Golden Gate, 1966; *Wallace the Wandering Pig,* Harcourt, 1967; *Higher Than the Arrow,* Golden Gate, 1969; *To the Rescue,* Harcourt, 1969; *The Gray Mare's Colts,* Golden Gate, 1971. Stories, articles, and poems have been published in magazines and included in anthologies.

JUDY VAN der VEER

WORK IN PROGRESS: More books based on "the ideas I receive from knowing animals and people."

SIDELIGHTS: "I live in the country with lots of animals and see lots of people. I hate to travel but have done some although I have more fun at home. I also hate all hunters, trappers and poisoners. I am interested in things like the importance of the individual, whether animal or human, and like all races and/or colors of people, but hate people who destroy land and animals."

FOR MORE INFORMATION SEE: Christian Science Monitor, November 6, 1969; *Horn Book,* December, 1969.

Van ORDEN, M(erton) D(ick) 1921-

PERSONAL: Born February 24, 1921, in Austin, Tex.; son of Merton Leroy and Thelma (Murphy) Van Orden; married Nancy Platt, June 9, 1944; children: Anne (Mrs. Stanton Paine Coerr), Richard Platt. *Education:* U.S. Naval Academy, B.S., 1944; Massachusetts Institute of Technology, B.S.E.E., 1949; George Washington University, M.B.A., 1964. *Religion:* Protestant. *Home:* 2027 Highboro Way, Falls Church, Va. 22043.

CAREER: U.S. Navy, midshipman, 1941-44, Officer, 1944—, with current rank of rear admiral. *Member:* United States Naval Institute, San Diego Yacht Club.

M. D. Van ORDEN

WRITINGS: The Book of United States Navy Ships (juvenile), Dodd, 1969. Contributor to *U.S. Naval Institute Proceedings* and other military and technical journals.

WORK IN PROGRESS: Research on new ships for a revised edition of *The Book of United States Navy Ships.*

SIDELIGHTS: "I have long been interested in ships, from sail to steam to nuclear power, particularly U.S. Navy ships. I felt the need for communicating to young people the interesting traditions associated with Navy ships and some of the characteristics of modern ships of the Navy. Discussions of ship terminology, ships' names and how they are arrived at, and some brief descriptions of the different types and their missions are believed to be of interest to young men contemplating a Navy career— These motivated my writing of *The Book of United States Navy Ships.*"

VERNOR, D.
See CASEWIT, Curtis

WAGNER, Sharon B. 1936-

PERSONAL: Born December 16, 1936, in Wallace, Idaho; daughter of Moses Ross (a drilling contractor) and Dorothy A. (Stephens) Wagner. *Education:* Colorado Woman's College, student, 1955-56; Famous Writers School, diploma in fiction, 1965; Mesa Community College, further courses, 1967—. *Politics:* Republican. *Home:* 2137 East Bramble Ave., Mesa, Ariz. 85204. *Agent:* Scott Meredith Literary Agency, Inc., 580 Fifth Ave., New York, N.Y. 10036.

CAREER: Clerical worker in Shelby, Mont., 1957-58; secretary in Cheyenne, Wyo., 1958-62, and Denver, Colo., 1962-63; Arizona State University, Tempe, part-time clerk, 1966-68; full time writer, 1968—.

WRITINGS: Prairie Wind (juvenile), Meredith, 1968; *The Dude Ranch Mystery* (juvenile), McKay, 1969; *Curse of Still Valley* (adult), Lancer, 1969; *Country of the Wolf,* Lancer, 1970; *Maridu,* Lancer, 1970; *Circle of Evil,* Lancer, 1971; *Winter Evil,* Lancer, 1972; *Silly Filly from Nowhere* (juvenile), Western, 1972; *House of Shadows* (adult), Beagle, 1972; *Moonwind* (adult), Lancer, 1972; *Shadow on the Sun* (adult), Lancer, 1972. Contributor of seventy short stories to periodicals.

WORK IN PROGRESS: Four gothics: *Cry of the Cat, Legacy of Loneliness, Echo of A Dream,* and *Shadow of Her Eyes;* an untitled Haitian gothic.

SIDELIGHTS: "Though I had always loved to write, it wasn't till 1961 that a personal crisis forced me into an evaluation of my life and goals. I decided then to become a professional writer. With the aid and guidance of the Famous Writers' School fiction course and my own determination, I began.

"A year later my first short story sold. It was followed by a slow, but fairly steady stream of sales, so that by the end of 1963, I quit my full-time job and moved to Arizona. With the extra hours provided by part-time

SHARON B. WAGNER

work, I felt free to try my first novel. Since I'd been raised in the prairie town of Cut Bank, Montana, I decided to do a children's book about the kind of life I'd wanted to live during my childhood. So *Prairie Wind* was born, making real the day dreams of horses I'd had for so long.

"The acceptance of that novel and *The Dude Ranch Mystery* soon convinced me that I was a novelist rather than a short story writer and I began trying new types of books."

HOBBIES AND OTHER INTERESTS: Reading, animals (horses, dogs, and cats in particular), history, sewing, and all needlecraft.

WALKER, Barbara K(erlin) 1921-
(Beth Kilreon)

PERSONAL: Maiden surname is pronounced Ker-*lin;* born October 13, 1921, in Ann Arbor, Mich.; daughter of Oscar Fahnestock (a school administrator) and Mildred M. (Baldwin) Kerlin; married Warren Stanley Walker (Horn Professor of English at Texas Tech University), December 9, 1943; children: Brian, Theresa Sue (adopted). *Education:* State University of New York at Albany, B.A., 1943, M.A., 1947; Cornell University, graduate courses in folklore. *Religion:* Disciples of Christ. *Home and office:* 3703 66th St., Lubbock, Tex. 79413.

CAREER: Junior high school teacher in Cornwall, N.Y., 1943-45, and Ithaca, N.Y., 1948-49; Albany Academy for Girls, Albany, N.Y., teacher, 1947-48; Cornell University Press, Ithaca, N.Y., editor and first reader, 1949-51; Blackburn College, Carlinville, Ill., professor in English and education, 1952-59; Parsons College, Fairfield, Iowa, instructor in English and education, 1959-61, 1962-64; teacher of English as a foreign language at elementary school in Ankara, Turkey, 1961-62; Parsons College, instructor in English and education, 1962-64. Member of board of directors, Project Impact, government-sponsored program at Library-Learning Center, Lubbock.

Member: American Folklore Society, Authors Guild, Texas Folklore Society, Phi Kappa Phi, Theta Sigma Phi, Delta Zeta, Lubbock City Panhellenic. *Awards, honors:* Cited by Turkish Ministry of Education for acquainting American children with Turkish culture, 1967; named Texas' most distinguished Delta Zeta alumna, 1970.

WRITINGS—Adult: (Editor with husband, Warren S. Walker) *Nigerian Folk Tales,* Rutgers University Press, 1961; (editor with Warren S. Walker) *The Erie Canal: Gateway to Empire,* Heath, 1963.

Juvenile: *Just Say Hic! A Turkish Silly Tale,* Follett, 1965;

BARBARA K. WALKER

"... any man who sits on the outside end of a branch he is chopping is certain to fall." ■ (From *Watermelons, Walnuts and the Wisdom of Allah* by Barbara Walker. Illustrated by Harold Berson.)

Hilili and Dilili: A Turkish Silly Tale, Follett, 1965; (with Mine Sumer) *Stargazer to the Sultan*, Parents' Magazine Press, 1967; *Watermelons, Walnuts, and the Wisdom of Allah, and Other Tales of the Hoca*, Parents' Magazine Press, 1967; *Once There Was and Twice There Wasn't*, Follett, 1968; *The Dancing Palm Tree and Other Nigerian Folktales*, Parents' Magazine Press, 1968; *I Packed My Trunk*, Follett, 1969; (with Naki Tezel) *The Mouse and the Elephant*, Parents' Magazine Press, 1969; *Pigs and Pirates: A Greek Tale* (Junior Literary Guild selection), David White, 1969; *The Round Sultan and the Straight Answer*, Parents' Magazine Press, 1970; *Korolu, the Singing Bandit*, Crowell, 1970; *The Courage of Kazan*, Crowell, 1971; *The Ifrit and the Magic Gifts*, Follett, 1972; *How the Hare Told the Truth About His Horse*, Parents' Magazine Press, 1972.

Contributor of more than 200 stories and articles to folklore, education, and children's periodicals, including *Child Life, Journal of American Folklore, Horn Book, Children's Digest,* and *Humpty Dumpty's Magazine;* the pseudonym, Beth Kilreon, has been used chiefly in *Humpty Dumpty's Magazine,* for which she supplied the "At Home with the Humpty Dumpty Family" page each month, 1958-70. Member of editorial board, *New York Folklore Quarterly*, 1951-55; yearbook editor, *Lubbock City Panhellenic,* 1969-73.

WORK IN PROGRESS: To Set Them Free: The Story of Mustapha Kemal Ataturk; a collection of Samoan tales; with Mabel Ross, a collection of Congalese tales, completion expected in 1973; with Wolodymyr Zyla, a collection of Ukrainian tales, 1973.

SIDELIGHTS: "At the age of seven, I decided on seven goals for myself, to be achieved at some time during my adult life. I wanted to become a wife, a mother, a teacher, a missionary, a storyteller, a journalist, and an author of children's books. At one time or another, I have achieved each of these goals, but I have since discovered that achieving goals is very much like eating peanuts: one peanut makes you want another peanut, and one achievement of a goal makes you want another achievement of that goal. Since books were a very important part of my childhood and youth, I have been especially pleased with those parts of my work that have involved bringing books and children together: teaching courses in children's literature over a period of twelve years, many years of storytelling in schools and public libraries and to groups of all kinds and all ages, collecting tales from other lands that would be of interest to young people, and writing and publishing stories, songs, plays, and books for children and those adults who work with children. It seems to me that children are the most important audience in the world because they *grow* on what they read and hear and watch; I like to think that what I write gives room for children of all ages to grow. Since folktales have something special and something lasting to say to all ages, I prefer to work with folktales. They are a treasure meant to be shared.

"At the age of seven, I also chose my penname, Beth Kilreon—*Beth* because I especially liked that name and *Kilreon* because it is an earlier spelling of my Scots-Irish maiden name *Kerlin*. My penname has appeared fairly often in *Humpty Dumpty's Magazine,* but I have never used it on a book. Why? I have discovered that librarians 'track down' pennames and provide the author's real name on the title page anyway, so there seems very little point in using one.

"We chose to go to Turkey for a year's Fulbright experience because my husband and I had been folklorists and writers ever since our college days, and we knew that almost no Turkish folk materials had appeared in American publications. We felt sure there must be thousands of good stories in Turkey just waiting for someone who knew Turkish and liked good stories—and indeed there were. We are *still* collecting Turkish folktales and we probably shall as long as we live. My husband uses some of the tales we have collected in scholarly books and with the exception of various articles in *Horn Book,* I have used our Turkish tales and other materials in books for children. My favorite story is *Stargazer to the Sultan*, although I have enjoyed collecting and retelling the others, too.

"The African, Samoan, and Ukrainian tales have come to me in various ways, largely from students in my college classes, but sometimes from hours of thumbing through dusty folklore journals and records kept by nineteenth-century missionaries, explorers and anthropologists. *Pigs and Pirates,* my retelling of a Greek legend, grew out of a little note in an agricultural textbook, *Pigs from Cave to Corn Belt;* when I first told it to my son, then three years old, he said: 'Tell it again, and tell it bigger.' After I had told him the story till it became big enough to suit him, I tried it out with twenty-seven different book publishers, one after another. Since no one seemed to want it, I put it away and tried other books. Finally, Pat Kienzle Ross, a new editor at David White Co. who had published many of my pieces in *Humpty Dumpty,* asked me for a book manuscript and I sent her *Pigs and Pirates.* She liked it and David White published it. You never can tell about manuscripts.

"I am sure of one thing: my work in writing for children's magazines has been a great help to me in my apprenticeship as a writer of children's books. It has taught me the importance of meeting publication deadlines and the necessity of polishing what I write until I cannot possibly make it any better and what I suppose is a lesson every author learns sooner or later: there is no substitute for 'seat of pants to seat of chair' on a regular working-day schedule if one intends to write books that are publishable.

"Several editors have been very helpful to me in my growth as a children's author: Esther K. Meeks and Bertha Jenkinson at Follett, Alvin Tresselt at Parents', Pat Kienzle Ross (then at White, now with Knopf), and Lilian Moore Reavin and Matilda Welter at Crowell. Though the editor rarely is mentioned in a children's book, he (or she) is constantly at work helping the author and the illustrator create books to grow on.

Mrs. Walker expressed her viewpoint on children's reading in a letter to *Horn Book:* While visiting a library in a Dallas suburb she observed "the librarian 'counsel' a fourth-going-on-fifth-grade girl about the books she was to read in the Children's Room this summer. 'You needn't think you're going to read those 'thin books' with all those pictures,' she said. 'We're not interested in your going around saying you read a hundred or more books. We'll think a lot more of you if you read at your own level.' The child's shoulders slumped perceptibly, but she dutifully stepped off toward the bookcases pointed out to her by the librarian.

"I'm an author of 'thin books' myself, and I winced at the implicit condemnation of such books. But, more, I've been a teacher for seventeen years, and of courses in children's literature for twelve, and I felt the librarian might be missing a very important factor in her summer reading program—in *any* summer reading program. To her surprise, I spoke my mind. I think 'thin books,' if the books in the Children's Room have been wisely selected, have a very definite place in the summer reading of a child at *any* grade level—and for adults, too, for that matter. As someone—May Hill Arbuthnot, I believe—has said, 'A book worth reading at five is worth rereading at fifty.' And indeed it is true. Many of the books which appear in the States as 'thin books,' picture-books, are retellings of traditional tales, folk tales, which are told—in Turkey, at least—by adults to and for adults, with the children sitting by, remembering them for their own children. What can a fifth-grader do but *gain* by absorbing the very basic understanding that people around the world are, after all, very much alike in the things they enjoy and remember and value?

"Quite apart from those 'thin books' are others acquainting young readers with the questions and delights and experiences of early childhood, which the child was too busy living to know how to appreciate at the time. At the very advanced age of eight or nine or ten, if he is permitted by the librarian, he can go back and discover what he had before been too young to relish and appreciate: the privilege and dimension and immense value of being a young child. If he had met these books before, he can reread them with a new eye for their meaning and beauty. If they have come along since his own early childhood—and, of course, *many* books of enduring value for children *have*—he can claim his rightful heritage as an American child with a treasury of fine books at his disposal.

"Reading should please the heart, the spirit, of the child. This, to me, seems far more important than his measuring up to the 'ruler' of any given children's librarian. At that crucial stage in that particular child's life, she is making up her mind whether reading for pleasure is something she will choose as refreshment for the rest of her life. She already *has* reading as a tool, if she ever will; now she will decide whether she will count it also a treasure. Perhaps she is *tired* of 'thick books,' after nine months of school exposure to 'thick' textbooks crammed with facts to be memorized, crowding out her own questions with too many answers. Perhaps she *needs* the 'thin books' in order to rediscover her own questions, to bathe herself in pure delight, to escape the pressure of 'required reading.' And is there something wrong in being able to claim that she has read a hundred books? Would that *many* youngsters yearned to make that claim! (It's almost a bow to The Establishment, with its everlasting one-up-manship . . .) In what better, more lasting area could *any* child really benefit from claiming 'the most' ?"

Pigs and Pirates has been filmed by Weston Woods Studios, *Just Say Hic!* by Bailey-Film Associates, and *I Packed My Trunk* was used on "Sesame Street." Manuscript and production materials of five of Mrs. Walker's books have been placed on permanent loan to the Kerlan Collection at University of Minnesota Library. All of her juveniles are included in the International Youth Library in Munich.

HOBBIES AND OTHER INTERESTS: Fishing and boating off an island in Georgian Bay, Ontario, where the Walkers homesteaded in 1954 and built their own cottage.

FOR MORE INFORMATION SEE: Horn Book, February, 1970, December, 1970, October, 1971, December, 1971; *Lamp* (Delta Zeta publication), summer, 1970.

WALLACE, Barbara Brooks

PERSONAL: Born in Soochow, China; daughter of Otis Frank and Nicia E. Brooks; married James Wallace, Jr.

BARBARA BROOKS WALLACE

(in U.S. Air Force), February 27, 1954; children: James. *Education:* Attended schools in Hankow, Tientsin, and Shanghai, China, in Claremont, Calif., and Pomona College; University of California, Los Angeles, B.A. *Religion:* Episcopalian. *Home:* 2708 George Mason Pl., Alexandria, Va. 22305. *Agent:* Johnson & Thompson, 28th & O St., Washington, D.C.

AWARDS, HONORS: National League of American Pen Women Juvenile Book Award, 1970, for *Claudia*.

WRITINGS: *Claudia* (juvenile), Follett, 1969; *Andrew the Big Deal* (juvenile; *Weekly Reader* Book Club selection), Follett, 1971; *The Trouble with Miss Switch* (juvenile), Abingdon, 1971; *Victoria* (juvenile), Follett, 1972; *Missy Charlie* (juvenile), Follett, 1973.

SIDELIGHTS: "Nothing in my childhood that I can think of pointed toward an interest in writing. I'm told that I wrote highly amusing letters, but by my parents, not a very reliable source. Though I treasured books (the newest 'Oz' book from Grandmother in America or the latest 'Tiger Tim Annual' from England—both books that were joyfully discovered under the Christmas tree each year), I didn't read avidly, at least not hundreds of books. Nor did I start writing at eight, or some other wonderfully early age. I envy all writers who have done both these things, as so many have.

"As for writing for children, I'm not certain what brought that on either. Although my sister and I had what one might call an exciting childhood in China, it was also a very protected childhood. I hardly remember a moment when there wasn't an anxious amah hovering over us.

Claudia simply stood and stared, completely immobilized by the enormity of the mess she had created and by the fact that she really couldn't decide which dog to capture first. ■ (From *Claudia* by Barbara Wallace. Illustrated by Charles Liese.)

"There have never been many children in my life. As a child I had few playmates. The classes I was in in school were so small they didn't provide for many friends. My sister, Connie, whom I idolized, was luckier in finding friends. I spent a great deal of time haunting *them*, the kind of thing that doesn't add to a younger sister's popularity.

"My husband and I have only one child, Jimmy, who has been my main source of material for almost all my book children, three-year-old girls, twelve-year-old boys, all of them. (Even my witches, dragons, and talking mushrooms tend to sound like Jimmy.)

"I do, however, have a clear recollection of how I felt as a child about many things, Christmas, the terror of waking alone at night, having a friend, and an understanding, I believe, of why I felt as I did. And I love children, especially the ages of seven to twelve. They are eager, enthusiastic, and so tremendously responsive. *And* honest. One little girl brought back a manuscript she was trial-reading for me and said, 'I never got past chapter one because I didn't know what you were talking about.' Just like that! These are the reasons, I think, why what I write will probably always be for children."

WALSH, Jill Paton
See PATON WALSH, Gillian

WALTON, Richard J. 1928-

PERSONAL: Born May 24, 1928, in Saratoga Springs, N.Y.; son of Richard James (a salesman) and Gertrude (Boyle) Walton; married Margaret Hilton (a teacher), June 8, 1957 (now separated); children: Richard Mackay, Catherine Anne. *Education:* Brown University, A.B., 1951; Columbia University (school of journalism), M.S., 1954. *Politics:* "Reform Democrat." *Home:* 14 Cornelia St., New York, N.Y. 10014. *Agent:* Knox Burger Associates, 39½ Washington Square South, New York, N.Y. 10012.

CAREER: WICE (radio station), Providence, R.I., news editor and chief announcer, 1952-53; *Providence Journal-Bulletin,* Providence, R.I., reporter and photographer, 1954-55; *New York World-Telegram & Sun,* New York, N.Y., reporter, feature writer, columnist, and on occasion, assistant city editor and makeup editor, 1955-59; Voice of America, Washington, D.C., writer, producer, and narrator of "Report to Africa," 1959-62, principal United Nations correspondent, 1962-67. Western Connecticut State College, part-time lecturer in international relations, political science, and creative writing, 1968—; New School for Social Research, New York, N.Y., lecturer in international relations, 1969—. Caucus of Connecticut Democrats, member; Connecticut State Interim Planning Committee, member of executive committee, 1968-69. *Military service:* U.S. Navy, journalist, 1946-48. U.S. Naval Reserve, now lieutenant junior grade (retired).

WRITINGS: *The Remnants of Power: The Tragic Last Years of Adlai Stevenson,* Coward, 1968; *America and the Cold War* (young adult), Seabury, 1969; *Beyond Diplomacy* (young adult), Parents' Magazine Press, 1970; *Cold War and Counterrevolution: The Foreign Policy of John F. Kennedy,* Viking, 1967; *The United States and Latin America* (young adult), Seabury, 1972; *Canada and the U.S.A.* (young adult), Parents' Magazine Press, 1967; *Congress and American Foreign Policy,* Parents' Magazine Press, 1972. Writer and narrator of nine documentaries on Africa for Voice of America. Contributor to *Nation, Village Voice, New York Times, Saturday Review, Esquire, New Leader, Nugget, Liberator, Playboy, Vista, Book World.*

WORK IN PROGRESS: *Henry Wallace and the 1948 Campaign,* for Viking; *The United States and the Far East,* a young adult book for Seabury, which looks at U.S. involvement with Asia over the centuries.

SIDELIGHTS: "I write young adult books as well as adult books because I believe that young people in the U.S., as elsewhere, get a distorted view of their country, a narrow, even chauvinistic view, in their education. I believe they want to, and must, know the whole story about the American past, the less edifying as well as the good.

"I write these books with no condescension whatsoever; the only difference with adult books is that they are shorter, less detailed. I am totally convinced that teenagers today can, and must, be treated as adults, particularly since they are so much more activist than their parents were at a like age. I like them, admire them and have great faith in them, without, however, subscribing to the cult of youth, that so many kids must find embarrassing in their elders."

FOR MORE INFORMATION SEE: *Book World,* October 20, 1968, January 23, 1972; *New York Times Book*

Review, October 20, 1968, March 19, 1972; *The Nation*, January 20, 1969; *Life*, February 11, 1972; *Saturday Review*, May 20, 1972.

WARE, Leon (Vernon) 1909-

PERSONAL: Born February 21, 1909, in Plainview, Minn.; son of William L. and LaVerne (McGaan) Ware; married Elizabeth Hull, 1937; children: Elizabeth. *Education:* Northwestern University, B.S., 1930. *Religion:* Presbyterian. *Address:* Box 831, San Juan Capistrano, Calif. 92675. *Agent:* Harold Ober Associates, 40 East 49th St., New York, N.Y.

CAREER: Title insurance business, 1930-33; free-lance writer, 1933—. *Military service:* U.S. Navy, 1944-45. *Member:* Delta Tau Delta, Lido Isle Yacht Club (past commodore), N Club (Northwestern University), Balboa Power Squadron, International Beer Tasting Society. *Awards, honors:* Edgar Award of Mystery Writers of America, 1966, for *The Mystery of 22 East*.

WRITINGS: Crazy Dog, McGraw, 1945; *Shifting Winds,* McGraw, 1948; *Phantom of the Bridge,* Westminster,

The gulls appeared from everywhere, wheeling and screaming overhead as they recognized a familiar source of food. ■ (From *The Threatening Fog* by Leon Ware. Illustrated by Edward J. Smith.)

LEON WARE

1954; *The Man on a Stick* (play), Samuel French, 1957; *Threatening Fog* (Junior Literary Guild selection), Westminster, 1962; *The Rebellious Orphan,* Westminster, 1964; *The Mystery of 22 East,* Westminster, 1965; *The Jade Monkey Mystery,* Westminster, 1969. Film, radio and television scripts, and stories in national magazines, including *Saturday Evening Post, McCall's, Ladies' Home Journal, Redbook, Cosmopolitan, Collier's, Liberty, Country Gentleman, American;* contributor of travel articles to *Orange Coast Illustrated.*

WORK IN PROGRESS: A new juvenile, *The Delta Mystery.*

SIDELIGHTS: "The first five juveniles all began as *Saturday Evening Post* adult stories. Almost all my stories have a factual basis buried in them—*Crazy Dog* from a dog I had that acted nuts; *Shifting Winds* from when my daughter first began racing her boat; *Phantom of the*

Bridge from a remembered incident about climbing a small bridge when I was a youngster; *Threatening Fog* from a hair-raising experience in the Santa Barbara Channel; *Rebellious Orphan* from a young chap I knew who'd been raised by three maiden aunts; *Mystery of 22 East* from a German freighter trip with a regular bear of a captain who terrified everyone but Betsy, my wife—and she had him eating out of her hand; and *Jade Monkey* from our latest freighter trip to the Orient. (We've had fourteen. I met my wife in 1936 on a Norwegian ship enroute to Shanghai.)

"I gave up teaching creative writing at Orange Coast College to instruct on the *first* University-around-the-world cruise. That one folded, but believe me, it was an experience I'll never get over. I had been out of college a long, long time—the permissiveness, the morals, the academic indifference almost broke my heart. What a shocking lack of personal discipline. (I know that over-thirty attitude, but I don't *feel* sixty-two.)"

HOBBIES AND OTHER INTERESTS: Fishing, and "spending a lot of time trying to break 100 on the golf course that surrounds us in this lovely old mission town."

WATERS, John F(rederick) 1930-

PERSONAL: Born October 27, 1930, in Somerville, Mass.; children: Herbert, Sandra, Lane, Duane. *Education:* University of Massachusetts, B.S., 1959. *Residence:* Mount Desert Island, Me.

CAREER: Cape Cod Standard Times, Hyannis, Mass., reporter, 1959-60; elementary teacher in Falmouth, Mass., 1960-66; full-time writer of books for young people, 1966—. *Military service:* U.S. Army, 1952-54; became sergeant.

WRITINGS: Marine Animal Collectors, Hastings House, 1969; *The Sea Farmers,* Hastings House, 1970; *What Does an Oceanographer Do?,* Dodd, 1970; *Saltmarshes and Shifting Dunes,* Harvey House, 1970; *The Crab from Yesterday* (Junior Literary Guild selection), Warne, 1970; *Turtles,* Follett, 1971; *Neighborhood Puddle* (Junior Literary Guild selection), Warne, 1971; *Some Mammals Live in the Sea,* Dodd, 1972; *Green Turtle Mysteries,* Crowell, 1972; *The Mysterious Eel,* Hastings House, 1972; *The Royal Potwasher,* Methuen, 1972.

SIDELIGHTS: "I lived in Woods Hole, Mass., home of the Woods Hole Oceanographic Institution, Marine Biological Laboratory, National Marine Fisheries Service, for twenty years and during that time I became interested in marine subjects and marine science.

"We are presently living in a large and very old house overlooking Northeast Harbor on Mt. Desert Island on

Other boys, and girls too, ran up to see what was in the wagon. When they saw only an old horseshoe crab, they giggled and walked away. ■ (From *The Crab from Yesterday* by John F. Waters. Illustrated by W. T. Mars.)

JOHN F. WATERS

the Maine Coast. I still write every day because that is how I support my wife and four children. My workroom overlooks the harbor and I have time for dreaming and writing—especially in winter. In the winters of 1970 and '71 we had 113 inches of snow. What else could I do but write? It was either that or shovel snow."

WATT, Thomas 1935-

PERSONAL: Born June 17, 1935, in Toronto, Ontario, Canada; son of William L. (a printer) and Isabel (Wright) Watt; married Mabs MacPherson, December 19, 1959; children: Kelly, Ruth Anne, Robert. *Education:* University of Toronto, B.P.H.E., 1959, M.Ed., 1969. *Religion:* Christian. *Home:* 73 Elwood Blvd., Toronto 12, Ontario, Canada. *Office:* R. 208 Hart House, University of Toronto, Toronto 12, Ontario, Canada.

CAREER: Board of Education, Toronto, Ontario, teacher in secondary schools, 1959-65; University of Toronto, Toronto, Ontario, lecturer of physical education and hockey coach, 1965-71, assistant professor, 1971—. *Member:* Canadian Hockey Coaches Association, American Hockey Coaches Association, Canadian Association for Health, Physical Education and Recreation, North American Society for Sports Psychology. *Awards, honors:* Named Canadian college coach of the year by Canadian Hockey Coaches Association, 1970-71.

WRITINGS: How to Play Hockey: A Guide for Young Players and Their Coaches, Doubleday, 1971.

WORK IN PROGRESS: A day by day account of problems involved in college coaching.

WATTS, (Anna) Bernadette 1942- (Bernadette)

PERSONAL: Born May 13, 1942, in Northampton, England; daughter of Bert (a surveyor) and Josephine (Roberts) Watts. *Education:* Attended Ashford County Grammar School for Girls; Maidstone College of Art, National Diploma in Design. *Politics:* Socialist. *Religion:* "None of the established churches—rather a very personal view of life and belief in good things, responsibility towards ones neighbors, love and humanity to be expressed to those around us, and work towards liberation of all peoples in this world." *Home:* Tyr Odyn, Golan, Garndolbenmaen Caernarvonshire, N. Wales.

CAREER: Free-lance illustrator. *Awards, honors:* Premio Graphico (Bologna, Italy), 1969, for illustrations in James Reeves' *One's None.*

BERNADETTE WATTS

When I was a little boy, I had but little wit.
It is some time ago, and I've no more yet,
Nor ever, ever shall, until that I die,
For the longer I live, the more fool am I. ■ (From One's None by James Reeves. Illustrated by Bernadette Watts.)

WRITINGS—Author and illustrator under name Bernadette: Hans Millermann, Nord Sud Verlag [Zurich], 1969, published in America as *Hans the Miller Man*, McGraw, 1969; *Varenka*, Nord Sud Verlag, 1970, Oxford University Press, 1970; *Mother Holle*, Nord Sud Verlag, 1972.

Illustrator under name Bernadette: Ruth Ainsworth, *Look, Do and Listen*, Watts, 1969; Grimm Brothers, *Little Red Riding Hood*, World Publishing, 1969; James Reeves, *One's None*, Watts, 1969; Tennyson, *Lady of Shallott*, Watts, 1969; Reinhold Ehrhard, *Kikeri: The Proud Red Rooster*, World Publishing, 1970; Grimm Brothers, *Jorinda and Joringel*, World Publishing, 1970; Rhoda Power, *The Big Book of Stories from Many Lands*, Watts, 1970; George Mendoza, *The Christmas Tree Alphabet Book*, World Publishing, 1971; Reinhold Ehrhard, *The Clocktower*, Nord Sud Verlag; *Cinderella*, Watts [London]; *Snow White and the Seven Dwarfs*, Watts [London]; *The Lord's Prayer*, Parents' Magazine Press, in press. Also illustrated little "zig-zag" books for Kauffmann Verlag, posters, book jackets, and educational materials.

WORK IN PROGRESS: Now working on Herr Fiedler, the story of a Viennese musician who forsakes true love for fame and success; illustrating *Hansel and Gretel*, for Nord Sud Verlag; painting towards an exhibition.

SIDELIGHTS: "I am generally interested in travel and do go abroad whenever possible, usually combined with work.
I read a great deal of travel and exploration books and watch similar programs on television. My visit in 1969 to South Africa opened my eyes to the distress and underpriviledged condition of so many people all over the world today and I have a permanent involvement with these people.

"I enjoy music of many kinds, reading, cinema, looking at every kind of art in galleries and museums. Seeing bushman paintings in caves in Cape Peninsula was a great occasion for me. My ambition eventually is to leave the city and live in the country with the things I love: my work, my home, a garden with trees, and maybe a river and all the life it supports. [Achieved exactly—March, 1972—in a mountain cottage in Wales.]"

Ms. Watts takes part in the illustration exhibitions in Bologna, Italy each year and has been invited to take part in the next Biennale in Bratislavia, Czechoslovakia. She also took part in Graphic Design Britain, the largest graphics exhibition held in London each year.

FOR MORE INFORMATION SEE: Graphis 155, Volume 27, Graphis Press, 1971/72.

We are on Tom Tinker's ground
 Picking up gold and silver.
You pick weeds and I'll pick seeds
 And we'll pick caraway comfits. ■ (From One's None by James Reeves. Illustrated by Bernadette Watts.)

WERNER, K.
See CASEWIT, Curtis

WHITEHEAD, Don(ald) F. 1908-

PERSONAL: Born April 8, 1908, in Inman, Va.; son of Harry Ford (a merchant) and Elizabeth (Bond) Whitehead; married Marie Patterson, December 20, 1928; children: Ruth (Mrs. H.E. Graham). *Education:* University of Kentucky, student, 1926-28. *Home and office:* 3636 Taliluna Dr., Knoxville, Tenn.

CAREER: Harlan Daily Enterprise, Harlan, Ky., city editor, 1929-33; *Knoxville Journal*, Knoxville, Tenn., reporter, 1934-35; Associated Press, New York, N.Y., reporter, 1935-42, war correspondent, 1942-45, bureau chief in Hawaii, 1945-48, special correspondent in Washington,

The Klan controlled the whole of northern Louisiana by terror. The Klan's membership included law enforcement officers and leading townspeople. The agents began working under cover, themselves hunted by klansmen at times. ■ From the movie "The FBI Story," © 1959 by Warner Bros. Pictures Corp.

D.C., 1948-56; *New York Herald Tribune,* New York, N.Y., chief of Washington bureau, 1956-57; *Knoxville News-Sentinel,* Knoxville, Tenn., columnist, 1959—. As war correspondent was attached to British Eighth Army in Egypt, made assault landings with American troops in Sicily, and at Salerno and Anzio, Italy, landed in Normandy with spearheading forces on D Day, remained with First Army until it joined with Russians on the Elbe.

MEMBER: Gridiron Club, Sigma Delta Chi. *Awards, honors:* Medal of Freedom from U.S. Army for work as war correspondent during World War II; honorary LL.D. from University of Kentucky, 1948; Pulitzer Prize for war reporting in Korea, 1951; Sigma Delta Chi Distinguished Service Award, 1951; George Polk Award for outstanding wire service reporting, 1951; Pulitzer Prize for national reporting, 1953; Christopher Award for *The FBI Story,* 1957.

WRITINGS: *The FBI Story,* Random House, 1956, juvenile edition, 1963; *Journey Into Crime,* Random House, 1960; *Border Guard—The Story of the U.S. Customs,* McGraw, 1963; *The Dow Story,* McGraw, 1968; *Attack on Terror: The FBI Against the Ku Klux Klan in Mississippi,* Funk, 1970.

SIDELIGHTS: "A plain case of curiosity led me to write *The FBI Story.* In 1954, I was a special correspondent for the Associated Press working out of Washington, D.C., writing politics and special feature stories. Early that year I read somewhere that J. Edgar Hoover would observe his thirtieth anniversary as director of the Federal Bureau of Investigation. The anniversary was important because few if any men had ever held a high government position for such a length of time.

"In April, I requested an interview with Mr. Hoover. The interview was granted and for one entire afternoon Mr. Hoover talked to me of his years in office, the Presidents under whom he had served, his views of law enforcement and why the FBI operated as it did. The interview was one of the first he had given in several years. From my book of notes, I wrote a series of five stories on Hoover's career which were distributed throughout the country by the A.P. They created quite a bit of excitement and comment, as they were given prominent play in the newspapers.

"After completing the series, I realized I had barely scratched the surface of the FBI's history. I returned to the FBI and said I would like to do a history of the Bureau from its beginning in 1908. Several months later the Bureau said it would cooperate with me by giving me access to letters, memoranda, case histories on criminal investigations, and other necessary information that would reveal the FBI's methods of operations through the years.

"I began work on the book in early 1955 and completed it in the early fall of 1956—sometimes working eighteen hours a day on the research and writing. It became an immediate bestseller.

DON WHITEHEAD

"Where does the material come from for my books? It comes from numerous interviews with people who know something of the story I want and who were a part of that story; it comes from libraries, newspapers, magazines, letters, reports, files and any source that can shed light on a certain place, event or person. The research is the key to how interesting and how informative a story is.

"I am not a speedy writer. I am a 'bleeder.' I write rather slowly and do much rewriting. I work in my office at my home, and when working on a book keep 'office hours.' I am not one who believes that a writer can wait for the proper 'mood.' You create the mood by sitting at a typewriter and forcing yourself to write. The professional writer who sits around waiting for 'a mood' will starve to death."

The FBI Story was filmed by Warner Bros. in 1959 with Jimmy Stewart in the lead.

WILKINSON, (John) Burke 1913-

PERSONAL: Born August 24, 1913, in New York, N.Y.; son of Henry and Edith (Burke) Wilkinson; married Frances Proctor, June 11, 1938; children: Eileen Burke, Charles Proctor. *Education:* Harvard University, B.A. (magna cum laude), 1935; Cambridge University, graduate study, 1935-36. *Politics:* Independent. *Religion:* Episcopalian. *Home:* 3210 Scott Pl., Washington, D.C. *Agent:* International Famous, 1301 Avenue of the Americas, New York, N.Y. 10019. *Office:* 1518 K Street, N.W., Washington, D.C. 20005.

CAREER: Lord & Thomas (advertising agency), copywriter, 1936-38; Reynal & Hitchcock (publishers), assistant advertising manager, 1938-39; Little, Brown and Co., Boston, Mass., advertising manager, 1939-41; free-lance writer, 1946-50, 1952-54; with U.S. Department of State, Washington, D.C., 1954-58, deputy assistant secretary for public affairs, 1956-58; Supreme Headquarters, Allied Powers Europe, public affairs adviser, 1958-62; novelist and biographer, 1962—. Foreign Students Service Council, director; U.S. Lawn Tennis Hall of Fame, vice-president and director. *Military service:* U.S. Naval Reserve, 1941-46, 1950-52; became commander; received Navy Commendation Ribbon for work in preparing for Normandy Invasion.

MEMBER: Authors Guild, National Press Club, International Lawn Tennis Club of United States (director), International Lawn Tennis Club of United Kingdom (honorary), International Lawn Tennis Club of France (honorary), Phi Beta Kappa, St. Botolph's Club (Boston). *Awards, honors:* Commendatore, Italian Order of Merit for Italian sections of *By Sea and by Stealth; The Helmet of Navarre* was chosen by the *New York Times Book Review* as one of the twelve best juveniles of 1964.

WRITINGS: Proceed at Will, Little, Brown, 1948; *Run, Mongoose,* Little, Brown, 1950; *Last Clear Chance,* Little, Brown, 1954; *By Sea and By Stealth* (nonfiction), Coward, 1956; *Night of the Short Knives,* Scribner, 1964; *The Helmet of Navarre,* Macmillan, 1965; *Cardinal in Armor,* Macmillan, 1966; *Cry Spy!* (anthology), Bradbury; 1969; *Young Louis XIV,* Macmillan, 1970; *Francis in All His*

Glory, Farrar, Straus, 1972. Contributor of articles to magazines and some one-hundred reviews to *New York Times Book Review.*

WORK IN PROGRESS: "I am preparing a sequel to *Cry Spy!* (titled *Cry Sabotage!*) which contains some twenty-seven famous spy stories written in good part by the operator himself. It is mainly for the young but has had a good general reception as well. Also plan another suspense novel like *Night of the Short Knives.* I did finish a State Department novel three years ago but it needed re-working as it lacked suspense. The basic working theme of arms control was a bit complicated and not too dramatic, but expect to have a new, more adventurous, draft by mid-1973."

SIDELIGHTS: "The four biographies for the young are all drawn from French history. For each I visited the battlefields and castles and towns that figure in the story. No dialogue is made up—it is taken from contemporary memoirs and diaries, and in good part translated by me. All together, with the new one on Francis I, the splendid Renaissance king, they cover a span of nearly two-hundred years—from 1474 to 1662, when young Louis XIV started to rule in his own right. Grown-ups seem to like them too and there is talk of putting the first three together in one volume for all ages. Quite a switch on the usual procedure!"

Wilkinson sold his first article to *Yachting* in 1943, and then continued to write a series of Navy articles; a self-described "in-and-out" author of books since 1948, Wilkinson feels that his brand of fiction profits by first-hand experience, and has drawn heavily on his own activities for "backgrounds and foregrounds."

BURKE WILKINSON

Conde took off his plumed hat in salute to the fallen foe. "If I had not won, I would wish to have died as honorably as he who lies here." ■ (From *Young Louis XIV* by Burke Wilkinson, Illustrated by Doreen Roberts.)

WISE, William 1923-

PERSONAL: Born July 21, 1923, in New York, N.Y. *Education:* Yale University. B.A., 1948. *Agent:* Brandt and Brandt, 101 Park Ave., New York, N.Y. 10017.

CAREER: Free-lance writer.

WRITINGS—Juvenile: *Jonathan Blake,* Knopf, 1956; *Silversmith of Old New York: Myer Myers,* Farrar, Straus, and Jewish Publication Society, 1958; *Albert Einstein: Citizen of the World,* Farrar, Straus, and Jewish Publication Society, 1960; *The House with the Red Roof,* Putnam, 1961; *The Cowboy Surprise,* Putnam, 1961; *Alexander Hamilton,* Putnam, 1963; *The Story of Mulberry Bend,* Dutton, 1963; *In the Time of the Dinosaurs,* Putnam, 1964; *Detective Pinkerton and Mr. Lincoln,* Dutton, 1964; *The Two Reigns of Tutankhamen,* Putnam, 1964; *The World of Giant Mammals,* Putnam, 1965; *The Spy and General Washington,* Dutton, 1965; *Franklin D.*

Roosevelt, Putnam, 1967; *Monsters of Today and Yesterday,* Putnam, 1967; *When the Saboteurs Came,* Dutton, 1967; *Sir Howard, the Coward,* Putnam, 1967; *Killer Smog* (adult nonfiction), Rand, 1968; *Monsters of the Ancient Seas,* Putnam, 1968; *Aaron Burr,* Putnam, 1968; *Booker T. Washington,* Putnam, 1968; *Secret Mission to the Philippines,* Dutton, 1969; *Nanette: The Hungry Pelican,* Rand, 1969; *Giant Birds and Monsters of the Air* (Junior Literary Guild selection), Putnam, 1969; *The Terrible Trumpet,* Norton, 1969; *The Amazing Animals of Latin America,* Putnam, 1969.

The Amazing Animals of Australia (Junior Literary Guild selection), Putnam, 1970; *The Lazy Young Duke of Dundee,* Rand, 1970; *Fresh as a Daisy, Neat as a Pin,* Parents' Magazine Press, 1970; *From Scrolls to Satellites,* Parents' Magazine Press, 1970; *Giant Snakes and other Amazing Reptiles,* Putnam, 1970; *Charles A. Lindbergh: Aviation Pioneer,* Putnam, 1970; *Monsters of the Middle Ages,* Putnam, 1971; *Amazing Animals of North America,* Putnam, 1971; *Fresh, Canned, and Frozen,* Parents' Magazine Press, 1971; *All on a Summer's Day,* Pantheon, 1971. Author of television scripts; contributor of fiction to *Harper's, Yale Review,* and other periodicals, and of reviews to *New York Times* and *Saturday Review.*

SIDELIGHTS: "I really do not like to discuss writing, or why I write books. I think most writers talk a good deal of nonsense when they get on such topics. So let me say just one or two things; I write fiction, in prose or verse, because I very much enjoy telling a story. Biographies, or tales based on historical fact are a different matter; I've written them, at least in part, because I think Americans are far too indifferent to the past. I write books about animals, particularly with an ecological bias, because animals are very important to human beings, and many

He brings cookies to eat (in case he is caught).... ■ (From *Sir Howard the Coward* by William Wise. Illustrated by Susan Perl.)

Something about the Author

species are rapidly disappearing from our world—destroyed by mankind.

"The above leaves out a major truth: writers write to support themselves and their families. Why can't we tell children this?—that writers spend a great deal of time, worrying about money. If we don't tell children the truth, how can we expect them to grow up with the attitudes and values that we would like them to have?"

WISEMAN, B(ernard) 1922-

PERSONAL: Born August 26, 1922, in Brooklyn, N.Y.; son of Abraham Z. and Yetta (Goldstein) Wiseman; married Geraldine Manners, 1958; married Susan Nadine Levin, May 9, 1970; children: (first marriage) Peter Franklin. *Education:* Attended schools in Brooklyn, N.Y. *Politics:* Republican. *Religion:* Hebrew. *Home and office:* 15 Buena Vista Dr., Westport, Conn. 06880.

CAREER: Contract cartoonist for *New Yorker,* 1948-56; cartoonist and illustrator, 1948—, with Spadea Syndicate, then McNavgat's Syndicate, now partner and art director with Crown Syndicate; other cartoons for *Punch, Saturday Evening Post, True, Look, This Week, Playboy, Rogue;* comic illustrations for *Cosmopolitan* and other magazines; advertising illustrations for American Airlines, New York Transport Authority, Woolite, and other companies and organizations. *Military service:* U.S. Coast Guard, four and one-half years, World War II.

WRITINGS: Morris the Moose, Harper, 1959; *Morris Is a Cowboy,* Harper, 1959; *The Log and Admiral Frog,* Harper, 1961; *Morris Goes to School,* Harper, 1970; *Ninety-Six Cats,* Hale, 1970. Writes and illustrates stories about "Sir Nervous Norman" for *Boys' Life Magazine.*

"Fun to Learn" Series: *The Nutty Nature Book, The Silly Science Book, Detective Dog,* and *Hats and Coats, Cows and Goats* (all published by Platt & Munk).

Cartoon books: *Cartoon Countdown,* Ballantine, 1959; *Boatniks,* Dell, 1961; *Irwin the Intern,* Dell, 1962; (with Sandy Brier) *Sadness is a Back View,* Citadel, 1964; *The Hat That Grew and Grew,* R. Hale, 1965. Illustrated "The Boy Who Found Xmas" by James A. Michener.

SIDELIGHTS: "I was a cartoonist long before I was a writer, in fact, before I was a civilian, for I began selling cartoons while I still wore the uniform of a bosen's mate in the U.S. Coast Guard. That was way back during World War II.

"I thought of the cartoon ideas while on watch, while working at various sailor tasks and, when I couldn't get to New York myself—where the big cartoon markets were—I sent my drawings to my mother who mailed them

B. WISEMAN

Morris the Moose wanted candy.
He went to the wrong store. ■ (From *Morris Goes to School* by B. Wiseman. Illustrated by the author.)

to appropriate magazines. I particularly remember her selling one to *Look* Magazine because she trimmed the top off the picture to make it fit an envelope, and thereby improved the drawing by eliminating some unnecessary background.

"The *New Yorker* Magazine gave me a contract after I became a civilian, and for about a dozen years I drew cartoons for them and for almost all other publications. With the rarest of exceptions—perhaps a half dozen in all—my drawings were of my own ideas.

"I became interested in writing long before I actually did any. Doing ideas is quite similar in some ways, since you are constructing scenes and writing dialogue—though only one or two lines of it, of course. I began to seriously engage in writing after Harold Ross died, the great editor of the *New Yorker,* and my interest in the magazine slackened. Under his guidance, the *New Yorker* was something mystical to me, and I took pride in working with the very small and special group he had assembled, people like Peter Arno, Sam Cobean, Charles Addams, etc. After Ross was gone the doors opened to many artists I did not respect, and I felt standards had dropped. Therefore, I turned to stories for small children, which were closest to cartoon ideas in their creation.

"As to those stories, I work slowly when I think them out, fast when I write them, and polish most slowly of all. The drawing part of it is a pleasure for me and I relax a bit when I get to that.

"The 'Sir Nervous Norman' tales, I write and illustrate for *Boys' Life,* follow much the same pattern as the books for young children. Think slow, write fast, correct slow. For the future, I plan more of all that I'm doing, as well as a few short novels for older children."

Booklets that Wiseman illustrated for Radio Free Europe were dropped by balloons in Communist satellite countries. Recently he has been active in Karate, and has a color belt. He studies with sensei (teacher) Shigern Oyama.

WOHLRABE, Raymond A. 1900-

PERSONAL: Born April 25, 1900, in Superior, Wis.; son of Adolph Gustav and Flora (McCallum) Wohlrabe. *Education:* University of Washington, Seattle, Wash., B.S. 1922; additional studies at Purdue University, 1923-24, and at University of Southern California, University of Washington, University of British Columbia. *Address:* P.O. Box 6625, Seattle, Wash. 98116.

CAREER: Public schools, Burlington, Wash., science teacher, 1922-23; Purdue University, West Lafayette, Ind., laboratory instructor, 1923-24; public school teacher, Port Townsend, Wash., 1924-25, Portland, Ore., 1925-26, Seattle, Wash., 1926-66. Subject area for last ten years of teaching was chemistry. *Member:* National Retired Teachers Association.

WRITINGS: (With Werner Krusch) *The Land and People of Austria,* Lippincott, 1956; (with Krusch) *The Land and People of Germany,* Lippincott, 1957; (with Krusch) *The Land and People of Venezuela,* Lippincott, 1959, revised edition, 1963; (with Krusch) *The Land and People of Portugal,* Lippincott, 1960, revised edition, 1963; (with Krusch) *The Land and People of Denmark,* Lippincott, 1961; (with Krusch) *The Key to Vienna,* Lippincott, 1961; *Crystals,* Lippincott, 1962; *Metals,* Lippincott, 1964; *Exploring Electrostatics,* World Publishing, 1965; *Exploring Solar Energy,* World Publishing, 1966; (with Krusch) *Picture Map Geography of Western Europe,* Lippincott, 1967; *The Pacific Northwest,* World Publishing, 1968; *High Desert and Canyon Country,* World Publishing, 1969; *Fundamental Physical Forces,* Lippincott, 1969; *Exploring Giant Molecules,* World Publishing, 1969. Contributor of travel articles to magazines and newspapers, other articles to juvenile publications.

WORK IN PROGRESS: Working on the second editions of some of the Lippincott "Portraits of the Nations" series.

SIDELIGHTS: "My interest in photography and in travel as a hobby led to my becoming an author. After teaching photography in high school and adult evening school I was selected to serve as a Seattle exchange teacher for a year in one of the Los Angeles high schools. While there, I took advantage of the opportunity to study photography under Ansel Adams at the Art Center School. My first writing was for the Eastman Kodak Company's little magazine, *Kodakery,* which was discontinued quite a number of years ago.

"Eventually I became interested in making use of my years of experience in teaching science in high school in writing books about science that would be popular with young people. Experiments that youngsters could do were worked into the text of each science book. All of these were tried out on students in my own classes to make certain youngsters would be able to do them at home or in the school laboratory. An effort was made to use purely scientific terms only where these were absolutely necessary

RAYMOND A. WOHLRABE

Parachutes opened after entering the earth's atmosphere increase the effectiveness of air resistance in slowing down the spacecraft before splashdown. ■ (From *Fundamental Physical Forces* by Raymond A. Wohlrabe. Illustrated by Edward A. DeVille. Reprinted by permission of J. B. Lippincott Co.)

and where scientific terminology had to be used, to include simple explanations that could be easily understood. This made factual science books far more interesting to the young reader than the regular textbooks normally used in their class activities.

"Emphasis is placed in my travel books on the way of life, the traditions, legends, and culture of the people of a nation as well as the geography, economy, and historical development from earliest times to the present. Information for these books is obtained through extensive research supplemented by the experiences and observations gained by traveling through the country, living in the homes and country inns, and attending festivals, sports events, and pageants."

Several of Wohlrabe's books in the Lippincott "Portrait of Nations" series have been published in Urdu, Bengali, Persian, and other languages in the Franklin Book program. Other books have been translated and published in Brazil and Italy.

HOBBIES AND OTHER INTERESTS: Photography, hiking, travel, art.

YATES, Elizabeth 1905-

PERSONAL: Born December 6, 1905, in Buffalo, N.Y.; daughter of Harry and Mary (Duffy) Yates; married William McGreal, November 6, 1929 (died December, 1963). *Education:* Attended schools in Buffalo, N.Y., and Mamaroneck, N.Y. *Home and office:* Shieling, R.F.D. 1, Peterborough, N.H. 03458.

CAREER: Writer, lecturer. Staff member at writers conferences at University of New Hampshire, University of Connecticut, Indiana University, 1956—; instructor at Christian Writers and Editors conferences, Green Lake, Wis., 1962—; Trustee, Peterborough Town Library. *Member:* New Hampshire State Library Commission, New Hampshire Association for the Blind (executive board member), Delta Kappa Gamma. *Awards, honors:* New York Herald Tribune Spring Book Festival juvenile award, 1943, for *Patterns on the Wall;* John Newbery Medal, 1951, and William Allen White Children's Book Award, 1953, both for *Amos Fortune, Free Man;* Boys' Clubs of America gold medal, 1953, for *A Place for Peter;* Jane Addams Children's Book Award from U.S. section of Women's International League for Peace and Freedom, 1955, for *Rainbow 'Round the World;* Sarah Josepha Hale Award, 1970; Litt. D.: Aurora College, 1965, Eastern Baptist College, 1966, University of New Hampshire, 1967, Ripon College, 1969, New England College, 1972.

WRITINGS: High Holiday, A. and C. Black, 1938; *Gathered Grace,* W. Heffer, 1938; *Hans and Frieda,* Nelson, 1939; *Climbing Higher,* A. and C. Black, 1939, Knopf, 1940; *Haven for the Brave,* Knopf, 1941; *Under the Little Fir,* Coward, 1942; *Around the Year in Iceland,* Heath, 1942; *Patterns on the Wall,* Knopf, 1943; *Mountain Born,* Coward, 1943; *Wind of Spring,* Coward, 1945; *Nearby,* Coward, 1947; *Once in the Year,* Coward, 1947; *The Young Traveller in the U.S.A.,* Phoenix House, 1948; *Beloved Bondage,* Coward, 1948.

Amos Fortune, Free Man, Dutton, 1950; *Guardian Heart,* Coward, 1950; *Children of the Bible,* Alladin, 1950; *Brave Interval,* Coward, 1952; *David Livingstone,* Row, Peterson & Co., 1952; *A Place for Peter,* Coward, 1953; *Hue and Cry,* Coward, 1953; *Your Prayers and Mine,* Houghton, 1954; *Rainbow 'Round the World,* Bobbs, 1954; *Prudence Crandall, Woman of Courage,* Dutton, 1955; *The Carey Girl,* Coward, 1956; *Pebble in a Pool: The Widening Circles of Dorothy Canfield Fisher's Life,* Dutton, 1958; *The Lighted Heart,* Dutton, 1960; *The Next Fine Day,* Day, 1962; *Someday You'll Write,* Dutton, 1962; *Sam's Secret Journal,* Friendship, 1964; *Carolina's Courage,* Dutton, 1964, published in England as *Carolina and the Indian Doll,* Methuen, 1965; *Howard Thurman: Portrait of a Practical Dreamer,* Day, 1964; *Up the Golden Stair,* Dutton, 1966; *Is There a Doctor in the Barn?,* Dutton, 1966; *An Easter Story,* Dutton, 1967; *With Pipe, Paddle, and Song: A Story of the French-Canadian Voyageurs,* Dutton, 1968; *On That Night,* Dutton, 1969; *Sarah Whitcher's Story,* Dutton, 1970; *Lady From Vermont,* Stephen Greene, 1971.

Editor, adapter: Enys Tregarthen, *Piskey Folk,* Day, 1940; Tregarthen, *The Doll Who Came Alive,* Day, 1942, new edition, 1972; *Joseph,* Knopf, 1947; Tregarthen, *The White Ring,* Harcourt, 1949; *The Christmas Story,* Knopf, 1949; George MacDonald, *Sir Gibbie,* Dutton, 1963. Contributor of articles, essays, and reviews to magazines and journals.

SIDELIGHTS: "Although I was born in Buffalo, New York, the most memorable days of my childhood and youth were the long summers spent on my father's many-acred farm in the rich rolling country south of Buffalo. Being next to the youngest of seven children, there were always playmates as well as horses and dogs, and there were always tasks—gardening, butter-making, caring for the animals.

"I used to go off on my horse for a day at a time, rambling through the countryside, a sandwich in my pocket and the knowledge that any fresh-running stream would give us both a drink; but I was never lonely, for there was the horse to talk with and in my head I was writing stories. On the next rainy day, I would climb the ladder to an unused pigeon loft that was my own secret place and there write down in a series of copy books all that I had been thinking.

"From kindergarten through the twelfth grade I attended school in Buffalo; this was followed by a year at boarding school and a summer abroad, then there were three years of work in New York. About this time a poem of mine was published in F.P.A.'s [Franklin Pierce Adam's] 'The Conning Tower,' and that confirmed my long-held desire to be a writer.

"At twenty-three I married an American whose business was in England, and for the next ten years our life was based in London. I continued my apprenticeship writing, spending much time in the British Museum and the London Library; but there were months of travel throughout the British Isles and on the Continent, and there was mountain climbing in Switzerland and Iceland. My first book, *High Holiday,* was published in England in 1938.

ELIZABETH YATES

Amos learned to read and write and cipher, but still he did not speak easily though the expression in his eyes and the mobility of his face spoke for him. ■ (From *Amos Fortune, Free Man* by Elizabeth Yates. Illustrated by Nora S. Unwin.)

"A year later we returned to the United States to live in Peterborough, New Hampshire. We found an old farmhouse with a farm of fields and woodland. There were mountains nearby, forest lakes to swim in, and a green countryside with many lovely white villages. A little loft in the far end of the house is my workroom, furnished with a wide table, two chairs and an old-fashioned wood stove. Writing is my joy, but gardening claims much of my time as do community activities."

While the majority of the fifteen foreign editions of Ms. Yates' books are British, they also include translations into Dutch, Japanese, Israeli, Bengali, and German.

FOR MORE INFORMATION SEE: *Junior Book of Authors*, edited by Kunitz and Haycraft, H.W. Wilson, 2nd edition, 1951; *Horn Book*, summer, 1951; *Newbery Medal Books: 1922-1955*, edited by Miller and Field, Horn Book, 1955; *Commonweal*, May 26, 1967; *Library Journal*, September, 1968; *Friends Journal*, October 15, 1969; Hoffman and Samuels, *Authors and Illustrators of Children's Books*, Bowker, 1972.

YOLEN, Jane H. 1939-

PERSONAL: Born February 11, 1939, in New York, N.Y.; daughter of Will Hyatt (author, public relations man) and Isabelle (Berlin) Yolen; married David W. Stemple (computer expert), September 2, 1962; children: Heidi Elisabet, Adam Douglas, Jason Frederic. *Education:* Smith College, B.A., 1960. *Politics:* Liberal Democrat. *Religion:* Quaker. *Mailing address:* Phoenix Farm, 31 School St., Hatfield, Mass. 01038.

CAREER: Saturday Review (magazine), New York, N.Y., production asistant, 1960-61; Gold Medal Books (publishers), New York, N.Y., assistant editor, 1961-62; Rutledge Books (publishers), New York, N.Y., associate editor, 1962-63; Alfred A. Knopf, Inc. (publishers), New York, N.Y., assistant juvenile editor, 1963-65; full-time professional writer, 1965—; teacher of writing and lecturer, 1966—. *Member:* American Civil Liberties Union, Society of Children's Books Writers, Society of Friends, International Kitefliers Association, American Kite Fliers Association, Smith College Alumnae Association, Citizens for Participation Politics.

WRITINGS—All juveniles: *See This Little Line*, McKay, 1963; *Pirates in Petticoats*, McKay, 1963; *The Witch Who Wasn't*, Macmillan, 1964; *Gwinellen, The Princess Who Could Not Sleep*, Macmillan, 1965; *Trust a City Kid*, Lothrop, 1966; *The Emperor and the Kite* (Caldecott Honor Book), World Publishing, 1967; *The Minstrel and the Mountain*, World Publishing, 1967; *The Longest Name on the Block*, Funk, 1967; *Greyling* (Horn Book Honor List), World Publishing, 1968; *World on a String*, World Publishing, 1968; *Isabel's Noel*, Funk, 1969; *The*

Wizard of Washington Square, World Publishing, 1969; *Hobo Toad and the Motorcycle Gang,* World Publishing, 1970; *It all Depends,* Funk, 1970; *The Inway Investigators,* Seabury, 1970; *The Seventh Mandarin* (Junior Literary Guild selection), Seabury, 1971; *The Bird of Time,* Crowell, 1971; *The Fireside Song Book of Birds and Beasts,* Simon & Schuster, 1972; *Friend: The Story of George Fox and the Quakers,* Seabury, 1972; *The Girl Who Loved the Wind,* Crowell, 1972. Contributor of poetry to *Poetry Digest, Grecourt Review,* and other periodicals, and of articles to *American Weekly, This Week, The Writer, Publisher's Weekly,* and other periodicals. Contributor of book reviews to *New York Times* and *Book World.*

WORK IN PROGRESS: *The Wizard Islands, The Boy Who Had Wings,* and *The Girl Who Cried Flowers and Other Tales,* all for Crowell; *Writing Books for Children,* for the Writer Press; *Zoo 2000,* for Seabury.

SIDELIGHTS: "Whenever someone asks me 'Why Juvenile books?' I always answer, 'It's better than senile books.' But the real answer is that children's books—and especially fantasy and folktales—give me a chance to say what I want poetically and allegorically. I am a very aural person. I love music and respond to spoken poetry with a delicious feeling that must be love. I write for myself. Never for children, or even—though I love my three—for any particular child. And, if what I write turns out to be a

"I must have run out of magic," said Isabel at last. ■ (From *Isabel's Noel* by Jane Yolen. Illustrated by Arnold Roth.)

chlidren's book then, as Arthur Ransome says, I am a children's book writer. 'No special credit to me, but simply thumping good luck.'

"My great-grandfather was the storyteller in his village in Fino-Russia. My parents were both writers. My brother is a journalist. So writing came early and easily to me. It has taken me ten years to educate myself out of that facility. Whenever I write—especially with the folktales and picture stories—I read the work in progress outloud to the walls over and over until it sounds well, reads well, and means well. Since picture stories are (or should be) an extension or a redirection of the old campfire tales and songs, it is important for them to sing.

"If I had to pick one word to describe books for children, I would pick 'honesty.' A book that is not made honestly for children, made for reasons other than storytelling (for example, propaganda) will be a book that the children themselves will reject. I hope that I write honest books. I think I do. And the generations of children will be the ultimate judges of my (and my books') honesty."

HOBBIES AND OTHER INTERESTS: Folk music and dancing, politics, camping, and the Elizabethan Age.

FOR MORE INFORMATION SEE: Horn Book, August, 1970; *Publishers' Weekly,* February 22, 1971; *New York Times Book Review,* September 10, 1972.

JANE H. YOLEN

South Hunterdon Regional
High School Library

R   Vol. 4
920.003
So

Something about the author